The LCP Handbook to the Late Roman Amphora 1 (LRA1)

The Levantine Ceramics Project Handbooks

Number 1

Editors
Andrea M. Berlin
Matthew J. Adams
William Caraher

The LCP Handbook to the Late Roman Amphora 1 (LRA1)

Samuel Grady Gillett
Veronica Iacomi

Published under the auspices of
The Center for the Mediterranean World and the
American Society of Overseas Research

LOCKWOOD PRESS
Columbus, GA • 2025

Cover design by Susanne Wilhelm.

ISBN: 978-1-957454-64-1 (paper)

Library of Congress Cataloging-in-Publication Data

Names: Gillet, Samuel Grady, author. | Iacomi, Veronica, author.
Title: The LCP handbook to the late Roman amphora : LRA (1) / Samuel Grady Gillet, Veronica Iacomi.
Other titles: Levantine Ceramics Project handbook to the late Roman amphora
Description: Columbus, [Georgia] : Lockwood Press, 2025. | Series: LCP handbooks ; 1 | Includes bibliographical references and index. | Summary: "This handbook to the Late Roman Amphora 1 (LRA1) is a publication of the Levantine Ceramics Project (https://www.levantineceramics.org/), an open-access resource for the study of Levantine pottery, its societies, cultures, and economies, from the Neolithic era (ca. 5500 BCE) until today. For four hundred years (fourth-seventh centuries), the LRA1 served as both agent and symbol of the deeply entwined, far-flung economic network of the later Roman and Byzantine worlds. The handbook offers an up-to-date overview and user-friendly identification guide to known production sites, petrographic data, and current information on distribution, which stretches from Scotland and Wales to Yemen and India"-- Provided by publisher.
Identifiers: LCCN 2025011247 (print) | LCCN 2025011248 (ebook) | ISBN 9781957454641 (paperback) | ISBN 9781957454658 (pdf)
Subjects: LCSH: Amphoras--Rome. | Amphoras--Mediterranean Region. | Excavations (Archaeology)--Mediterranean Region. | Rome--Antiquities.
Classification: LCC DG97.2 .G555 2025 (print) | LCC DG97.2 (ebook) | DDC 666/.680937--dc23/eng/20250620
LC record available at https://lccn.loc.gov/2025011247
LC ebook record available at https://lccn.loc.gov/2025011248

Printed in the United States of America.

Table of Contents

Series Editor's Foreword

The Levantine Ceramics Project (LCP) is an open-access resource for the study of Levantine pottery—and its societies, cultures, and economies—from the Neolithic era (ca. 5500 BCE) until today. The LCP's mission is to provide present and future archaeologists and ceramicists with a dynamic digital platform that will enable us to help build the future of ceramic research—together.

With this handbook, we take a new step forward in the collaborative, open-ended experiment that is the LCP. LCP Handbooks are meant to be user-friendly, value-added resources, a combination up-to-date overview and helpful identification guide to vessel types and wares commonly found on archaeological sites throughout the wider Levant. For the first volume in this series, there could be no subject more suitable than the Late Roman Amphora 1 (LRA1). For four hundred years, this single vessel type served as both agent and symbol of the deeply entwined, far-flung economic network of the later Roman and Byzantine worlds. Versions are known to have been produced in over 20 workshops, spread over four countries; the jars themselves have been found at over 500 sites ranging from Scotland to India. These precise aspects—long duration, geographic range, tremendous ubiquity—mean that when an archaeologist finds an LRA1 on site, it is simultaneously familiar and challenging. It's easy to identify an LRA1 but hard to answer the many questions it raises. Who made it, and when? What did it hold? By what route and for what reason did it arrive? The jar itself is something like the tip of an iceberg: a recognizable object with much additional meaning behind it.

The LRA1 is exceptional but not unique. The "tip of the iceberg" analogy pertains to many ceramic forms, wares, and styles that archaeologists regularly find. So, along with summary overviews and identification guides, these handbooks will also provide the kind of fundamental information that helps scholars and students raise, frame, and begin to address bigger questions. Pottery has always been an essential wayfinding tool to the vast and varied landscape of the past. We see this series as a kind of navigation system, a twenty-first-century resource aimed at that past landscape.

The engine propelling this twenty-first-century resource is the LCP itself. The contents are built from data on the LCP's stable digital platform: every site, kiln/workshop, vessel, petrographic sample, and ceramic ware/ware family/style cited in this handbook also appears there. Each book will be available in hard copy as well as in a free, open-access download. Readers of the online version can toggle directly between the handbook and the LCP and there find additions, for example, new photographs, petrographic data, an LRA1 from a new site or different country, and so on. LCP contributors can set notifications to keep abreast of new information pertaining to LRA1s specifically (or late Roman/Byzantine amphoras or pottery in general). In this regard, we hope that LCP Handbooks offer a new model for print/digital partnership.

When I launched the LCP in 2011, the focus was archaeological ceramics from the Levant—the modern countries of Turkey, Syria, Lebanon, Cyprus, Israel, the Palestinian Authority, Jordan, and Egypt—from the Neolithic era (ca. 5500 BCE) through the present day. I hoped that a tool that made it easier to find information and connect with other archaeologists would spark new ideas, spur collaborations, answer old questions and inspire new ones. Yet I could not have imagined that the site itself would become a seedbed for an even newer mode of communication—or that its geographic range would become so expansive. That this has come to pass is thanks to many, many people, beginning with the 744 contributors (as of this writing) who have submitted data to the LCP.

There is not enough space for the long roll call of people whose energy, efforts, and time have gotten us to this juncture. Collaboration takes multitudes! Here I give special shout-outs to the LCP's earliest adopters, people whose work and belief helped turn a big idea into reality: Austin Alexander, Peter Stone, Matthew Spigelman, Güzin Eren, Brigitte Keslinke, Sabine Ladstätter, Débora Sandhaus, Patrick Degryse, and Anastasia Shapiro. Thank you! Everlasting gratitude to Sharon Herbert, whose support has made the difference time and again, and who remains a deep well of sage advice. Deepest, dazzled thanks to Raoul Alwani, the engineering mastermind who makes it all work.

Finally, there is the indispensable team behind this volume. Tremendous thanks to Matt Adams and Bill Caraher, whose willingness to jump on this train has been instrumental to its forward momentum. The last bow must go to Grady Gillett and Veronica Iacomi, for their dedication, creative energies, and wide-angle vision. Thank you all.

Andrea M. Berlin
Founder and Editor, The Levantine Ceramics Project

An invitation to Become an LCP Contributor!

The LCP is not just a resource designed *for* researchers as they reference the data and tools freely available on our platform. It was built and is constantly growing thanks to the contributions *by* scholars around the world. Every individual who uploads their original data to the LCP is a verified author of this digital publication and always receives full credit for all information submitted. We invite you to join us and hundreds of LCP contributors as we collaborate to make Levantine pottery easily available and thus propel dialogue and facilitate research.

There are three key things to know about the LCP: (1) contributors can edit their entries at any time; (2) all entries have a stable URL to ensure long-term accessibility; and (3) all entries are digital publications linked to their specific authors/contributors. For example:

Jackson, Mark; Meyza, Henryk; Late Roman D-E/Cypriot red slip (LRD-E/CRSW), *The Levantine Ceramics Project*, https://www.levantineceramics.org/wares/160-late-roman-d-e-cypriot-red-slip-lrd-e-crsw.

Registering as a contributor on the LCP takes less than one minute. Go to the homepage at https://www.levantineceramics.org/. Click the "register" button in the top right corner.

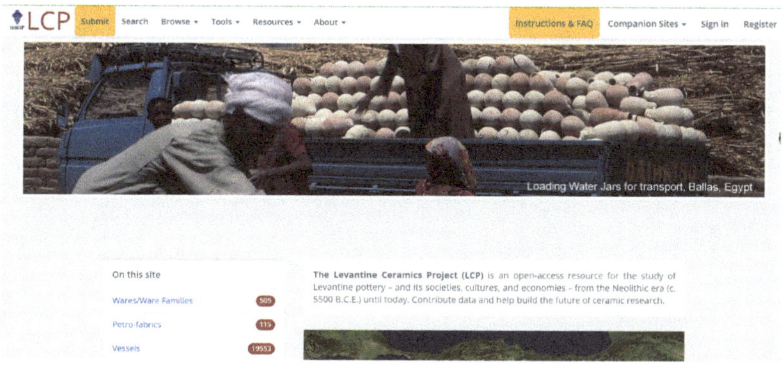

The default settings register you as an LCP user. Click the checkbox at the bottom of the registration page to *also* register yourself as a contributor. This will create a profile page where you, along with all LCP users and visitors can see all of the data you upload.

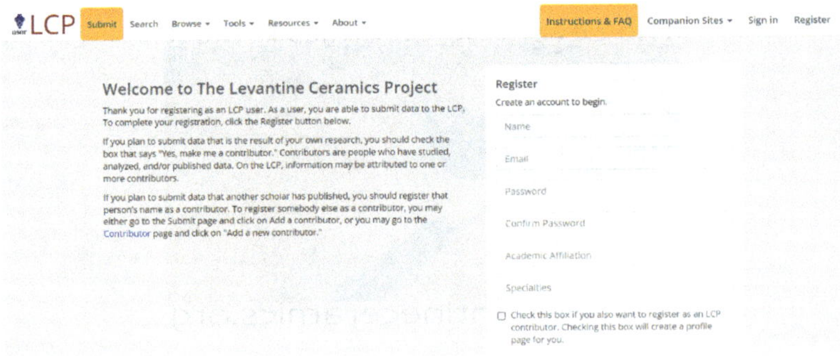

Contributing ceramic data to the LCP is intuitive. Select your category from the main submission page, and then follow the step-by-step prompts to submit your information. LCP editors and interns are available to help answer any questions or concerns you might have.

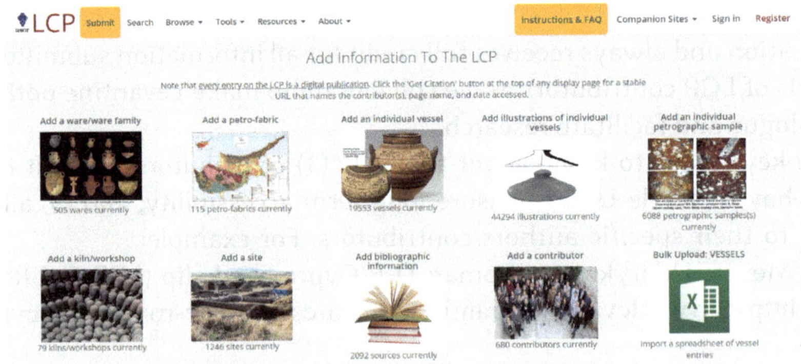

We invite you to register on the LCP, contribute data, and help build the future of ceramic research!

Preface

There are few other vessels of late antiquity, or indeed any historical period, so ubiquitous and representative of their own age as the Late Roman Amphora 1 (LRA1). Mass-produced and widely distributed, these amphoras are found in assemblages all over the Mediterranean and beyond from the 4th–8th centuries, and occasionally even later.[1] LRA1s are well attested in the main centers of Mediterranean trade (Athens, Alexandria, Antioch, Beirut, Caesarea Maritima, Carthage, Rome and Ostia, Marseille, etc.), in tiny "opportunistic harbors" frequented by local merchants, and inland agricultural villages alike. This range has made LRA1s an important proxy for analyzing social and economic connectivity. In the two decades following John Riley's creation of the Late Roman amphora typology (1979), scholarly attention began moving toward the identification of production centers deduced by ceramic "wasters" (Peacock 1986; Empereur and Picon 1989), until actual kilns and production facilities started to be excavated (e.g., Paphos in Cyprus, see Demesticha and Michaelides 2001; Elaiussa-Sebaste in Cilicia, see Burragato et al. 2007, Borgia and Iacomi 2010). In recent years, petrographic analyses on specimens from a wide variety of assemblages, including Cyprus, Cilicia, Spain, and Israel (e.g., Leidwanger 2014; Diamanti 2010; Gillett 2023) have added new information to the picture. Eminent scholars have produced important synthetic studies (Opaiţ; Demesticha), and a glance at the index of the LRCW annual publications shows the intensity and variety of LRA1 research.

Despite such a rich body of literature, we have still only scratched the surface of this complex and long-lived exchange network. We believe that by synthesizing the existing literature and supporting it with robust open-sourced ceramic data, we can create a state-of-the-art assessment of the "LRA1 question" that will grow more precise as more data are contributed. That is the mission behind this handbook. Stemming from data published on the Levantine Ceramic Project (LCP), and conforming to the LCP's guiding principles (i.e., building the future of collaborative and open-access ceramic research), this handbook is your handy and compact—but at the same time comprehensive and updated—field guide to the comprehensive and updated-field guide to the LRA1.

After a short introduction (ch. 1), we discuss the typological features, together with a reasoned presentation of the different typological subdivisions, and present a simplified solution (ch. 2). A detailed catalog of all known production centers follows (ch. 3), including data on the workshops' associated petrography, typology, and inscriptions (when available). Separate chapters are dedicated, respectively, to petrographic studies on various LRA1 assemblages (ch. 4) and extra data on inscriptions (*tituli picti*, stamps, and graffiti; ch. 5). After a concise presentation of the current scholarly discussions on contents (ch. 6), we present an overview of LRA1 distribution patterns through the synchronic and diachronic mapping of relevant assemblages (ch. 7). The closing chapter (8) is the synopsis of additional studies where the LRA1 question is analyzed from the wider perspective of the socioeconomic and political implications, alongside some final considerations stemming from the present book. Lastly, references to other ceramic databases are provided to encourage scholars to contribute to these practical digital resources (ch. 9). Are you a field archaeologist, researcher, or student who has come across LRA1s in your work? If so, we cordially invite you to join us and contribute data to this innovative digital pub-

1. All dates in the handbook are to be considered CE unless specified otherwise.

lication via the LCP, and become a part of the future of ceramic research! Please see above for a quick guide on how to become a contributor.

Veronica Iacomi
Grady Gillett

Chapter 1. Introduction

The LRA1 was a maritime transport container characterized by two ˥-shaped handles and inverted pear-shaped to cylindrical body, often featuring a pinched waist, and covered with wide ribs. Produced by potters across the eastern Mediterranean during late antiquity, the vessel was used primarily to ship liquids (see ch. 6). Scholars have interpreted the massive production and vast distribution of the LRA1 as evidence for the workings of the *annona* and *annona militaris*, the state-level system of taxation in kind and redistribution of foodstuffs—most frequently grain, but also wine and olive oil—given as an allowance for some Roman citizens and the military (Rostovtzeff 1957: 158–63; Peacock and Williams 1986: 186; McCormick 2001: 85–86; Iacomi 2010; Bezeczky 2013: 159; Rauh, Autret, and Lund 2013: 164). While the state controlled the *annona* and therefore had a role in the production of LRA1s (see Diamanti 2023: 282–86), the container was also a common part of regional and local merchants' toolkits as they conducted smaller-scale private trade or co-opted the container for their own secondary uses, according to a pattern that has been outlined for Late Roman Amphora 2s (LRA2; Karagiorgou 2001). The widespread network of LRA1 producers and far wider network of consumers, both on a state and private level, mean that this amphora is one of the best proxies for reconstructing intangible social and economic connections across the Mediterranean during late antiquity (Karagiorgou 2009: 37).

This is not to say that this proxy is readily understood. Questions abound concerning nearly every aspect of the LRA1. What was the main use of the amphora: to carry wine or olive oil (or even dry goods)? Did Cypriot production of the form largely replace Cilician production in the 6th century? Is it possible to connect the LRA1s found in an excavation to a particular workshop? And, above all, how can we define an LRA1—*What is* an LRA1? In the following pages, we hope to offer evidence to help address each of these queries and more by presenting new data alongside an overall view of existing research.

During the process of synthesizing the considerable range of LRA1 chronologies, typologies, workshops, and primary uses, we encountered several issues that should be noted. What at first sounds like the easiest question to answer, "What is an LRA1?," under scrupulous analysis produces a rather convoluted definition that includes a wide range of possible components. As a matter of fact, despite a few distinctive features, the form exhibits considerable variability in terms of volume, size, and production areas, not to mention contents. It is therefore not surprising that the first typology assigned to this amphora, the "Dressel 34," did not survive for long, unlike the many other amphora names coined by this eminent scholar. Many different typological classifications exist to describe the LRA1: the Ballana 6;[1] British B2/Bii;[2] Agora M333;[3] Michel Egloff's Kellia 164 and 169;[4] Georgi Kuzmanov's type XIII;[5]

1. After Emery and Kirwan 1938.
2. After Thomas 1959.
3. After Robinson 1959.
4. After Egloff 1977.
5. After Kuzmanov 1973.

Constantin Scorpan's type 8B;[6] Avshalom Zemer's type 66;[7] Yassı Ada 1;[8] David Peacock's and David Williams' type 44;[9] Simon Keay's type 53;[10] John Hayes' type 5[11] (see Reynolds 2005: 565; Bezeczky 2013: 158; Demesticha 2014: 600 for more). Some of these are obsolete (e.g., Ballana 6), while others are regional types that still appear in the modern literature of their respective area (e.g., B2/Bii). The widely used LRA nomenclature, including the LRA1 name that has become the standard, comes from John Riley's work at Berenice and Carthage, where large numbers of amphoras from the "Late Roman" period were found and classified (cf. Riley 1979, 1981). However, it remains difficult to apply it universally due to the vast variability mentioned above: Andrei Opaiţ (2004: 8) recognized "at least six subtypes, each of it divided into many other variants"; Dominique Pieri (2005a) devised two primary groups and a considerable array of subgroups and *sous-modules*; Stella Demesticha (2013) suggested three generations of LRA1s, the second comprising at least three different forms. These typologies are further explored and synchronized in chapter 2.

The "late Roman" portion of the name seems to represent a constant characteristic of the form throughout all modes of inquiry, thus defining the amphora in a chronological, rather than typological, way. But late Roman is a loose and flexible period that is used in myriad ways, often as a synonym for "late antique" and "early Byzantine," and usually to indicate the time from the foundation of Constantinople to the rise of Islam and subsequent Islamic conquests (conventionally 330 and 622, respectively). As this is not a book delving into historical periodization, we will explicitly define the chronology we use and share the rationale behind it. While the peak of LRA1 production and consumption does fall neatly into the general Late Roman period, there are ongoing debates on when and from which parent form the LRA1 evolved.[12] It seems probable that a "proto-LRA1," itself an influential form that might have spurred imitations (Poblome et al. 2008: 1004–5), was developed in eastern Cilicia (see examples from Elaiussa in Ferrazzoli and Ricci 2010), while "canonical" LRA1 production started in the late 4th century, according to stratigraphic data. The earliest LRA1 identified outside Cilicia was found in the "Earthquake House" at Kourion in a context dating to the last third of the same century (Costello 2011: 38; LCP vessel 34825). Therefore, for the purposes of this handbook, the term LRA1 refers to all subtypes within this group *after* roughly 370–380.

By the end of the LRA1's lifespan, the picture is considerably less defined, indeed it is much more blurred. While the data indicate that eastern Cilician and Cypriot production came to an end soon after the mid-7th century, LRA1 manufacturing had begun in other regions around the same time or beforehand, and in some of these regions the industry continued for at least another half-century (see ch. 3). Undoubtedly, the influence and sheer ubiquity of this amphora made a significant impact on ceramic-producing communities in the eastern Mediterranean and Black Sea regions. There are numerous instances of workshops incorporating morphological components of the LRA1 into their

6. After Scorpan 1975.
7. After Zemer 1977.
8. After Bass and van Doornick 1982.
9. After Peacock and Williams 1986.
10. After Keay 1984.
11. After Hayes 1992.
12. The main hypotheses are either that the LRA1 is an evolution from the Pompeii V/Late Pompeii V amphora or the Gauloise 4 amphora. For a thorough discussion and references therein, see Reynolds 2008: 70–72; Opaiţ 2009: 284–85; Marchand, Reynolds, and Bomin 2022.

repertoire of shapes—thence the production of what are frequently referred to as imitations, variants, *sous-modules*, and derivatives (see Pieri 2007b: 614–15). The type D Snp I amphora[13] produced at the Demirci workshop in the hinterland of Sinop, alongside the Cretan TRC9 and Antonova types 5/6 (likely produced in the Pontic area, see Smokotina 2015: 129–32) and 9 (sometimes defined as LRA1 imitation, Opaiț 2017: 594 and n. 226), offer prime examples in this regard. The question then arises: At what point does a ceramic phenomenon cease to contain meaning pertinent to archaeologists, beyond which we are simply observing similar-looking containers? Obviously, there is no discrete endpoint, but the strands of influence are so far-flung that we finally decided to implement a clear cutoff in defining an LRA1. Therefore, we excluded LRA1-adjacent forms for which *production* demonstrably began after the late 7th century (i.e., definitely falling into the mid-Byzantine period).

The Sinopean, Cretan, and probable Bosporan LRA1-equivalent amphoras mentioned above are fascinating examples of the long-distance diffusion and coevolution of technological and artistic styles. They are morphologically and chronologically compatible with LRA1s. Often, these parallel amphoras were part of the same exchange systems and imported by the same consumers (e.g., type D Snp I amphoras and LRA1s in the Levant). However, each one of these types developed within a distinct milieu of local communities of potters that had their own well-developed styles and repertoires displaying some broad similarities to LRA1s. Thanks to the strong ties established by Mare Nostrum and her sister the Black Sea, these forms grew to resemble each other even more from the 6th century onward in terms of morphology. Nevertheless, we decided to exclude each type from the LRA1 designation used in this book due to their demonstrable connections to distinct local amphoras.

We also incorporated late antique geopolitical and economic realities as we defined the scope of our LRA1 analysis. As mentioned above, the data suggest a connection between the core LRA1 manufacturing areas and the Constantinopolitan *annona* system, although this connection was not the original economic force driving the early development and movement of the vessel. The provinces of Cilicia and Cyprus, and the southern Aegean were the most productive for the LRA1 tradition (see ch. 3); 18 of the 21 known workshops that produced these containers are found there (Empereur and Picon 1989; Manning et al. 2000; Demesticha and Michaelides 2001; Borgia and Iacomi 2010; Papavassiliou, Sarantidis and Papanikolaou 2014). The implications of the Abydos tariff (Iacomi 2010) point to a progressive cooptation of Cilician wine merchants—who had an already-established trade network since the early/mid-Roman period, as suggested by local industry of pottery production (an overview in Komar 2016: 159–72) into the imperial foodstuff supply chain revolving around Constantinople (a nascent system compared to the centuries-old *annona* of Rome). A similar process occurred in 536, when Justinian's 41st Novel codified a new administrative district led by a *quaestura exercitus* that included the LRA1-producing regions of Caria, Cyprus, and the Cyclades, intended to optimize *annona* shipments to military outposts on the empire's northwestern fringes (see Demesticha 2015: 68 and Opaiţ et al. 2020: 391 and references therein for further discussion). In both cases, preexisting and well-worn commercial trade routes and ceramic manufacturing centers were folded into the state's administrative machine, seemingly increasing the flow of traffic. An often-overlooked LRA1 production site in the imperial breadbasket of Egypt (see Saint Jeremiah's Monastery) might offer even further evidence for this trend, although the connection is murkier.

13. D Snp I amphoras—a part of broader long-lived ceramic traditions in the southern Pontic region (see Kassab Tezgör 2020: 15–43)—have very similar handles and a conical body covered in ribs of varying width that make it difficult to distinguish from later LRA1s.

Outlining the LRA1 productive mechanism and its dynamics as a whole demands dealing with the current state of archaeological research. Many sites have been proposed to be LRA1 production centers in recent decades, some corroborated via excavation but often assumed based on a large number of LRA1 sherds found in surveys or similarities between the fabric and local raw clays. Only through the clear presence of facilities and other "strong" indicators like waster deposits (see the discussion in ch. 3), can their identification as production centers, as opposed to storage or transshipment *entrepôts*, be confirmed.

Another important element for the definition of the amphora class (and dictated by its manufacturing areas) is its contents. Whether LRA1s were primarily utilized for wine, olive oil, even garum, honey, or grain remains a debate among some scholars, but the ambiguity of evidence is itself a clue that is frequently overlooked (but cf. Panella 1993: 665–66 n. 220). Our approach to the question of what LRA1s transported has been to concurrently examine the corpus of inscriptions, a dataset frequently understudied and referenced only in passing, alongside the macro- and microdistribution patterns of the LRA1s. We strongly believe that characterizing the full spectrum of patterns and conclusions that may be elucidated via the LRA1 must include an accurate record of all reported attestations within, and just as importantly, *beyond* its areas of production.[14]

LRA1s have been found along the Mediterranean coast of southern Europe, northern and eastern Africa, and western Asia as well as the Black Sea region; their long-range diffusion includes the British Isles, North Sea littoral, and the southern Arabian peninsula, and even sporadically the Sahara and the Indian subcontinent (see the site index). We have recorded 575 sites where the amphora is attested, and this number is undoubtedly an underestimate. In order to assemble and synthesize useful data for cross-referencing, we reviewed a huge mass of literature, beginning with the classics on the subject (Peacock and Williams 1986; Empereur and Picon 1989; Pieri 2005a, among many others) and the conference papers of the relevant periodical meetings on ceramics (e.g., the series Late Roman Coarse Wares [LRCW], and Rei Cretariae Romanae Fautorum Acta). We combed through excavation reports and pottery studies devoted to single regions, areas, and sites; relevant entries on the LCP; and material personally provided to us by many collaborative colleagues.[15] Our goal was to define distribution patterns through consistent diachronic and synchronic mapping, based upon the widest possible catalog of attestations.

One of our main challenges in the creation of this catalog regarded the definition of coherent regions that best reflect the diffusion of LRA1s within the colorful and variable mosaic of milieus of which they were a part. The easiest choice would have been to abide by a model using modern nations' boundaries, but projecting the realities of 21st century borders onto late antiquity seemed rather arbitrary from a historical perspective. On the other hand, LRA1s are attested over a long period that saw frequent changes in terms of political borders, economic structures, administrative organization, and religious ideologies within multiple imperial and independent polities. It is impossible to draw a single regional map that represents and conveys all of these changes. Accepting these shortcomings, we fi-

14. Such a holistic analysis of a single amphora form is unprecedented: Pieri 2005a, e.g., is not limited to LRA1 but includes several different late antique amphoras, wonderfully analyzed but not at the resolution presented here. Öniz 2016, on the other hand, defined his survey with precise geographical limits in the eastern Mediterranean, while Reynolds 2010a is geographically circumscribed and chronologically wider in scope. A good synopsis of the *status quaestionis* is offered in Pacetti 1995: 273–79, which nonetheless needs to be updated in light of the new evidence stemming from the uninterrupted research of the past 30 years.

15. We offer our deepest thanks to all of the many scholars who contributed to this research in the index.

nally opted for a hybrid approach. With the Barrington Atlas (Tolbert 2000: map 102) as a reference, we distinguished a series of macroregions (see ch. 7) that loosely reflect the political situation during the 6th century, the LRA1's most representative period in terms of both production and consumption. In this way, the contents provided for each of our regions can be effectively used for reasonable historical evaluation as well as for quick interregional comparisons. To avoid confusion or misleading ambiguous definitions, we labeled each region according to their more widespread historical-geographical names (e.g., "Levant," "Asia Minor"), adding a reference to both the late antique/early Byzantine denomination and the modern countries in whose territories they fall.

Another frequent dilemma we faced was the inconsistency of the available literature: sometimes even small assemblages are fully analyzed and published, whereas some larger sites still await detailed final publication. Moreover, nomenclature (see above), statistics, and even vessel measurements are reported in diverse ways, as there are no broadly accepted standards to reference or address these data points. Notwithstanding such challenges, in this handbook we chose to consider *all* sites where LRA1s are even only mentioned,[16] so as to propose the most comprehensive possible mapping. We see this as a starting point, one we hope can be expanded in future editions of this handbook. The distinctive power and flexibility of the open-access LCP enabled and empowered us to achieve this, and we emphasize that knowledge will continue to grow so long as integration between publications and digital databases becomes standard operating procedure for scholars in this internet age.

16. Or where their presence is cross-referenced in reliable sources.

Chapter 2. Typology

Over centuries of production, the essential shape of the LRA1 remains constant. All forms have two ˥-shaped handles and horizontal ridges or ribs running across the body. The body is roughly cylindrical to pear-shaped, sometimes with a "cinched" waist that has a smaller diameter than the upper body. The handles project perpendicularly from under the rim, turning down in a curve that varies from rounded to a sharp right angle. That said, potters did make different sizes and volumes, as well as change certain small details. These variations, a result of the form's long lifespan and its being manufactured in many different workshops across the eastern Mediterranean, can complicate the creation of neat typologies.

The standard typological subdivision was devised by Pieri (2005a). Broad in scope, it has proven durable and remains the most cited. In this handbook, we use a modified version of Pieri's typology, which we explain below. We have introduced a few adjustments and additions (i.e., the LRA1 type C and the late LRA1 *survival*) to account for new discoveries in the two decades since Pieri's classification. In some cases, individual workshops produced LRA1s with characteristics sufficiently distinctive to allow for their products to be specifically distinguished; these particular cases inform our adjusted typology (e.g., Laggeri and Kambos, see the production centers catalog below).

Our objective is not to create the most detailed typological series, but to convey the most current overall picture of the amphora's morphology. We offer this synthesized breakdown of the LRA1 type as a contribution to the ongoing dialogue and iterative process of refining the typology as more data are published (and shared on the LCP).

The LRA1 is notably diverse in its morphology, size, and volume. The seminal study on LRA1 capacities was conducted by Peter van Alfen (1996) and focused on type Bs in the Yassı Ada assemblage. Just within this subtype (which van Alfen breaks into 11 more subtypes), at least three discrete capacities existed: ca. 6 l, 7.1 l, and 9.5 l. No significant correlation could be made between the amphoras' volume and common volumetric measurements in the Late Roman and Byzantine periods, leading to the suggestion that the dominant metrological system was measured not by volume, but by weight (the Byzantine λίτρα, or *litra*). This hypothesis too, however, did not always explain the variations, as the empty weight of the vessels within the same subtype varied substantially (van Alfen 1996: 205–7). Inscriptions do not seem to agree with this hypothesis, as several indicate *sextarii* as the metrological system (although this is irrelevant in the recycling/secondary use case). The situation only becomes messier when the other subtypes are incorporated, with capacities ranging from 18–36 l (Lund 2023: 45); see figure 1.

It is sometimes observed that capacities tended to decrease over the LRA1's lifespan (e.g., Bădescu and Cliante 2014: 174), and this is generally true for our types A–C, but does not apply for the 6th–8th century production in the Aegean.

LRA1-specific stands or pedestals were sometimes produced alongside the container itself, such as at Elaiussa (Ferrazzoli and Ricci 2007: 677, fig. 2b) and Soli-Pompeiopolis, and potentially at Mastichari, though at the latter they might have been intended for LRA3s. These objects, sometimes bearing inscriptions, are understudied, and at present it is unclear if they were associated with a specific production region, type, or time period of the LRA1 phenomenon. All subtypes of the amphora were

Concordance of LRA1 Typologies

Our typology/ subtype	Major characteristics	Chronology	Other typologies
LRA1 type A (see fig. 47.1–4)	The earliest iteration of the "standard" LRA1 is type A. This form has a pear-shaped body, a tall narrow neck (5–7.5 cm, sometimes narrower in the midsection), grooved handles, a button on the base, and a narrow mouth with a fold rim. There is a good deal of variability within the necks and rims of type A—this probably attests to the variety of workshops producing it. We include Pieri's type A *sous-module* within this type.	Mid-4th to the late 5th or early 6th c.	Pieri LRA 1A and LRA 1A *sous-modules*; Demesticha LR1/a or LR1 first generation; Kourion type 5 (KT V); Egloff/Kellia 169; Dressel 34; Opaiţ LRA 1A2
LRA1 transitional type (see fig. 50)	The body of this type is cylindrical, not ovoid, and the handles are thicker. In general, LRA1 handles are attached at an obtuse angle during the 4th c. (type A), but became right angles in the 5th c. Starting in the 5th c., potters begin to widen the mouths of the LRA1. This results in shorter, wider neck walls and a more robust protruding rim around the vessel's mouth. Note that the cylindrical body does not yet feature the "pinched" lower half, a classic feature of type B.	5th–6th c.	Pieri LRA 1A transition or late LRA 1A; Tamás Bezeczky's type 52B
LRA1 type B (see fig. 48)	A pinched waist, often wider neck (6–12.5 cm), and round base are defining characteristics of LRA1 type B (Pieri 2005a: 75). The rim flares out more than type A, but the handles remain grooved. The center of the neck frequently features a sort of rib or ridge. This is the most common form, and most LRA1 variants made outside the core production area adhere to this template (e.g., LRA1s produced in the Aegean Islands and Egypt). We include some of Pieri's type B *sous-modules* within this type. The Egyptian LRA1 type B may be reliably distinguished as a further subtype on the basis of fabric (see fig. 21 below). Nile silty clay is the raw material used to produce it, which appears brown to reddish brown (it is iron-rich) in section with quartz grains and some mica.	Late 5th to early 7th c.	Pieri LRA 1B and 1B *sous-modules* (note that some of these fit into our LRA1 type C); Bezeczky type 52C; Yassi Ada 1 (YA1) and its subtypes; Demesticha LR1/b or LR1 second generation; Opaiţ 2004 LRA 1A3–4; Egloff/Kellia 164; note that Cretan TRC9s are morphologically very similar to type B

LRA1 type C (LRA1c) (see fig. 49)	Type C is smaller in volume than the typical type A or B and the body's pear shape (the pinched waist) is even more pronounced. The neck is cylindrical and varies significantly in diameter from ca. 5–12 cm. The base may be rounded or feature a slight nipple, but less pronounced than the type A. We divide type C into the Cypriot and Cilician forms.	mid 6th–7th c.	Pieri LRA 1B *sous-modules*; Demesticha LR1/C or LR1 third generation; Jean-Yves Empereur's Amathus LRA 1B2; Bezeczky "later forms"; note that type D Snp I amphoras are morphologically very similar to Cypriot type C LRA1s
LRA1 *survival* (see fig. 50)	The LRA1 *survival* is almost globular, and the distinctly pear-shaped or pinched waist body of previous forms is less pronounced. The diameter of the amphora increases past the joint between the handle and shoulder before angling inward in a similar manner to the type A and transitional LRA1. The handles may form a right angle or more of a curve. The neck and mouth tend to be narrower than type B. This subtype has clear parallels with the growth of the LRA13 and the Byzantine Globular Amphora (BGA).	7th–early 9th c.	Byzantine globular-ovoid amphora; LRA1 *survival*; Hayes type 44–45 at Saraçhane

most likely sealed either with a ceramic disk or a cork and an adhesive agent such as pitch or plaster (Pieri 2005a: 77–78; Brennan et al. 2020: 303). Over 160 ceramic stoppers were found in the Yassı Ada shipwreck, ranging from 4–9.7 cm in diameter (van Alfen 1996: 190). They seemed to fall into four categories, aligned with the Byzantine δάκτυλος (*daktylos*, or finger), which correlates with van Alfen's conclusion of multiple size standards within the type B. Ceramic stoppers showing the same fabric as the locally produced amphoras are attested in 7th century assemblages at Elaiussa—but not in contexts of the previous century (Burragato et al. 2007: 690; Ferrazzoli and Ricci 2007: 677, fig. 2c).

The lack of stringent standardization in the LRA1, particularly in contrast to its frequent travel companion the LRA2, reflects how manufacturers in different regions co-opted the container in flexible and dynamic ways to fit their needs. While it may have originally been designated to carry a single specific liquid (i.e., wine), "LRA1 types of all sizes were manufactured to hold specific measures of different liquid commodities, effectively making this class of amphora, as a whole, a general-purpose container" by the end of its lifespan (van Alfen 1996: 209).

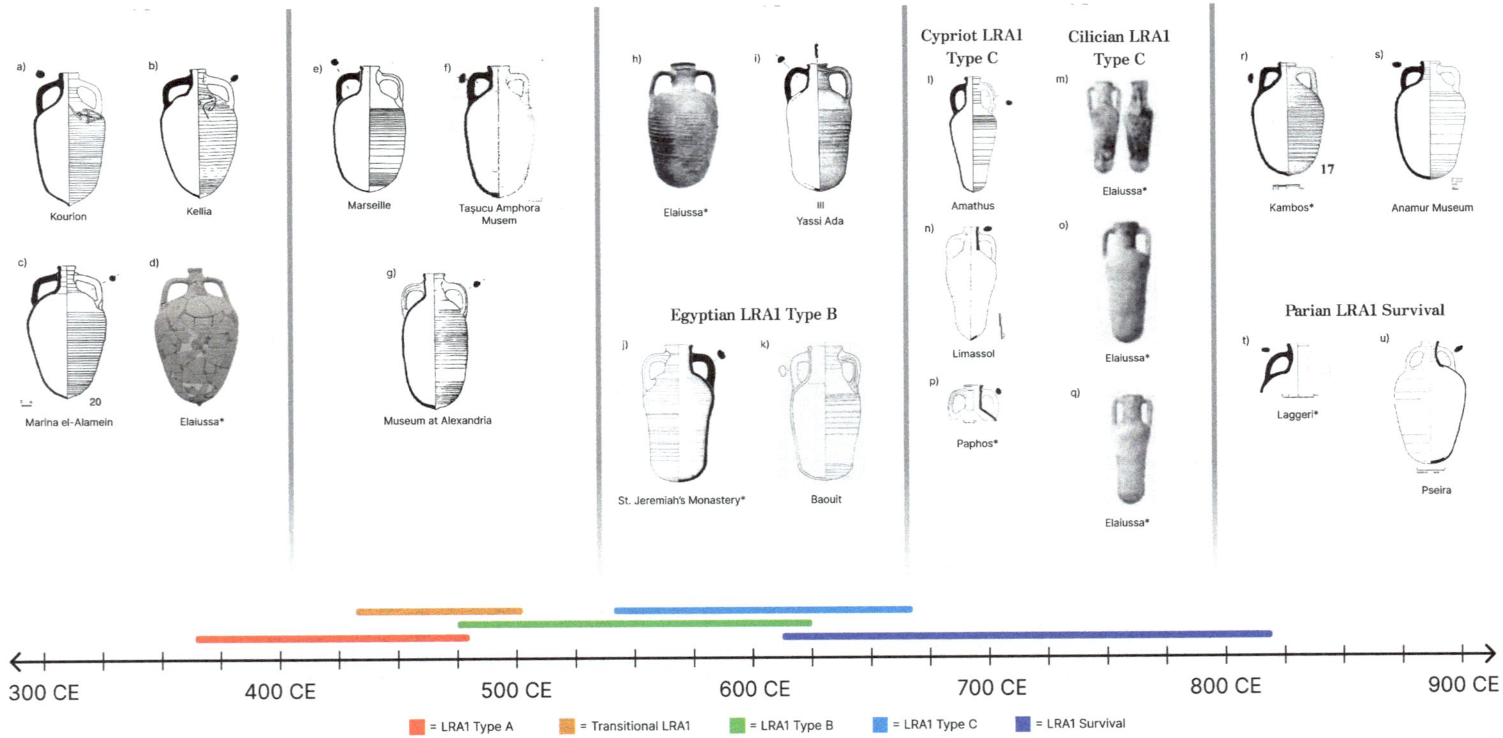

Figure 1. A chart displaying the various LRA1 subtypes within our typology. Each vessel is labeled with the site where it was excavated (or the museum where it currently resides. Note that not all images are to scale. The asterisk * denotes LRA1s manufactured at the findspot.

(a) Williams 2005a: fig. 2; (b) Pieri 2005a: fig. 27; (c) Majcherek 1993: fig. 11; (d) Ferrazzoli and Ricci 2010: fig. 4.21; (e) Pieri 2005a: pl. 14; (f) Şenol 2009: 232, catalog #58; (g) Empereur and Picon 1989: fig. 15; (h) Ferrazzoli and Ricci 2010: fig. 6.26; (i) van Alfen 1996: fig. 5; (j) Ghaly 1992: fig. 16b; (k) Marchand and Dixneuf 2007: fig. 23; (l) Empereur 2018: fig. 1.F3; (m) Ferrazzoli and Ricci 2010: fig. 7.27; (n) Demesticha 2013: fig. 4; (o) Ferrazzoli and Ricci 2010: fig. 7.27; (p) Demesticha and Michaelides: 2001, fig. 10; (q) Ferrazzoli and Ricci 2010: fig. 7.27; (r) Poulou-Papadimitriou and Nodarou 2014: fig. 5a; (s) Rauh 2023: fig. 31; (t) Diamanti 2016: fig. 8; (u) Poulou-Papadimitriou and Nodarou 2014: fig. 5a.

Chapter 3. Production

Since the publication of the pivotal study by Peacock and Williams (1986), the Syro-Cilician coastland and Cyprus have been regarded as the main production areas of LRA1s. Large scale surveys by Empereur and Maurice Picon in the 1980s provided solid support for this assumption, with a catalog of 15 production centers identified along the eastern Mediterranean coastland from northern Syria to the eastern Aegean, including Cyprus (Empereur and Picon 1989).[1] In this catalog, we include all these production centers even when no further evidence can be provided, unless their conclusions have been reasonably challenged in the decades since. Regrettably, archaeological excavations to further examine their findings have been conducted in only a few of their listed sites (notably, at Elaiussa Sebaste and Yumurtalik); the majority of the reported kilns remain unstudied. Some have even disappeared as a consequence of the urban development of the modern centers in the meantime (see Tarsus, and it may well be the case of Seleucia Pieria).[2]

LRA1 production has been suggested in other regions, though these areas tend to lack more systematic studies and clear archaeological evidence. Michel Bonifay mentions *en passant* some 5th–6th century African imitations of LRA1, but provides little context and no further comment (2004: 151).[3] Recent petrographic studies by one of the authors (G.G.) offer tantalizing evidence of a possible production in the southern Levant, but no actual workshop has yet been identified in the area (see ch. 4). The latter also applies to the Cypriot "Workshop X," a class of LRA1s from sites across Cyprus that bear petrographic similarities assumed to be the product of an unknown Cypriot workshop (Demesticha 2003: 471; 2015: 59). In all three cases, strong archaeological markers are so far missing (see below) and therefore no African nor southern Levantine production center could be included in the present catalog. Finally, we do not include Sinop as a production center because although the formulation of the type D Snp I amphora was clearly informed by the LRA1, it was a component in the evolution of the well-established local amphora repertoire. The systematic study of the rich epigraphic corpus associated with LRA1s (in particular, *tituli picti*) will help shed further light on the areas of production, as the first steps in this direction are promisingly starting to demonstrate.[4]

Apart from the manufacturing sites and regions mentioned above, we evaluated potential LRA1 production centers using a set of rigorous standards. The strong indicators we selected are as follows:

1. In an earlier report of their survey, some more LRA1 production centers are included (notably: Olympos, Phaselis, and Side; see Empereur and Picon 1988: 35, fig. 21) that were not mentioned again in the publication of the following year. The 1988 map is reproposed again in Williams 2005a and Williams 2005b. As to Syedra, a fourth site mentioned in the 1988 but not in the 1989 reports, the Rough Cilicia Survey Project did in fact report a kiln there, though tentatively dated to the Roman period (Rauh et al. 2023).

2. As they had foreseen: "There is a certain urgency about this type of fieldwork throughout the Mediterranean because the pace of agricultural and other development is threatening small sites like workshops.... Several important workshops deposits at Alexandria have already been destroyed" (Empereur and Picon 1988: 34). Similar considerations in Pieri 2007b: 612.

3. The reference must be to Henchir Ech Chekaf, in Tunisia, where reportedly LRA1 imitations were produced (Nacef 2007: 583), but there seems to be no strong indicator of a kiln or a workshop; however, Pieri (2012: 47; cf. also 2007b: 614–15) lists it as an active workshop producing LRA1 imitations.

4. See Fournet (2021: 66) about Apamea and an estate in the vicinity of Anazarba.

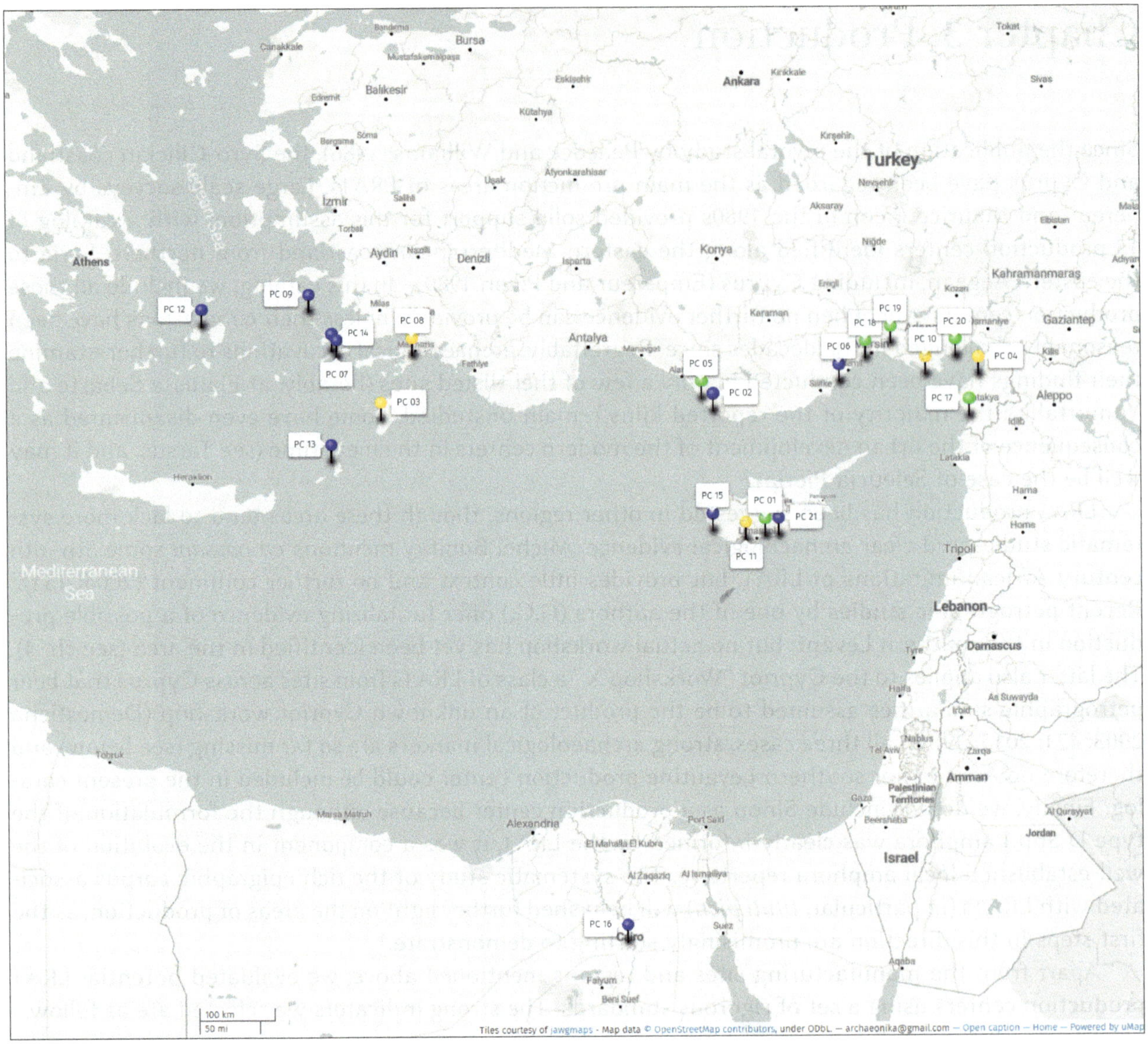

Figure 2. Kiln/workshop identification criteria. Blue: excavated/investigated kilns; green, presence of wasters; yellow: NA. Numbers correspond to the entries in the catalog.

1. The presence of kiln structures containing evidence of LRA1s, and/or
2. Significant deposits of misfired or vitrified LRA1 wasters, which can be related to the firing processes occurring in situ or close by, and/or
3. Deposits of overfired and pulverized clay (*concotto*)—a good indicator of the former presence of a ceramic kiln—alongside LRA1 sherds.

Following the criteria above, there are 21 production centers we can reasonably confirm to date. These sites are described in the catalog below.

§3.1. Catalog

Each LRA1 production center in the catalog presented here will follow the format below and is how they appear on the LCP.

Site characterization: An introduction to the settlement, with information relevant to contextualizing the LRA1 production (e.g., whether a massive urban center, a port, or a little village).

Background: Generic notes on data related to production.

Location: Of the workshop/kiln within the larger site.

Number of kilns: When known.

Period of activity: Of the workshop for LRA1 manufacturing, defined by the stratigraphy of the facilities or assumed on the typology of its products.

Description of facilities: A concise overview of the workshop and its components, when attested, that is, kiln(s), settling tanks/water storage, and other facilities such as storehouses. Particular emphasis is given to the relationship of the workshop to its surroundings, especially in terms of connective infrastructures, when known.

Typology: Of the LRA1s produced at the workshop.

Local fabric: A visual description of the fabric as seen in a "fresh break," and references to petro-fabric analyses when available.

Distribution: Of the products of the particular workshop, when known.

LCP contributors: Names of scholars who have added relevant data to the LCP.

Production center 01: Amathus

Site characterization: Located on the southern coast of Cyprus, Amathus was a sizable port city in the Late Roman period and a key node on intraisland and Mediterranean exchange, with active trade relationships to the southern Levant, north Africa, and Asia Minor (Kaldeli 2008: 153–55; Empereur 2018: 186).

Background: While no LRA1 kiln structure has been found at Amathus, wasters and the results of ceramic petrography strongly corroborate Empereur and Picon's (1989) proposal of LRA1 production at the site.

Location: Unknown, but hypothesized to be on the "slopes of the acropolis" of Amathus (Empereur and Picon 1989: 242)

Number of kilns: Unknown.

Period of activity: Mid-6th–mid-7th c.

Description of facilities: Unknown.

Typology: LRA1 type B (including a smaller "submodule," see Pieri 2005a), and type C (Empereur 2018: 183–85).

Local fabric: The local clay can vary from gray to green to beige, with mostly dark but also red and white inclusions visible to the naked eye. The fabric is nearly identical to that of Zygi-Petrini (see §4.2).

Distribution: Unknown, but see §4.2.

LCP contributors: Stella Demesticha; Maria Dikiomitou Eliadou; Paula Waiman-Barak; Grady Gillett; Veronica Iacomi

Production center 02: Antiocheia ad Cragum

Site characterization: Located along the coast of western Rough Cilicia, Antiocheia ad Cragum began as a major center of the famed Cilician pirates of the 2nd–1st centuries BCE. The settlement was taken over by the Romans in the 1st century and was a prosperous city well into the 9th century. The numerous wine presses and extent of amphora production illustrate that a thriving ceramic industry complemented the city's wine production.

Background: Amphora production at Antiocheia ad Cragum was revealed during surveys conducted by the Rough Cilicia Archaeological Survey Project in the 1990s. Recent excavations by Asena Kızılarslanoğlu (personal communication, 2023) show that the local repertoire includes LRA1s, as well as Zemer 41 ("pinched handle") and Agora M239 amphoras (Rauh 2023: 15–20). Forthcoming publications by the excavator will undoubtedly shed more light on the workshop here.

Location: Above the former Great Bath complex from the Roman period.

Number of kilns: At least seven kilns have been identified in late antique to Byzantine strata in the city.

Period of activity: ca. 4th–8th centuries.

Description of facilities: See Kızılarslanoğlu in Hoff et al. 2018: 7; Rauh 2023.

Typology: A late LRA1 *survival* (but with some different characteristics than the Aegean *survivals*), Agora M239 amphoras, and other coarse wares.

Local fabric: Nicholas Rauh and Kathleen Slane identified at least two different fabrics of locally produced wares. One is deep red and the other orange, and coarser. Both have however a very micaceous fabric and present traces of a white engobe, and are frequently referred to as Antioch fabrics (Dodd 2020: 52).

Distribution: Unknown.

LCP Contributors: Caroline Autret; Asena Kızılarslanoğlu; Nicholas K. Rauh; Grady Gillett; Veronica Iacomi

Production center 03: Apolakkia

Site characterization: Located about two kilometers from the coast on the southwestern side of Rhodes, Apolakkia was a small settlement with some large-scale architecture in the Hellenistic period, and had a Christian presence by the 5th century at the latest, shown by a basilica potentially dedicated to a local saint.

Background: In their survey of LRA1 workshops, Empereur and Picon describe "une petite production de LR1" near Apolakkia (1989: 242). Unfortunately, no further evidence is given, and no archaeological work has been conducted at Apolakkia. *Dipinti* on LRA1 found in Rome and Ballana might corroborate the assumption of Rhodian production (see ch. 5).

Location: Unknown.

Number of kilns: Unknown.

Period of activity: Unknown.

Description of facilities: Unknown.

Typology: Unknown.

Local fabric: Unknown, but petrographic research on ceramics and local clay deposits on Rhodes may provide useful reference data (see for instance Betina 2019).

Distribution: Rome.

LCP contributors: Grady Gillett; Veronica Iacomi

Production center 04: Arsuz

Site characterization: The village of Arsuz (present-day Uluçınar), located on the coast a few kilometers south of Iskenderun, is usually identified with ancient Rhosos (or Rhodiopolis). There have been no systematic investigations of the ancient ruins that are, in some cases, still visible today (Hild and Hellenkemper 1990: 392). Even though the productive facilities recognized by Empereur and Picon may have originally been related to more than one urban center (see below about the location of kilns), we have grouped them under the Arsuz entry to best align with the previous literature, until new research allows a better assessment of the matter.

Background: During their surveys, Empereur and Picon identified at least three production centers in the coastal stretch immediately south of Iskenderun, clustered around the village of Arsuz (Empereur and Picon 1988: 35, fig. 21, nos. 17–19). The state of preservation and the exact locations cannot be further ascertained.

Number of kilns: Three.

Period of activity: Unknown.

Typology: Unknown, but the workshop(s) may have produced tiles and bricks as well (Empereur and Picon 1989: 237).

Local fabric: Williams analyzed some of the sherds collected by Empereur and Picon, and described the fabric as hard and rough, ranging from pink to red (5YR 8/4–2.5YR 6/6). The main attribute was "the mixture of frequent small, dark green to black glassy grains of pyroxene and red pieces of serpentine that are scattered throughout a fairly clean-looking clay matrix" (Williams 2005a: 163–66). He also noted the occasional presence of limestone, mica, iron oxides, and voids with reaction rims.

Distribution: At least part of the assemblage of the Plaka shipwreck (see §7.2) may be related to Arsuz: results from chemical and petrographic analysis match with samples collected during the survey by Empereur and Picon in the 1980s (Waksman et al. 2014).

LCP contributors: Veronica Iacomi; Grady Gillett

Kiln #01

Location: Six kilometers south of the harbor of Arsuz, in open countryside (1980s) and on the seashore; wasters deposit.

Description of facilities: Unknown.

Kiln #02

Location: Between Arsuz and Iskenderun, in the heart of the modern village (the description given does not specify if the "village" is Arsuz).

Description of facilities: It seems that at least part of the kiln was still visible at the time of Empereur and Picon's surveys, but the facility was already, reportedly, very badly damaged.

Kiln #03

Location: 13 km north of Arsuz, in open countryside and by the seashore.

Description of the facilities: Reported as "damaged during the construction of modern road."

Production center 05: Delice

Site characterization: Located about four kilometers north of the modern town of Gazipaşa, this probable kiln site sat adjacent to a large walled enclosure that has not been excavated.

Background: The site was first identified by the Rough Cilicia Archaeological Survey Project in 1997, and a later reassessment of overfired pottery and fired clay fragments by one of the surveyors determined a ceramic kiln likely existed there in the Late Roman and Byzantine periods.

Location: Behind a line of dunes, beyond which is the mouth of the Delice River, "several hundred meters (m) south of the site" (Rauh 2023).

Number of kilns: Unknown.

Period of activity: It seems that the production center was already active during the 1st–4th centuries (Agora M239), and the original surveyors write that activities were later resumed in the Early to mid-Byzantine periods (8th–10th c.). We disagree with this dating of the second phase, as the ceramic assemblage identified generally dates to the 4th–7th centuries (LRD-E).

Description of the facilities: No kiln structure has been located, but a clay pit with "large lumps of fired clay" and overfired pottery was found at the southern end of the ruined structure (Rauh 2023: 20).

Typology: LRA1 *survival* (which the excavators assert should be dated to the 8–10th c., though this chronology seems late to the present authors).

Local fabric: Consistent, fine, reddish-brown fabric (2.5 YR 6/4–6/6, light red) with numerous medium red specks and small white lime inclusions. The fabric is very hard and often appears overfired on the surface (2.5 YR 5/1; Rauh 2023; LCP vessel 30597).

Distribution: Unknown.

LCP contributors: Nicholas Rauh; Veronica Iacomi; Grady Gillett

Production center 06: Elaiussa Sebaste

Site characterization: Known simply as Sebaste in late antiquity, Elaiussa was an original mid-Hellenistic foundation on the coastline of eastern Rough Cilicia. As a medium-sized and strategically located urban center, it thrived throughout the Roman Imperial and Early Byzantine periods until its abandonment, which must have occurred during the second half of the 7th century. The settlement was characterized by a promontory with two natural bays exploited as harbors, and communication routes with the hinterland may have been facilitated by the presence of a stream just outside the city center and quite close to the southern harbor. Background: Elaiussa was a major node in Mediterranean ceramic exchange networks already by the 1st century (Ferrazzoli and Ricci 2009). Ceramic material, wasters, and actual kilns show that the city's workshops were primarily used to produce LRA1, oil lamps, lanterns, carved decorated pottery, and *unguentaria*, all sharing the same clay/fabrics. The six known kilns/workshops are located in close proximity to the basin and/or the facilities of the southern harbor of the city, and were active in different periods, for the greatest part overlapping, proving the quite considerable extent of the local production.

Number of kilns/workshops: Six.

Typology: LRA1 type A (Ferrazzoli and Ricci 2007), type B, and type C.

Local Fabric: Hard, sandy fabric varying from light yellow (7.5YR 8/2–4) to red (5YR 7/6) with limestone inclusions and a rough surface.

Distribution: Based on preliminary petrographic investigations, Itanos and Pseira (Crete); Tarraco (Spain); Cibalae (Croatia); and Nea Paphos (Cyprus).[5]

LCP contributors: Asena Kızılarslanoğlu; Veronica Iacomi; Grady Gillett

Kiln #01;

Location: Western end of the southern harbor.

Period of activity: Unknown.

Description of the facilities: The kiln is located at the western end of the southern harbor (mentioned in Burragato et al. 2007), by the mouth of the seasonal stream of the Paşa Deresi. It is mostly unpublished, and was identified in 2003 during construction works on the coastal road (cf. Borgia and Iacomi 2010: 1034 n. 9).

Kiln #02

Location: Northwestern necropolis.

Period of activity: Beginning of the 5th to the mid-7th centuries

Description of the facilities: Brief notes on this kiln are given in chapters by Chiara Morselli and Marco Ricci (2009: 103) and Adele Federica Ferrazzoli and Ricci (2010: 815–16). The northwestern necropolis seems to have been dismissed by the end of the 4th century, when a series of productive facilities (most notably, an installation interpreted as an olive oil press) were created along the hillside once

5. For the preliminary petrographic investigations, see Gillett 2023: 53–59, but further petrographic analyses are needed to clarify and refine the provenance proposed there. For the locations, see Poulou-Papadimitriou and Nodarou 2014: figs. 18, 19 (Crete); Fantuzzi et al. 2019: fig. 2b (Spain); Nagy and Szakmany 2019: fig. 6A (Croatia); and Kaldeli, Williams, and Michaelides 2022: fig. 14 (Cyprus, and note that we disagree with the authors' petrographic provenance of a local Paphian origin for this LRA1 sample).

Figure 3. Sebaste kiln #02 by the northwestern necropolis. Photograph by V. Iacomi, Archive of the Italian Mission at Elaiussa Sebaste, after Morselli and Ricci 2009.

accommodating the tombs. The kiln itself, built of bricks and rectangular in plan, apparently conforms to the type of kiln #06 and preserved part of the arched covering of the combustion chamber, built out of bricks. It is said to have been installed on an earlier one, but either way, it was built after the olive oil facility went out of use.

Kiln #03

Location: Area of the Byzantine palace—northwestern end.

Period of activity: Mid-6th–mid-7th centuries.

Description of the facilities: Located just outside the palace walls and close to the southern harbor basin, the kiln was later replaced by #04 nearby, as they were seemingly part of the same atelier (Iacomi and Cassiani 2016; cf. notes in Borgia and Iacomi 2010: 1034 and in Iacomi 2020).

Kiln #04

Location: Area of the Byzantine palace—by the polygonal wall.

Period of activity: 7th century.

Description of the facilities: Built in stone and bricks exploiting a preexisting polygonal wall, the kiln is basically unpublished (Iacomi and Cassiani 2016).

Kiln #05

Location: Eastern front of the southern harbor.

Period of activity: 5th to late 6th–early 7th centuries.

Description of the facilities: Located along the southern harbor front, in an area still not thoroughly investigated, the structure remains basically unpublished (Iacomi and Cassiani 2016).

Kiln #06

Location: Residential sector by the southern harbor.

Period of activity: Late 4th–second third of the 7th century.

Description of the facilities: Workshop in the lowermost terrace of the domestic block investigated 2005–2016 by Veronica Iacomi and others (Missione Archeologica Italiana a Elaiussa Sebaste, Sapienza University of Rome; see the detailed description of the complex in Borgia and Iacomi 2010). Just outside the limits of the southern harbor basin, a large portion of a preexisting terrace, formerly used for domestic purposes, was arranged to accommodate the workshop at least by the end of the 4th century (cf. Iacomi 2020: 83). It includes a large kiln for amphora production and a smaller kiln (maybe for lamp production?). The large kiln (unit Ia) is enclosed by preexisting walls, covering an eight meter by five meter area. Two series of eight short pillars built in bricks are preserved, in some cases to the arch spring; these were meant to support the arches on top of which there was the "slab" of the firing chamber. Compacted clay forms two massive jutting *antae* on the front, marking the inverted-V-shaped entrance. A sondage on the floor of the combustion chamber showed that both the floor itself and the pillars were periodically raised in new construction phases (at least four were identified for the floor only).

In the rest of the terrace, preexisting rooms were used as related facilities. In a unit adjoining the kiln (If) the settling and then storage of clay was taking place; here an underground rock-cut cistern must have been exploited for the process as well. Later, the cistern was used to dispose of misfired vessels, hence the large deposit (in two different and separate heaps), almost exclusively made of LRA1 (about 800), uncovered here. The crafting must have happened in one of the northern units (Ic), next to which a large room (Id) might have been worked as storage for the different materials entering (firing wood among the others) and exiting (the crafted and fired amphoras) the workshop. The connection to docking or mooring station(s) along the shore is still unclear, but it seems that the amphoras (already filled with their content?) were brought outside and toward the sea through narrow passages.

The capacity of this kiln has been calculated in a possible load of up to 250 or 500 amphoras per firing process. The workshop fell out of use together with the final abandonment of the whole domestic block investigated so far; the kiln was filled with its (last) firing load when it collapsed; the event must have occurred around 630–660.

Production center 07: Halasarna

Site characterization: Located on the southwestern coast of Cos, Halasarna was a wealthy and well-connected village in the 5th century with a relatively small-scale LRA2/LRA13 production industry. This industry suddenly and exponentially grew after a large earthquake and tsunami in 554, and the ceramic repertoire was expanded to include LRA1s and Byzantine Globular Amphoras (BGAs).

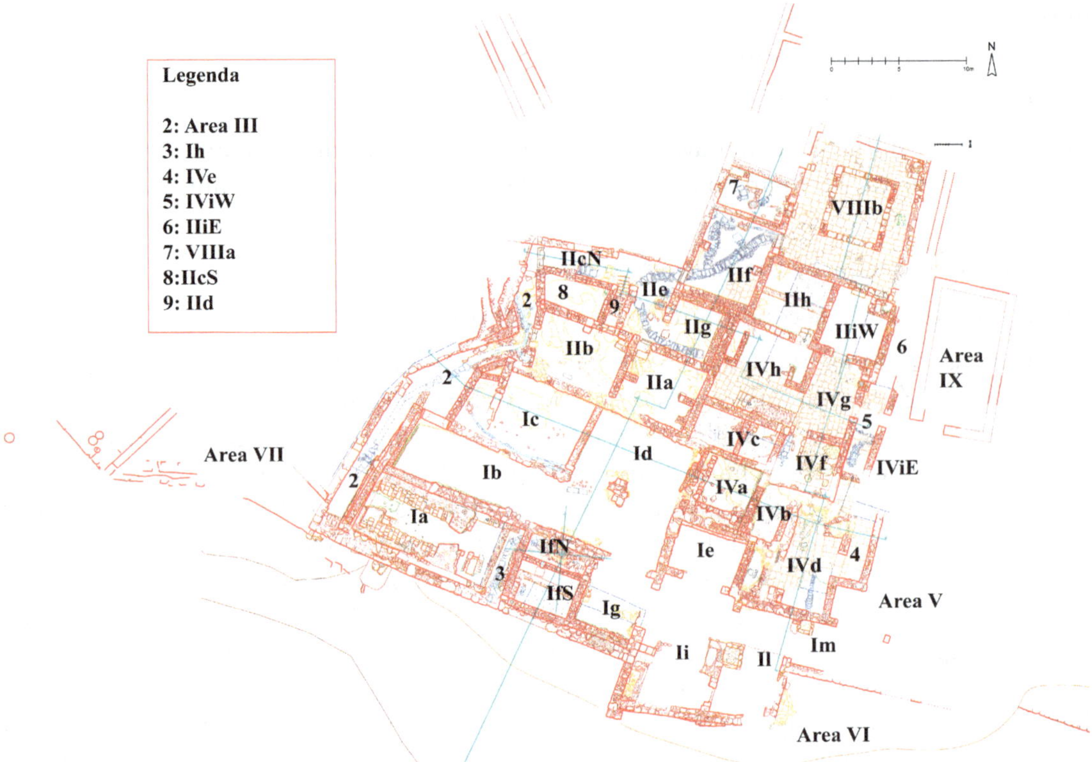

Figure 4. A plan of the residential district by the southern harbor at Elaiussa, location of kiln #06 (= unit Ia). Revised after Iacomi 2020: 81, fig. 2.

Figure 5. Kiln #06, from northeast. Photograph by V. Iacomi, after Iacomi 2010: fig. 5.

Figure 6. Discarded misfired LRA1s from the cistern deposit by kiln #06. Photograph by V. Iacomi, after Borgia and Iacomi 2010: fig. 9.

Background: The University of Athens has been excavating Halasarna for the past 35 years. A thorough analysis of the LRA1 industry was published in 2010 (Diamanti 2010).

Number of kilns: At least two, but possibly three. One kiln structure has been excavated and another is strongly attested through the presence of ceramic wasters, molds, and the peripheral features of a ceramic workshop. It has been suggested that a workshop existed near the basilica of presbyter Photeinos, but none of our strong indicators are present, and thus it will not be included here (see Didioumi 2014: 170, citing unpublished data.

Local fabric: The local fabric at Halasarna is reddish-orange to the naked eye, "moderately hard, with few inclusions with the exception of whitish, gray nodules and numerous golden micas (Munsell, reddish yellow 5YR 6/6)" (Poulou-Papadimitriou and Didioumi 2010: 742). The concentration of mica is characteristic of the local products (see §4.5 for the petrographic details).

Distribution: Caesarea Maritima (Israel; LCP vessel 28119)

LCP contributors: Grady Gillett; Veronica Iacomi

Kiln #01: Aghia Theotis (sometimes called Tsoukalaria, Kaminia, and Liopyra) kiln

Location: In the middle of the modern village Kardamaina, sitting ca. 300 m north of the Early Byzantine basilica of Aghia Theotita (Poulou-Papadimitriou and Didioumi 2015: 401).

Period of activity: Mid-7th century.

Description of the facilities: The kiln is circular with an inner diameter of 2.8 m and a preserved height of 1.9 m. The combustion chamber, dug directly into bedrock, was constructed of stone and mortar and covered in ceramic plates. North of the kiln, there were four rectangular rooms, some of which were

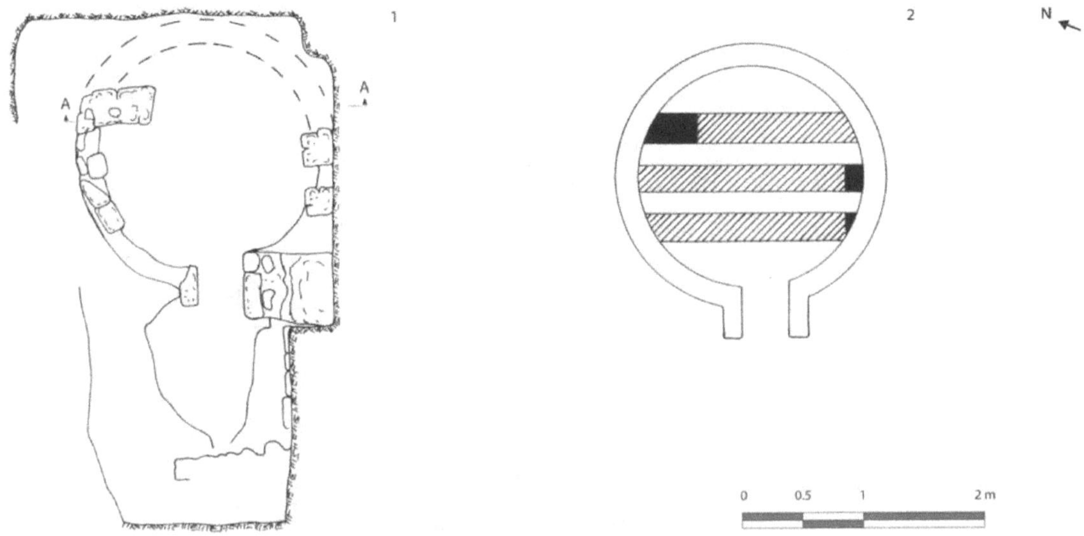

Figure 7. Left: a plan of the actual Aghia Theotis kiln; right: a reconstruction of the Aghia Theotis kiln (from Poulou- Papadimitriou and Didioumi 2015: fig. 2).

used for clay preparation as seen by layers of clay on the floor and inside an in situ pithos (Poulou-Papadimitriou and Didioumi 2010: 742).

Typology: LRA1 (referred to as *survivals* by the excavators, but in the authors' opinion better fits as type B), LRA2 and LRA13 (also known as LRA2C), cooking pots, lamps, and unguentaria. The LRA2 was the main product of the workshop during the 5th–6th centuries, and then there was a major transition that involved an increase to industrial-level production of LRA1 and LRA13 (Diamanti 2023: 275–82).

Kiln #02: Ancient Halasarna kiln

Location: Roughly "250 m west of the [Aghia Theotita] kiln ... and 500 m from the basilica" (Didioumi 2014: 170).

Period of activity: Second half of the 6th to the first half of the 7th century.

Description of the facilities: The "ducts and tanks" related to a kiln were found by the University of Athens team, but not the kiln architecture itself (Papavassiliou and Didioumi 2017: 48)

Typology: Unknown.

Production center 08: Içmeler, Ismeler

Site characterization: The modern town of Içmeler is located on the southern coast of the Datça Peninsula in Turkey. The origin of the site is not well studied, but a long-lived Christian basilica was constructed there around the mid-5th century, which aligns with the trend of LRA1 production alongside church estates.

Background: Empereur and Picon (1989) describe the "poor remains of a small workshop" at Içmeler without adding further reference. The site has not been excavated and LRA1 production there has not been explored further.

Location: Unknown.

Number of kilns: Unknown.

Period of activity: Unknown.

Description of the facilities: Unknown.

Typology: Unknown.

Local fabric: Unknown.

Distribution: Unknown.

LCP contributors: Veronica Iacomi; Grady Gillett

Production center 09: Kambos (Lipsi)

Site characterization: Kambos is located on the southern coast of the island of Lipsi. Little is known about the history of Lipsi, or Lepsia, apart from its connection to the Calypso myth and its famed "brusco-like wine" (Papavassiliou, Sarantidis, and Papanikolaou 2014: 161). It was a part of a series of outposts of ancient Miletos, in southwest Turkey.

Background: A rescue excavation that began in 2008 uncovered the LRA1 workshop at Kambos, after which a more thorough dig was completed by the Fourth Ephorate of Byzantine Antiquities.

Location: A "considerable distance" from a settlement at Kousselio, on the other side of Lipsi's small bay. It is notably located next to a clay deposit, which might be the source of the raw material potters used in the workshop.

Number of kilns: Four.

Typology: Kambos-type LRA1 *survival.* The excavators described the Kambos products as poorly made with little care for symmetry or quality. The pronounced rolled rim and pear-shaped body make Kambos products distinct from other LRA1 *survivals.*

Period of activity: At least from the mid-7th century onward, but the full lifespan of the workshop remains unknown (Papavassiliou, Sarantidis, and Papanikolaou 2014: 161).

Local fabric: "Reddish yellow, mediocre, clean, incorporating whitish small inclusions and abundant golden mica (Munsell 5YR, 6/6 or 6/4)" (Papavassiliou, Sarantidis, and Papanikolaou 2014: 160)

Distribution: Emporio; Paphos (based on typology).[6]

LCP contributors: Grady Gillett; Veronica Iacomi

Kiln #01

Location: West of, almost abutting a larger rectangular structure that might have been the workshop storeroom or drying facility (fig. 8).

6. See Ballance et al. 1989: fig. 43.280–81 (LCP vessel 33664); Hayes 2003: fig. 32.341.

Description of facilities: Rectangular structure measuring 5.3 m × 5.2 m, with walls built of "medium and small-sized rubble bound together with pebbles, pottery sherds, and clay mortar" (Papavassiliou, Sarantidis, and Papanikolaou 2014: 159). Benches lined the long walls, and there was evidence of a central pillar.

Kiln #02

Location: Just south of kiln #01, sitting on a natural clay deposit (fig. 8).

Description of facilities: Rectangular structure measuring 4.2 m × 2.8 m s built on a clay deposit with the same masonry as kiln 1. The firing floor was made of "clay plaques and of rectangular blocks coated with clay," and the floor from clay and pumice (Papavassiliou, Sarantidis, and Papanikolaou 2014: 159).

Kiln #03

Location: On the north side of the workshop complex, possibly outside of it (fig. 8).

Description of facilities: This kiln is significantly smaller than the others at 2.1 m × 1.2 m, but constructed with the same method as ##1–2. This kiln was seemingly used for the firing of small vessels like oinochoai.

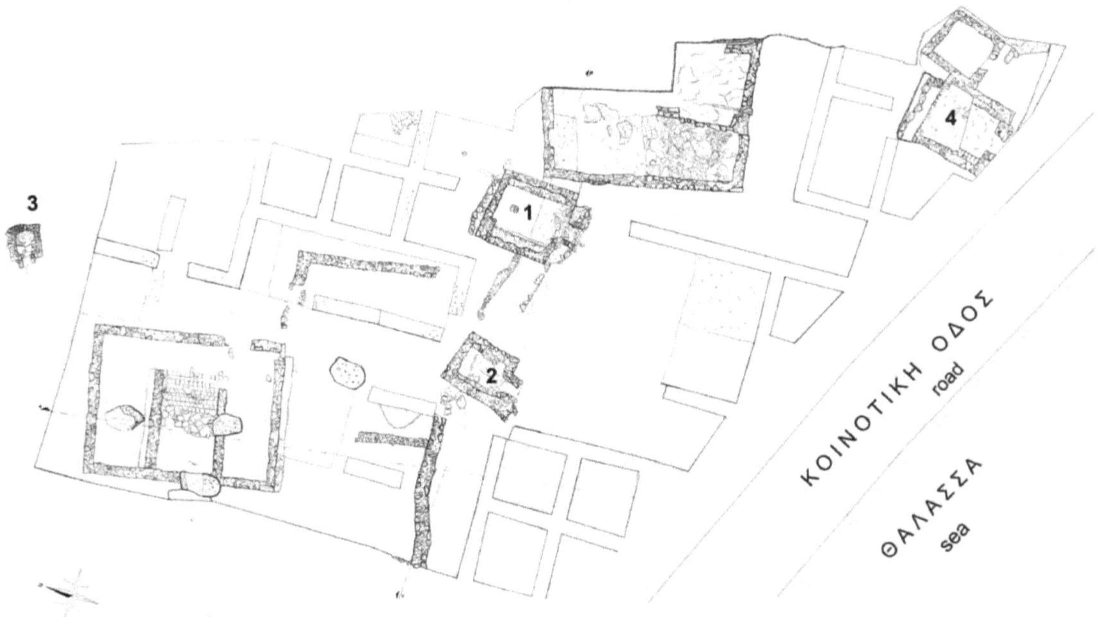

Figure 8. A plan of the excavations of the kilns found at Kambos (from Papavassiliou, Sarantidis, and Papanikolaou 2014: fig. 3).

Kiln #04

Location: At the eastern edge of the workshop complex, built over a clay deposit like kiln #02 (fig. 8).

Description of facilities: Rectangular structure measuring 4.8 m × 3.9 m, and built with mortar-coated walls of "medium and small-sized rubble held together by pebbles, pottery fragments, and lime mortar" (Papavassiliou, Sarantidis, and Papanikolaou 2014: 160). This kiln was built on top of a natural clay deposit and was used to fire LRA1s, pithoi, and lekanides.

Production center 10: Karataş

Site characterization: Located at the mouth of the Pyramus River, the area of Karataş was a key hub for trade routes into Plain Cilicia from at least the 4th century BCE. The strategically important area was occupied by a number of cities and towns before the Roman period, but Magarsos (Antiochia ad Pyramum) was the major settlement until the Byzantine times (Hild and Hellenkemper 1990: 335, "Magarsos").

Background: Reported in the survey by Empereur and Picon (1989)

Location: The only available information places the workshop "to the right of the mouth of the Pyramos" (i.e. modern Ceyhan Nehri).

Number of kilns: Unknown.

Period of activity: Unknown.

Description of the facilities: Unknown.

Typology: Fineware and tiles, in addition to LRA1s of an unknown type.

Local fabric: Unknown. However, there are numerous examples of petrographic thin sections and fresh break photographs from pottery produced at other sites in Plain Cilicia (e.g., Kinet Höyük).

Distribution: Unknown.

LCP contributors: Veronica Iacomi; Grady Gillett

Production center 11: Kourion

Site characterization: Located on the northwestern edge of Cyprus's Akrotiri Peninsula, the urban district of Kourion (or Curium) was founded in the Late Bronze Age. The city had significant trade contacts with the dominant powers in the eastern Mediterranean and prospered over the following centuries, and particularly during the Roman period until an earthquake completely leveled the city sometime in the late 4th century (Kaldeli 2008: 59; Costello 2011: 17–39). It already had a Christian presence by this point, but when the city was rebuilt a few decades later it was explicitly reorganized as a Christian city (Costello 2011: 39–40). Kourion was likely abandoned after the mid-7th century Arab raids in the region.

Background: The site has been subject to archaeological excavations for nearly a century, but LRA1 production was first suggested by Empereur and Picon, who described a workshop outside the city (1989: 242). Williams (2005a: 166–67) petrographically analyzed several LRA1 samples from Kourion and argued that they represented the local Kourion fabric, and that it can be distinguished from Cilician or northern Syrian fabrics.

Location: Unknown—Empereur and Picon report that the workshop was "a few kilometers (km) west of the city," but nothing has been excavated (1989: 242).

Number of kilns: Unknown.

Period of activity: Unknown.

Description of the facilities: Unknown.

Typology: Unknown.

Local fabric: "A hard, rough, sandy fabric, pinkish-white in colour (5YR 8/2). Small to medium-sized pieces of white limestone, or sometimes voids with reaction rims, are scattered throughout the fabric, together with some small quartz, serpentine, and dark-coloured ferromagnesian minerals" (Williams 2005a: 166).

Distribution: Unknown.

LCP contributors: Grady Gillett, Veronica Iacomi

Production center 12: Laggeri

Site characterization: Paros's location along various maritime trade corridors in the Aegean Sea made it a prosperous island with multiple settlements from at least the Late Bronze Age onward. It is home to one of the oldest Christian churches in the Aegean (Diamanti 2016: 691). The amphora workshop was associated with a near late Roman port from which its products could conveniently be exported, since the island was included in the *Quaestura justiniani exercitus* in the 6th century.

Background: Rescue excavations on Paros unearthed a considerable amount of ceramic wasters and debris, and a later rescue excavation revealed two kilns.

Location: Less than 100 m from the coast and very close to the settlement of Laggeri, attested by the remains of a few buildings and storerooms of "a very active Late Roman port" (Diamanti 2016: 691).

Number of kilns: At least three, two of which are published.

Period of activity: Late 6th to the late 7th or early 8th century, according to the excavator (Diamanti 2016). The workshop produced LRA1s (also called the Parian type 1) until the first half of the 7th century and LRA13s (Parian type 2) until the end of the workshop's existence. However, this chronology has been challenged, and Poulou-Papadimitriou (2018: 35) asserts that the workshop's date should be pushed back to the second half of the 7th to the 8th century.

Description of facilities: The layout of two of the three kilns is nearly identical: a ca. 7 m × 4 m rectangular blueprint with three square piers on each of two opposite walls, which supported arches that held the firing chamber floor which lay above (fig. 9).

Typology: The types produced were variations of the LRA1 and LRA 2C (LRA13), which are locally called the Parian type 1 and type 2 amphoras, respectively. The Parian type 1 has "a rim diameter of 7–8 cm, a cylindrical neck up to 10 cm in height, not perfectly but often grooved handles, a cylindrical

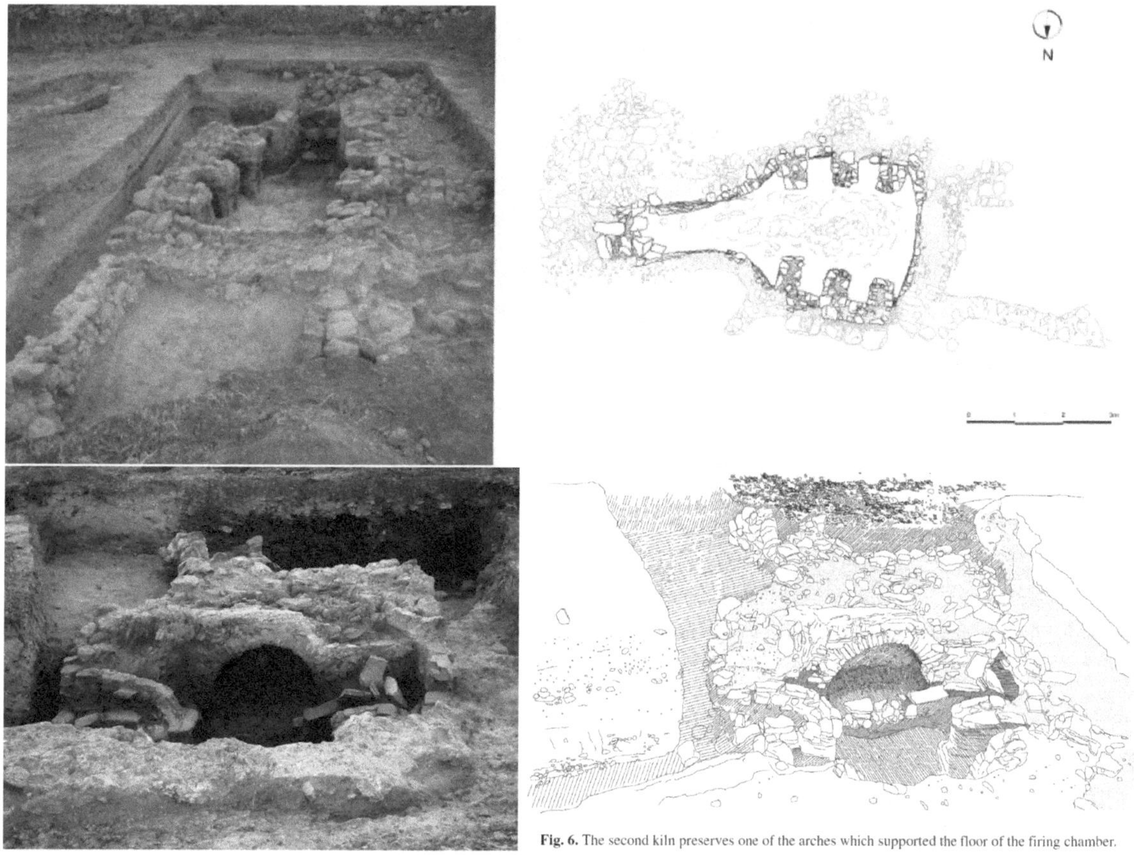

Figure 9. Photographs and drawings of the two published kilns excavated at Laggeri (top, from Diamanti 2023: fig. 16; bottom, from Diamanti 2016: fig. 6).

and not so strongly ribbed body of ca. 20 cm diameter at its maximum, and a rounded base" (Diamanti 2023: 286–87). The Parian type 2 has "an ovoid body, elongated conical neck up to 9–10 cm in height, a rim with a maximum diameter of 7–8 cm and sometimes hook-shaped interior, and more horizontal and sometimes arched handles that are oval in section and often grooved" (Diamanti 2023: 287–89). This local typology is a key piece of data in understanding the transition from the set of common Roman-Byzantine amphoras—the LRA 1 and 2—to a single type, the BGA, in the later Byzantine period.

Local Fabric: "Brown in colour (7 YR 6/6) and quite fine with several calcareous particles, mica flakes and other inclusions" (Diamanti 2016).

Distribution: Priniatikos Pyrgos (based on typology; LCP vessel 35016).

LCP contributors: Grady Gillett; Veronica Iacomi

Figure 10. Photographs of the kiln at Leukos (left: from Papavassiliou and Didioumi 2017: fig. 10; right: from Nelson et al. 2015: fig. 8)

Production center 13: Leukos

Site characterization: A port settlement sitting on rugged white cliffs on the western coast of Karpathos, Leukos has been proposed to be the fourth city of the Hellenistic to Classical period tetrapolis on the island (Nelson et al. 2015: 321–22). However, the earliest archaeological evidence around the site dates to the 1st century. What is certain is that the town flourished as a Christian trade hub (though perhaps not a large-scale manufacturer) in the 4th–7th centuries in large part due to the three natural harbors near it and its position on intersecting shipping lanes.

Background: An Italian archaeologist suggested Leukos was the fourth city of Strabo's tetrapolis on Karpathos in 1923, a proposal that eventually resulted in a thorough survey of the area from 2008–2011 (Nelson et al. 2015). The kiln at Leukos, however, was excavated in a separate project conducted by the Fourth Ephorate of Byzantine Antiquities in October 2012 (Christidou-Stylianou 2013).

Location: Southwest of the basilica, the kiln is roughly 10–15 m east of Liani Pounta Bay.

Number of kilns: At least one.

Period of activity: 1st–9th centuries. (Christidou-Stylianou 2013; Papavassiliou and Didioumi 2017: 52).

Description of facilities: An exceptionally well-preserved circular updraft-type kiln constructed with a combination of limestone rubble, flat clay-coated stones, and clay. The diameter of the upper firing chamber is ca. 1.78 m, with walls about 30 cm thick and a perforated firing floor. The combustion chamber was not excavated (fig. 10).

Typology: LRA1 *survivals* and an unknown short and wide-mouthed amphora type (see Papavassiliou and Didioumi 2017: fig. 11, although it must be noted that there are no photographs or drawings of pottery found within the kiln).

Local fabric: Unknown.

Distribution: Unknown.

LCP contributors: Grady Gillett; Veronica Iacomi

Production center 14: Mastichari

Site characterization: Sitting on the northern coast of Cos, a basilica contemporaneous with those at Kardamaina and various "Early Byzantine settlements and workshop installations" existed at Mastichari (Poulou-Papadimitriou and Didioumi 2015: 403). The site was inhabited since "the Prehistoric period," but well-dated occupation is first attested in the 3rd century BCE (Poulou-Papadimitriou and Didioumi 2015: 411). Throughout its entire inhabitance it seems to have been a small agricultural-based village in a fertile area between two streams.

Background: The area was repeatedly excavated by the Fourth Ephorate of Byzantine Antiquities.

Number of kilns: Four kilns, two of which are located within one complex and two immediately adjacent but outside of it. LRA1 wasters have, thus far, only been found at Kiln D.

Typology: Tiles, mud brick, LRA1 (unknown type), LRA3, BGA, Bezeczky's Ephesus 56 amphora, and pot stands.

Local Fabric: Sandy with gold mica and gray inclusions, soft and reddish yellow (5YR 6/6, 7/6, and 8/4). The slip is brown-red (5YR 5/6), as observed on the LRA3s.

Distribution: Unknown.

LCP contributors: Grady Gillett; Veronica Iacomi

Kiln #01: Kiln A

Location: At the northwestern corner of the unroofed southern wing of the complex, ca. 10 m southeast of kiln D and less than 10 m northwest of kiln B.

Period of activity: Perhaps active in the Hellenistic and Early Byzantine periods based on the ceramics found within the kiln, but its exact chronology is uncertain.

Description of facilities: A circular updraft kiln constructed with stone, quicklime, clay, and fragments of tiles, pithoi, and other vessels. The underground combustion room is 2.20 m in diameter and 1.73 m tall. Two pillars once supported a vaulted entrance to the kiln, and three equally spaced openings allowed air into the firing chamber (fig. 11).

Typology: Mud bricks, tiles, and an unidentified combed Byzantine ware.

Kiln #02: Kiln B

Location: Near the southern edge of the unroofed southern wing of the complex, less than 10 m southeast of kiln A.

Period of activity: Certainly in use until the early 7th century, though it is unclear when production began.

Description of facilities: A circular updraft kiln constructed with mud bricks. The structure is 2.90 m in diameter with a tile-paved stoking channel projecting out to the north. Near the channel were "shallow pits with combustible material," perhaps used to start the fires used to stoke the furnace (fig. 11; Poulou-Papadimitriou and Didioumi 2015: 408).

Typology: Mud bricks and tiles.

Kiln #03: Kiln C

Location: Outside and east of the complex where kilns A and B were found.

Period of activity: Early Byzantine period.

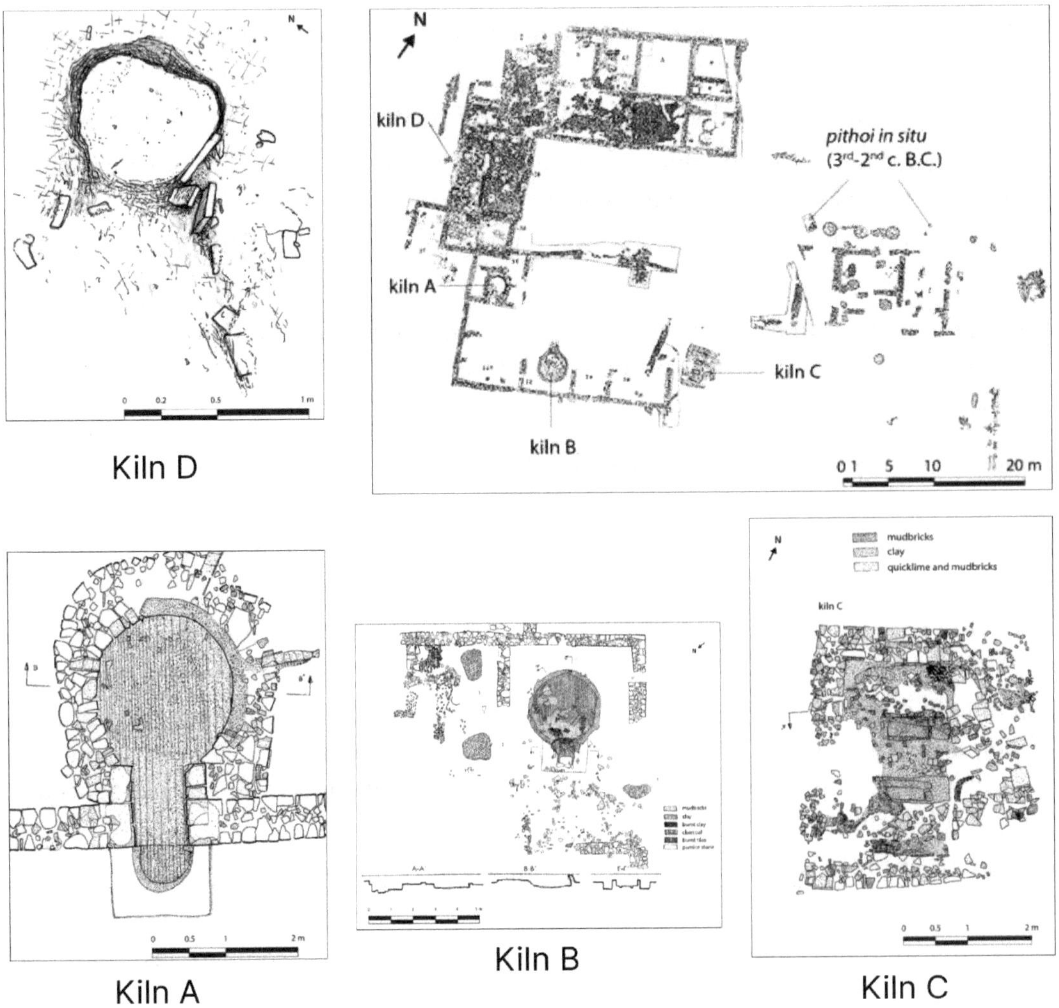

Figure 11. Plan of the ceramic workshop at Mastichari, showing the larger complex (top right) and individual kilns. After Poulou-Papadimitriou and Didioumi 2015: figs. 8–11.

Description of facilities: A rectangular updraft kiln with a firing floor supported by pillars (fig. 11).

Typology: Tiles and an unidentified combed Byzantine ware.

Kiln #04: Kiln D

Location: Kiln D is the northernmost at Mastichari, and sits in a northwest–southeast-oriented wing connecting the northern and southern portions of the complex.

Period of activity: Natalia Poulou-Papadimitriou and Sophia Didioumi propose that this simple kiln operated "only in prehistoric times" (2015: 411), but we find this hypothesis incomplete. Several intact LRA3s were found inside it and LRA1, LRA3, and Bezeczky's Ephesus 56 type amphoras were found to the west of kiln D, all of which are dated to the late 4th to early 7th century. It could be that this former kiln, unused in early Byzantine times, was used as a dump for products of the other kilns, but the authors do not describe the stratigraphy within the kiln.

Description of facilities: A basic kiln with minimal architecture, made from a shallow firing pit dug into the earth and lined with clay, heated by a combustion pit adjacent to it (fig. 11).

Typology: If kiln D was in fact active in the 4th–7th centuries, LRA3s were probably produced there, and LRA1 and Bezeczky's Ephesus 56 as well.

Production center 15: Nea Paphos

Site characterization: Nea Paphos sits on a natural harbor on the southwestern coast of Cyprus, making it an active trade hub throughout most of its occupation. The city was a wealthy and cosmopolitan administrative center on the island in the Late Roman period, though no longer the rich capital, as it had been in from the 3rd century BCE to the 4th century CE (Kaldeli 2008: 52).

Background: Unfortunately, the LRA1 workshop at Paphos was found after most of it had been completely destroyed by a hotel development in 1988–1989. Dr. Demetrios Michaelides was nearby and luckily stopped the workers before the kiln was entirely lost.

Location: The kiln at Paphos was "built outside the city walls, fairly far from the harbor but very near the coast ... right next to the area that was extensively used during the Hellenistic and Roman periods as a cemetery" (Demesticha and Michaelides 2001: 290).

Number of kilns: Only one kiln was excavated, but the excavators proposed that more likely existed and were destroyed by the same development that destroyed most of the single known kiln (Demesticha and Michaelides 2001: 290).

Period of activity: Unknown. Due to the cemetery immediately adjacent to the kiln, it is assumed that the structure was built after the 3rd century when the cemetery fell out of use.

Description of facilities: The kiln was built from soft bricks, stone, plaster, and amphora fragments against a preexisting stone wall. The floor of the underlying furnace (?) was a curved depression sunk directly into bedrock, above which were five brick pillars that supported the kiln's firing floor. A tunnel connected this area to a stone "upside down truncated cone, and its bottom opened into the understructure of the kiln" (Demesticha and Michaelides 2001: 290). Because the kiln was built between the coast and the cemetery complex, the potters probably did not collect their clay on site (fig. 12).

Figure 12. Photographs of the kiln excavated in Paphos (left: from Demesticha and Michaelides 2001: fig. 3; right: from Demesticha and Michaelides 2001: fig. 4).

Typology: LRA1, LRA13 (also known as LRA2C), and potentially Oziol's type 19 lamps (Demesticha and Michaelides 2001: 290). The LRA1s have necks of two different shapes: (1) narrow and slightly conical, and (2) broader, lower, and cylindrical. The excavators identified the LRA1s as Riley's type A, but it seems to us that our type B was also produced here.

Local fabric: The ware is hard, light brown to red in color, with many medium red and black inclusions and small lime inclusions, often densely concentrated close to the surface, sparse dark brown pieces. See §4.1 for petrographic analysis of Paphian LRA1s or on the LCP as Cyprus/Mamonia Complex/calcareous clay/carbonates, quartz, ophiolitic suite.

Distribution: Unknown.

LCP contributors: Stella Demesticha; Anthi Kaldelis; Grady Gillett; Veronica Iacomi

Production center 16: Saint Jeremiah's Monastery

Site characterization: The monastery, part of a larger Coptic Christian settlement near Saqqara in Egypt, dates from the end of the 5th to the mid 9th century. The site was home to a small self-sustaining Christian community, likely not just monks but women as well.

Background: The ceramic workshop was discovered in a test pit, and excavated in 1988–1989. The results were published by Holeil Ghaly in 1992 who called for further research of the area to clarify the chronology, but nothing has been published since.

Location: Southwest of the monastery, roughly "200 m from the Unas Valley Temple" (Ghaly 1992: 161).

Number of kilns: Eight kilns have been found at the workshop, but only six are described by Ghaly, the other two being "kilns of middle size ... west of this area" (1992: 161).

Typology: The productions of individual kilns cannot currently be distinguished. Overall, the workshop produced coarse tablewares, including plates and shallow bowls; cooking pots; painted water jugs, featuring geometric and floral motifs; thick basins; and LRA1 type B (LCP vessel 30652).

Period of activity: The workshop is "older than the 6th century," and the associated ceramic assemblage (including LRD, and North African "sigillée claire D") generally dates to the 5th–7th centuries (Ghaly 1992: 161). It is unclear if all the workshop's kilns are contemporaneous or not, and the chronology of each kiln cannot currently be distinguished. The close proximity of six of the kilns may suggest they were not all operating synchronously. The site was abandoned around 850 (Ghaly 1992: 171).

Local fabric: Alluvial clay, commonly known as Nile silt, tempered with straw (see §4.6 for a petrographic description).

Distribution: Dime / Soknopaious Nesos near Fayyum (Caputo and Davoli 2023: 741), Kellia, and Baouît (Marchand and Dixneuf 2007: 316).

LCP contributors: Grady Gillett, Veronica Iacomi

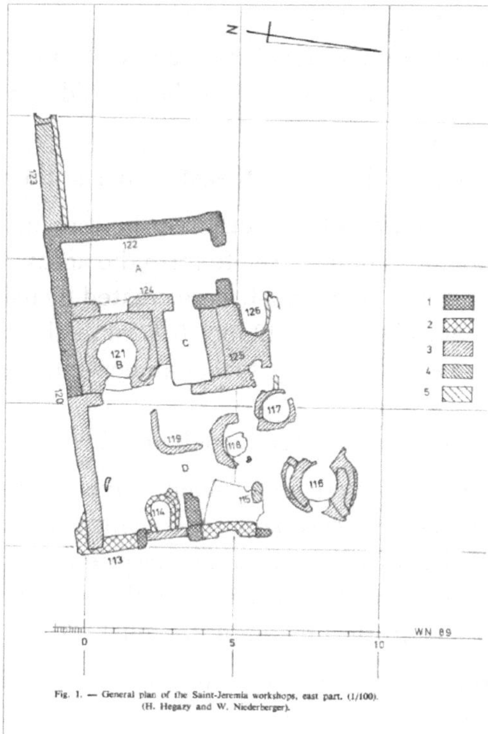

Figure 13. Plan showing the layout of the ceramic kilns within the monastery (from Ghaly 1992: fig. 1).

Kiln #114

Location: At the northwestern corner of the structure which enclosed the workshop, ca. 2 m northwest of kiln 118.

Description of facilities: The floor was dug into the ground, and walls were built from "half bricks" but did not wrap around the entire kiln—the east side was open, presumably for loading fuel (Ghaly 1992: 161).

Kiln #116

Location: In the southwestern corner of the workshop, ca. 1.5 m southwest of kiln 117.

Description of facilities: Constructed with three round walls roughly 1.2 m in diameter, with no evidence for "distinction between the fuel room and the firing chamber" (Ghaly 1992: 161). The space between the second and third walls was filled with sand. There were two openings, one in the east and one in the west.

Kiln #117

Location: About 1.5 m northeast of kiln 116.

Description of facilities: This kiln is a "kind of hole dug in the ground but consolidated with mudbrick" (Ghaly 1992: 163). The structure was one meter in diameter, and potentially used to create lime.

Kiln #118

Description of facilities: 1.2 m wide and constructed of bricks, this kiln is not described in detail by the author but seems to have been used as a refuse pit after it went out of use.

Kiln #121

Location: In the northeast corner of the workshop, ca. 4 m east of kiln 114.

Description of facilities: Was built in an abandoned mud-brick room in which what had once been the door was repurposed to form the access hole to stoke the fuel chamber. The firing floor had many perforations in it, which were created by using the necks of vessels. In addition to these holes, trapezoidal shapes "flues" (0.12 m × 0.27 m at the base and 0.15 m × 0.25 m at the top) allowed more hot air to travel between the fuel chamber and the firing room.

Production center 17: Seleucia Pieria

Site characterization: Seleucia Pieria was founded as a port city in the late 4th–early 3rd century BCE, and several decades later became the chief port of Antioch. The city was an important node in eastern Mediterranean exchange, despite recurring problems with its harbor silting up, up until the early to mid 6th century when multiple earthquakes ravaged the city to the point of abandonment in the late 6th century (Erol and Pirazzoli 1992: 320–25).

Background: Reported in the survey by Empereur and Picon (1989), who identified it based on a large deposit of wasters.[7]

Location: Wasters were noted over an area larger than a dozen hectares, by the west and southwest limits of the *kothon* of the ancient harbor, outside the walls.

Number of kilns: Unknown.

Period of activity: Unknown.

Description of the facilities: Unknown.

Typology: Unknown.

Local fabric: "A hard, rough sandy fabric, ranging in colour from pinkish-white (Munsell 7.5YR N8-8/2) to reddish brown (2.5 YR 6/4). Many large dark green to black glassy grains of pyroxene are scattered throughout a fairly clean-looking matrix. In thin section this fabric is characterized by the large size (some grains are over 0.70 mm across) and frequency of green and colourless pyroxenes. Also present are some small fragments of lava, discrete grains of potash and plagioclase feldspar, shreds of mica, a little serpentine, cryptocrystalline limestone, or voids with reaction rims where the limestone body has dissolved out, and some opaque iron oxide. These are all set in a groundmass of silt-sized quartz grains" (Williams 2005a: 163)

Distribution: Unknown.

LCP contributors: Grady Gillett, Veronica Iacomi

7. Fresh break photographs of an LRA1 recovered from Seleucia by Empereur and Picon are available on the ADS database, though it is unclear if this specimen is also hypothesized to be a local product.

Notes: Paul Reynolds (2005: 566) has challenged Empereur and Picon's identification of an LRA1 workshop at Seleucia Pieria, arguing that: (1) he did not observe any wasters when he conducted a pedestrian survey of the site and, (2) what they observed might have been a warehouse or storage depot for the busy port city. However, it cannot be ruled out that ruins visible in the 1980s disappeared at the progressive growth of the modern urban center (see the considerations in this regard by Empereur and Picon 1988, and by Pieri 2007b).

Production center 18: Soli-Pompeiopolis

Site characterization: Located on a harbor at the border between Rough and Plain Cilicia, settlement at Soli-Pompeiopolis dates back to at least the 2nd millennium BCE. Deserted in the 1st century BCE, the city (then called Soloi) was rebuilt as Pompeiopolis and prospered under Roman and Byzantine rule until destroyed by early 6th century earthquakes, the same that wrecked Seleucia Pieria. It remained abandoned until the 19th century (Sarıkaya Levent 2022: 276–78).

Background: First identified as a kiln site by Empereur and Picon's survey (their 'Soles-Ouest' kiln).[8] LRA1 production was confirmed by Caroline Autret in 2009–10 (Autret, Yağci, and Rauh 2010).

Location: The Soli-Pompeiopolis workshop was close to the harbor, "100 m west of the [city's] ancient harbor mole" and ca. 650 m from "the center of Soli itself" (Autret, Yağci, and Rauh 2010: 203–4).

Number of kilns: Unknown, but perhaps two. Empereur and Picon write that they observed "double installation" at the site during their survey, but then only describe a single kiln (1986: 241). Excavations in the 21st century revealed no intact kiln structures.

Period of activity: Based on the morphological features of the examples studied, the LRA 1 production at Soli-Pompeiopolis began around the late 4th or early 5th century, and continued up to the early 7th century.

Description of facilities: Unknown, as construction work destroyed any kiln structures.

Typology: Production started with LRA1 type A and expanded with LRA1 type B. The workshop also produced roof tiles and basins with a Y-shaped rim in section. Amphora stands were also manufactured, which is similar to the production of both amphora and stand at Elaiussa Sebaste, situated about 45 km southwest along the shore.

Local fabric: The entire assemblage exhibits a relatively fine fabric with color ranging from a yellowish beige (5Y 7/3–8/3) to a somewhat orange-beige tint (10YR 6/4). All samples exhibit sparse, very fine fragments of silvery micas, very fine brown speck inclusions, as well as small lime holes. Some sherds also display grayish-white inclusions (LCP vessels 20496, 20497).

Distribution: LRA1s that match the macroscopic fabric characteristics of Soli-Pompeiopolis have been identified in Cyprus, Cilicia, Yassı Ada, Egypt, Crete, Crimea, Moesia (?), Thrace, and Dalmatia (see Autret 2022: 166–68; note that these parallels are tentative and have not been petrographically confirmed).

LCP contributors: Caroline Autret, Grady Gillett, Veronica Iacomi

8. Fresh break photographs of LRA1s recovered from Soli-Pompeiopolis by Empereur and Picon are available on the ADS database, though it is unclear if these specimens are also hypothesized to be local products.

Notes: A note from the excavator, Caroline Autret: "I should specify that so far only a short study of the Soli kiln site has been done, so the results presented here are preliminary. There are not yet any drawings due to lack of time. Research should be continued in order to identify the locally manufactured typology. It would also be very helpful for the identification of local ceramics to conduct analyses of the clay composition, and if possible to compare them with other LRA 1 manufactured along the shore of Cilicia."

Production center 19: Tarsus

Site characterization: Located on the Cydnus River (modern Tarsus Çayï), Tarsus has been occupied since the 3rd millennium BCE and was consistently the major center and/or administrative capital of the Cilician plain from the 5th century BCE through the Roman period (a general overview, despite being outdated, is in Hild and Hellenkemper 1990: 428–39). The city's location on the river made it a de facto port.

Background: The scanty remains of a kiln were identified by Empereur and Picon (1989) near the Kleopatra Kapısı (Cleopatra's Gate).

Location: At a close distance from the Kleopatra Kapısı, almost by the ancient wall.

Number of kilns: Unknown.

Period of activity: Unknown. Nonetheless, it seems worth noting that early Type A LRA1s (termed proto-LRA1s by the excavators) have been recently found in urban excavations by the northern sector of the city; interpreted as an import from Elaiussa on the basis of macroscopic observation of their fabric (a hypothesis that would require further investigation), they represent a good indicator of the very early presence of the amphora at Tarsus (cf. Alkaç-Işık and Adibelli 2024, who seem not to be aware of a local Tarsus production of LRA1s; LCP vessel 33435).

Description of the facilities: Probably disappeared without being documented, as already in the 1980s Empereur and Picon stressed the impact of modern urbanization on the site.

Typology: Unknown.

Local fabric: Unknown. However, ceramics produced in Iron Age Tarsus kilns have a medium to fine fabric with "diverse mineral temper[s], probably natural in the alluvial clays carried by the rivers" (see Cilician Iron Age Plain Ware produced in Tarsus on the LCP).

Distribution: Unknown.

LCP contributors: Grady Gillett, Veronica Iacomi

Production center 20: Yumurtalik/Aigai (Cilicia)

Site characterization: Known as Aigai in antiquity, the pre-Seleucid history of the ancient city is not well understood. Located on a natural harbor on the western side of the Gulf of Iskenderun, Yumurtalik grew from a small village in the 1st century to an important city well integrated with the militant, economic, and religious infrastructure of Cilicia in the Late Roman to Byzantine period (Hild and Hellenkemper 1990: 160–64).

Background: In their survey, Empereur and Picon (1989) identified two kiln sites—one located east of the city's harbor and the other "2 km from the city"—which produced LRA1s, after earlier pseudo-Coan and Dressel 4 amphora manufacturing. More recent investigations at Yumurtalik have located two discrete deposits of LRA1 wasters, one sitting one kilometer east of Aigai near the Ayaş Hotel and the other 200 m east of the Ayaş Hotel, at a site called Domuz Burnu ("pig cape" or "pig snout" in Turkish; Şenol and Alkaç 2017).

Number of kilns: Two.

Typology: LRA1 type B.

Local fabric "A hard, rough sandy fabric, ranging in colour from pinkish-white (7.5YR 8/2) to pinkish-grey (5YR 7/2). This fabric is much more granular in texture than [Seleucia Pieria and Arsuz], with a visibly much higher small white limestone content or voids with reaction rims. Small dark-coloured pyroxene and reddish serpentine can also be seen" (Williams 2005a: 166).[9] In their analysis, Ahmet Kaan Şenol and Erkan Alkaç found a very similar fabric at Aigeai, which contained "common white limestone, a little mica and round cryptocrystalline limestone, with less reddish serpentine, iron oxide and grains of quartz. These amphoras are coated with a thin white coat and the fabrics range from light brown to yellowish-red, due to different firing" (Şenol and Alkaç 2017: 833).

Distribution: Unknown.

LCP contributors: Grady Gillett, Veronica Iacomi

Kiln #01

Location: 200 m east of the Ayaş Hotel at a place called "Domuz Burnu."

Period of activity: Mid-5th to 6th century.

Description of the facilities: Wasters deposit.

Kiln #02

Location: Near the Ayaş Hotel in Yumurtalik.

Period of activity: Mid-6th to 7th century.

Description of the facilities: Wasters deposit.

Production center 21: Zygi-Petrini

Site characterization: Zygi-Petrini is located ca. 17 km east of Amathus at the mouth of the Vasilikos Valley on the southern Cypriot coast. It was a small village during the late Roman period, probably not much bigger than two hectares, that likely engaged in maritime trade and cabotage through a small "opportunistic port" (see Leidwanger 2013a).

Background: The Maroni Valley Archaeological Survey Project (MVASP) discovered a kiln and in situ LRA1s at the site in 1990 (Manning et al. 2000).

9. Fresh break photographs of LRA1s recovered from Yumurtalik are available on the ADS database, though it is unclear if these specimens are also hypothesized to be local products.

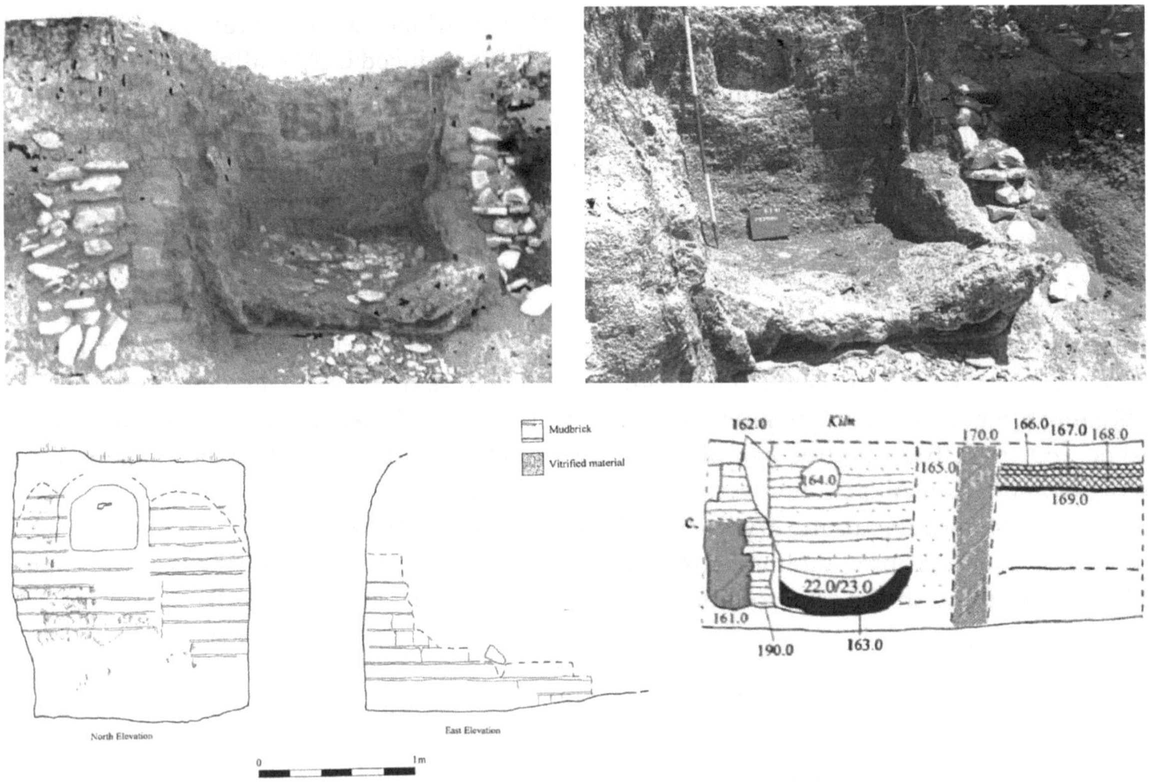

Figure 14. Photographs, drawings, and profiles of the LRA1 kiln at Zygi. Top left: photograph of kiln before cleaning; top right: close-up photograph of kiln after cleaning; bottom left: drawing of the surviving kiln architecture; bottom right: profile of the kiln and surrounding strata (from Manning et al. 2000: figs. 8.1, 8.4, 10, and 6, respectively).

Location: When the kiln was discovered, it was on the western side of the site, directly on a coastal scarp against the sea. Coastal erosion over the past two decades has destroyed the kiln site, and no sign of it was visible when one of the authors examined it in 2022 (G.G.).Number of kilns: One.

Period of activity: 6th–mid-7th century, perhaps with more production occurring in the 7th century.

Description of facilities: Geomagnetic surveys and excavation at Zygi-Petrini revealed at least seven multiroom buildings and a "standard updraught type" kiln structure (Manning et al. 2000). Built of roughly hewn river stones, boulders, and gypsum rocks, the stone components of the wall were fixed together with mortar and lined with mud brick. The inner kiln chamber was rectangular and connected to a plaster-lined firing chamber. There were open and covered courtyard areas southwest of the kiln that likely operated as working or storage facilities for the kiln (fig. 14).

Typology: LRA1 type C (Pieri 2005a *sous-modules*)

Local fabric: The excavators distinguished two fabrics in their excavation: (1) "Brown-red with many small dark inclusions, scarce white ones, often with small pieces of clay in the matrix" and (2) "light brown to buff, relatively condensed with various small inclusions (red, white, dark)" (Manning et al. 2000: 251). Later analyses show that the latter is the primary local fabric, ranging from light brown or buff to gray-green, with mostly dark inclusions visible to the naked eye. The fabric is nearly identical to that of Amathus (see §4.2).

Distribution: Unknown, but see §4.2

LCP contributors: Stella Demesticha; Maria Dikiomitou Eliadou; Grady Gillett; Veronica Iacomi; Paula Waiman-Barak

§3.2. Some Considerations on Production

A single aspect is shared by all production centers: proximity to water transport. Most workshops are situated near harbor facilities or close to the shore. The two exceptions (Saint Jeremiah's Monastery and Tarsus), both lay by a major river that allowed easy access to the wider Mediterranean network. Four production centers (Delice, Elaiussa, Halasarna, and Zygi-Petrini) share proximity to both a harbor and a river or freshwater streams facilitating efficient connections with the hinterland where raw materials and produce came from.

While the linked agricultural activities that lay behind the LRA1 production have not yet been well investigated (for the hinterland of Elaiussa, see Baratta 1999; Iacomi and Cassiani 2016), it seems clear that urban centers represented the system's primary nodes—at least 13 of the attested workshops are located by major settlements (Amathus, Antiocheia, Elaiussa, Halasarna, Karataş, Kourion, Laggeri, Leukos, Paphos, Seleucia Pieria, Soli, Tarsus, Yumurtalik).

In a couple of cases, kilns were built in these cities' previously undeveloped, peripheral, or dismissed areas with marginal perceived economic value (see Elaiussa and Paphos). There are six workshops near small settlements or villages—enough to indicate that rural sites were also important actors in LRA1 production (Apolakkia, Arsuz, Delice, Içmeler, Mastichari, Zygi-Petrini). Interestingly, there is evidence that workshop infrastructure at both urban and rural sites, but particularly the latter, was tied to the early Christian church. This correlation is seen at Içmeler and Mastichari, which were essentially the agricultural estates of local churches, and of course at Saint Jeremiah's monastery. LRA1 manufacturing has also been proposed at a basilica in Halasarna (though this locale does not meet our criteria). Data from many inscriptions on LRA1s (see ch. 5) also illustrate the influence of ecclesiastical institutions, showing Christian textual formulas or symbols. In some cases the church might have controlled the entire "vertical supply chain": from viniculture to grape harvesting to wine pressing, from the production of the containers to ship the wine to the marketing of that wine to consumers. The captain of the Yassi Ada ship may have even been a church official, as suggested by an inscription on board reading "*Georgiou Presbyterou Nauklerou*" (Bass and van Doornick 1982: 314; full discussion in van Doornick 2015: 205–6).

Examining the layout of LRA1 workshops in closer detail, we see variability especially among the kilns. All are circular at Halasarna and Leukos, as are some at Saint Jeremiah's (kilns #116 and #117) and Mastichari (kilns A and B). Others are rectangular, such as those at Elaiussa (whose kilns all conform to the same layout), Kambos, Laggeri, and Paphos. Kiln construction also differs. Some are made from river stones, mud bricks, ceramic sherds, partially hewn in bedrock, or any combination of them. However, nearly each excavated kiln *operated* in the same way: an updraft-style kiln in which fuel was loaded into a lower combustion chamber and stoked, transferring heat through a gridded floor into the ceramic firing chamber. Kiln #06 at Elaiussa offers a rare complete picture of the *chaîne opératoire* of

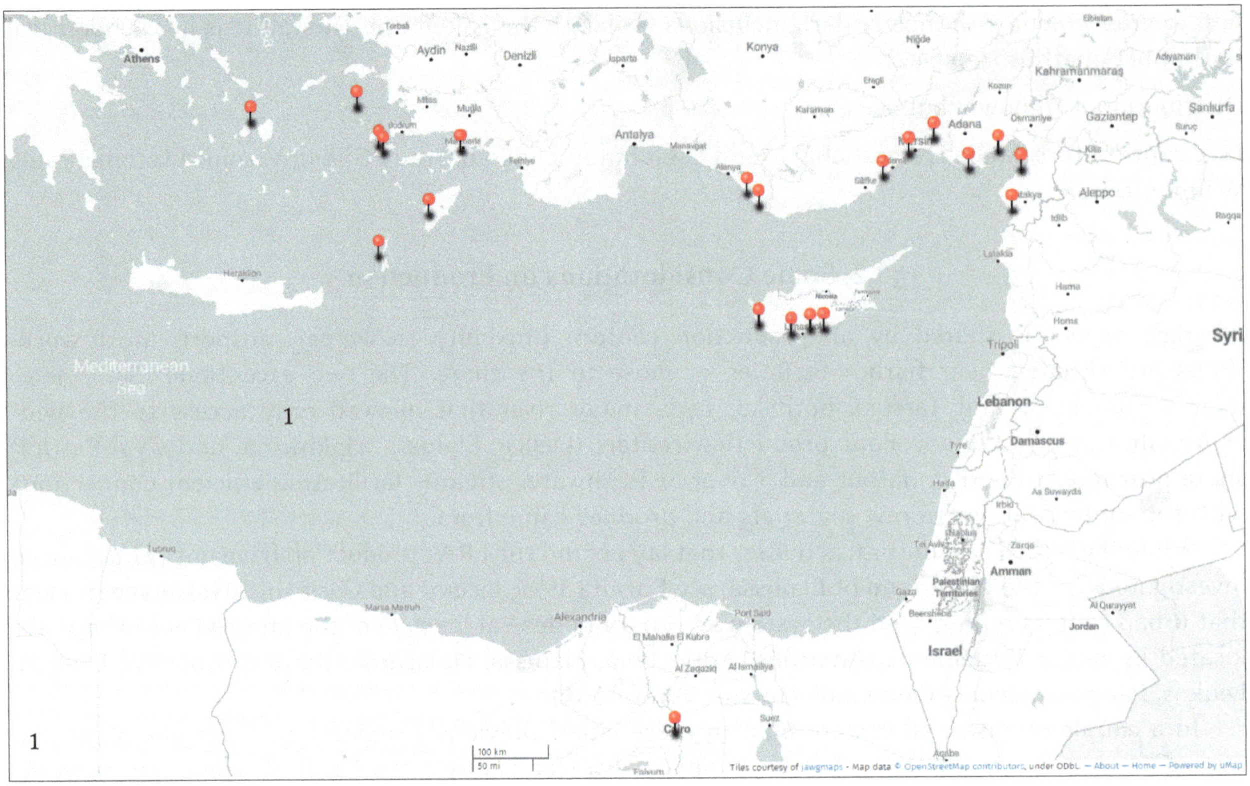

Figure 15. Maps of all known production centers, according to our three criteria. (1) Geographic distribution; (2) Cilician and Cypriot workshops; (3) Aegean workshops.

production, with a clay settling tank and related storage and crafting rooms. Unfortunately, it remains an isolated case, to which we can add only the clay deposit noted by the excavators at Kambos.

Finally, the last and possibly most important element to consider is the attested chronology, which represents a key factor for the evaluation of the historical dynamics behind LRA1 production. Based mainly on those workshops with relatively well-established chronologies, LRA1s were first made in Cilician sites during the late 4th century (Antiocheia ad Cragum; Elaiussa; Soli), while an early beginning in the Dodecanese remains undetermined. Over the course of the 5th century, production began at other Cilician and Aegean centers (Yumurtalik, Halasarna). In the (late?) 6th century production began in Cyprus as well (Amathus; Zygi-Petrini), and developed further in the Aegean into the Cyclades (Laggeri, Mastichari). By the mid-7th century, some of the Cypriot (Amathus; Zygi-Petrini), Aegean (Halasarna, Mastichari), and maybe Cilician (Soli; Yumurtalik ?) workshops came to an end, while other Cilician workshops remained active (Antiocheia; Elaiussa Sebaste), and production started in a new Aegean center (Kambos, and potentially Leukos). By the end of the second third of the 7th century, the last operating kiln at Elaiussa Sebaste was abandoned abruptly. Production continued along the western coast of Cilicia and in the southern Aegean with LRA1 *survivals* (Antiocheia ad Cragum and Delice in Cilicia; Kambos and Laggeri in the Aegean), which seem to flourish up to the 8th century and possibly even later (see §10.1 for maps, tables, and diagrams on production).

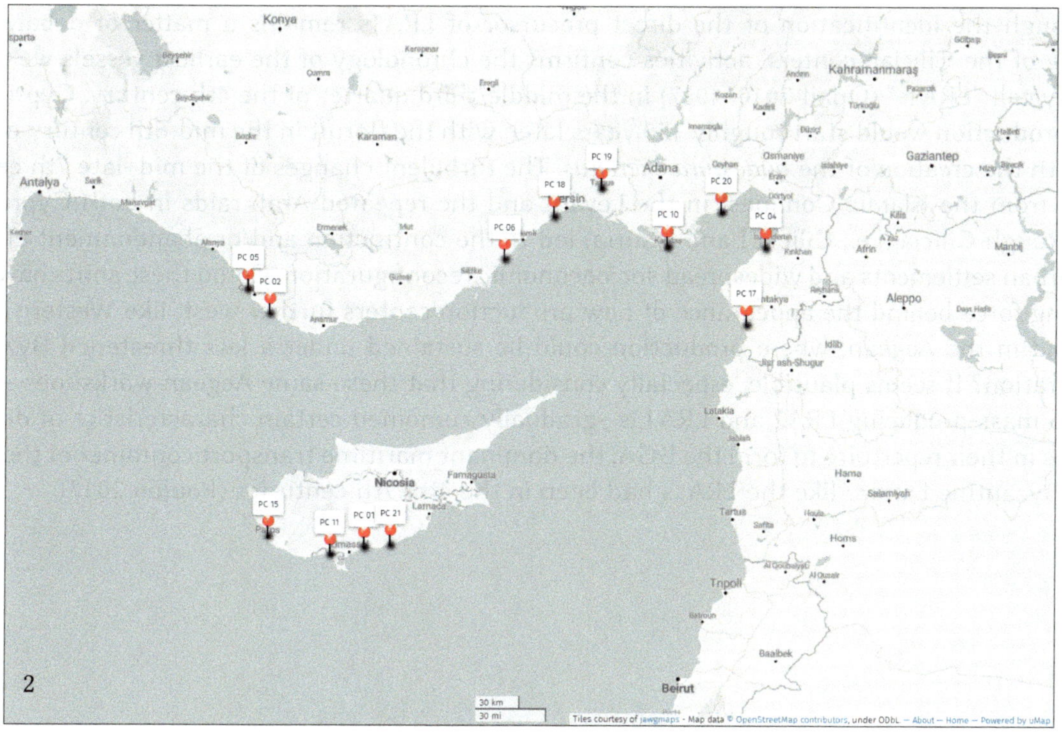

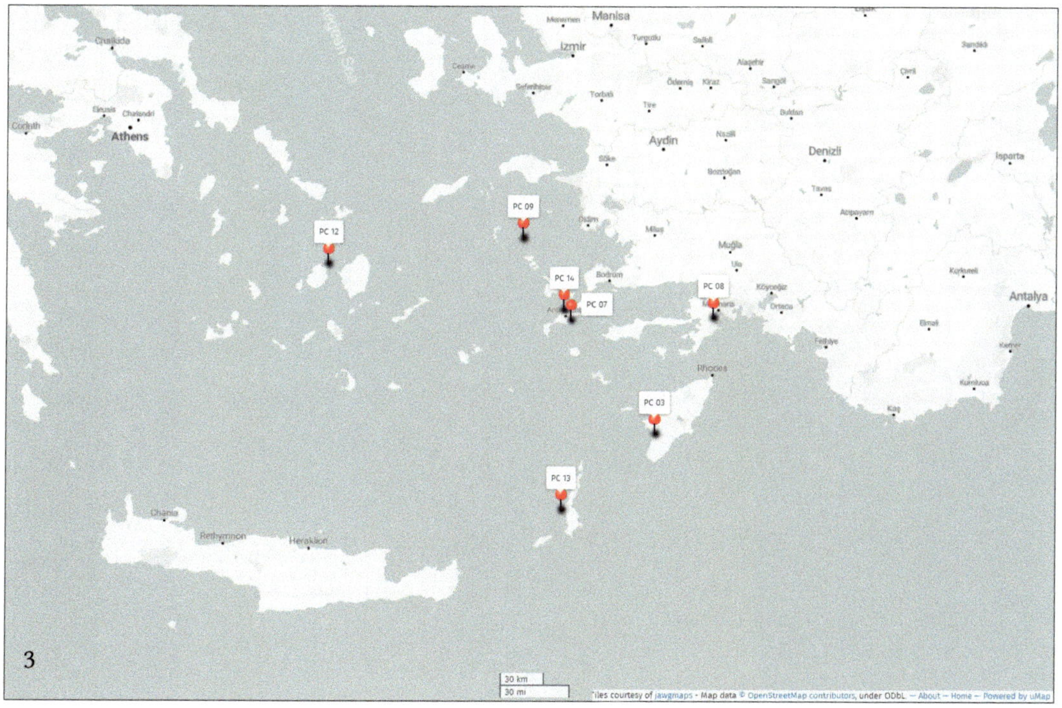

See caption on previous page

Although the identification of the direct precursor of LRA1s remains a matter of debate,[10] the beginning of the Cilician centers' activities confirms the chronology of the earliest vessels we can legitimately call "LRA1s" (Opaiț 2010: 1017) in the middle/third quarter of the 4th century. Cypriot and Aegean production would start roughly 150 years later, with the floruit in the mid-6th century concurrently with the creation of the *quaestura exercitus*. The turbulent changes of the mid–late 7th century resulting from the Islamic Conquest in the Levant and the repeated Arab raids in both Cyprus and Eastern Rough Cilicia (i.e., Cilicia I and Isauria) led to the contraction and/or abandonment of many coastal urban settlements and widespread socioeconomic reconfiguration. Could these shifts have been the driving force behind the appearance of new production centers further west, like Western Rough Cilicia and in the Aegean, where production could be sustained under a less threatened Byzantine administration? It seems plausible, especially considering that these same Aegean workshops—which were also mass-producing LRA2 and LRA13s—gradually combined certain characteristics of different amphoras in their repertoire to form the BGA, the dominant maritime transport container of the 8–9th century Byzantine Empire like the LRA1s had been in the 4th–7th centuries (Poulou 2017).

10. A good assessment of the questions in light of recent discoveries at Taposiris is in Marchand, Reynolds and Bomin 2022. See also the chart for a proposed evolution of LRA1s from earlier forms in Reynolds 2018: 359, fig. 12.5.

Chapter 4. Petrographic Data

As detailed in chapter 3, LRA1 production sites are primarily clustered in Cilicia, Cyprus, and the southern Aegean, with others in the western littoral of Anatolia, Lower Egypt, and northern Syria. Ongoing work in the southern Aegean is highlighting both that production extended further west and perhaps for over a century later than previously thought. The study of each centers' typical clay petro-fabrics is one of the key themes of current LRA1 research, particularly because the combination of calcareous clay, ophiolite-derived minerals, and igneous rock that characterizes many LRA1 fabrics is commonplace in *both* Cilicia and Cyprus, thus requiring high-resolution analysis to differentiate them. Notable exceptions are the variety of micaceous fabrics of southwest Turkey and the Aegean—including the workshops Halasarna, Kambos, and Laggeri (Diamanti 2010: figs. 15–16; Papavassiliou, Sarantidis, Papanikolaou 2014; Diamanti 2023). In this chapter, we identify and describe LRA1 petro-fabrics that can be clearly demonstrated to originate in a specific geological area; in other words, the results of *petrographic analysis* (with a polarized light microscope, not macroscopic analyses with a magnifying glass) conducted on LRA1 specimens, primarily those excavated in the context of a local production center. The two exceptions to this rule are:

1. The "Nile Clay" petro-fabric family, where the local LRA1 products have not been analyzed petrographically but are included here because the petro-fabric family itself is well known through years of detailed study, and
2. The Carmel Coast red *hamra* which has been identified in LRA1s and has been proven to be a local petro-fabric, although no production center in the coastal southern Levant is currently known.

Notably, there are far fewer LRA1 petro-fabrics that can be confidently connected to known production centers than there are known petro-fabrics overall; this is a gap in the research that remains understudied and should be a target for future analyses.

§4.1. Paphos Petrographic Characteristics and Distribution

Paphian products may be identified via their yellowish color in both plane polarized light (PPL) and cross polarized light (XPL), a result of the calcareous and bioclastic clay that is available in marls near Paphos. There is a wide range of materials included in the aplastic components, such as shell, microfossils, chert, red serpentine, and pillow lavas. These components usually occupy 15–25% of the total fabric, are moderately to poorly sorted, and range from subangular to rounded in shape. These characteristics align with the raw clays and parent rock in the vicinity of Nea Paphos, sourced from the Mamonia Complex. Petrographic analysis of these local rocks and sediments conducted by one of the authors matched with the main compositional features of locally produced LRA1s, providing a good template for identifying Paphian types at any consumption site.[1] Two LRA1s found in Israel (Sepphoris [LCP vessel 27979] and Caesarea Maritima [LCP vessel 28117) appear very similar to this fabric, but are distinct enough to suggest a different *chaîne opératoire* or slightly different raw material selection.

1. Local clays, sediments, and LRA1s from the Cypriot production centers were made available to us thanks to the generous contributions and guidance of Stella Demesticha, Maria Dikomitou-Eliadou, Paula Waiman-Barak, and Zeza Zomeni.

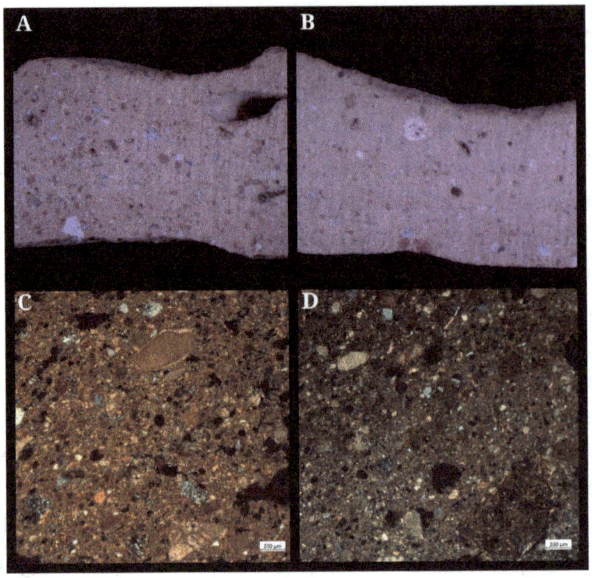

Figure 16. Fresh break photographs and petrographic thin sections of two LRA1s produced in Paphos (from Gillett 2023: fig. 17).

Petro-fabric	Workshop(s)	Clay	Silt	Aplastic components	General description
Cyprus/Mamonia Complex/calcareous clay/carbonates, quartz, ophiolitic suite	Paphos	Highly calcareous, light reddish brown to tan yellow-brown fabric in PPL, yellow in XPL	Silty (15–20%), including iron nodules, quartz, mica, limestone, and feldspar	Shell, *foraminifera*, limestone, serpentine, quartz, pillow lava, chert	A silty fabric with many bioclastic inclusions and a wide array of igneous, sedimentary, and meta-morphic components

§4.2. Amathus and Zygi-Petrini Petrographic Characteristics and Distribution

LRA1s from Amathus and Zygi-Petrini cannot be distinguished via petrography due to their close proximity in the same geological area. The petro-fabric associated with this area is quite characteristic, featuring greenish-gray to brown calcareous clay that is frequently sintered or vitrified from high firing temperatures and/or duration. The variability in color is also likely due to firing temperature and time (see Erten et al. 2004). The aplastic components present in the fabric are primarily minerals deriving from ultramafic rocks from the Troodos Mountains, including pyroxene, pillow lava, and basalt. Calcareous grains, like micritic limestone and microfossils, are also common throughout the fabric. This collection of sand-size grains tends to fall into two clear morphological categories, either very angular or well-rounded, though both are often stained with iron. Analysis of fluvial soils and bentonitic clays around the two production centers and cross-examination with locally made LRA1s confirmed that this petro-fabric can be tied to Amathus and Zygi. While this petro-fabric's appearance may seem unique and easily identifiable with the naked eye, microscopic examination is vital, as fabrics that have been hypothesized to originate in other regions, such as Sinop on the Black Sea, appear very similar. A LRA1 of this petro-fabric has been found at Ashkelon (LCP vessel 28238).

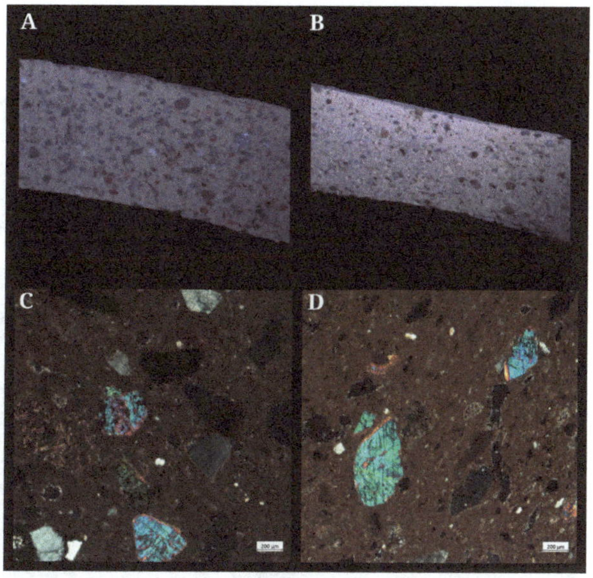

Figure 17. Fresh break photographs and petrographic thin sections of an LRA1 produced in Amathus (left) and another produced in Zygi (right) (from Gillett 2023: fig. 18).

Petro-fabric	Workshop(s)	Clay	Silt	Aplastic components	General description
Cyprus/Eastern South Coast/ Pakhna Basin/river lithology	Amathus and Zygi-Petrini	Calcareous, usually highly fired, which results in a gray-green color in PPL, gray in XPL	Ca. 5% silt, consisting primarily of iron nodules and some quartz	Pyroxenes, pillow lava, and basalt grains dominate	A fine carbonatic clay tempered with weathered material from the Troodos Mountains

§4.3. Cilician (Elaiussa Sebaste?) Petrographic Characteristics and Distribution

Petrographic analyses of petro-fabrics and local clays from Cilician LRA1 workshops are rare (but see Burragato et al. 2007 for a characterization of petro-fabrics at Elaiussa Sebaste). However, recurring patterns observed in imported LRA1s' fabric excavated in other areas closely align with both the known petrographic traits of Elaiussa's products as well as the regional geology in eastern Cilicia. Furthermore, an imported LRA1 excavated in Sepphoris, analyzed by one of the authors (G.G., LCP vessel 27983), was preliminarily identified as an Elaiussa product by petrographers studying that assemblage (Murat Eroğlu, pers. comm.). This methodology of connecting petro-fabric to region is not ideal, however, and future research is vital to confirming these hypotheses.[2] The broad Cilician petro-fabric category is always composed of reddish marly clay with aplastic components of limestone and bioclastic carbonates and an orange-red mineral, likely serpentine. The common calcareous grains tend to be larger than the others, and voids within the fabric occur frequently. LRA1s of this fabric have been found in northeastern Spain,[3] Croatia,[4] Jordan,[5] Crete,[6] the Burgaz shipwreck,[7] and the famous Yassı Ada shipwreck.[8]

Figure 18. Photographs, fresh break photographs, and petrographic thin sections of two LRA1s excavated in Israel likely produced in Cilicia, maybe at Elaiussa Sebaste.

2. Forthcoming work should provide much needed clarification on the Elaiussa petro-fabrics, as key photographs from the previous study at Elaiussa are published in black and white and not openly accessible on a platform like the LCP for cross-examination
3. See Fantuzzi, Ontiveros, and Reynolds 2017: fig 4a, 4b; Fantuzzi et al. 2019: fig. 2b.
4. Nagy and Szakmany 2019: fig. 6A (LCP vessel 34479)
5. Hudson and Hartman 2020: 245 (LCP vessel 28954).
6. Poulou-Papadimitriou and Nodarou 2014: figs. 18–19.
7. Leidwanger, Greene, and Tuna 2015: fig. 7 (LCP vessel 33674).
8. Leidwanger 2014: fig. 2a–d.

Petro-fabric	Workshop(s)	Clay	Silt	Aplastic components	General description
Rough Cilicia/red clay/red mafics, foraminifera, limestone, igneous rock	Unknown	Red to red-brown marly clay in both PPL and XPL, filled calcareous components	5-8% of the fabric, mainly calcareous material, quartz, and iron nodules	Micritic limestone is the most frequent, and foraminifera and serpentine (?) are common	Many large, well-rounded carbonates alongside bright red inclusions (serpentine) in a marly red clay

§4.4. General "Aegean" Petrographic Characteristics and Distribution

A large portion of petro-fabrics from the southeast Aegean, including some of the Cycladic and Dodecanese Islands, as well as the western coast of Anatolia may be broadly characterized as featuring a moderately to highly micaceous and noncalcareous clay with metamorphic rock-derived inclusions (e.g., LCP Turkey/Southern Lydia/metamorphic/schist and mica). These general attributes do not represent a single petro-fabric but rather a group of loosely related petro-fabrics from a large and geologically heterogenous area. It is difficult to connect any member of this group with a specific geological region or LRA1 manufacturing center, not because of universal geological features (though petro-fabrics from different sites in this region can be quite similar), but because of the scarcity of high-resolution petrographic analyses conducted at production sites (but see below) and the tendency of scholars to label any brown to pink micaceous clay as "Aegean." When rigorous studies are conducted, however, they often allow for a more precise identification of provenance. LRA1s of this petro-fabric group have been found at Pseira (Poulou-Papadimitriou and Nodarou 2014: fig. 11; LCP vessel 34069), Caesarea Maritima (LCP vessel 28122), and Sepphoris (LCP vessel 27991).

Figure 19. Photographs, fresh break photographs, and petrographic thin sections of two LRA1s excavated in Israel likely produced at one of the Aegean workshops.

Petro-fabric	Workshop(s)	Clay	Silt	Aplastic components	General description
Aegean/Micaceous/quartz, iron, metamorphic rock	Unknown	Noncalcareous clay studded with mica laths, light red-brown in PPL, slightly darker in XPL	Ca. 5–8% silt, including mica, quartz, hornblende, feldspar, calcite, and iron oxides	Quartz dominates, with some feldspars and limestone, and occasional mica schist	A combination of frequent mica laths in a red-brown noncalcareous clay

§4.5. Halasarna Petrographic Characteristics and Distribution

Close study of the local LRA1s of Halasarna prove that Aegean petro-fabrics can sometimes be differentiated, with the proper analysis (see Diamanti 2010: 204). Previous analyses of a variety of Koan amphoras show that there are at least three distinct petro-fabrics used on the island, all featuring yellow-brown to gray-colored clay, a concentration of micas and quartz grains (Whitbread 1995: 87–94; Diamanti 2010: figs. 10–16; Diamanti, Kouzeli and Petridis 2014: 183–84). It is without a doubt

Charikleia Diamanti's work, however, that clearly defined the Halasarna LRA1 petro-fabric, what she terms "Group B." The clay is noncalcareous and dense with occasional voids, appearing gray with greenish hue in PPL and darker in XPL. Occasional rounded clay pellets or grog could suggest the incomplete mixing of multiple clays before usage. The fabric contains quartz and mica silt, and the few aplastic components are similarly dominated by quartz and preferentially aligned mica. The infrequency of inclusions led Diamanti to describe the fabric as relatively "clean," which is noticeable to the naked eye. Calcareous components sometimes occur, and based on their presence or absence Diamanti defines the subgroups B1 and B2, with carbonates present in the former but not in the latter (Diamanti 2010: 142–43). A probable example of this petro-fabric was found at Caesarea Maritima (LCP vessel 28119); it featured the same clay matrix with about 15% quartz silt and mica laths with some iron grains, while aplastic components are present at roughly 5% and include quartz (60%), plagioclase feldspar (15%), chert (10%), and basalt grains (>5%).

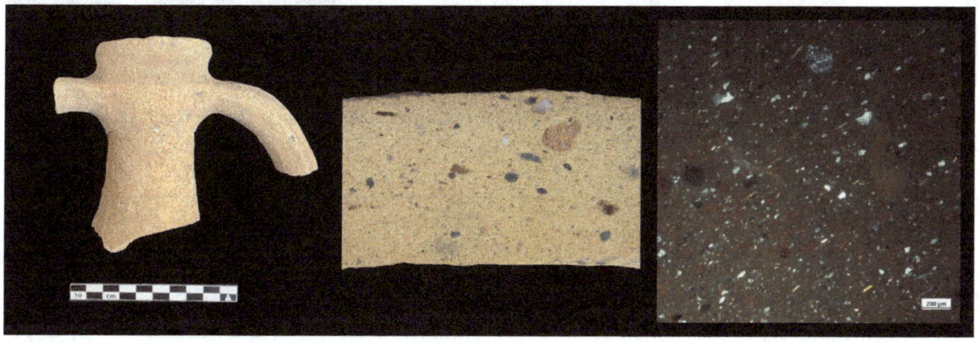

Figure 20. A photograph, fresh break photograph, and petrographic thin section of an LRA1 excavated in Israel that matches the Halasarna petro-fabric.

Petro-fabric	Workshop(s)	Clay	Silt	Aplastic components	General description
Halasarna/ micaceous/quartz and mica	Halasarna	Noncalcareous, fine grained/ clean clay, grayish green to brown PPL and darker in XPL	Ca. 10–15%, predominantly mica laths	Quartz and mica (grains and laths) are the most common	Mica and quartz in a fine noncalcareous gray-green clay

§4.6. Egyptian Nile Clay Petrographic Characteristics and Distribution

It is nearly impossible to differentiate petro-fabrics produced from Nile clay collected at different spots along the river due to the homogeneity of its lithology, but the overall family of petro-fabrics is easy to spot, sometimes even with the naked eye. A type B LRA1 found at Saint Jeremiah's Monastery was made out of a "coarse, alluvial Nile silt" (Ghaly 1992: 168) version of this fabric. It is highly probable that this macroscopically identified petro-fabric belongs to the well-known Nile clay category, although this has *not* been corroborated by petrographic studies and figure 18 displays a Nile Silt red-slipped open vessel from the Byzantine period. Nile clay fabrics are characterized by the silty iron-rich clay (usually dark and inactive in XPL and PPL) sourced from the river with a myriad of aplastic components in variable quantities, including quartz, feldspars, mica, pyroxene, and opaques. None of these Egyptian LRA1s have been found outside the country, though they are found at other Egyptian sites, such as Dime / Soknopaious Nesos (Caputo and Davoli 2023: 741), Kellia, and Baouît (Marchand and Dixneuf 2007: 316; LCP vessel 34776).

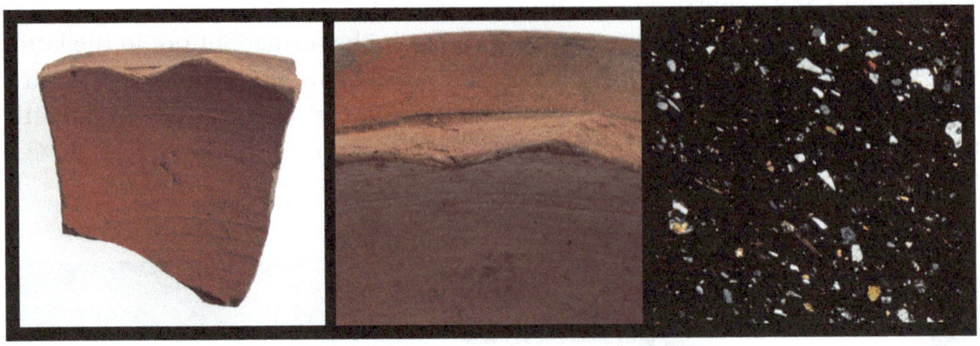

Figure 21. A photograph, fresh break photograph, and petrographic thin section of an open vessel excavated in Aswan with a Nile Clay petro-fabric (LCP vessel 18154).

Petro-fabric	Workshop(s)	Clay	Silt	Aplastic components	General description
Egypt/Nile Clay	Saint Jeremiah's Monastery	Iron-rich red clay with common silt grains, typically appearing dark and optically inactive in polarized light	Varies. Mainly quartz, occasional feldspars, iron oxides, and opaques	Varies. Frequent quartz, and smaller amounts of feldspar, chert, pyroxene	A variable group of petro-fabrics with silty iron-rich Nile clay

§4.7. A Suggestion for Carmel Coast Petrographic Characteristics and Distribution

Several LRA1s excavated at Sepphoris, Israel, were produced using clay that originated along the northern coast of Israel. This suggests that an LRA1 workshop existed somewhere in this region in addition to the widespread local production of other amphora types, like the well-known LRA4 or Gaza jar, although no such kiln has yet been found. The fabric is identified by its reddish-brown clay, derived from the coastal paleosol *hamra*, and dominant—indeed almost exclusive—quartz sand inclusions. Other aplastic components are occasional foraminifera, clay pellets, calcareous materials, iron oxides, and chert. The foraminifera and carbonates derive from *kurkar* (calcareous aeolianite sandstone) ridges that line the Carmel Coast (Frechen et al. 2004: 41–52; Zviely et al. 2009: 240). LRA1s of this fabric have not been found anywhere outside of Sepphoris, although Agora M334 amphoras with the same petro-fabric have been found in Caesarea Maritima (Ratzlaff et al. 2017). We include it here because petrographic studies must be integrated and put in conversation with archaeological ceramic studies in order to continue refining our understanding of past human's relationship with pottery. Indeed, the very first proposal that LRA1 kilns be sought for in regions with ophiolitic outcrops like Cyprus and east Cilicia, rather than Egypt, came from petrographic reasoning (Peacock and Williams 1986: 186)!

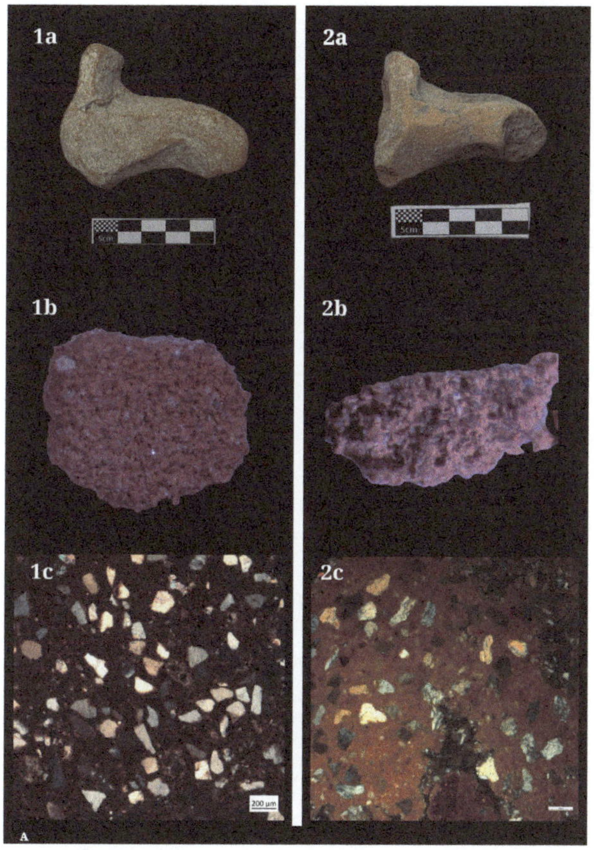

Figure 22. Photographs, fresh break photographs, and petrographic thin sections of two LRA1s excavated in Israel with a local Carmel Coast petro-fabric.

Petro-fabric	Workshop(s)	Clay	Silt	Aplastic components	General description
Israel/Northern Coastal Plain ferruginous/quartz and biogenic sand	Unknown	Red, iron-rich clay that appears orange-red to red-brown in PPL and XPL	<5% silt, made up of quartz and carbonates	Quartz is ca. 60% of the total, with clay pellets, carbonates, and few microfossils	Quartz and carbonitic components in a red, iron-rich clay

Chapter 5. Inscriptions

§5.1. "Dipintology"

Within the world of epigraphic corpora on ceramics, Greek *tituli picti* on amphoras in late antiquity are regrettably understudied (Derda 1992, Fournet 2021).[1] *Dipinti* on LRA1s are no exception. Epigraphists and paleographists have conducted few systematic studies, mostly stemming from the detailed analysis of LRA1s found in Egypt (Fournet and Pieri 2008; Fournet 2012, 2021).[2]

Typically, inscriptions on LRA1s range from a few letters to three or four lines painted in ochre, red, or black on the neck, under the handle, or on the upper body of the amphora. Greek is by far the predominant language used. Some occurrences of Latin are reported at Ravenna (Cirelli 2014: 543), while the Aramaic (?) and Hebrew inscriptions on vessels from, respectively, Ashdod (Freedman 1967: 34 and 69, fig. 14.2; LCP vessel 33473)[3] and Ravenna (Cirelli 2014: 551, fig. 8; LCP vessel 34988) remain, so far, isolated cases.

The following is a schematic summary of the nature and contents of LRA1 inscriptions (after Fournet 2021), where the letter (*x*) correlates with a particular location on the amphora and the subscript (x_1) represents the most frequent inscription types found in that location/line.

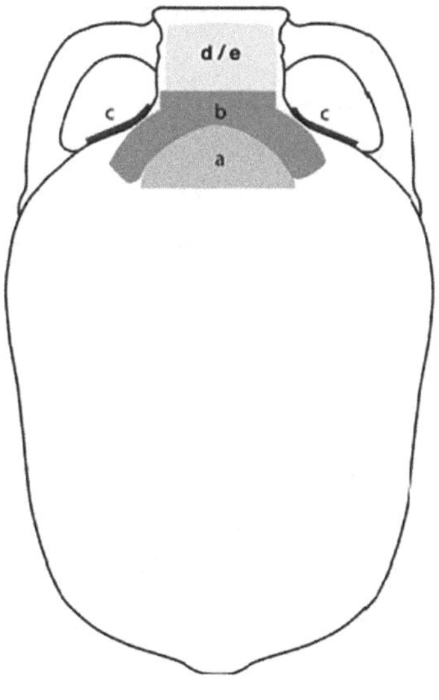

Figure 23. Diagram of the typical locations of *dipinti* on LRA1s (after Fournet 2021: 64).

1. We are following here the evocative proposal suggested by Fournet (2012) for the study of this class of inscriptions; on the use of *tituli* or *dipinti*, used here as synonyms, see the clarification and explanation in Fournet 2021: 63 n. 1.
2. See also Diamanti (2010) and Gerousi (2015) for broader considerations on the inscriptions on late Roman amphoras in general.
3. Which can be possibly associated with the type (d) attested in Egyptian contexts, see below.

a. On the shoulders, centered between the handles:
   - a_1: Date (the indiction, or fiscal, year).[4]
   - a_2: Christian formulas: an isopsephism;[5] or the acrostic χμγ, which stands for "Christ born of Maria";[6] other abbreviations for Θεός, "God"; or κύριος, "Lord" are also recurrent.
   - a_{3+4}: The quantity contained in the vessel; it usually consists of (a_3) an abbreviation for the unit of measure (commonly *sextarii*)[7] followed by (a_4) a figure often including fractions; a_3 is more commonly found on earlier types, and tends to be replaced by very stylized letters, interpreted as a reference to the content (Gascou 1978: 26; cf. De Rossi 1890: 40–41) or other religious formulas (Fournet 2021: 65).

b. In the area between the shoulders and neck surrounding (a), sometimes perpendicularly to the latter. A few letters, interpreted as a quantity because of the presence of fractions. These symbols very likely represent the tare of the vessel.

c. Under the handles (and therefore difficult to read), usually painted in red, on three or four lines, using small characters:
   - c_1: Personal name (abbreviated or in genitive), possibly the vine grower's.
   - c_2: A second name, possibly a patronymic or a toponym (the estate where the contents are produced?).
   - c_3: (Occasionally) the word ὀρινίου/ὀρ(ινίου), which provides an indication of the vine growing technique ("high-trained vines," following a rare lemma in Hesychius).[8]
   - c_4: A number, interpreted as the content's batch number.

d. On the neck, in black letters:
   - d_1: Two–three lines, Christian formulas akin to $a_{3.}$
   - d_2: Personal name in the genitive case.
   - d_3: Usually ἐμάτι(ο)ν or ἐμάτινον (for αἱμάτιον or αἱματίνον)–a characteristic of the wine ("red as blood"?), sporadically with another adjective (like πρωτεῖον) to describe its quality, a sort of label.

e. On the neck, large letters, in red: a figure (number?). So far attested only in Antinoupolis, maybe written at destination.

The recurring presence of c_3 and, to a lesser extent, of d_3, led Jean-Luc Fournet to assume that the primary content of the amphoras must be unequivocally considered wine (see also Opaiţ 2017). Explicit mentions of wine come from specimens excavated in Athens (cf. Lang 1976: 83, I45, but the amphora might have been reused; LCP vessel 35026)[9] and, possibly, Rome (see below). In Fournet's interpre-

4. One of the inscriptions from the Athenian Agora, so far an isolated example, seems to base the date on the ascension of Diocletian (Lang 1976: 72, Hc 23; LCP vessel 34495).

5. The most common in the Egyptian dossier is υπδ = 484 = Θεοῦ "from God" (Fournet 2021: 64).

6. Χ(ριστός) Μ(αρίας) γ(έννα)/γ(έννημα) in the current interpretation (discussion in Derda 1992: 136 n. 6; cf. instead the old reading as Χ(ριστός), Μ(ιχαήλ), Γ(αβριήλ) in, e.g., De Rossi 1890: 42).

7. On the value of the *sextarii*, to be interpreted as the Alexandrine or Syriac measure, see Whitehouse et al. 1985: 191. Lang (1976: 57) focuses on the oil *sextarium* stressing the different standards in use, with adjustments to allow an easy conversion to *litrai*; cf. van Alfen 1996: 204, the "fluctuations of the *xestes*-value" might be regarded as "an attempt to equate 1 *xestes* of oil or wine to 2 *litrai*."

8. Fournet 2021: 66 with references and discussion; LCP vessel 35173.

9. We could not check the inscription on an amphora found in Milan that, reportedly, bears the inscription "from Chios," interpreted as a reference to the wine produced on the island (mentioned in Auriemma 2007: 148).

tation, (a), (b), and (c) were possibly written at the same time: the departure of the filled amphora (Fournet 2021: 67). He suggests these markers were added after filling the amphoras with their content at the shipping location where the tare (b) and the quantity (a) had been verified and the name of the producer/production zone was noted (c). Sometimes, these were followed by the addition of (d), which could even totally replace the (a)–(b)–(c) sequence. Finally (e), an unloading batch number or control mark(?), was scribbled at arrival.

The practice of inscribing (a) and (b) on the vessels would have been vital to ensure the accuracy of shipments, considering the variability in size and volume of LRA1s (see ch. 2). Mabel Lang noted that capacity might have been "defined not by the number of standard units it [the amphora] could hold but by the net weight of the particular contents" (1976: 59). In some cases, the standard metrological unit was the Cypriot *modius* (see Lang 1976: 63, H44, an inscription where the abbreviation *mo-* is used), corresponding to 17 and a fraction (½ or ⅔) *sextarii*, a figure recurring in inscriptions on some LRA1s from the Athenian Agora with the same estimated capacity (9.8 L; Lang 1976: 62, Ha 36; 63, Ha 43 and Ha 44).

In our catalog, inscriptions are attested in 71 sites (see table 10.2).

The corpus is incomplete and heterogeneous, particularly concerning the full analysis and publication of the inscriptions. A preliminary evaluation of the available evidence suggests that the interpretative template envisioned and refined by Fournet remains valid as more *dipinti* are found. Iatrus—one of the largest fully studied and published corpora outside of Egypt (Conrad 2007: 64–65)[10]—and the Palatine Hill contexts in Rome (Pensabene 1981; detailed analysis by Simon Pratt in Whitehouse et al. 1985), are good confirmations in this regard.

A remarkable exception is a group of LRA1s and other vessels from Egypt, Romania, and Bulgaria, all of which feature various inscriptions that share the recurring formula Θεοῦ χάρις κέρδος, "God's grace [is a] gain" (Derda 1992).[11] Interestingly, other common elements in this group of inscriptions indicate that these containers carried "sweet" olive oil, and sacred oil in at least one case (i.e., to be used for liturgical purposes; Derda 1992: 138). The typology of the amphoras and paleographic analyses point to a 6th century date, with only one exception from Naqlun, a Peacock-Williams 36/Tripolitana I amphora, which cannot be dated later than the 4th century. The Naqlun vessel was utilized as wall-building material in a later context (6th–7th c.), so it might have been inscribed during a phase of reuse. While scanty, this evidence suggests that some LRA1s (as well as other common transport amphoras), whatever their original content/purpose, were *refilled* with olive oil and exported (specifically, to the Danubian regions).[12] Does this possibility offer an additional framework, beyond wine consumption, to interpret the large quantities of LRA1s found in olive-oil-producing regions (whether specializing in the mass-produced commodity or "boutique" holy oil) of the late Roman world (see ch. 6)?

Inscriptions on LRA1s from the Royal Tombs of Ballana and Qustul in the Nile Valley show another pattern: written in red and occasionally black ink, some of these *dipinti* have been read as κριθῆς/κριθῶν ἀρταβαί, "artabs of barley" (Hautumm 1981: 63, with references) and in at least one case, there is a direct mention of olives (Emery and Kirwan 1938: 403, no. 9, table 117.9; non vidi). Measurements of the capacity of these LRA1s have shown they could actually carry about half of the volume and weight

10. In particular, the entries 1304–1309, 1311 (tables 15–16).

11. Three LRA1 are in Derda's list (I.1, II.1, II.6; see the entries for Naqlun, Sacidava, and Sucidava in our table), alongside various LRA2, spatheia, and Peacock-Williams 36 amphora; Derda 1992: 139.

12. An assumption already expressed, e.g., in Gerousi 2015: 129.

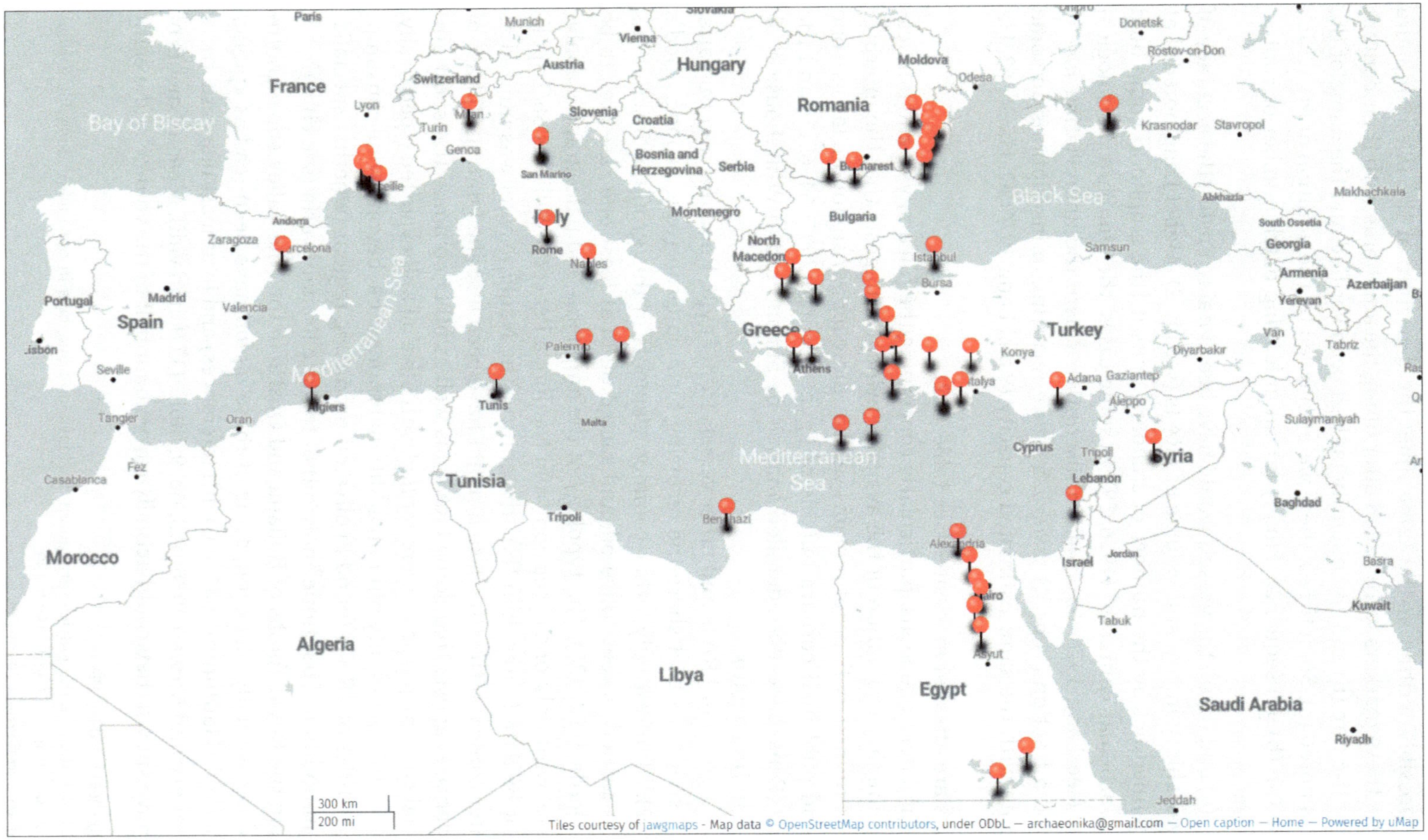

Figure 24.1. Distribution maps of *dipinti* attestations in our catalog, including sites: A05 Apamea, A32 Palmyra, A33 Qal'at Sem'an, A40 Sergilla, B11 Dhiorios, B27 Skouriotissa-Vouppes, C02 Ashdod, C09 Capernaum, C16 Horbat 'Aqav, C25 Ma'agan Mikhael B (shipwreck), C34 Rehovot-in-the-Negev, C41 Upper Zohar, D01 Aegyssus, D05 Callatis, D10 Constantinople, D12 Dinogetia, D14 Halmyris/Murighiol, D16 Histria, D17 Iatrus, D24 Novae, D27 Orgame/Argamum, D31 Sacidava, D35 Sucidava/Corabia, D36 Tomis, D37 Topraichioi, D39 Tropaeum Traiani, E14 Pantikapaion, Bosporus/Kerch, E24 Tyritake, F03 Aphrodisias, F06 Arykanda, F07 Assos, F12 Ephesus, F13 Halasarna, F28 Kyme in Aeolis, F38 Patara, F42 Sagalassos, F44 Sardis, F49 Troy/Ilion, F50 Xanthos, G06 Athens, G16 Corinth, G18 Dion, G21 Gortyn, G24 Itanos, G52 Thessaloniki, G56 Torone, H15 Cefalù (shipwreck), H16 Classe, H40 Milan, H42 Neapolis/Naples, H60 Ravenna, H61 Rhegion, H63 Roma, I04 Alexandria, I05 Antinoupolis, I08 Berenice/Benghazi, I12 Deir el-Naqlun, I13 Dime/Soknopaiou Nesos, I20 Kellia, I27 Oxyrhynchus/Bahnasa, I29 Saqqara, I30 Taposiris Magna, J02 Carthago, J34 Tipasa, K24 Tarraco, L04 Arelatum/Arles, L07 Avignon, L29 Massalia/Marseille, L39 Saint-Blaise, L43 Saint-Martin-de-Crau, N03 Ballana, N05 Firka, N06 Kalabsha, N15 Wadi Qitna.

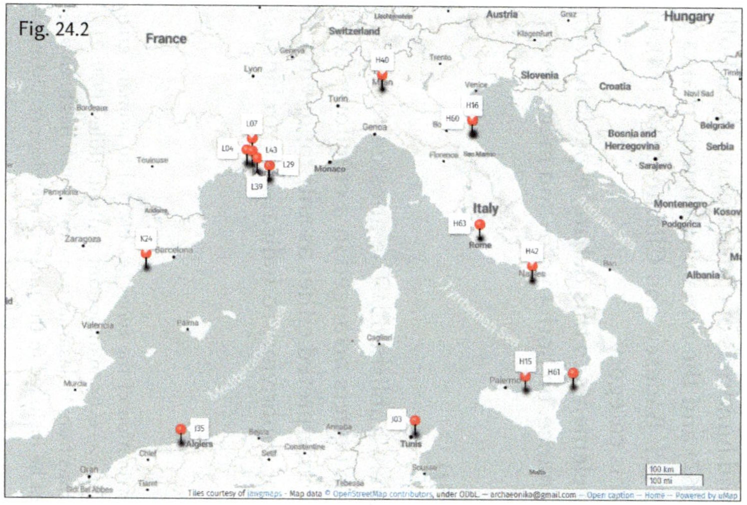

Fig. 24.2

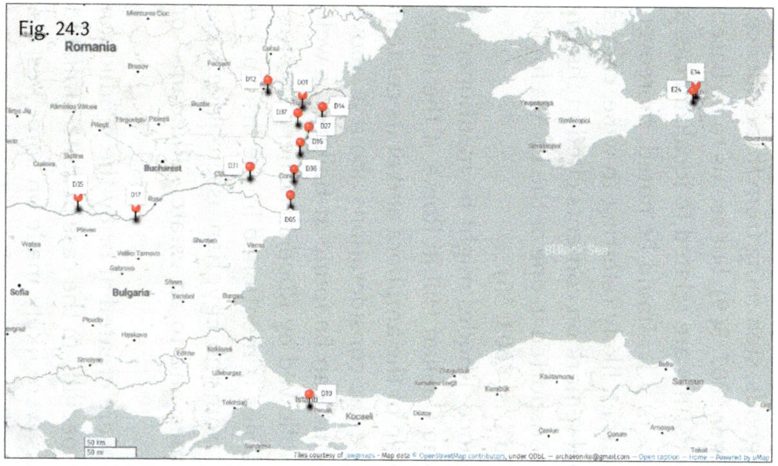

Fig. 24.3

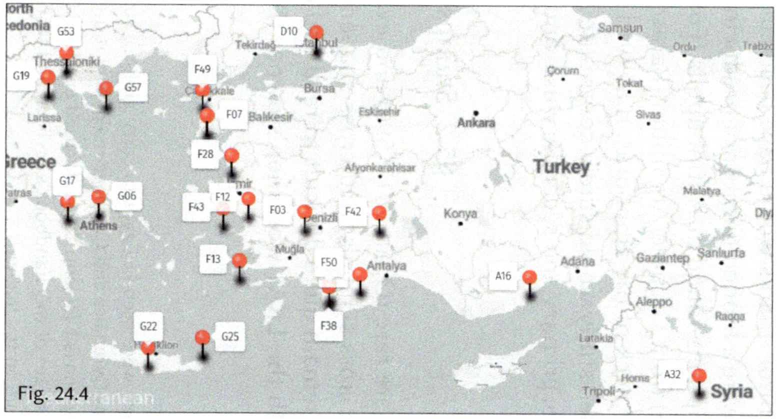

Fig. 24.4

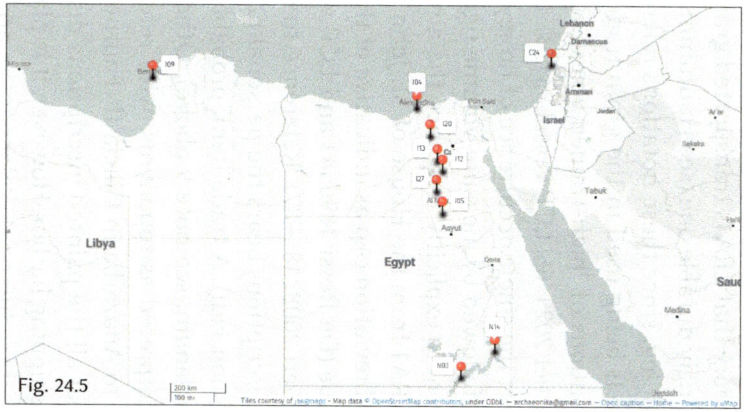

Fig. 24.5

Figure 24.2–5. See previous page for caption.

of an artab. The theory that LRA1s transported grain or other dry goods, stemming from this evidence, has been a surprisingly durable one (see Hautumm 1981; Leidwanger 2007: 309), but seems to be based on a misunderstanding, since these notations referencing dry foodstuffs are related to localized cases of repurposed LRA1s being used in the grain trade (see below, ch. 6).[13] It should be noted, moreover, that one of the mentions of "high-trained vines" discussed by Fournet, likely referring to wine, comes from Ballana (Fournet 2021: 66; LCP vessel 35173). Lastly, as a final remark on contents cited in the *titulus*, we must report the single occurrence of honey as the good transported in one of the LRA1s found at Classe (*méllitos* followed by measure/volume figures; Cirelli and Lasi 2003: 55).

Few *dipinti* seem to explicitly reference the amphora provenance. Rhodes might be mentioned in the *titulus* on an LRA1 from the House of St. John and Paul on the Caelian Hill in Rome, if the interpretation of the abbreviation c+ρ as indicative of the Rhodian origin of the amphora and of its content can still be held true (De Rossi 1890: 41 and LCP vessel 35174; see the considerations about a_3 above and Fournet and Pieri 2008: 186–87). Reference to the Aegean island can be found at Ballana as well, where one of the inscriptions bears the personal name *Iōann(ēs)* followed by *Rhodion* (Emery and Kirwan 1938: 404, 19; non vidi). A trade item, probably wine, from Chios is mentioned in the inscription from Milan (Mediolanum; see note 9 above). Other inscriptions from the Egyptian assemblage have been read and interpreted as toponyms, with reference to Apamea and to an estate ("Rhadam-" or "Randama") close to Anazarba in Cilicia II (Fournet 2021: 66).

We assume that all the painted inscriptions discussed so far were created at or by the production center and/or the shipping harbor. However, it is plausible that, especially in the case of state-affiliated trade, verification procedures took place upon arrival, and marks were likely made on some vessels. Clearly, these "control" marks would have been considerably more diverse than the rest of the written apparatus; there were a limited number of producing centers, and hundreds of consumption sites. Both the (e) type inscriptions found at Antinoupolis (Fournet 2021: 67) and the nonalphanumeric marks (a red painted circle) from Orgame/Argamum (Paraschiv 2006: 89; cf. Bădescu and Cliante 2014: 174), in either case on the neck of the amphoras, may well fall under this category.

A more detailed study would surely contribute meaningful elements to this debate, especially with regard to contents, primary and secondary use, and even provenance, on both micro- and macrolevels.

§5.2. Stamps and Graffiti

Stamps on LRA1 are rare (Opaiţ 2017: 596) and even more rarely published.[14] The attested forms are crucigrams (plain cross symbols) and cross-shaped monograms (letters arranged in a cruciform fashion). These latter remain quite difficult to read and are usually interpreted either as anthroponyms, to be associated with the LRA1 workshop's owner (Kara 2015), or toponyms, to indicate the (religious)

13. "Amphoras certainly were used in Egypt to carry grain ... but the wide distribution of the type [i.e., LRA1s] to primary grain producing areas such as Cyrenaica and Carthage make [sic] it unlikely that grain was ever an important content" (Riley 1979: 215).
14. A meaningful exception is Diamanti 2024a (focused on LRA1 and LRA13 stamps from Halasarna; non vidi), which has been published during the last stages of this handbook's revision and therefore could not be included in the present overview; cf. Diamanti 2024b (non vidi) for more on the matter.

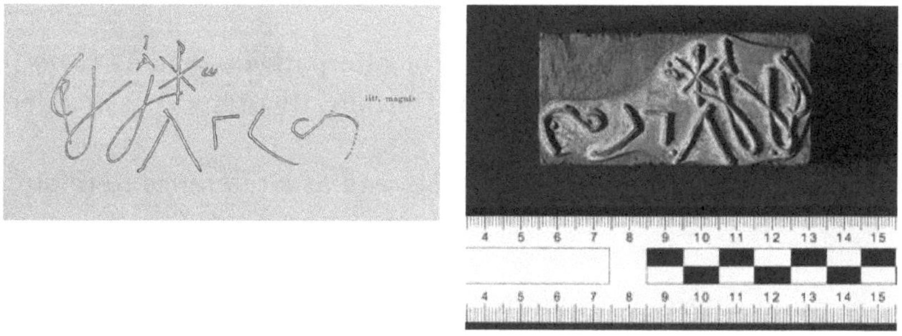

Figure 25.1–2. Inscription on LRA1 from Rome, possibly mentioning Rhodian wine, and the zincograph used by H. Dressel to reproduce the inscription later published in *CIL* 15 4893 (image: Corpus Inscriptionum Latinarum (CIL), BBAW. https://berlin.museum-digital.de/object/103044).

estate to which the workshop belonged (Pieri 2012), or else more generically the city where the amphoras were manufactured (Opaiţ 2017). Some examples include:[15]

- Crucigram stamp from late 6th century Antinoupolis (Pieri 2012)

Figure 26. Neck of a stamped LRA1 found in Antinoupolis (LCP vessel 35048).

- Monogram stamp from Constantinople, Yenikapi (Kara 2015: 247). It finds comparisons with some Scythian examples (see below), so we suggest reading it as *Sebaste* as well.

Figure 27. Neck of a stamped LRA1 found in Constantinople (LCP vessel 33954).

15. Other known and partially/totally published stamps: Opaiţ 2004: 8–9 (Histria); Autret 2022: 163–64 (Korykos, Elaiussa Sebaste, Soli-Pompeiopolis); see Kara 2021 for a wider discussion of stamps from Constantinople. Bes, Diamanti, and Dolea 2023 (Limyra) became available during the draft revision of this handbook, so it could not be discussed extensively in the text, but the authors present a stamp containing a monogram that has been read as ΚΩΡΥΚΟΥ, or Korykos

- Monogram stamps from Sucidava:
  (a) monogram dated to late 4th–early 5th century, alternatively read as *Kyros* (Gherge and Amon 2011) or as *Korykou*, either a reference to the Cilician city of Korykos or a personal name (Opaiţ 2017: 596)
  (b) monogram read as *Sabeinos*, more likely to be read as a reference to (Elaiussa) *Sebaste* (Opaiţ 2017).

Graffiti seem to be rarely attested or reported. Some are known on LRA1s from, respectively, Berenice (Riley 1979: 215, fig. 91:338; LCP vessel 34770), Gortyn (Portale and Romeo 2001: 330), and Emporio on Chios Island (Ballance et al. 1989: 114, no. 280, figs. 43 and 45, and pl. 25; LCP vessel 33664); reportedly, there are several on LRA1 pedestals produced at Elaiussa (Ferrazzoli and Ricci 2007). Maybe the best-known instance of LRA1 graffiti is on board the Yassi Ada: it reads EΛE, interpreted as an abbreviation for ἔλαιον, and was marked "after the amphora was fired" (van Alfen 1996: 201–2 and fig. 15).

Chapter 6. Transported Goods (and Uses)

The debate on the contents that LRA1s were designed to carry is by no means settled. Were they used to transport wine (Pieri 2005a; Opaiţ 2017: 596) or olive oil (Waliszewski 2014)? Perhaps dry foodstuffs (like grain and barley; Hautumm 1981) or other products like garum (Zoroğlu 2020) or even honey? Are we even asking the right question: Did the LRA1 have a designated set of contents? As mentioned above (see introduction), certain ambiguities in the available evidence make the question hard to solve unequivocally. This evidence ranges from archaeometric characteristics to inscriptions, from traces of original contents and of pitch-lining (or the absence thereof) to considerations of the agricultural background of the producing regions. In this chapter we summarize the *status quaestionis* and outline a tentative interpretative model.

Some LRA1s from Cyprus, France, Egypt, and multiple Mediterranean shipwrecks were found with a coating of impermeable pitch on the interior, indicating that these particular vessels were optimized for liquid contents rather than dry goods (van Alfen 1996: 209; Pieri 2005a: 612; Fournet and Pieri 2008; Reynolds 2010b).[1] Indeed, out of seven LRA1s from Sagalassos subjected to residue analysis, five tested positive for pine resin biomarkers (Romanus et al. 2009: table 1). Such inner pitch-lining is usually regarded as a clue that the amphora's original purpose was to carry wine (Brennan et al. 2020: 323), while its absence is sometimes used as evidence for olive oil being the original content.[2] After the surveys by Empereur and Picon and the massive deposits of wasters they reported in the Gulf of Alexandretta—an area renowned in late antiquity for intensive olive monoculture—the "Antioch thesis" (van Alfen 1996: 208) gained popularity for a while and olive oil was regarded as the possible main product carried in LRA1s (see the acute analysis in Panella 1993: 665–66 n. 220; and the synthesis in Pacetti 1995: 273). Reportedly, a specimen found at Sabratha, on the coast of North Africa had traces of olive oil residue (Williams 2005a: 161; mentioned as a personal communication in Williams 2000), and as we have seen, some occasional *dipinti* and graffiti mention olive oil (see ch. 5), reinforcing the assumption that in some circumstances LRA1s were produced to ship olive oil or could have been reused to do so. Opaiţ (2017: 596) argues though that "the thickness and permeability of the walls of LRA1 require an internal coating", and that usually olive oil-designated amphoras (like Dressel 20 and 24, San Lorenzo 7, or Zeest 80) had much thicker walls than the LRA1s. Moreover, as Olga Karagiorgou (2001: 149) has pointed out, comparing the capacities of LRA1s and LRA2s suggests that the latter, definitively bigger, vessels could carry a commodity not subject to spoilage once opened, like olive oil, while the former, being smaller, would have helped to preserve the quality of wine simply by allowing it to be emptied faster. The LRA2 was used to ship olive oil, and this type is very frequently found in the same assem-

---

1. A few instances of pitched LRA1s include some on the Yassi Ada (van Alfen 1996: 203), Avdimou Bay (Leidwanger 2007: 312), and Marmaris B shipwrecks (Brennan et al. 2020: 303).

2. However, it must be noted that residue analysis on pitch-lined amphoras has pointed to the opposite conclusion: that pitch did not prevent wine from penetrating into the ceramic matrix, and therefore might have been used to prevent *oil* cargoes from seeping into the ceramic container (Romanus et al. 2009: 908). Hopefully further research will be conducted in this direction to clarify the matter.

blages as LRA1s.[3] Why would all of the requisite coordination and effort be taken to equally utilize a different amphora type, primarily produced in different areas, to also carry olive oil?

The analysis of LRA1 distribution patterns in specific regions and alongside other specific amphora types (Karagiorgou 2001; Opaiţ 2004: 96–98; Pieri 2005a: 84–85; Opaiţ 2017: 596) further undermines the hypothesis of olive oil as primary content. LRA1s are frequently found at sites that had existing infrastructure to export locally produced olive oil (like Carthage and the coastal sites of Syria, for instance; cf. Riley 1979: 215; Williams 2005a: 161; Komar 2016: 161; Reynolds 2021: 335–43). Why would LRA1s carrying olive oil be shipped in huge numbers to sites that already produced olive oil in huge quantities?

The prime-use association with wine is much more prevalent in data from *dipinti* (Fournet and Pieri 2008; with the exceptions above). That said, this position is only rarely corroborated by cases of direct evidence, like the LRA1 found on the Ma'agan Mikhael B shipwreck off the Israeli coast (see below) that contained grape or raisin seeds (LCP vessel 33519), or the grape seed in an amphora aboard Yassi Ada wreck (van Alfen 1996: 203).[4] Still, in addition to all the reasons mentioned above, the wine hypothesis can be indirectly corroborated. All the regions involved in LRA1 production, from Cilicia to Cyprus, to Kos and Rhodes, had a well-documented history in winemaking (Opaiţ 2009: 283; see the overview about Cilicia and Cyprus in Komar 2016). This tradition continued well into late antiquity. There are, for example, at least 15 funerary inscriptions identifying the interred as wine merchants/traders at a Cilician site near Elaiussa (Korykos, itself a possible candidate as a production center;[5] 2010: 22–23), and the "*seriolae Ciliceses*" explicitly defined as "*vasa fictile vini*" by Isidore of Seville (Pacetti 1995: 274; Pieri 2005a: 69 and 175 with other references). Abundant textual evidence, such as the Aphrodito Cadaster (a tax appraisal/record of properties in a Byzantine Egyptian village; MacCoull 2010: 632), and excavated wine presses (e.g., Dayr Anba Hadra, Abou Mina) strongly attest to late antique wine production in Egyptian monasteries, juxtaposed with rather scant evidence for olive oil (Lewit 2023: 20–21).

Recently, it has been suggested that LRA1s found at Kelenderis (Cilicia) were used for shipping locally produced salted fish and *garum* (Zoroğlu 2020), although the interpretation of the workshop as a fishery and its association with the amphoras have yet to be demonstrated. Additionally, as we have seen, some *dipinti* have been read as abbreviations for measurements of dry goods, but this must have been an occasional and highly localized phenomenon. Eventually, it may be that amphoras were assigned a specific use or cargo on a local-regional basis (such as eastern Cilicia and Egypt; contra Pacetti 1995: 273–74), but in general the extent of second- or even multiple-uses should not be underestimated (see Abdelhamid 2013; Martin-Kilcher and Tchernia 2021: 35–36; Peña 2021: 79–81).[6] In this regard, an LRA1 assemblage from Florence offers a good example (Pecci, Salvini, and Cantini 2010). Analysis of

3. Even more telling are the shipwreck assemblages that show LRA1 and LRA2s being transported in the same shipment, like the Yassi Ada (van Alfen 1996: 191), the Knidos T (Brennan et al. 2020: 307–8), and the Burgaz wrecks (Leidwanger, Greene, and Tuna 2015: 303–5, also see 307–8 for a deeper discussion on the intermingling of LRA1 and LRA2 cargos).

4. It should be noted, though, that the more recent analyses on residuals of contents from Yassi Ada amphoras showed the presence of grape seeds also inside some LRA2s; see Ward 2015.

5. See the more recent interpretation of the stamped crucigram on an LRA1 from Sucidava presented above; it is worth stressing again that one rare designation for wine merchants occurring in Korykos epitaphs, *oinegos*, is the same used in the Abydos Tariff (Iacomi 2010: 27 and n. 46).

6. Peña (2021: 85) also mentions a written source (POxy. 55.3804, dated to 566) that helps in assessing the recycling of used amphoras as a common practice.

the seven LRA1s excavated in a rubbish dump revealed that all were coated with *Pinaceae* resin; five showed fermentation markers related to wine or fruit. Among these five, one presented traces of vegetable oil (potentially olive oil), while three might have carried fish products. The concurrent presence of different markers is often interpreted as evidence of the reuse of the vessels.[7]

In summary, we tend to agree with the original position of van Alfen (1996: 208), according to whom "at its introduction in the 4th century, the [LRA1] might have been produced to contain one regional commodity.... Through the course of three centuries, however, the function of the LRA1 amphora probably changed, or, to be more precise, may have been expanded *to serve better the ever-changing exchange systems in which it was used*" (emphasis added). We should therefore distinguish between original use and recycled use (i.e., after the vessel's first contents have been emptied). Furthermore, within the original use case we want to highlight prime-use(s) and secondary use(s). The most likely candidate for the primary original use of the LRA1 was to carry wine. The LRA1 was coopted into the imperial *annona* system at some unknown point in time, but certainly before the promulgation of the Abydos tariff at the end of the 5th century (Iacomi 2010, which remains valid despite some inaccuracy in addressing the *annona* question). The secondary original use was related to the synchronous private trade that "piggy-backed" upon the same vectors as state-subsidized exchange. Merchants engaging in long-distance *annona* shipping were not prohibited from conducting some business "on the side" at each port of call—indeed the existence of incentives like duty-free trade for shipowners who worked with the state apparatus makes it clear that such activity regularly occurred (McCormick 2001: 89–90; Gandila 2021: 318–19). This private LRA1 usage was likely either wine or olive oil.

After this mutualistic first exchange took place, a wide array of recycled uses became possible. Continued use as a wine or olive oil container was no doubt the most common recycling practice, but other probable options were as a vessel to ship dry foodstuffs, fish, garum, luxury oils, or even honey. There are also occasional examples of more unusual secondary uses, such as an infant burial in 5th–6th centuries Greece (Vasiliou and Tsigarida 2014: 726) and Genoa (Bellatalla, Bertino, and Gardini 1989: 395); LRA1s were frequently used as grave goods in the British Isles (see §7.1.M). At Elaiussa, in the mid-6th century a LRA1 was used to hide the coin hoard found in the theater (Borgia 2003: 33; Polosa 2003). Some cases of frequent recycling could have even been the reason behind the eventual genesis of local production of LRA1s; this might be the case in Egypt, where the association with (holy) olive oil and grain is readily apparent through *dipinti*. The variety of roles that the LRA1 fulfilled make it a harbinger of a broad transition in production and usage, from a wide pool of specific-use amphora forms to the later multipurpose BGA (Poulou 2017: 200–202; contra Opaiţ 2017: 596).

7. However, an experimental analysis of oil and wine penetration into ceramic materials sets forth the possibility that *both* products might have been combined in a single amphora, as an addition of oil to a wine amphora could have sealed the mouth and reduced the amount of wine that was lost to the seepage into the vessel (Romanus et al. 2009: 908).

Chapter 7. Consumption and Distribution Patterns

§7.1. The Regional Perspective

In this chapter we survey the LRA1s' wide geographical span. After brief historical notes, we provide a concise comment on the broad distribution patterns for each region. A full list of sites where LRA1s are attested is included in the accompanying maps (figs. 28–41) and tables (tables 10.3.A-N, S1, S2).[1] Additional data on some sites may be found in the relevant entry on the LCP.

It is certain that we have overlooked some LRA1 consumption sites, thus leading to some regions being underrepresented in this overview. We hope that this volume will serve as a catalyst for people to add missing and additional information to the LCP. While every site mentioned below has its own page published on the LCP, many do not yet contain much data. We encourage all ceramicists, field directors, archaeologists, and students to contribute data on the pottery they have uncovered or studied to the LCP. With more data on the platform, this book (and others like it) will have a constantly updated digital analogue, while also allowing the texts themselves to be regularly refined to reflect the current state of research, making future projects even more robust and impactful (see p. xi on how to become a contributor on LCP).

A. Cilicia/Isauria and northern Levant (southeastern Turkey, Syria, northern Lebanon) —Diocese Orientis

§10.3.1. Table A

The Northern Levant and Cilicia (Cilicia I, Cilicia II, and Isauria in late antiquity and early Byzantine times) experienced troubled times throughout the span of LRA1 production and circulation, marked by indigenous social uprisings (the Isaurians) and periodic invasions (the Sasanians), along with several catastrophic earthquakes. Despite these challenges, urban and rural life continued to thrive without major interruptions until the mid-7th century. The Islamic Conquest in the eastern part and frequent Arab raids in the west seemingly caused many cities to be abandoned and the consequent shifting to more rural lifeways.[2] Recent research is even suggesting that this period was not as tumultuous as is frequently assumed for "life on the ground." The relative stability is reflected in the large productive system of the region accounting for nine out of the 21 known LRA1 workshops, which implies a wider network of solid agricultural and communication infrastructures (Iacomi and Cassiani 2016).[3] Finally, it is worth noting the very recent discovery of hundreds of previously unknown Roman to Umayyad

1. We will not be discussing here the historical development of each region in detail, as it evidently goes beyond the purposes of this handbook. Nonetheless, we also hope that this section could be implemented and expanded in future editions to provide an even more accurate and historically valid contextualization of the "LRA1 question."

2. For a general overview of the history of the region, Hild and Hellenkemper 1990 remains a great resource; on the vitality of the countryside settlements even after the mid-7th c. see, e.g., Varinlioğlu 2013.

3. The countryside of both Isauria and Cilicia I (former western and eastern Rough Cilicia) is in fact characterized by a large number of rural productive installations, so far poorly investigated and reported (Varinlioğlu 2013; see also the recently published wine press at Eirenoupolis, quite inland in the Dekapolis district but well linked to the coast through roads connecting with Anemurium: Aşkın 2022).

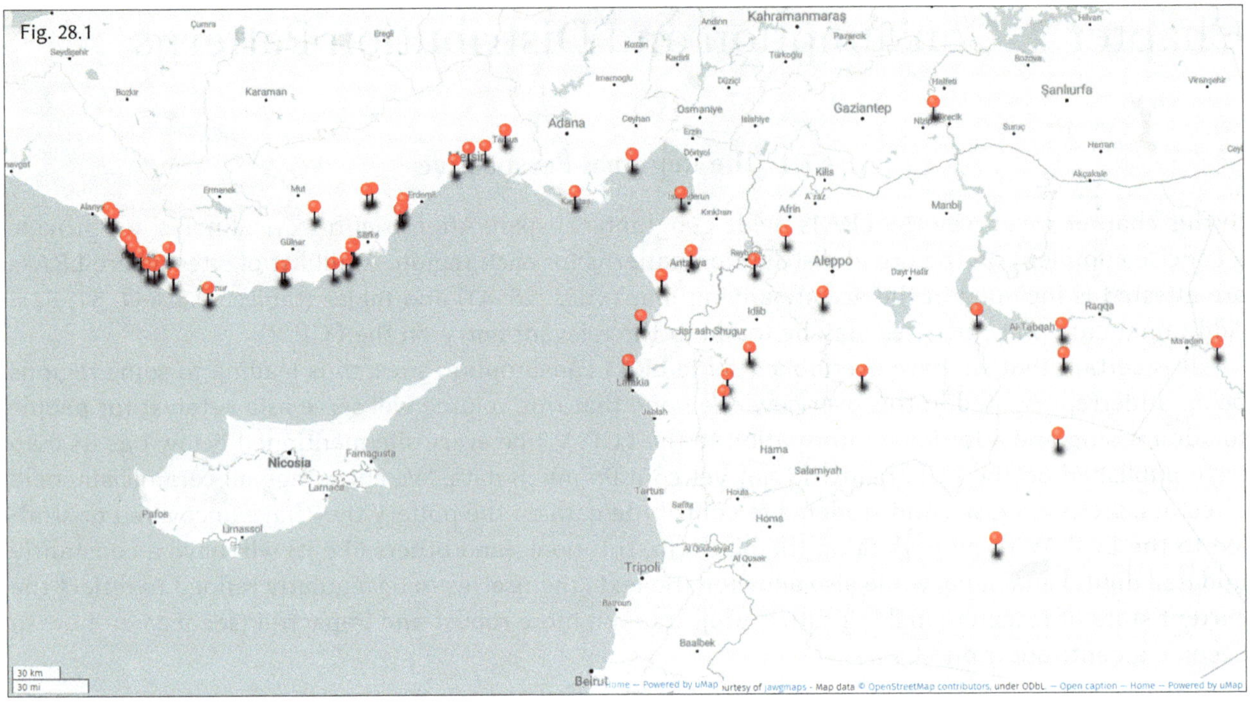

Figures 28.1–6. Maps showing LRA1 consumption sites in our region A, including: A01 Androna; A02 Anemurium; A03 Antiocheia ad Cragum; A04 Antioch; A05 Apamea; A06 Aphrodisias/Ovacık; A07 Arzus; A08 Asar Tepe; A09 Boğsak Island; A10 Charadros; A11 Dana Island; A12 Dehes; A13 Delice kiln site; A14 Dibsi Faraji; A15 Diocaesarea; A16 Elaiussa Sebaste; A17 Gocuk Asari; A18 Hadir; A19 Halabiye/Zenobia; A20 Hawarte; A21 Iotape; A22 Kanytelis; A23 Karataş; A24 Kazanli; A25 Kelenderis; A26 Kestros; A27 Kilise Tepe; A28 Korykos; A29 Naula; A30 Nephelion; A31 Olba; A32 Palmyra; A33 Qal'at Sem'an; A34 Qusair al-Saila; A35 Ras el Bassit; A36 Ras Ibn Hani; A37 Resafa/Sergiopolis; A38 Seleucia Pieria; A39 Selinus; A40 Sergilla; A41 Soli-Pomepiopolis; A42 Syedra; A43 Tahta Limani; A44 Tarsus; A45 Terimini; A46 Umm el-Tlel; A47 Yılanlı Island (shipwreck); A48 Yumurtalik/Aigai (Cilicia); A49 Zephyrion/Mersin; A50 Zeugma.

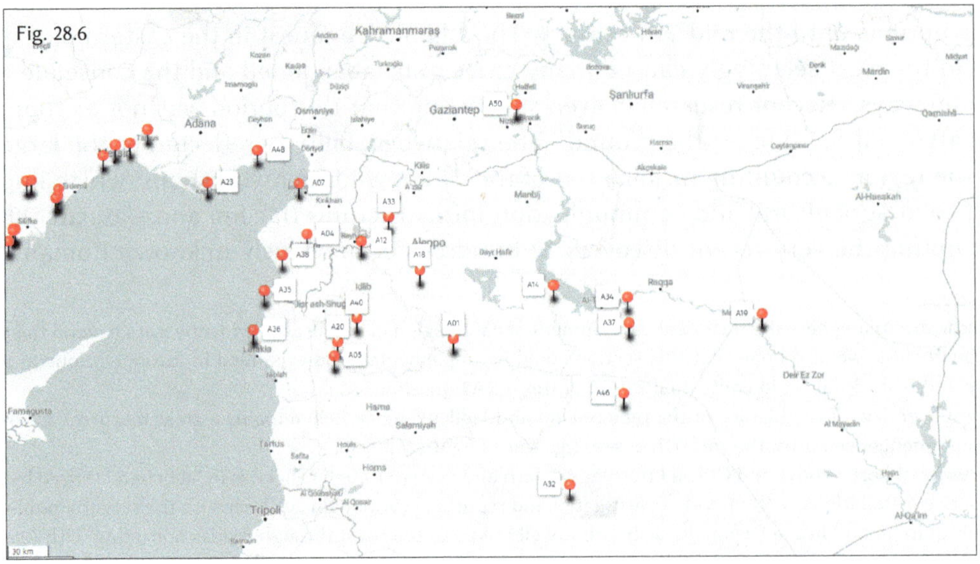

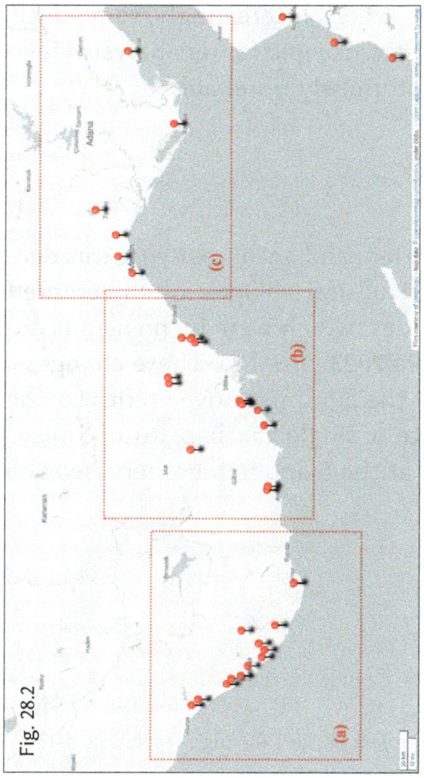

Fig. 28.2

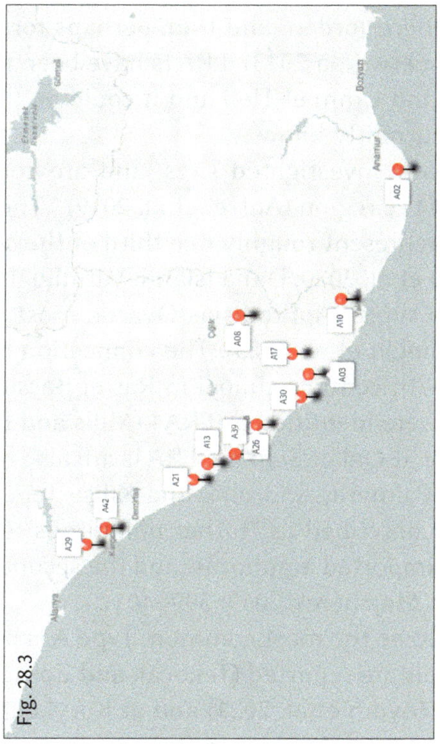

Fig. 28.3

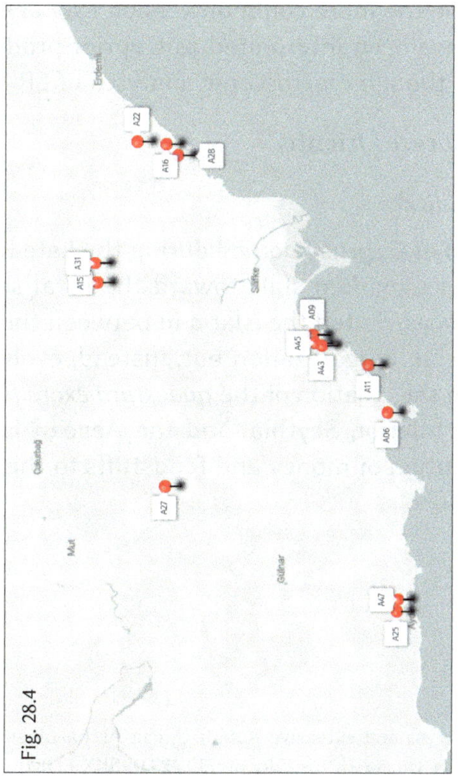

Fig. 28.4

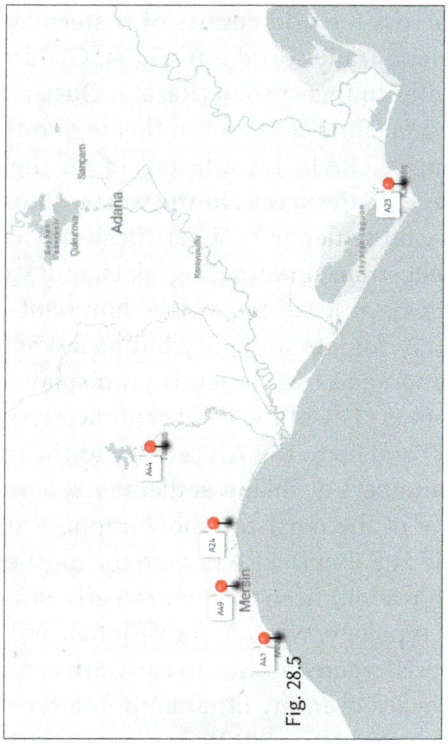

Fig. 28.5

See caption on page 66

fortified sites across the arid deserts of eastern Syria, northern Jordan, and Iraq, perhaps forming an east–west overland trade corridor (Casana, Goodman, and Ferwerda 2023). LRA1s have been found at several of the sites in this system (Resafa, Qusair al-Saila, and Umm el-Tlel) and it could be that they were exchanged far further inland in this region than we currently know.

Unsurprisingly, LRA1s are attested in all the extensively investigated sites, and are constantly found in the pedestrian surveys in the westernmost part of the region (Autret et al. 2019).[4] They occur primarily in coastal settlements, where in some cases they represent roughly one third of the collected pottery from pedestrian surveys (Boğsak Island: Varinlioğlu et al. 2020; Dana Island: Varinlioğlu, Rauh, and Pejša 2022), or at least one of the dominant amphora types (Aphrodisias/Ovacık, most attested amphora not only for late antiquity but as a whole: Varinlioğlu et al. 2023). The connection between LRA1 consumption and the church is on display at a 6th–7th century chapel in Ras el Bassit, where all of the amphoras (17% of the total ceramic assemblage) were identified as LRA1 (Mills and Beaudry 2010: tables 6, 7) and up to the 7th century at the monastery at Qal'at Sem'an. LRA1s are also recorded in significant numbers at inland settlements, like Resafa, Palmyra, Androna, and Kilise Tepe. At the latter it was one of the most common amphora types and described as "rather ubiquitous" (Jackson 2015: 360), while at Palmyra LRA1s were the most common imported amphoras (and the second largest amphora group overall) from the 2nd to early 9th century (Majcherek 2019: 399–401).

In terms of typology, types A, transitional, and B seem to be the most common. Type A is predominant at Kelenderis, where late 4th to early 5th century vessels are reported (Tekocak and Zoroğlu 2013: 119); type B prevails over any other amphora type at Olba (Aydın et al. 2021) and at Korykos (surface pottery from surveys, Alkaç 2012). At Apamea both the transitional type and type B are present, and type B might be the more common version (Vokaer 2017: fig. 1.1–7). Interestingly, some of the Kelenderis LRA1s have been interpreted as Cypriot products via macroscopic fabric analysis (Tekocak and Zoroğlu 2013), though macroscopic analyses of LRA1s are notoriously unreliable.

B. Cyprus—Diocese Orientis

§10.3.2. Table B

The population of Cyprus boomed during the Late Roman period, and accompanying this demographic increase was a marked shift toward the rural sector. Agricultural villages, often centered around Christian basilicas, dotted the island in between the major cities, which were by no means abandoned during this social reorganization but, instead, evolved (Vionis 2023: 163–65). These changes occurred in parallel with the creation of the *quaestura exercitus* in 536—the administrative unification of Cyprus, Caria, Moesia Inferior, Scythia, and the Aegean Islands into a single tax base to optimize the empire's redistribution of money and foodstuffs to the military at the Danubian borders (see Curta 2017; Penchev 2021).

4. See the open-access and extensive Rough Cilicia Archaeological Survey Project (RCSP) for high-resolution data on ceramics, including LRA1s, in Cilicia (https://doi.org/10.4231/9SKX-FD80).

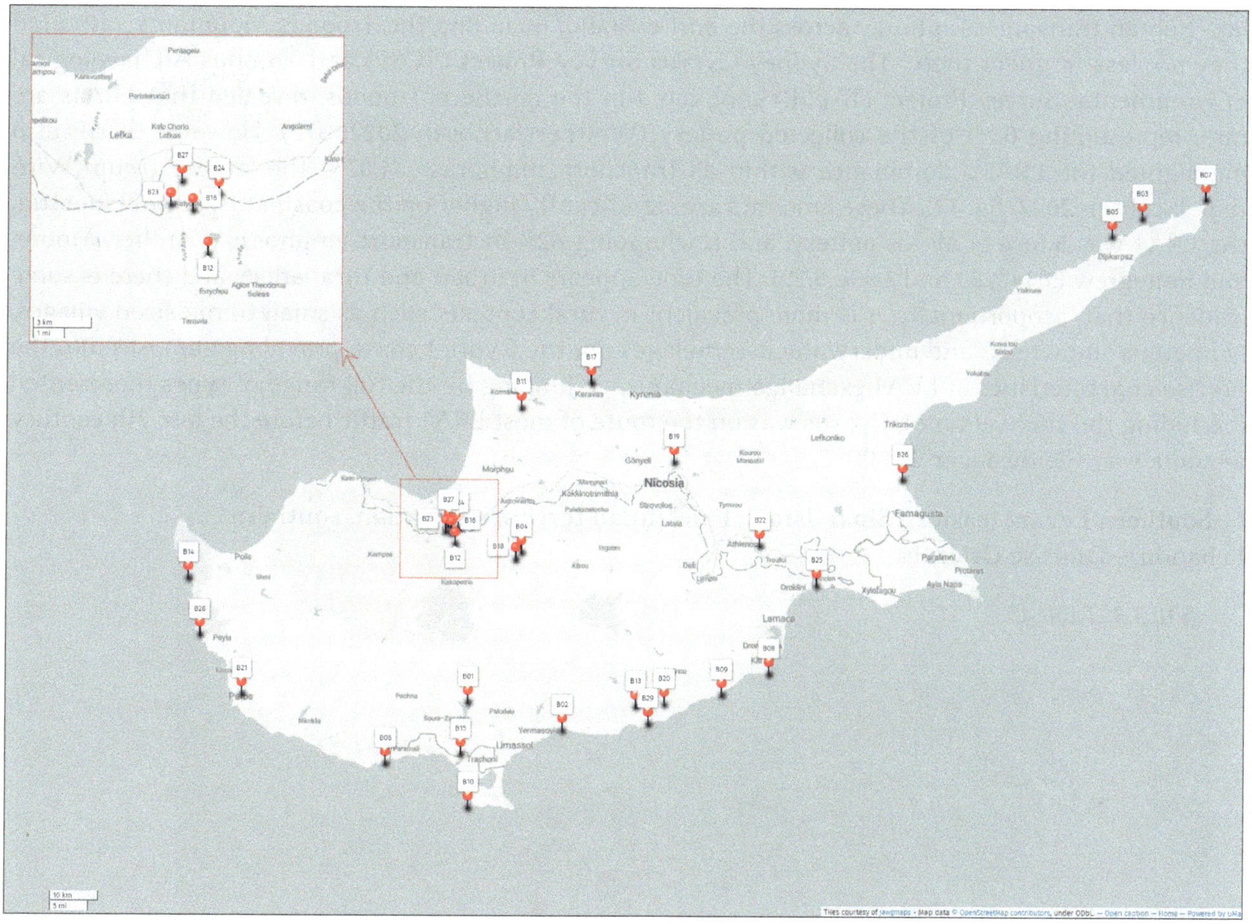

Figure 29. Map showing LRA1 consumption sites in our region B, including: B01 Alassa; B02 Amathus; B03 Aphendrika; B04 Ayia Marina-Mavrovouni; B05 Ayios Philon; B06 Avdimou Bay (shipwreck); B07 Cape Andreas, Green's Site 17 (shipwreck); B08 Cape Kiti/Kition; B09 Cape Petounda; B10 Cape Zevgari (shipwreck); B11 Dhiorios; B12 Dodekaskala; B13 Kalavassos-Kopetra; B14 Keratidhi; B15 Kourion; B16 Laonarka; B17 Lapithos; B18 Litharkies; B19 Mandres; B20 Maroni-Petrera; B21 Nea Paphos; B22 Panayia Ematousa; B23 Pano Limna; B24 Phoukasa; B25 Pyla-Koutsopetria; B26 Salamis; B27 Skouriotissa-Vouppes; B28 Thalassines-Spilies; B29 Zygi-Petrini.

The available evidence for LRA1 production and occurrence in Cyprus is uneven.[5] We only know of LRA1 manufacturing centers along the southern coast, and LRA1s themselves are more common at sites in southern and western Cyprus than in the northeast. Whether these patterns are due to the active choices of the island's Roman-Byzantine-era occupants or the relative lack of published ceramic assemblages from the self-proclaimed Turkish Republic of Northern Cyprus remains unclear;[6] the recent work at Aphendrika stands as an isolated case. That being said, LRA1s are often the majority of

5. Detailed and high-resolution data on ceramics, including LRA1s, in Cyprus are available in open access online repositories of local and/or regional projects; see below, §9.6.2: (https://doi.org/10.5284/1000271 and https://www.jstor.org/stable/j.ctv2xqng7r) for the Sydney Cyprus Survey Project (SCSP) and Troodos Archaeological and Environmental Survey Project (TAESP); and §9.6.3 (https://opencontext.org/types/dc84b645-90eb-466e-b4ea-8466a1f57673) for the Pyla-Koutsopetria Archaeological Project I: Pedestrian Survey (PKAP).

6. Cf. Kiessel, Saymanlier and Taluğ 2024: 147, in particular n. 17 with a (regrettably short) list of coastline surveys.

late Roman transport amphoras across the entire island, including the Troodos Mountains, although they are less frequent there. The Sydney Cyprus Survey Project (SCSP) and Troodos Archaeological Environmental Survey Project (TAESP) conducted in the northern Troodos, revealed that LRA1s are rare, representing 0.7% of the collected pottery (Winther-Jacobsen 2022: 377). However, SCSP also highlighted the LRA1's dominance within all transport amphoras—34.07%, the largest group (Winther-Jacobsen 2022: fig. 12). These amounts are significantly higher on the coast; at Pyla-Koutsopetria, the LRA1 was 5.68% of all LR pottery, and a whopping 62% of transport amphoras (Caraher, Moore, and Pettegrew 2014: 233 and table 5.29). The type appears in urban and rural areas, and there is some evidence that, proportionally, it is more prevalent in rural contexts such as small to midsized villages. Numerous shipwrecks and underwater assemblages dot the Cypriot coast, providing glimpses into the precise characteristics of LRA1 exchange mechanisms. Judging by the full range of types represented (excluding the survival type), Cyprus was on the route of most LRA1 traffic before the late 7th century in some way (Leidwanger 2013b).

C. Southern Levant (eastern Sinai, Israel, Palestinian territories, Jordan, southern Lebanon)—Diocese Orientis

§ *10.3.3. Table C*

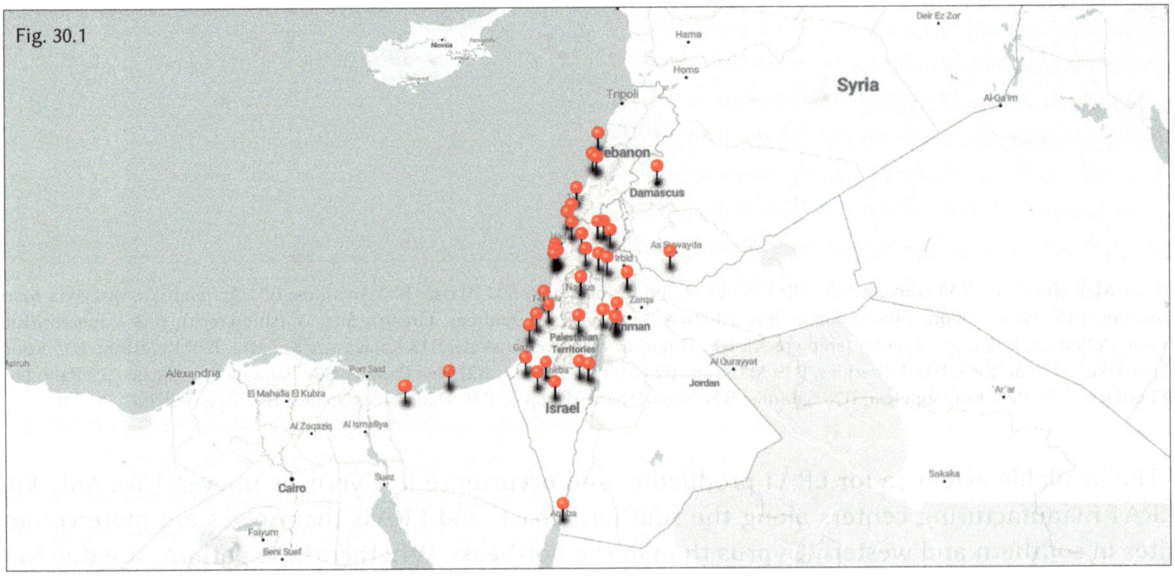

See caption on following page

The southern Levant prospered during the Late Roman period, in the midst of being subject to several administrative restructuring projects (Filipczak 2015: 5–11). The spread of Christianity was changing the cityscapes and economics of the region, as many Roman temples and Jewish synagogues were converted into churches and marketing of goods and services was targeted at Christian consumers and pilgrims (see Weiss 2010: 212; Decker 2012: 105–7, and references therein). While new research is showing that many urban and rural settlements continued to thrive after the tumultuous Islamic Conquest, it seems that LRA1 consumption dropped precipitously after the mid-7th century.

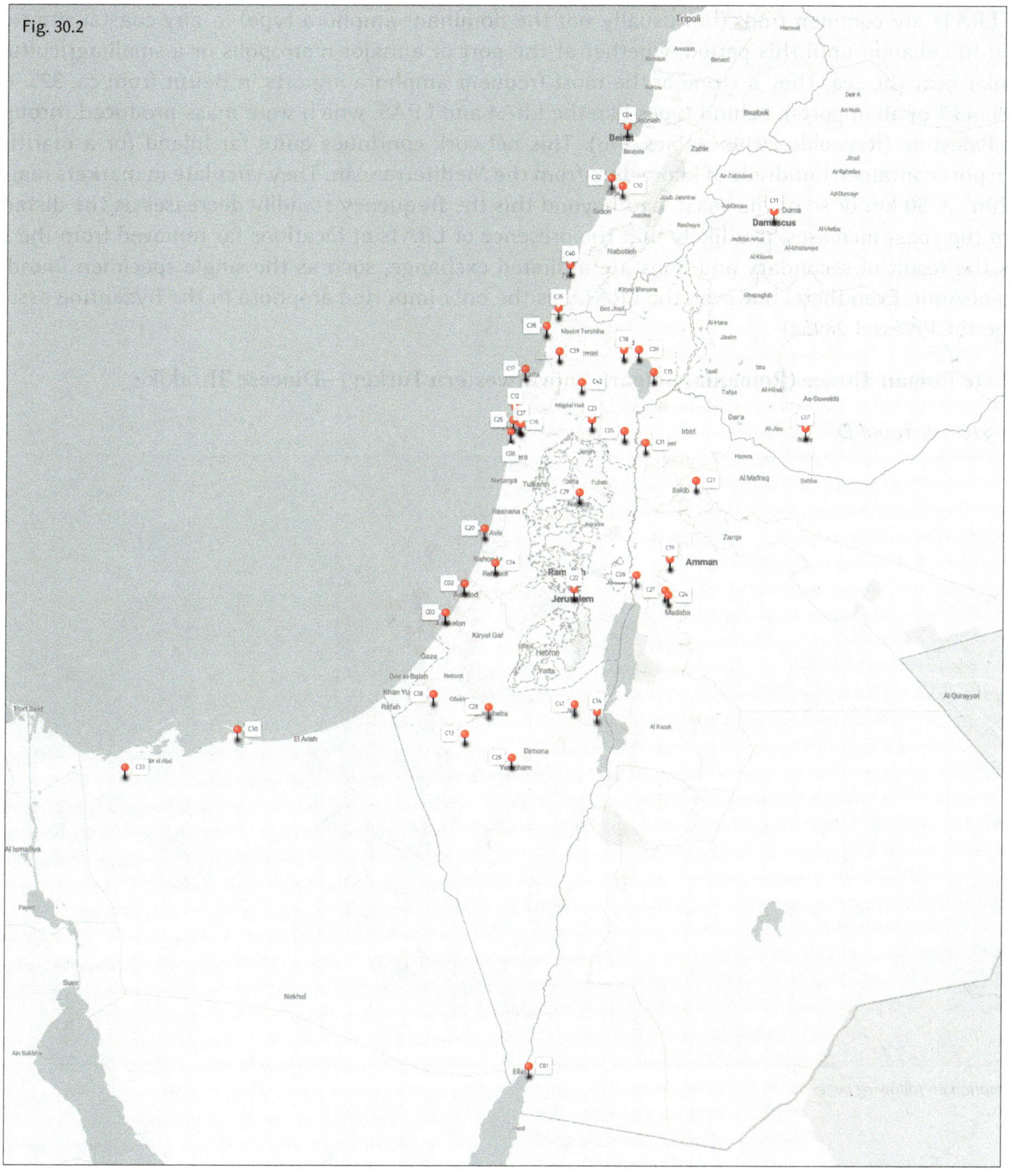

Figure 30.1–2. Maps showing LRA1 consumption sites in our region C, including: C01 Aila/Aqaba; C02 Ashdod; C03 Ashkelon; C04 Beirut; C05 Beisan/Scythopolis; C06 Bethany; C07 Bosra; C08 Caesarea; C09 Capernaum; C10 Chhim; C11 Damascus; C12 Dor; C13 Elusa; C14 Ein Boqeq; C15 Hippos-Sussita; C16 Horbat ʻAqav; C17 Horbat Castra; C18 Huqoq; C19 Iraq al-Amir; C20 Jaffa; C21 Jerash; C22 Jerusalem; C23 Jezreel/Esdraela; C24 Khirbet el-Mukhayyat; C25 Maʻagan Mikhael B (shipwreck); C26 Mezad Yerouham; C27 Mount Nebo; C28 Nahal Beqaʻ; C29 Neapolis/Nablus; C30 Ostrakine; C31 Pella; C32 Porphyreon; C33 Qasrawet; C34 Rehovot-in-the-Negev; C35 Shelomi; C36 Shavei Zion; C37 Shuni; C38 Tell Fara; C39 Tell Keisan; C40 Tyre; C41 Upper Zohar; C42 Zippori.

LRA1s are common finds (but usually not the dominant amphora type) at any coastal site from Sinai to Lebanon until this period, whether at the port of a major metropolis or a small agricultural hamlet near the sea. They are one of the most frequent amphora imports in Beirut from ca. 325–600 (6.09–43% of all imports), behind types like the LRA4 and LRA5, which were mass-produced throughout Palestine (Reynolds 2010b: tables 2–6). This network continues quite far inland for a maritime transport container, hundreds of kilometers from the Mediterranean. They circulate in markets mainly within ca. 50 km or so of the coast, and beyond this the frequency steadily decreases as the distance from the coast increases. It is likely that the presence of LRA1s at locations far removed from the sea was the result of secondary and nonstate-affiliated exchange, such as the single specimen found at Iraq al-Amir. Even there, however, the LRA1 was the only imported amphora in the Byzantine assemblage (LCP vessel 28954).

D. Late Roman Thrace (Romania, Bulgaria, northwestern Turkey)—Diocese Thrakike

§10.3.4. Table D

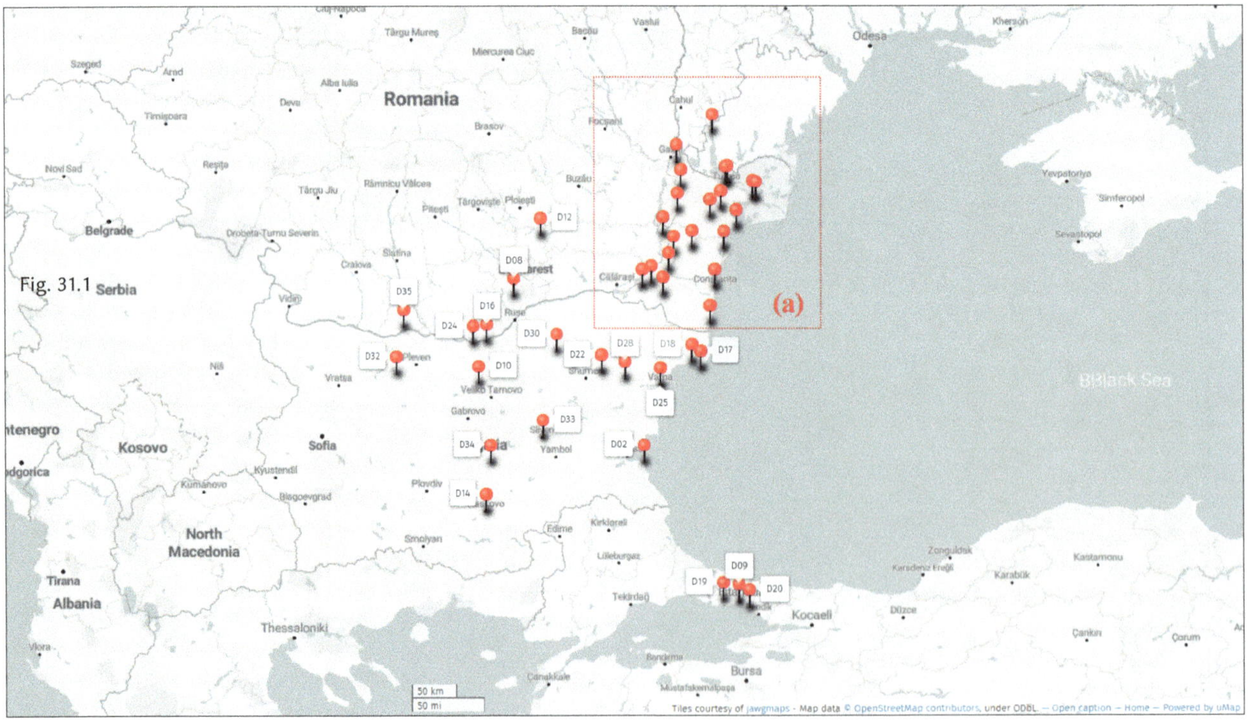

See caption on following page

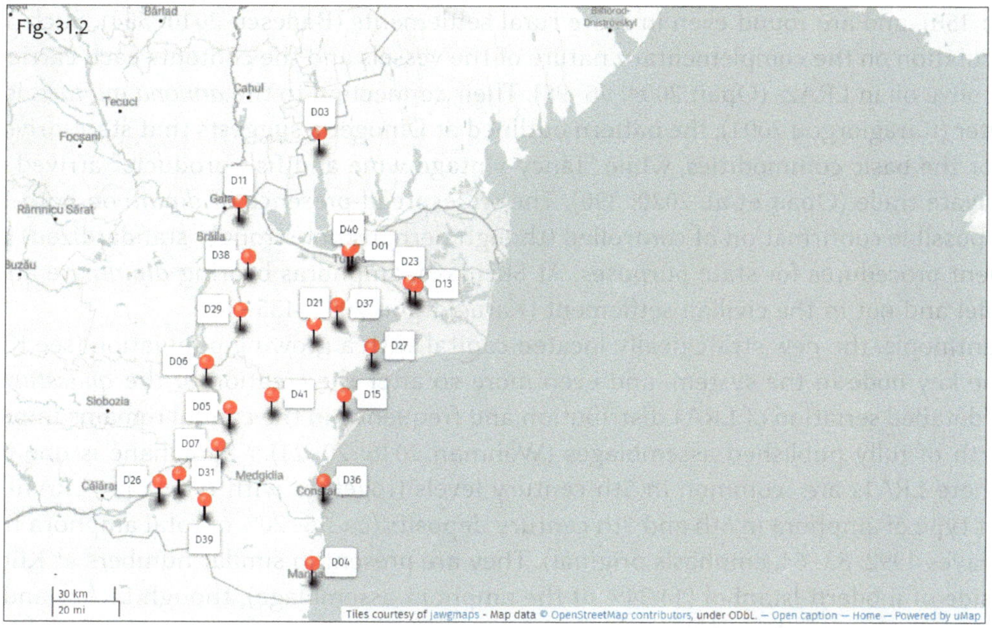

Figure 31.1–2. Maps showing LRA1 consumption sites in our region D, including: D01 Aegyssus; D02 Apollonia Pontica; D03 Anchialos; D04 Bjolgrad; D05 Callatis; D06 Capidava Fortress; D07 Carsium/Harsova; D08 Cernavodă/Axiopolis; D09 Cetatea; D10 Constantinople; D11 Dichin; D12 Dinogetia; D13 Gradiste; D14 Halmyris/Murighiol; D15 Haskovo; D16 Histria; D17 Iatrus; D18 Kaliakra; D19 Kavarna; D20 Küçükçekmece Lake/Bathonea; D21 Küçükyalı; D22 (L)ibida; D23 Madara; D24 Novae; D25 Odessos; D26 Oltina; D27 Orgame/Argamum; D28 Ovech Fortress (Provadia); D29 Piatra Frecăţei/Beroe; D30 Razgrad; D31 Sacidava; D32 Sadovec; D33 Sliven; D34 Stara Zagora; D35 Sucidava/Corabia; D36 Tomis; D37 Topraichioi; D38 Troesmis; D39 Tropaeum Traiani; D40 Tulcea, Villa Telita; D41 Ulmetum.

The foundation of Constantinople and the growing military distress along the Danubian border during the 4th century, along with an apparent contraction in the local production of commodities,[7] represented the main catalysts of imported goods and foodstuff traffic in late Roman Thrace and the eastern Black Sea (Karagiorgou 2001). Aegean and Levantine products[8] assumed a key role in supplying both the new capital and the army deployed around the Danube (Lewit 2015: 153–54), which might have reached some 90,000–100,000 men in the 4th and 5th centuries (Opaiţ 2017: 592–93, and references therein; 2023: 646–47), until the loss of the Lower Danube to Slavs and Bulgars at the beginning of the 7th century (Karagiorgou 2001: 135).

LRA1s are one of, and sometimes the most, common amphora found in the major military sites of the region, and their consumption increased from the 4th throughout the 6th century. At Halmyris they represent 2% of the amphora assemblage at the end of the 4th c., 17.3% in the 5th, nearly 45% in the 6th, then decreasing to 25% in the early 7th c. (Topoleanu 2000: 134; Opaiţ 1991; Pacetti 1995: 279). At the fortress of Capidava they count for 31% of the attested eastern Mediterranean amphoras (Opriş and Ratiu 2019). Generally associated with LRA2s, the two types usually represent the absolute majority (accounting for 84% of the whole pottery assemblage, e.g., at Dichin in the late 5th century;

7. The growth of urban population in the second half of the 5th c. has been associated with a progressive abandonment of the rural settlements (Bădescu 2010: 552); concurrently, pottery records seem to point to a diminished local wine production alongside the growing presence of LRA1s (Opaiţ 2023: 652).

8. Statistical analysis of pottery provenance in Scythia Minor shows that eastern Mediterranean products were the most frequent, 48% in general and 53.79% of the amphora assemblages (Bădescu 2010: 555).

Lewit 2015: 156), and are found even in more rural settlements (Bădescu 2010: 554). Such association allows speculation on the complementary nature of the vessels and the contents each carried—wine in LRA1s and olive oil in LRA2s (Opaiţ 2004: 96–98). Their connection to the *annona militaris* is a well-assessed matter (Karagiorgou 2001); the pattern outlined at Dinogetia suggests that state-driven supplies provided for the basic commodities, while "fancy vintage wine and fish products" arrived at the fort through private trade (Opaiţ et al. 2020: 390). The widespread presence of *dipinti* on both LRA1s and LRA2s is a possible confirmation of controlled (though perhaps not strongly standardized) production and shipment procedures for state purposes. At Sucidava, amphoras bearing *dipinti* are attested only in the citadel and not in the civilian settlement (Karagiorgou 2001: 135–36).[9]

Constantinople, the new strategically located capital with a growing population (see Külzer 2022: 77), was the key node in the system, and even more so after the creation of the *quaestura exercitus*. Creating a detailed seriation of LRA1 distribution and frequency in the capital remains impossible due to the dearth of fully published assemblages (Wohman 2016: 20–21).[10] Saraçhane is one of our best sources, where LRA1s are "common in 5th century levels (together with *type 3* [= LRA10]), and the commonest type of amphora in 6th and 7th century deposits (ca. 15–20% of total amphora finds of this period)" (Hayes 1992: 63–64, emphasis original). They are present in similar numbers at Küçükyalı, on the Asian side of modern İstanbul (14.34% of the amphora assemblage), though LRA2s and BGAs are more frequent (Wohmann 2016: 69).

Cilician *naukleroi* might have been the primary vectors shipping wine, in LRA1s, to Constantinople, as they are explicitly mentioned in the Abydos tariff as being subject to lower taxes when crossing the Dardanelles (see again Iacomi 2010: 27 for a detailed discussion; Diamanti 2010: 4). The possible inclusion of LRA1s in the package means that both the *annona militaris* as well as the *annona civica* remain to be investigated, as the extent of the amphora's distribution suggest it was a key component in both.[11]

E. Late Roman Pontica, and eastern and northern Black Sea (northern Turkey, Crimea, southern Russia, Ukraine, Georgia)—Diocese Pontike, Lazica

§10.3.5. Table E

The territory of the old Bosporan kingdom, covering Crimea and part of the northern Black Sea littoral, was considered the northernmost boundary of Christendom, and regarded as the empire's bastion against the attacks of invaders, like the Huns, Bulgars, and eventually the Khazars. This area, once believed to be a peripheral extension of the Mediterranean exchange system, has come in the past fifteen years to be understood as closely integrated with Mare Nostrum in the Late Roman and early Byzantine world (see Lewit 2015 and references therein).

9. On the "strong connection" between the Syrian-Palestinian and Asia Minor region with the *annona* in the Lower Danube, see the considerations by Opaiţ 2023: 653.

10. Forthcoming publications of the pottery from the excavations of the Theodosian Harbor at Yenikapi will likely shed more light on the matter. At least 5 of the 37 investigated shipwrecks in the harbor cover the timespan of LRA1s production and diffusion (YK 11, YK 34, YK 35, YK 22, YK 26, dated from the 5th to the 7th c.; Kocabaş 2015: 12, table 1; Külzer 2022: 86).

11. Many of the papers delivered at the recent (December 2022) congress "Provisioning of Late Antique Constantinople: *annona civilis* and Beyond" organized by the Boğaziçi University – Byzantine Studies Research Center have dealt with the matter; so far, only the abstracts have been published.

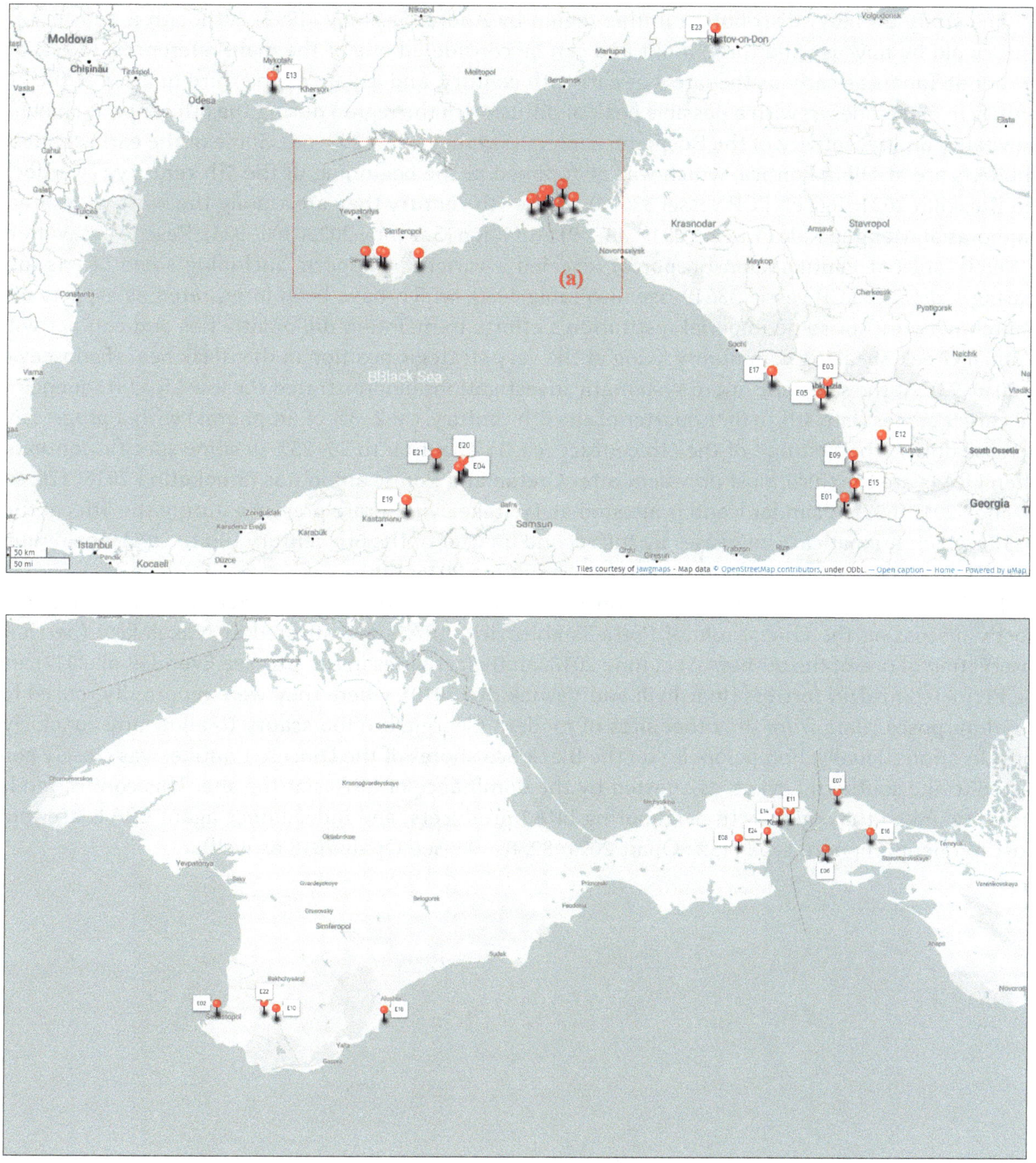

Figure 32.1–2. Maps showing LRA1 consumption sites in our region E, including: E01 Apsaros/Gonio; E02 Chersonesus; E03 Cibilium/Tsebelda; E04 Demirci; E05 Dranda; E06 Hermonassa; E07 Il'ich; E08 Kytaion; E09 Lake Palastiomi (Natechebi); E10 Mangup; E11 Myrmekion; E12 Nokalakevi/Archaiopolis; E13 Olbia Pontica, Borysthenes; E14 Pantikapaion, Bosporos/Kerch; E15 Petra/Tsikhisdziri; E16 Phanagoria; E17 Pitiunt/Bichvinta; E18 Plaka (shipwreck); E19 Pompeiopolis; E20 Sinop; E21 Sinop B (shipwreck); E22 Sivag-Kerman; E23 Tanais; E24 Tyritake.

The study on LRA1 distribution in this region by Andrei Sazanov (1999), although a quarter of a century old by now, is valid throughout and can be considered one of the main references. LRA1s are present at Tanais as early as the late 4 or early 5th century, and as late as the third quarter of the 7th century in Chersonesos, with a possible peak of diffusion in the region during the 6th century, showing the vitality and receptivity of the Bosporan centers (Sazanov 1999: 265–66). Some of the earliest attested LRA1s are at Olbia Pontica, which was abandoned at the beginning of the 5th century (Twardecki and Buiskikh 2021: 266; cf. LCP vessel 33617). In the 5th century they are among the most widespread amphoras at Mangup Kale (Yashna 2019: 48–49) and Il'ich (Sazanov 2023: 300–321). Rescue excavations at Kerch (ancient Pantikapaion-Bosporos) revealed a variety of imports, including some LRA1s (one bearing a *dipinto*, LCP vessel 33619, see also table 10.2), which have been interpreted as aspects of a "church network" or some imperial institution's efforts to maintain diplomatic ties and contact with "a small Greek-speaking community living at the very strategic position in the Black Sea" (Fedoseev et al. 2010: 93). At the same site, more systematic investigations demonstrated the low LRA1 frequency in the earlier stages (late 4th to first quarter of the 6th century, ca. 2–3% of amphoras) with a progressive increase during the first half of the 6th century (ca. 13%, but up to 20–25% in some specific contexts), when LRA1s are the third most prevalent after Cretan and Pontic amphoras (Smokotina 2015: 126; see Sazanov 2017: 653). A similar trend is attested at Tyritake, with a rare presence during the 5th century (1–3%) which dramatically increases by the second quarter of the 6th century (up to 25%), again numbering third after Cretan and Pontic vessels (Smokotina 2016: 716).

In the contested territory of Lazica on the eastern coast of the Black Sea (cf. Wieczorek 2023, mostly discussing the crucial role of Petra-Tsikhisdziri), LRA1s are attested at Nokalakevi (personal observation of one of the authors, V. I., June 2013; on the activities in the site, see Everill et al. 2017) and the Petra-Tsikhisdziri fortress (Inaishvili and Vashakidze 2010), where they were reportedly reused for burial purposes. Data from the other sites of modern Georgia are too scanty to allow any conclusive considerations. Finally, Pompeiopolis, on the Black Sea shores of the Diocese Pontike, was closely connected to the southern Levant, as attested by the dominance of LRA4s at the site. This connection by necessity linked the region with neighboring LRA1 producers, and indeed once again LRA1s are third most frequent amphora type (13%; Opaiţ 2021: 82, 89–90; see Opaiţ 2018 as well).

F. Asia Minor and Aegean Islands (central and western Turkey, insular Greece)—Diocese Asiane

§10.3.6. Table F

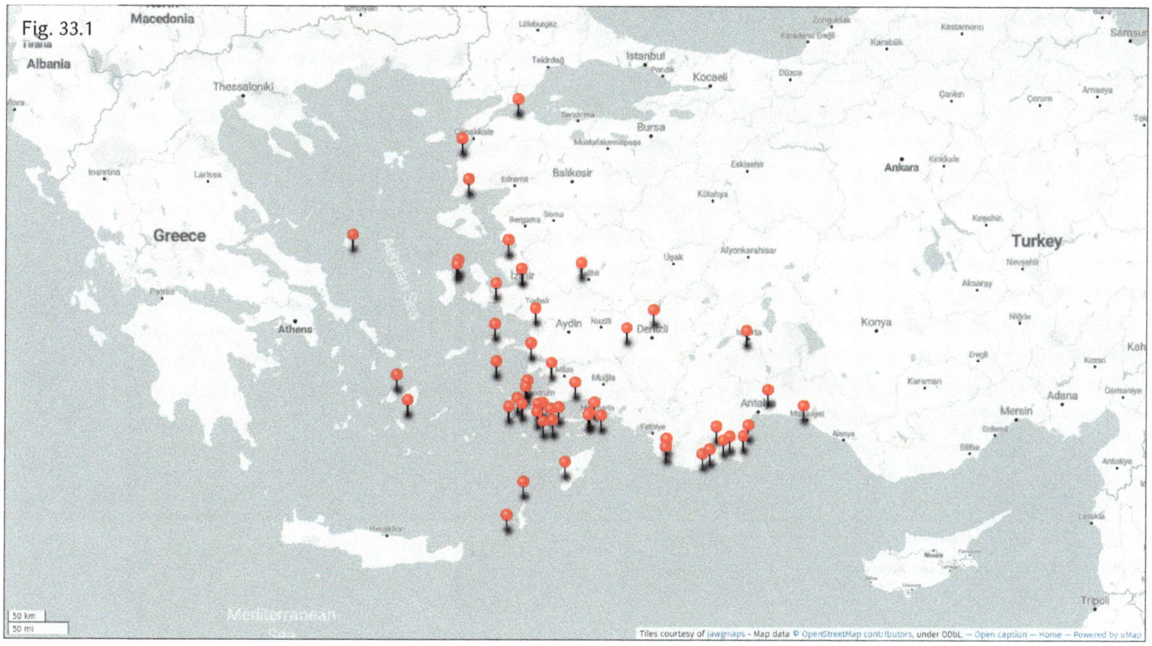

Fig. 33.1

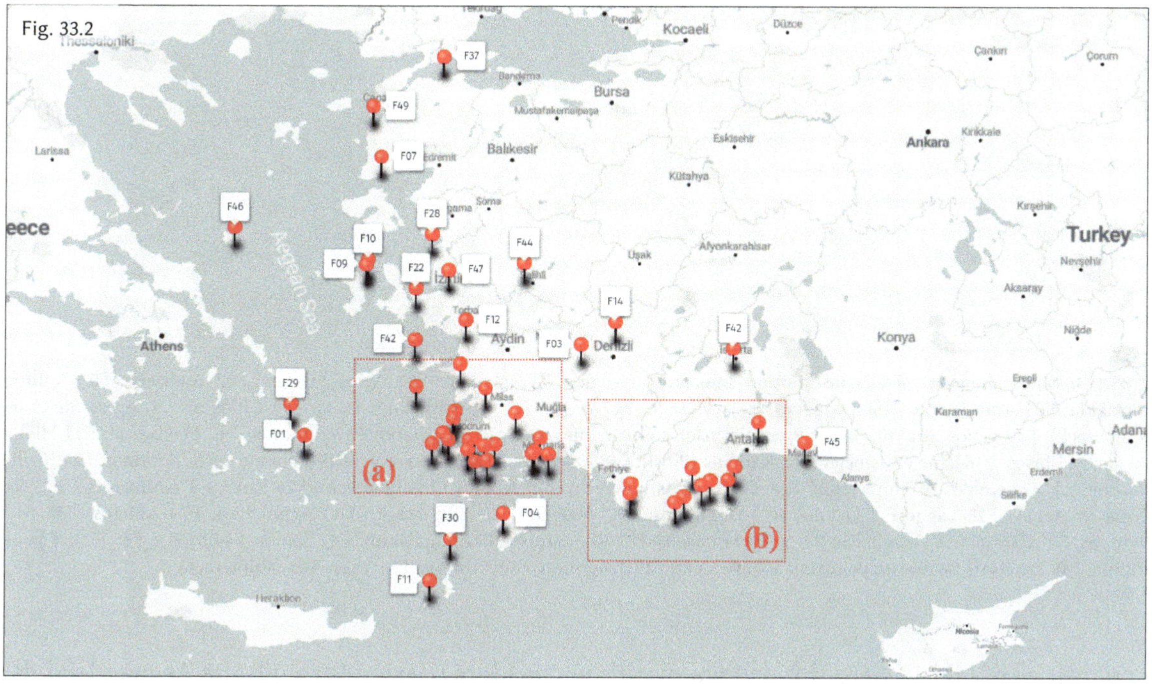

Fig. 33.2

See caption on following page

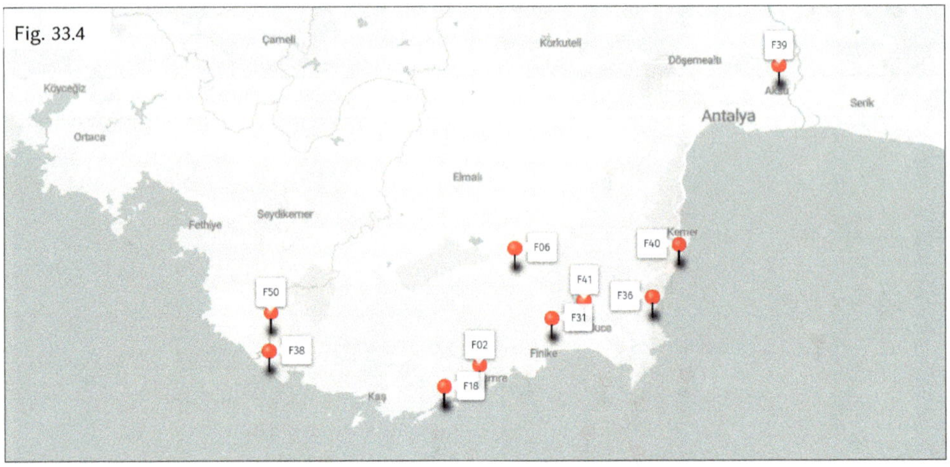

Figure 33.1–4. Maps showing LRA1 consumption sites in our region F, including: F01 Agios Ioannis; F02 Andriake; F03 Aphrodisias; F04 Apolakkia; F05 Arap Island (? shipwreck); F06 Arykanda; F07 Assos; F08 Burgaz (shipwreck); F09 Chios Site 9, Agios Stefanos Islet east (shipwreck); F10 Chios Site 10, South Prasonisi Islet south (shipwreck); F11 Emporio; F12 Ephesus; F13 Halasarna; F14 Hierapolis/Pamukkale; F15 Iasos; F16 Içmeler, Ismeler; F17 Kambos (Lipsi); F18 Kekova Island (shipwreck); F19 Kephalos; F20 Keramos; F21 Kizilburun; F22 Klazomenai; F23 Knidos A (shipwreck); F24 Knidos C (shipwreck); F25 Knidos O (shipwreck); F26 Knidos T (shipwreck); F27 Knidos; F28 Kyme in Aeolis; F29 Laggeri; F30 Leukos; F31 Limyra; F32 Marmaris B (shipwreck); F33 Mastichari; F34 Miletos; F35 Myndos; F36 Olympos; F37 Parion; F38 Patara; F39 Perge; F40 Phaselis; F41 Rhodiapolis; F42 Sagalassos; F42 Samos; F44 Sardis; F45 Side; F46 Skyros; F47 Smyrne; F48 TK05-AD Bozburun peninsula (shipwreck); F49 Troy/Ilion; F50 Xanthos; F51 Yassi Ada (shipwreck).

Vast quantities of LRA1s were shipped via maritime corridors passing through the Aegean Islands and along the coast of Asia Minor to fulfill *annona* obligations to Constantinople and her soldiers in the militarized frontier around the Danube, in addition to all manner of private and secondary exchange mechanisms. Though some Sasanian and Arab raids did reach the islands over the course of the 7th century, this region by and large remained the stable core of the shrinking empire throughout the LRA1 life cycle. In the islands, LRA1s are mainly found at coastal Christian sites, often fortified, that display clear ties to the Byzantine administrative infrastructure (e.g., Kephalos, Emporio).[12] These ties appear in myriad ways, such as urban *entrepôts* with state-operated warehouses to store and redistribute goods; or ecclesiastic complexes in removed rural areas collecting agricultural supplies for export (Poulou-Papadimitriou and Didioumi 2015; Poulou-Papadimitriou 2018). Local LRA1s are typically the second most common amphora in 6th–9th centuries contexts in the islands, with LRA2/13s being more abundant. However, they are sometimes rarer—at Emporio, for example, LRA13 and spatheion amphoras are far more common (each representing 21% of the amphora assemblage), with only one LRA1 *survival* (LCP vessel 33664).

On the mainland, LRA1s competed with the local LRA3, mainly produced in the Meander (Menderes) and Cayster River Valleys (see Bezeczky 2013: 26–31 and references therein). LRA1s are not very common at the late Roman agora in Ephesus overall, representing about 3.77% of amphoras dated to the 4th–8th centuries (Bezeczky 2013: fig. 27). This is not surprising, as LRA3 and similar type containers were produced around the city. Among imports, however, they are ca. 32.76%. The ratio between LRA1 versus LRA3 consumption in mainland sites is likely correlated with distance from the LRA3 producing areas. In a 5th century well deposit at Sardis, LRA3s are 40–44% of all amphoras, and LRA1s come in second at 13–18% (Rautman 1995: table 2); at the East and West Gates of Limyra, LRA1s are preferred, taking up 39.2–42.4% of the total, compared to 1.3–2.2% LRA3 (Bes 2020: table 1).

G. Western Balkans and central Mediterranean (Slovenia, Serbia, Croatia, Albania, Greece)—Diocese Moesia and Prefecture Illyricum

§10.3.7. Table G

The praetorian prefecture of Illyricum and the greater Balkan region (see §7.1.D on Late Roman Thrace) was witness to some of the more turbulent and violent historic episodes of the Late Roman and Early Byzantine periods. Frequent invasions—such as those of the Huns, Goths, Ostrogoths, Slavs, and indeed Romans from Constantinople—made the region "as ever ... contested territory" (Mitchell 2015: 18). Archaeological evidence, primarily from the 6th century, may corroborate this view of a highly militarized and nonurban region, characterized by small fortified settlements, few cities, and little evidence for complex agricultural or commercial activities (Curta 2017). Unsurprisingly in this scenario, LRA1s are commonly found in sites along the Danube, where, for instance, they can reach up to 54% of the assemblage as in 6th-century contexts at Viminacium (Pacetti 1995: 278–79), thus following a similar pattern as in Late Roman Thrace.

12. It has been argued that the LRA1s found at Kehpalos represent local production at the site (Didioumi 2014: 171). However, we found the evidence insufficient to corroborate this claim, hence Kephalos is not included in the production catalog.

Fig. 34.1

Fig. 34.2

Fig. 34.3

Figure 34.1–3. Maps showing LRA1 consumption sites in our region G, including: G01 Aliki (Thasos); G02 Antikythera; G03 Aquae/Prahovo; G04 Argos; G05 Askra; G06 Athens; G07 Belgrad; G08 Berat; G09 Bosman/ad scrufolas; G10 Brijuni Island; G11 Butrint; G12 Byllis; G13 Cezava/Novae; G14 Chinitsa; G15 Cibalae; G16 Corinth; G17 Dia Island (shipwreck); G18 Dion; G19 Dyrrachium, Epidamnos; G20 Gajtan; G21 Gortyn; G22 Gumenicë; G23 Hadrianopolis; G24 Itanos; G25 Iustiniana Prima; G26 Kallithea; G27 Kanistro; G28 Kastri/ Larymna; G29 Knossos; G30 Kostolac; G31 Križna gora; G32 Kryoneri; G33 Kula; G34 Kythera; G35 Marathon; G36 Nikopolis; G37 Olympia; G38 Onchesmos/Saranda; G39 Orikos; G40 Pefkochori; G41 Philippi; G42 Phoinike; G43 Pseira; G44 Rifnik; G45 Romuliana/Gamzigrad; G46 Ruginium; G47 Salona; G48 Scodra; G49 Sikyon; G50 Sirmium; G51 Thespiai; G52 Thessaloniki; G53 Thorikos; G54 Tiszavasvári; G55 Tonovcov grad; G56 Torone; G57 Velika; G58 Viminacium; G59 Zagabria.

Alternatively, the Greek mainland seems to have enjoyed a prosperous moment in this period, marked by an increase in occupied land and expansion of settlements. The overall picture might have been affected by modern surveying and interpretative frameworks unable to identify proper indicators for the early and middle Roman periods (full discussion in Pettegrew 2007: 745–49, tables 1–2, and 775–77). However, a clear trend for the period that emerges from archaeological surveys in Greece is the growth of imports (at the expense of local products); in this scenario, LRA1s are never predominant but constantly present, often immediately second in frequency to the LRA2s and sometimes a more rare import.

This picture is well defined, for instance, at Corinth and its hinterland (Sanders 1999: 460–61; Slane and Sanders 2005: 285), where only at the eastern harbor of Kenchreai do LRA1s reach a noteworthy amount (ca. 10%, against the ca. 70% of LRA2s; Heath et al. 2015: 7, table 1),[13] and confirmed at various sites on the Cassandra promontory in Chalcidice (Vasiliou and Tsigarida 2014). In a mid-to-late 6th century deposit at Iustiniana Prima, the LRA1 is ca. 1% of the amphora assemblage while LRA2s are closer to 20% (Bikić and Ivanišević 2012: 44). Only in rare cases like Dion are the former the most frequently attested amphora type (Fragoulis, Minasidis, and Mentzos 2014: 298). Years of analysis on assemblages at Butrint show a stark diachronic change in LRA1 consumption not observed elsewhere. The form was the most common imported amphora in the second quarter of the 6th century (34.6%), ahead of the LRA2 (21.1%, Reynolds 2010b: table 4). This radically shifts to 4.8–7.8% and 70%, respectively, in the mid-to-late 6th century (Reynolds 2010b: table 5). Work at Velika in Thessaly recorded LRA1s and other "international" amphoras in a structure interpreted as a state official's residence, highlighting the "connection with the state supplies network of this period and evidently shows the importance of the settlement for the collection and distribution of the *annona militaris*" (Sdrolia, Didioumi, and Koutsoyiannis 2018: 98). In Crete, data from Gortyn further emphasize the general swing in late antiquity toward an increasing dependence on imported foodstuffs in the central Mediterranean and western Balkans, though imports on the island never total more than 40% in the studied assemblages. LRA1s are attested early at Gortyn, since the post-365 earthquake strata in the *Praetorium*, but it is in the first seventy years of the 7th century that they appear to be the predominant vessel among the imports from the east, reaching up to 25–30% (Portale and Romeo 2001: 328, 398). However, LRA2s are often more frequent than LRA1s on the island, as in the monastic settlement on the islet of Pseira (Poulou-Papadimitriou and Nodarou 2007) and at Itanos (Greco et al. 1999: 528). The latter, strategically located at the northeastern-most tip of the island, might have represented the gateway and even redistribution point for LRA1s entering Crete (Poulou-Papadimitriou and Nodarou 2014: 877). Excavations of a 5th–6th century church complex at Knossos led to the proposal of local production of a "LRA1 imitations/*similis*" (Hayes 2001: 450, B61, LCP vessel 34082; Portale and Romeo 2001: 310, bearing some similarities to LRA1 *survivals*), but strong indicators for production have not yet been found.[14]

13. See the open-access Kenchreai Archaeological Archive (KAA) (http://kenchreai.org/kaa/typology/p-lra-1) for high-resolution data on ceramics, including LRA1s, at Corinth's harbor.

14. Portale and Romeo (2001: 310) had originally accepted the suggestion of a possible Cretan LRA1 production at Chersonesus (of Crete), based on the report by Marangou-Lerat (1995: 48); yet later, on the basis of more accurate petrographic observations, Portale rejected the idea and admitted the *survivals* might have been produced in the Aegean area (Portale 2014: 479).

H. Late Roman Italy (Italy, Austria, Malta)—Diocese and Prefecture Italia

§10.3.8. Table H

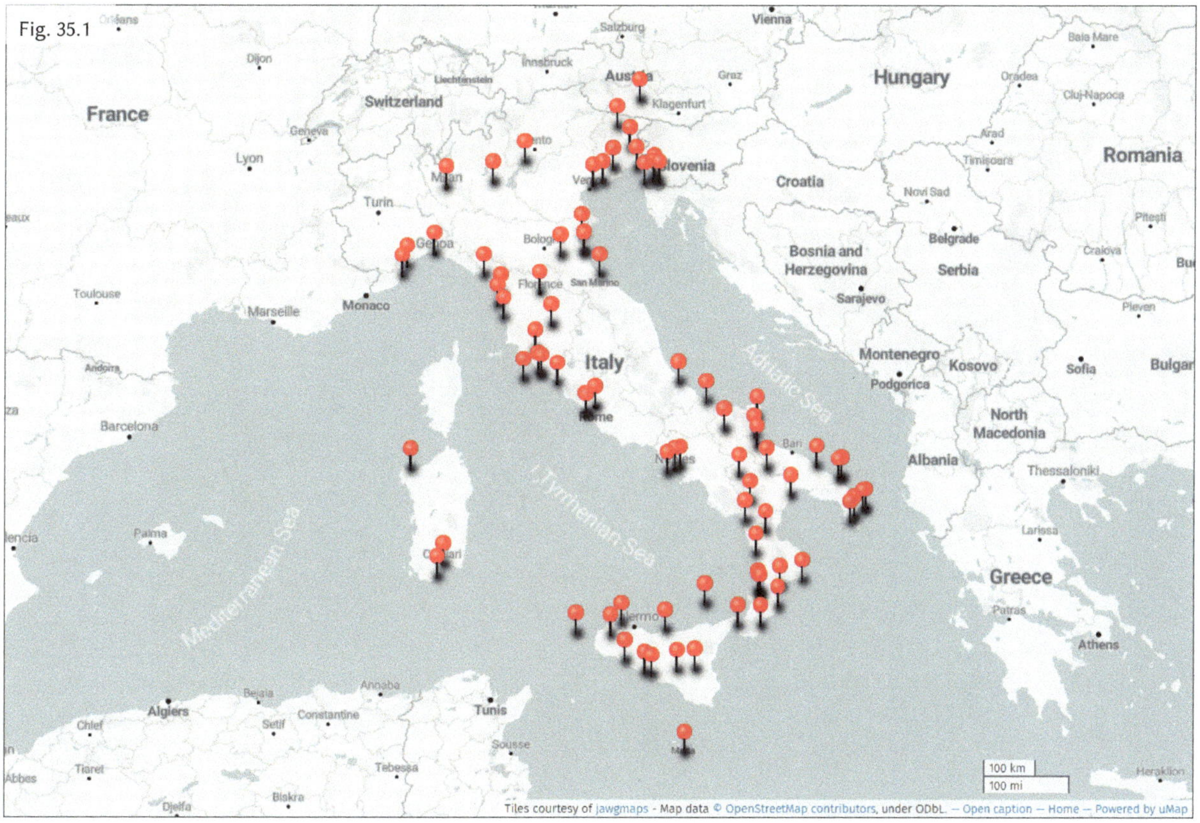

Figure 35.1–2. Maps showing LRA1 consumption sites in our region H, including: H01 Agnuli; H02 Akragas/Agrigento; H03 Albenga; H04 Aquileia; H05 Bivona; H06 Blanda Julia; H07 Brixia/Brescia; H08 Canusium; H09 Capo Rizzuto; H10 Capris, Iustinopolis; H11 Carales/Cagliari; H12 Casignana Roman Villa; H13 Caulon/Stilida; H14 Cazzanello Roman Villa; H15 Cefalù (shipwreck); H16 Classe; H17 Comacchio; H18 Concordia Sagittaria; H19 Contrada Cignana; H20 Cosa; H21 Crecchio; H22 Egnatia; H23 Finale Ligure (S. Antonino di Perti); H24 Florentia; H25 Genoa; H26 Giancola; H27 Giglio Island; H28 Giurdignano; H29 Grumentum; H30 Hala Milieri; H31 Imola; H32 Invilino-Ibligo; H33 Jesolo; H34 Lipari; H35 loc. Carabollace; H36 Loppio-S.Andrea; H37 Luna/Luni; H38 Marettimo Island; H39 Metapontum; H40 Milan; H41 Misenum; H42 Neapolis/Naples; H43 Nora; H44 Orbetello; H45 Ostia; H46 Otranto; H47 Palikè; H48 Paola; H49 Philosophiana; H50 Pievina; H51 Piran; H52 Pisa; H53 Piscino di Piscopio; H54 Pollena Trocchia; H55 Porto Torres; H56 Portus; H57 Portus Pisanus; H58 Predloka; H59 Punta del Serrone (shipwreck); H60 Ravenna; H61 Rhegion; H62 Rimini; H63 Roma; H64 Roselle/Rusellae; H65 Salapia; H66 S. Giacomo degli Schiavoni; H67 San Giusto; H68 Scolacium; H69 Segesta; H70 Sibari; H71 Supersano; H72 Tergeste; H73 Terrasini; H74 Teurnia; H75 Torcello; H76 Udine; H77 Ugento; H78 Vada Volaterrana; H79 Vagnari; H80 Vibo Valentia; H81 Villa S. Giovanni di Ruoti.

Fig. 35.2

See caption on previous page

The Italian peninsula underwent dramatic vicissitudes and evolutions between the 4th–7th centuries, bringing political instability, capital switches, invasions, and a long, consuming war between the Goths and Constantinople, to name a few (see Wijnendaele 2023). Notwithstanding these realities and a generalized contraction of urban populations, both major and minor centers still seem to have engaged in wide-ranging trade exchanges, including imports from the eastern Mediterranean.

In Rome, where a *praefectus annonae* is attested at least until the beginning of the 6th century (see the Paschasius mentioned in Martindale 2011: 1488), African imports prevail until the mid-5th century. At that point, eastern Mediterranean vessels such as LRA1s, already present in many assemblages from the late 4th century, progressively grow in frequency (see Reynolds 2010a: 218, table 17b; Casalini 2015: 543), despite never reaching major amounts (Panella 2013: 385). The highest percentage is registered at the *tabernae* of the temple of Cybele on the Palatine Hill at the end of the 5th century (12% in the whole excavated sector, Pacetti 1995: 274; up to 22% of all the eastern amphoras in certain contexts, Panella et al. 2010: 67). At Ostia "Eastern amphorae [are] of relatively minor importance, with somewhat more than 7% on average" (Martin and De Sena 2005: 387), though at Portus LRA1s seem to be a significant import in the 6th century, albeit at a lower rate than LRA3s and LRA4s (Pacetti 1995: 275, with references).

This seems to be a trend throughout the peninsula: LRA1s are consistently attested in small amounts, particularly (but not exclusively) at coastal sites. In the northeastern region, the largest assemblages come from 6th century strata in Tergeste—where they are the most widespread eastern amphoras, immediately followed by LRA4, both forming almost 70% of all amphoras (Auriemma 2007: 138)—and Classe, the harbor of the capital Ravenna (21% in mid-6th c., Reynolds 2010a: 229, table 3). LRA1s are attested sporadically in the Alpine region, at Loppio S. Andrea (Maurina and Capelli 2007: 482). Their widespread presence in southern Italy and Sicily, even with concurrent local production of the Keay 52 wine amphora, may be related to the region's reconquest by Justinian, especially when compared to the lower frequencies seen in the north. The Cefalù shipwreck (see §7.2), regrettably not yet extensively investigated, may provide key data to corroborate or disprove this hypothesis.

I. Late Roman Egypt (northern Egypt and the Nile, eastern Libya)—Diocese Aegyptu

§10.3.9. Table I

Egypt was an enormously wealthy and influential region during most of the Late Roman and Early Byzantine periods, as it had been since at least the early 3rd millennium BCE. The rise of Christianity, including desert monasticism, and imperial conflicts did little to change this until the early 7th century when Byzantine rule began to disintegrate for good under the Arab Conquest.

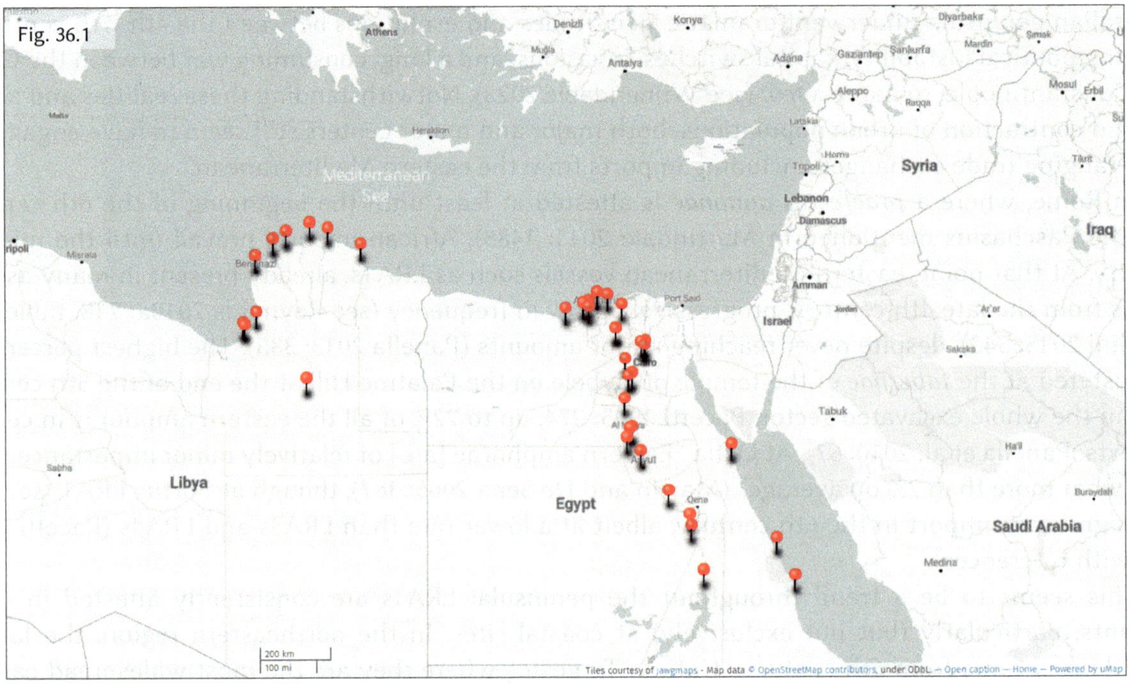

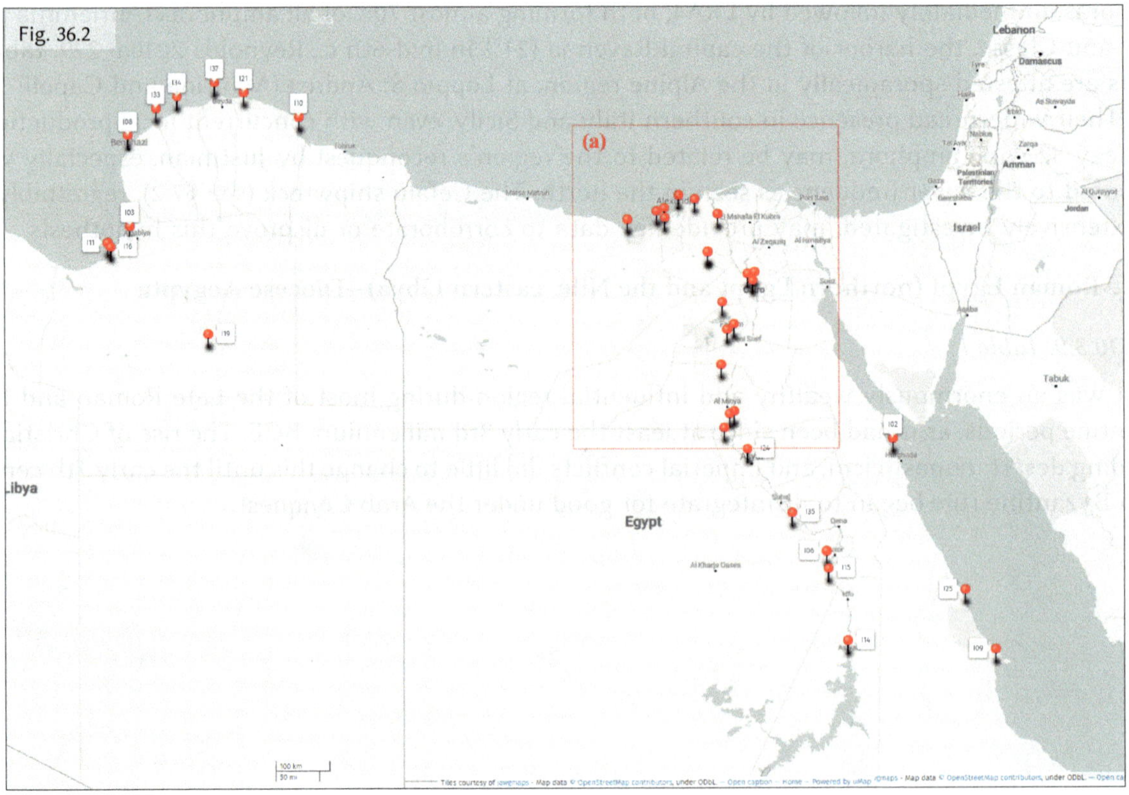

See caption on following page

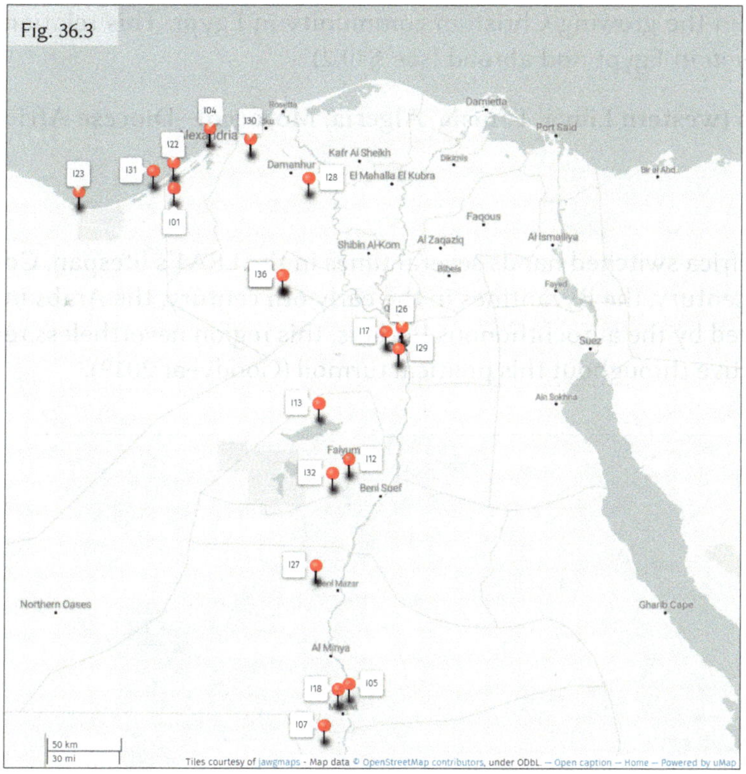

Figure 36.1–3. Maps showing LRA1 consumption sites in our region I, including: I01 Abu Mina; I02 Abu Sha'ar; I03 Ajdabiyah; I04 Alexandria; I05 Antinoupolis; I06 Armant/Hermonthis; I07 Baouît/Abba Apollotos; I08 Berenice/Benghazi; I09 Berenike/Bender el-Kebir; I10 Bomba/Plateia; I11 Boreum; I12 Deir el-Naqlun; I13 Dime/Soknopaiou Nesos; I14 Elephantine; I15 Esna/Latopolis; I16 Gasr el-Atallat; I17 Giza; I18 Hermopolis/El-Ashmunein; I19 Jalu; I20 Kellia; I21 Lamluda; I22 Marea; I23 Marina el-Alamein; I24 Manqabad; I25 Marsa Nakari/Nechesia(?); I26 Old Cairo; I27 Oxyrhynchos/Bahnasa; I28 Naukratis; I29 Saint Jeremiah's Monastery, Saqqara; I30 Schedia; I31 Taposiris Magna; I32 Tebtynis; I33 Tocra; I34 Tolmeta/Ptolemais; I35 Umm el Qa'ab; I36 Wadi Natrun; I37 Zaviet Hammama.

The LRA1 distribution in Egypt is directly connected to the Nile (along with most Egyptian economic activity), and the aforementioned Christian communities that grew starting in the mid-2nd century (Choat 2019: 450–56). All known sites sit on the Mediterranean or Red Sea coasts, or on the banks of the Nile, and the consumption and occasional production of LRA1s in monastic communities in Egypt was significant. The type was very popular in urban Egypt—it was the most common imported amphora at Naukratis and Giza (Thomas 2018: 16; Malykh 2007: 50); one of the chief imports at Alexandria and Antinoupolis (Majcherek 2007: 30; Fournet and Pieri 2008: fig. 26–27); and were also imported at other urban centers like Elephantine and Berenice (Katzjäger 2014: 600; Riley 1979: 213). The form is the most common imported (though some were local products from St. Jeremiah's Monastery) amphora at Baouît in the 7th century, representing 54% of that assemblage (Marchand and Dixneuf 2007: table 2). Riley echoes this assertion, writing that the type was the most common "amphora in Cyrenaica until the Arab conquest" (Riley 1979: 213). The LRA1 is among the most common imported types in many other rural Christian settlements, such as Kellia, Saqqara, and Abu Mina. All of these sites were monasteries or pilgrimage centers inhabited by ascetic Christian monks, highlighting the key role of the LRA1 in the growing Christian community in Egypt. This relationship is corroborated by the data from *dipinti* in Egypt and abroad (see §10.2).

J. Late Roman Africa (western Libya, Tunisia, Algeria, Morocco)—Diocese Africa and kingdom of the Vandals

§10.3.10. Table J

Dominion of North Africa switched hands several times in the LRA1's lifespan. Conquered by the Vandals in the early 5th century, the Byzantines in the early 6th century, the Arabs in the mid-7th, and all the while being resisted by the autochthonous Berbers, this region nevertheless remained wealthy and agriculturally productive throughout this political turmoil (Goodyear 2019).

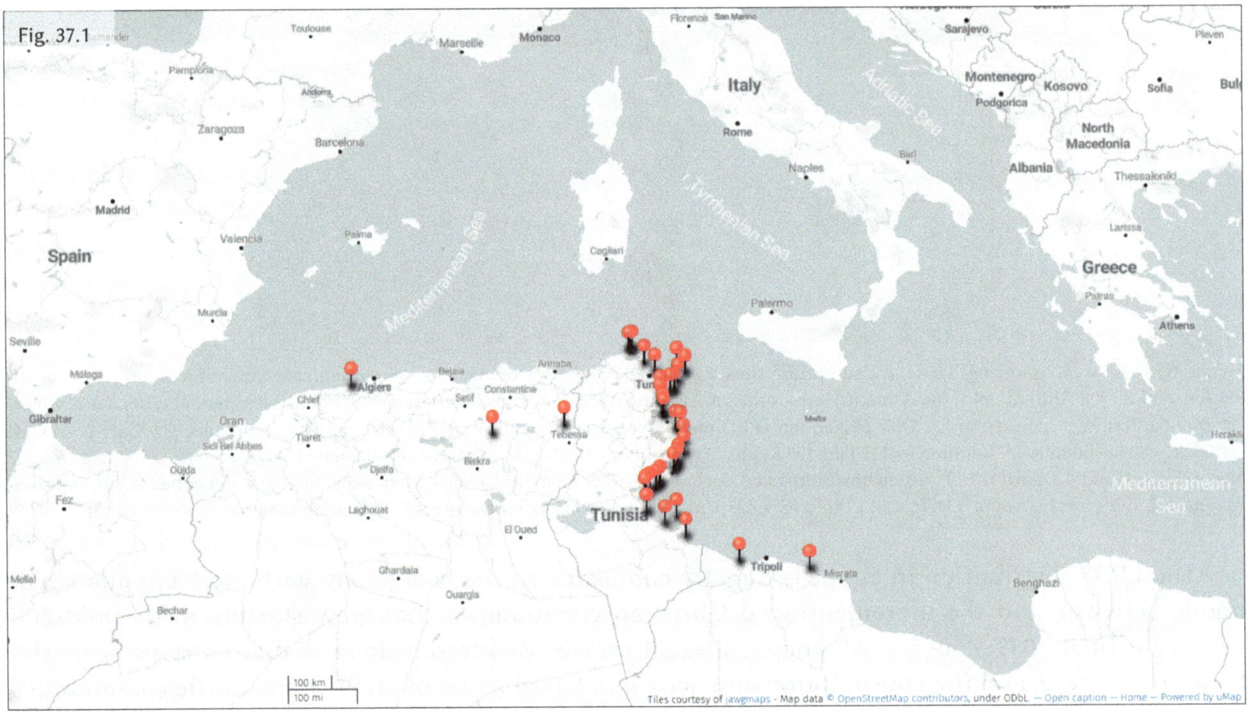

Figure 37.1–2. Maps showing LRA1 consumption sites in our region J, including: J01 Bir Flaguess; J02 Carthage; J03 Clupea; J04 Djerba; J05 El Aouabed/Koudiat Jaber; J06 En Nadour; J07 Gourine est; J08 Henchir Chougaf; J09 Henchir El Flouss; J10 Henchir El Hefair; J11 Henchir El Kebir; J12 Henchir Ferchatt; J13 Henchir Ech Cheggaf, Sidi Mansour; J14 Henchir Leich; J15 Horrea Caelia; J16 Khechad; J17 Leptiminus/Lamta; J18 Leptis Magna; J19 Maamoura; J20 Macomades Minores, Iunci; J21 Missua/Sidi Daoud; J22 Nabeul/Neapolis; J23 Naoura; J24 Oued Maltine; J25 Ras el Ain; J26 Ras el Koran; J27 Rass Enghela; J28 Rass Jezira; J29 Sabratha; J30 Sidi Aamer; J31 Sidi Ali Moujehed Sud; J32 Sidi Jdidi/Aradi; J33 Sullecthum; J34 Tipasa; J35 Themetra; J36 Utica.

Fig. 37.2

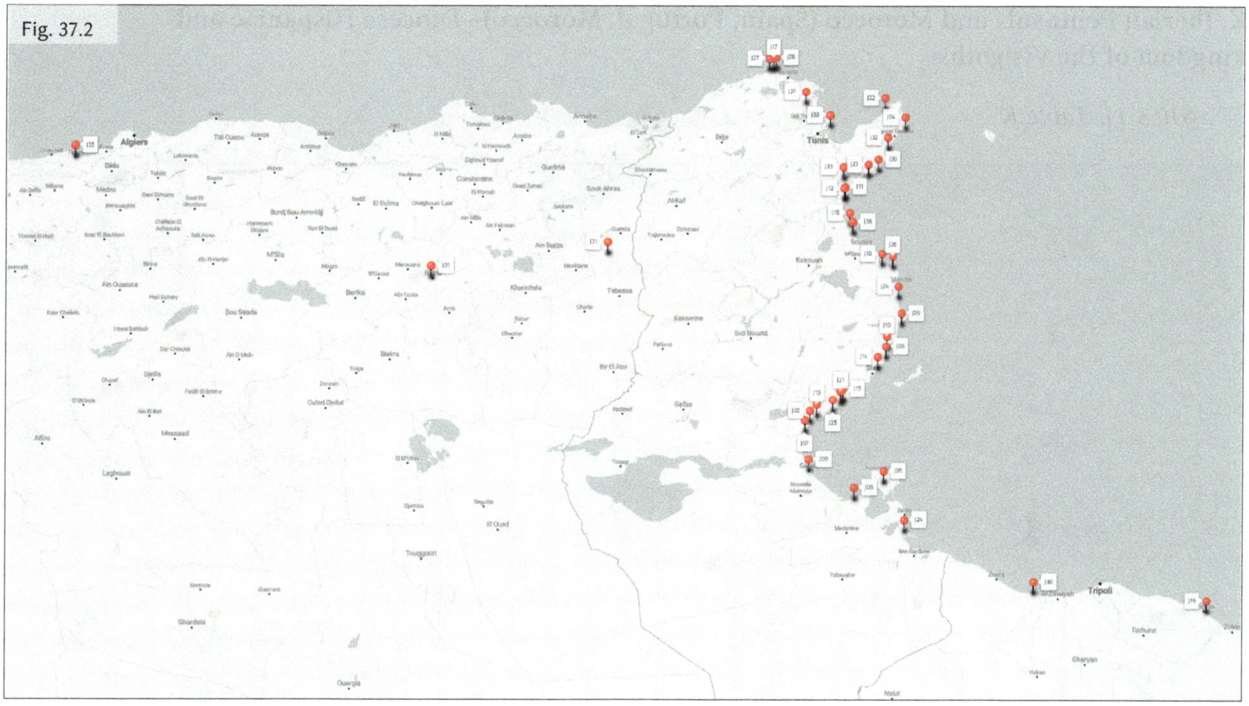

See caption on previous page

The dense concentration of LRA1 consumption sites within about 20 km of the North African coast, particularly Tunisia, is not a result of these historical events, but more likely a product of the region's geography and the current state of research. There are no major navigable rivers bisecting it as the Nile does in Egypt, and a notable dearth of archaeological excavations and surveys in the interior (Bonifay 2015: 531, 558). A survey in Sudan's Eastern Desert notably revealed multiple LRA1 consumption sites over 200 km from both the Nile and the Red Sea coast (see §7.N). The assumption that "extensive trade between the Roman world and the...Sahara" did not exist has been shown to be overexaggerated (Wilson 2012: 432). Could this be the case for the LRA1 in the following period? While possible, the data indicate that LRA1 diffusion in North Africa drastically decreases beyond 15–20 km from the Mediterranean–with the exception of Sidi Aamer. Unfortunately, most of these sites are not well published and quantified ceramic assemblages are quite rare, making detailed commentary impossible. In a major city like Carthage, however, LRA1s were important (though not dominant) containers at least in the first half of the 6th century, increasing from under 10% to ca. 15% by the middle of the century (Riley 1979: fig. 41).

K. Iberian Peninsula and Morocco (Spain, Portugal, Morocco)—Diocese Hispaniae and kingdom of the Visigoths

§10.3.11. Table K

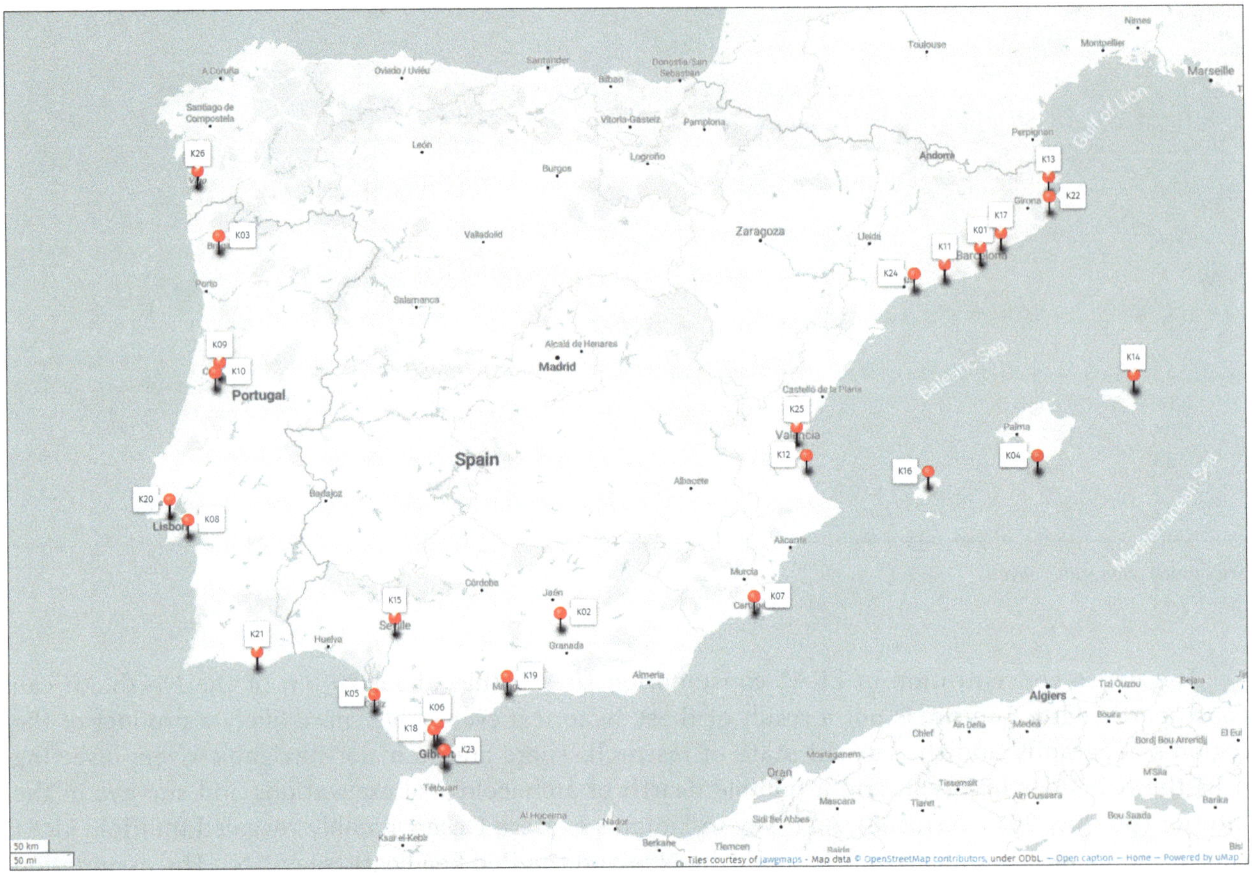

Figure 38. Map showing LRA1 consumption sites in our region K, including: K01 Barcino/Barcelona; K02 Benalùa; K03 Braga/Bracara Augusta; K04 Cabrera/Capraria; K05 Cadiz/Gades; K06 Carteia; K07 Carthago Nova, Karthago Spartaria; K08 Cetobriga; K09 Coimbra; K10 Conimbriga; K11 Cubelles; K12 Cullera Island; K13 Emporiae/Emporion; K14 Favatrix (shipwreck); K15 Hispalis/Seville; K16 Ibiza; K17 Iluro; K18 Iulia Traducta/Algeciras; K19 Málaga; K20 Olisipo; K21 Ossonoba; K22 Puig Rodon villa (Corça); K23 Septem/Ceuta; K24 Tarraco; K25 Valentia/Valencia; K26 Vigo/Vicus Spacorum.

While the exchange of specific commodities and economic ties with specific regions were reorganized when most of the Iberian Peninsula came under the rule of the Visigoths in the late 5th to 6th century, the region's overall economy was not radically altered (Jiménez and Narganes 2015: 266–72; and see Reynolds 2010a for a thorough discussion). A notable change between the Byzantine Mediterranean coast and northern Morocco, and the Visigothic north and west was probably related to the decline in participation in *annona* networks by the emerging Visigothic state(s) (Jiménez and Narganes 2015: 271–72; Reynolds 2010a: 92–94). Despite this, LRA1s appear frequently in both Byzantine and Visigothic administered areas, highlighting the resilience of the trade mechanisms on which it moved.

The LRA1 was the common amphora type at many of the Iberian consumption sites, including Barcelona (Carreras Montfort and Berni Millet 2005), Cartago Nova (Reynolds 2011), and Vigo (Fernández 2012: fig 4b). Notably, most of the LRA1 importing sites in this region are coastal urban centers with their own ports or harbors (with some key exceptions, like Seville and Braga). LRA1s do not seem to have penetrated far inland at all, mirroring the situation in North Africa. In his detailed analysis of the region, Reynolds observes the same pattern, "indicat[ing] that the vast majority of eastern amphoras were supplied to ports, where they remained..." (2010a: 108), but qualifying this with the northeastern coast of Spain where trade "was not restricted to major ports" (2010a: 107). This trend is also not entirely universal as it pertains to size—the occasional villa or monastic settlement in the region also acquired LRA1s, such as the villa of Puig Rodon.

L. Late Roman Gaul (France, Switzerland, the Netherlands, Germany)—Dioceses Galliae and Viennensis and kingdom of the Franks

§10.3.12. Table L

The core of this macro-region is Gaul, although we have also included the Roman provinces of Germania, still nominally part of the Western Roman Empire in the early 5th century. The masterful work by Pieri (2005a) remains unparalleled, a true milestone in the study of amphora circulation in the region during late antiquity. Thanks to recent excavations and research, we can add a handful of new sites to his detailed list of LRA1 occurrences throughout modern France (Pieri 2005a: fig. 33), updating the overall picture for the two periods he defined (5th to the beginning of the 6th c. and 6th to the first half of the 7th c.). As his considerations remain valid, we therefore point readers to his words and simply provide a short synthesis below.

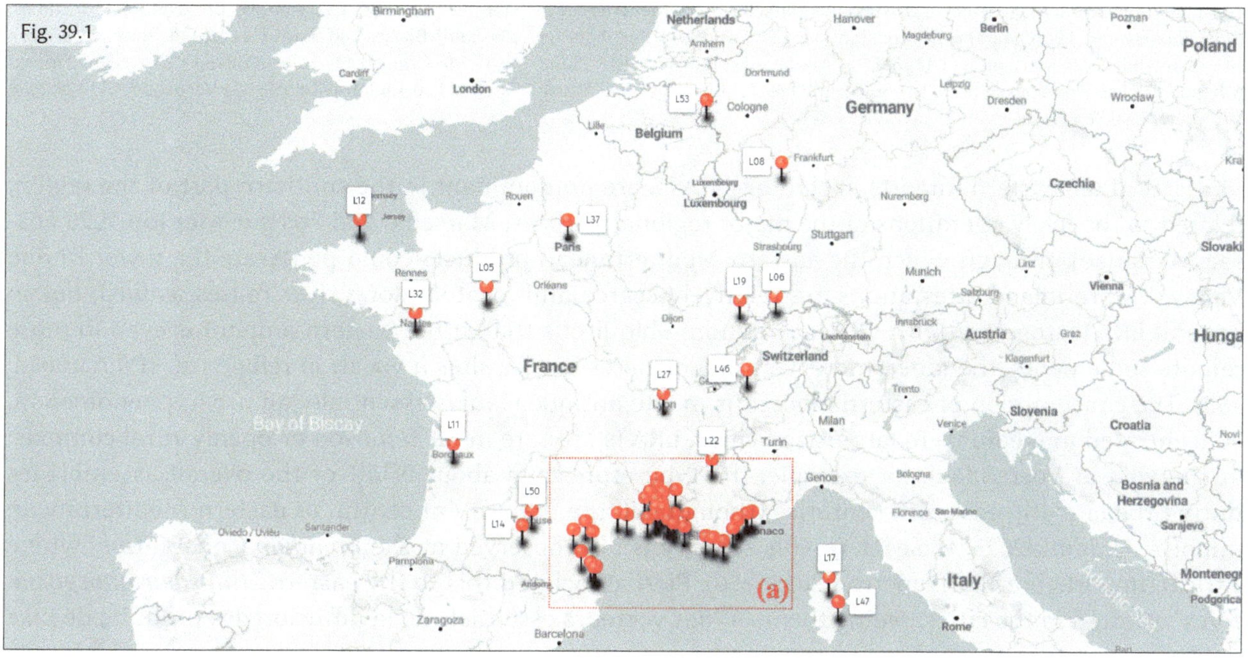

See caption on following page

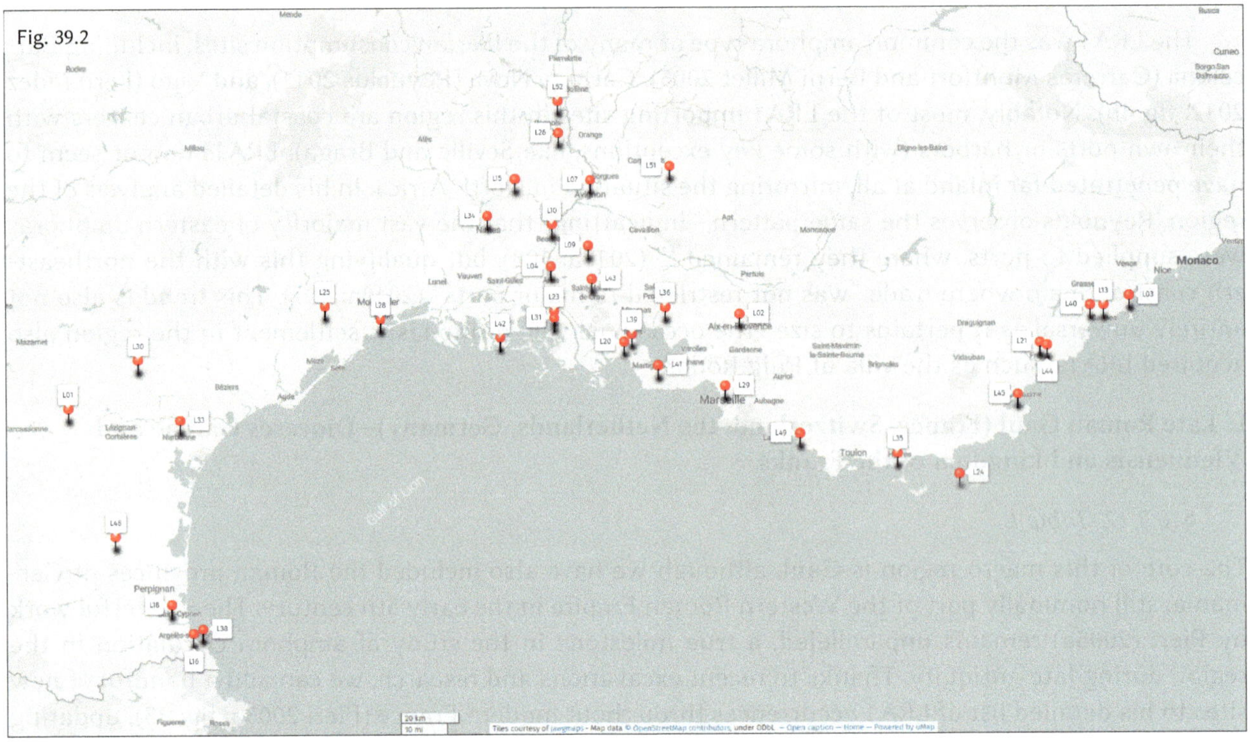

Figure 39.1–2. Maps showing LRA1 consumption sites in our region L, including: L01 Aigues-Vives; L02 Aix-en-Provence/Aquae Sextae; L03 Antibes/Antipolis; L04 Arelatum/Arles; L05 Aubigné-Racan; L06 Augst/Augusta Raurica; L07 Avignon; L08 Bad Kreuznach; L09 Baux-de-Provence; L10 Beaucaire; L11 Bordeaux; L12 Bréhat; L13 Cannes; L14 Carbonne; L15 Collias; L16 Collioure; L17 Corte; L18 Elne; L19 Epomanduodurum; L20 Fossae Marianae; L21 Frejús; L22 Gap; L23 La Capelière; L24 La Palud (shipwreck); L25 La Reille; L26 Laudun; L27 Lugdunum; L28 Maguelone; L29 Massalia/Marseille; L30 Menerbes; L31 Montille d'Ulmet; L32 Nantes; L33 Narbo; L34 Nîmes; L35 Olbia/Hyères; L36 Oppidum de Constantine; L37 Paris; L38 Port-Vendres; L39 Saint-Blaise; L40 Saint-Cassien/ad horrea (Cannes); L41 Saint-Julien-les-Martigues; L42 Saintes-Maries de la Mer; L43 Saint-Martin-de-Crau; L44 Saint-Raphaël; L45 Saint-Tropez/Athenopolis; L46 Sion-sous-le-Scex; L47 Solenzara; L48 Tautavel; L49 Telo Martius/Toulon; L50 Toulouse/Tolosa; L51 Venasque; L52 Vénéjan; L53 Voerendaal Ten Hove.

First of all, eastern imports, including LRA1s, are predominant in the southern part of the region, related to the lively operations of the major regional harbors, Marseille and Fos-sur-Mer (our L20 Fossae Marianae), through which the eastern Mediterranean products could penetrate the lower Rhône Valley.[15] More inland attestations are relatively scarce and located along river routes as well, but in general LRA1s, together with LRA4s, are more ubiquitous than other eastern amphoras even in more remote settlements–the latter, moreover, "majoritaires sur les sites à vocation religieuse" (Pieri 2007a: 152). The consumption of eastern foodstuffs in late antique Gaul is essentially an urban phenomenon, concentrated in medium- to large-sized cities. LRA1s are rare in far removed or openly rural contexts; at the villa at Voerendaal, for example, the type represents about 0.15% of the overall assemblages during the late 4th–early 6th centuries (though still the majority of central or eastern Mediterranean imports, Hiddink 2023: table 24.1). This scarcity is also observed at the *oppidum* Constantine, where African imports prevail (Duperron 2013: 256). Pieri associated this to the eastern "*transmarini negociatores*" attested in the cities, seeing them as "des vecteurs essentiels de la diffusion des produits de luxe

15. See www.romanopendata.eu for examples of LRA1 *dipinti* from the coast of southern France.

en Occident" (Pieri 2007a: 152). Indeed the presence of eastern merchants, as recorded by epigraphy, represents an important element to take into consideration for a general appraisal of LRA1 (and other eastern Mediterranean products) trade dynamics in the region. Pieri seems to imply that LRA1s (and other eastern Mediterranean products) are due to the presence of "*transmarini negociatores*." However, this assessment does not appear universally applicable in other regions, and therefore such a correlation based on LRA1s alone should likely be reconsidered.

M. British Isles (United Kingdom, Ireland)—Diocese Britanniae

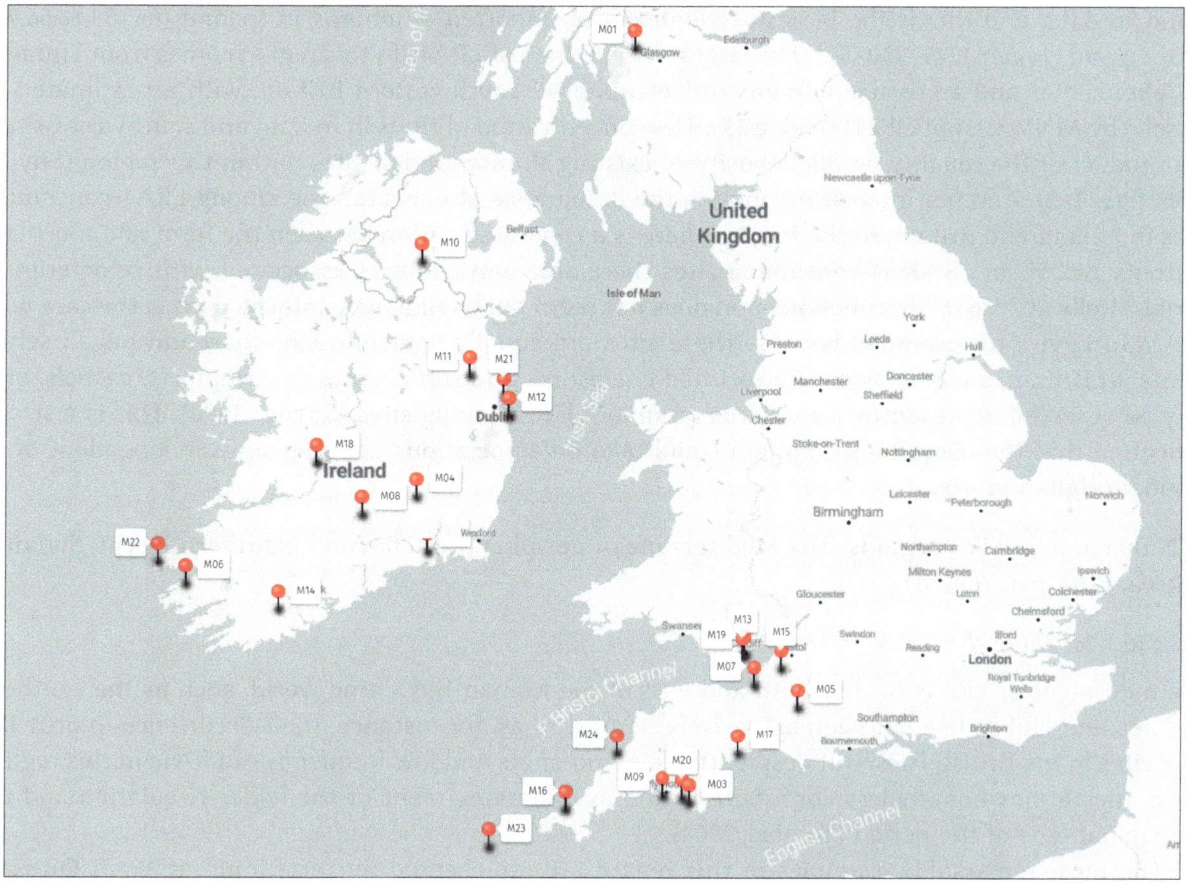

Figure 40. Map showing LRA1 consumption sites in our region M, including: M01 Alt Clut, Dumbarton Castle; M02 Ballygarran; M03 Bantham; M04 Blanchfieldsland; M05 Cadbury Castle; M06 Caherlehillan; M07 Cannington; M08 Cashel in Tipperary; M09 Cawsand; M10 Clogher; M11 Collierstown; M12 Dalkey Island; M13 Dinas Powys; M14 Garranes (Lisnacaheragh); M15 Glastonbury Tor; M16 Gwithian; M17 High Peak, Sidmouth; M18 Inis Cealtra; M19 Llandough; M20 Mothecombe; M21 Portmarnock; M22 Reask; M23 Sillina; M24 Tintagel.

The islands in *Britanniae* were always on the periphery of the Roman and Byzantine cultural sphere, and around the 5th century the power infrastructure morphed from an imperial administration to myriad small ethnicity-based kingdoms ruled by local Angles, Saxons, as well as Germanic peoples (Campbell 2010: 13). The prestige of "Romanness," however, clearly lived on within some of these polities, and ceramics (e.g., LRC, LRA1, LRA2) from the eastern Mediterranean continued to circulate in Ireland and southwest Britain well into the 7th century (Campbell 2010: 15–16; Kelly 2010: 52–54). Hypotheses vary on the nature of this exchange: Was it diplomatic gift-giving? Direct commercial trade? A demand for Christian-affiliated commodities? Secondary recirculation?

But whatever the case, the most recent analyses point toward direct commercial trade flowing from the Mediterranean up the Atlantic seaboard (see Duggan 2020; O'Brien and Hogan 2021: 256–59 and references therein). LRA1s are usually present in small quantities at the Irish and British sites, though the form was nevertheless one of the most frequently traded amphoras along this exchange route. At the Lisnacaheragh enclosure at Garranes, for example, "seven or eight" LRA1s have been found to date, and this is the largest assemblage of imported amphoras in Ireland (ca. 53.8–66.7%; O'Brien and Hogan 2021: 250–51). The largest assemblage of LRA1s in this region comes from Tintagel, the elite center and a possible administrative capital of southwestern Britain, with an estimated 29 vessels (by MNV, Campbell 2011: table 12). The concentration of finds in Ireland and southwest Britain is a product of the roughly parallel density of existing Roman-period sites within this region (Snyder 1996: figs. 1–2). Another interesting point is the dominance of one site-type among LRA1-consuming sites in Ireland and Britain. In the former, there is a clear association between the form and mortuary customs: 68.75% of all LRA1-consuming sites there are from contexts associated with cemeteries or burials (Kelly 2010: 61). This phenomenon does not seem to be religiously informed (as is the case with LRA1s in Egypt, for example) because these sites are equally split into Christian and pagan settlements. In Britain, a connection with fortified enclosures and settlements (i.e., ringforts, cashels, etc.) may be observed, representing two thirds of all LRA1-consuming sites (Snyder 1996). This is a strong indication that the ubiquitous amphora could take on associations and meanings independent of its original origin and use.

N. Nubia and Red Sea regions: The Mediterranean periphery and beyond (southern Egypt, Sudan, Eritrea, Ethiopia, Yemen)

§10.3.14. Table N

The movement of LRA1s to the south and east of the Roman-Byzantine world, such as the southern Red Sea and Nubia, has not been extensively addressed as, for instance, their occurrence in post-Roman sites in the British Isles. But despite the few find-spots and low frequency of LRA1s in this region, these attestations nonetheless contribute to the overall assessment of the wider circulation and exchange patterns of the period (Tomber 2004).

The most remarkable examples in this regard are represented by the tumuli at Wadi Qitna in Nubia (Strouhal 1984) and the so-called Royal Tombs of Qustul and Ballana; here the discovery of LRA1s birthed one of the vessel's typological identifications that remained largely in use throughout the 20th century ("Ballana 6," after Emery and Kirwan 1938: pl. 116). The presence of the amphoras in these burial contexts, alongside some other Byzantine "representative" objects (Kirwan 1984: 124–25), should be framed in the Constantinopolitan policies in Lower Nubia in the aftermath of the collapse of the Meroitic kingdom in the mid-4th century. The region was deemed strategic to protect Egypt from the expansion of the Sasanians and to assert control over the long-distance trade routes by the Red Sea, which had superseded the traditional land routes by then under Persian control (Zacharopoulou 2016: 233; for the competition between Constantinople and the Sasanians on the sea routes, see also Daryaee 2003). Byzantine influence might even have had a role in the emergence of the kingship of the

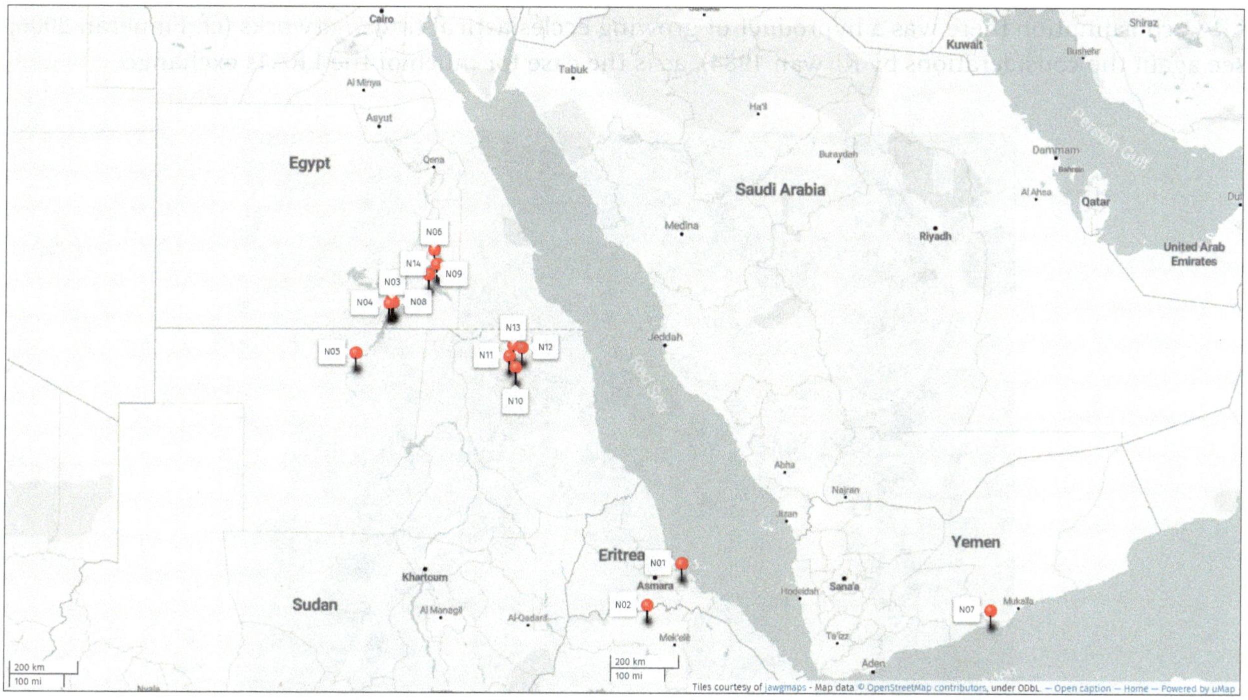

Figure 41. Map showing LRA1 consumption sites in our region N, including: N01 Adoulis; N02 Aksum; N03 Ballana; N04 Faras/Pachora; N05 Firka; N06 Kalabsha/Talmis; N07 Old Dongola; N08 Qana; N09 Qustul; N10 Sayala; N11 Sudanese Mine R37; N12 Sudanese Mine R45; N13 Sudanese Mine R57; N14 Sudanese Mine R60; N15 Wadi Qitna.

Nobades, one of the three post-Meroitic Christian kingdoms of Nubia, to whom the aforementioned Royal Tombs could pertain and who became formal allies of the empire by the mid-5th century (Zacharopoulou 2016: 237–41; Kirwan 1984: 126).

LRA1s accounted for in the Sudanese Eastern Desert survey, generally associated with other Mediterranean vessels (LRA2s, BGAs), are usually reported at mining settlements, a sign of the continuity—up to or beyond the 6th–7th centuries—of activity at sites previously considered abandoned since early Roman times (Massa 2020: 95). It is not clear though whether such activities were taking place under the imperial administration or local polities. The presence of these vessels, nonetheless, does illustrate the vitality of the caravan routes between the Nile and the Red Sea shore, "along the tracks connecting Egypt with the Ethiopian plateau" (Massa 2020: 85). LRA1s have been recognized at Aksum as well (Williams 2000), even though the Aila-Aksum amphoras are predominant. The former must have sometimes traveled along the exchange routes of these latter vessels, since they are found at Adulis, the harbor of the Aksumite capital (see references in Tomber 2004: 400),[16] and as far as Qana in the Yemenite Gulf (Tomber 2004: 401). Notably, the Aksumite kingdom had embraced Christianity as early as the 4th century (Seland 2014), and Aila, Adulis, and Aksum were all bishoprics, so it is possible that

16. LRA1s are also reported, possibly erroneously, aboard the Black Assarka shipwreck, in the coastal stretch immediately in front of Adulis, based on Pedersen 2000: 9, fig. 8 (Pieri 2005a, appendix 1, and 2007a: 614; Tomber 2004); the full account of the excavation of the wreck, though, does not mention nor illustrate any LRA1s, rather Aila-Aksum and BGAs (Pedersen 2008).

LRA1 consumption there was a byproduct of growing ecclesiastical trade networks (cf. Finneran 2006; see again the considerations by Kirwan 1984), as is the case for much of the LRA1s exchange.

Figure 42. Ballana, tomb 9, after Emery 1948: pl. 11.

§7.2. The Maritime Perspective: Shipwrecks

§10.3.15 and §10.3.16. Tables S1 and S2

While LRA1s are frequently identified as isolated finds in seabed deposits pertaining to jettisons or other dispersed underwater contexts (e.g., Leidwanger 2007), the contexts more valuable to our study are 18 investigated shipwrecks that transported LRA1s in the eastern Mediterranean and in the northern Black Sea. These closed archaeological assemblages offer us a rare "fine-grained and seemingly unparalleled glimpse into a moment frozen in time, a 'time capsule'" (Leidwanger 2017: 596; for more on the importance of shipwrecks in amphora and contents studies see Cibecchini 2021: 45–46).

Fig. 43.1

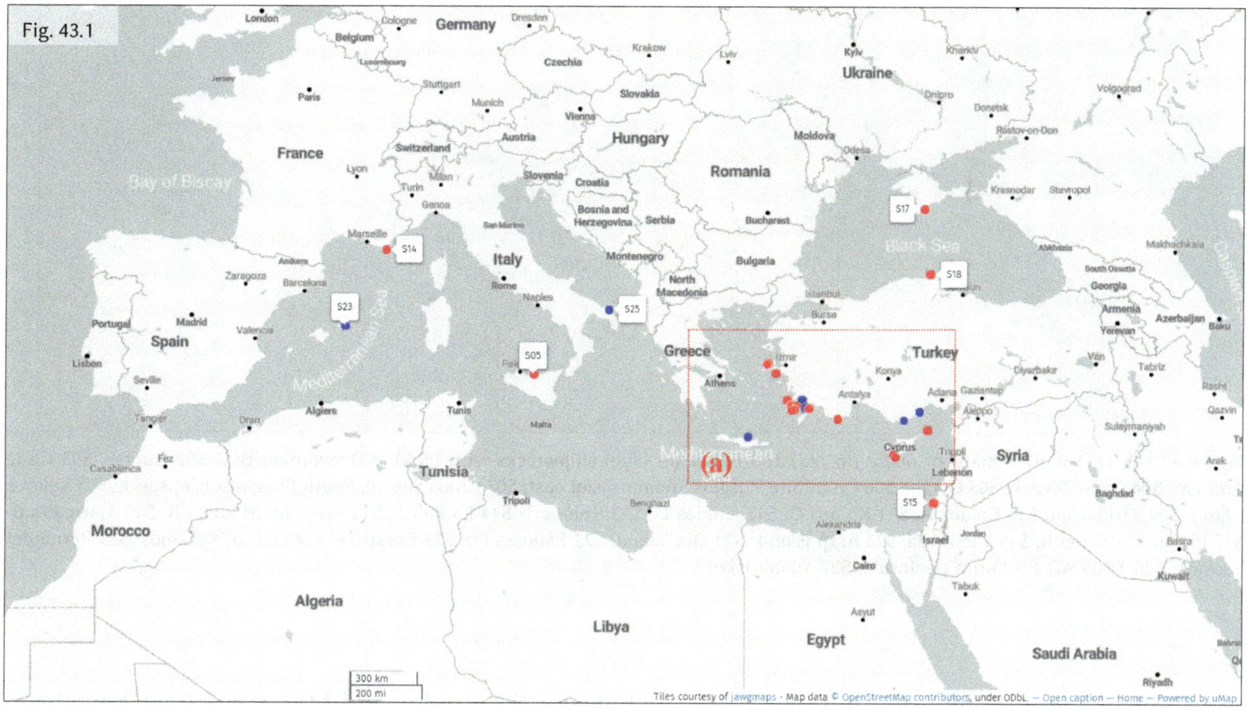

Fig. 43.2

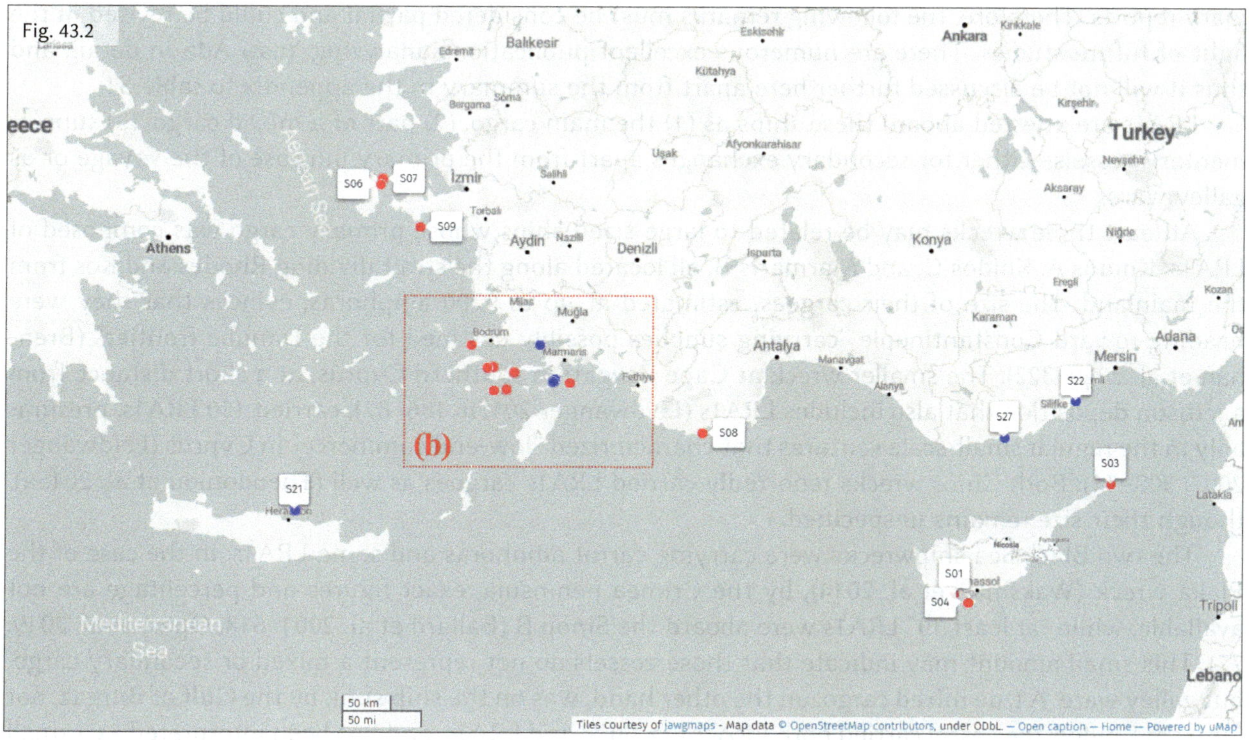

See caption on following page

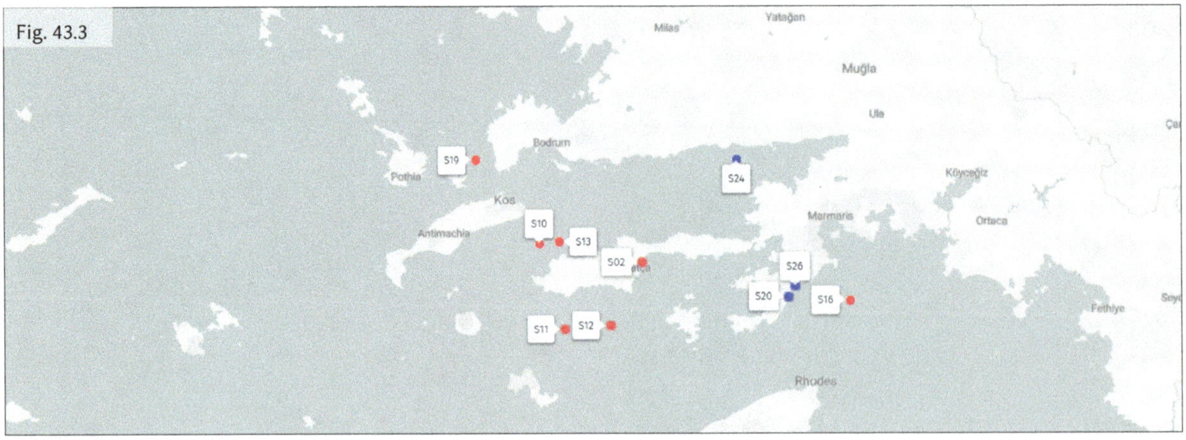

Figure 43.1–3. Distribution maps of major (in red) and minor (in blue) shipwrecks with LRA1: S01 Avdimou Bay; S02 Burgaz; S03 Cape Andreas; S04 Cape Zevgari; S05 Cefalù; S06 Chios Site 9, Agios Stefanos Islet east; S07 Chios Site 10, South Prasonisi Islet south; S08 Kekova Island; S09 Kizilburun; S10 Knidos A; S11 Knidos C; S12 Knidos O; S13 Knidos T; S14 La Palud; S15 Ma'agan Mikhael B; S16 Marmaris B; S17 Plaka; S18 Sinop B; S19 Yassi Ada; S20 Arap Island; S21 Dia Island; S22 Elaiussa (?); S23 Favatritx; S24 Gulf of Keramos; S25 Punta del Serrone; S26 TK05-AD Bozburun peninsula; S27 Yılanlı Island.

Some of these shipwrecks—notably Yassi Ada but also the Knidos and Marmaris sites—have been thoroughly studied and published; in other cases, the research is ongoing and we must rely on preliminary reports. Therefore, the following remarks must be considered partial and could be revised in the light of future studies. There are numerous excellent publications analyzing Yassi Ada in detail, and thus it will not be discussed further here apart from the summary in the appendix to table S1.

LRA1s are attested aboard these ships as (1) the main cargo, (2) part of a mixed cargo, (3) supplementary vessels—either for secondary exchanges apart from the primary purpose of the voyage or as galley ware.

At least three wrecks may be related to large-sized ships whose primary cargo was composed of LRA1s: Knidos A, Knidos C, and Marmaris B, all located along the strait dividing Rhodes and Kos from the mainland. The size of their cargoes, estimated at up to 1200 amphoras, evinces that they were heading toward Constantinople "carrying supplies possibly destined for the Danube frontier" (Brennan et al. 2020: 322). The smaller wreck at Cape Zevgari in southern Cyprus, at a short distance from a jettison deposition that also includes LRA1s (Leidwanger 2013b: 186–87), carried 150 LRA1s, presumably in the regular small-scale ventures that characterized "low-end commerce" in Cyprus (Leidwanger 2007: 308–14). Both Chios wrecks reportedly carried LRA1s cargoes as well (Theodoulou et al. 2015a), though their size remains unspecified.

The two Black Sea shipwrecks were carrying carrot amphoras and some LRA1s; in the case of the Plaka wreck (Waksman et al. 2014), by the Crimea peninsula, exact figures and percentage are not available, while "at least 10" LRA1s were aboard the Sinop B (Ballard et al. 2001: 618; Opaiț et al. 2019: 77). This small amount may indicate that those vessels do not represent a mixed or secondary cargo, but galley ware. A true mixed cargo, on the other hand, was on the ship sunk by the Gulf of Burgaz, not far from Knidos: the vessel carried both LRA1s (ca. 60%) and LRA2s, and has been interpreted as a small ship engaged in cabotage routes similar to the Zevgari ship (Leidwanger, Green, and Tuna 2015: 307).

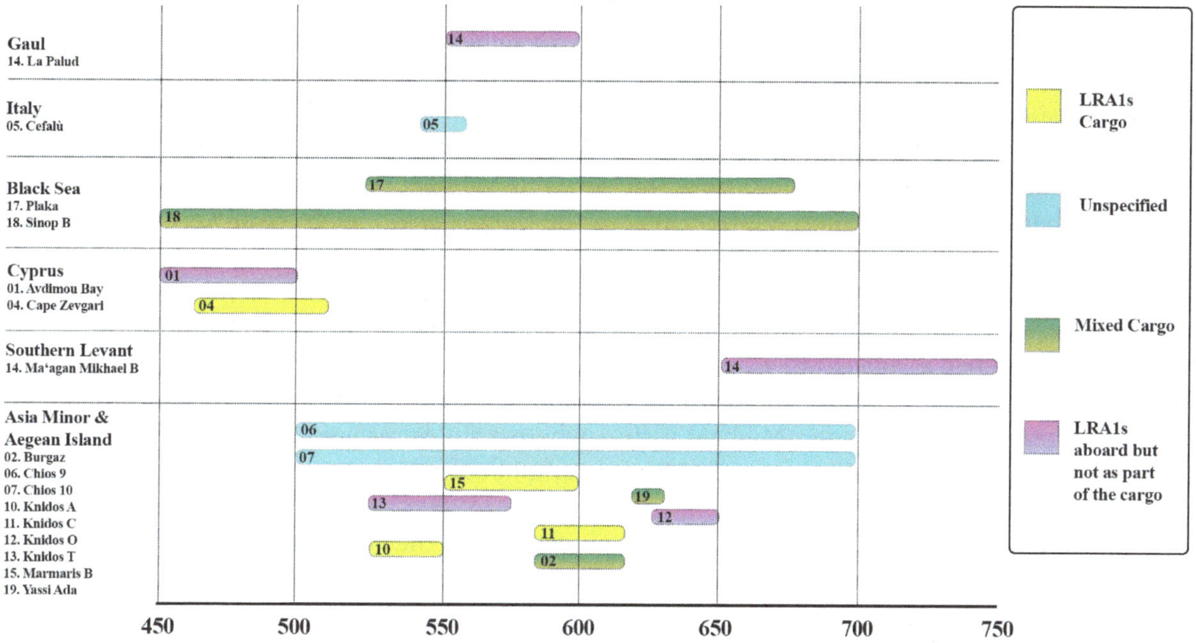

Figure 44. Chronology and cargoes of ships sunk in the Mediterranean and Black Sea carrying LRA1s; some context/assemblages are not included because of the incompleteness of the reports (graphics by V. Iacomi).

All the other shipwrecks suggest that LRA1s were a recurrent element of the galley ware, indicating that the eastern Mediterranean wine carried within these containers was a common component of these sailors' diet. Two LRA1s are attested at Avdimou Bay (actual cargo, a small batch of LRA4s and possibly millstones) and at Kekova (carrying also some late imitations); they were aboard La Palud, the Ma'agan Mikhael B (main cargo: LRA2s and LRA5s) and the Knidos T ships (a dozen approximately; main cargo: possibly grain); a singleton is attested even on the small Knidos O (carrying a small batch of LRA2s and probably engaged in local or regional trading) and in the Favaritx wreck (whose unstudied cargo made up of a disparate bronze objects may suggest that it was the accumulated hoard of pillaging pirates). LRA1s are reported onboard the Punta del Serrone shipwreck, which was carrying to Italy a large set of bronze statues, possibly for recycling purposes, from an undetermined location in Greece—plausibly an old shrine, related to Herod Atticus, at Delphi. Interestingly, the two LRA1s on the Kekova Island shipwreck conform to typologies pertaining to different periods (end of the 5th and 6th–7th c. respectively; Aslan and Orhan 2020), a further possible clue of widespread recycling practices, as demonstrated for some of the LRA1s and LRA2s aboard Yassi Ada (van Alfen 1996: 202–3; Leidwanger 2014: 898). It has been suggested that the Burgaz, Kekova, and Knidos A shipwrecks carried reused LRA1s and/or specimens from a range of production centers (Brennan et al. 2020: 295).

The shipwreck by Cefalù, in Sicily, unfortunately not excavated and actually even repeatedly plundered (Purpura 2004a), seems to offer a completely different scenario. Considering its remarkable size, Purpura (1983: 95; 2004b) suggested it was a military ship, possibly to be related to Justian's attempt to reconquer Sicily in 535. According to the preliminary report, LRA1s are the predominant amphora type (Purpura 1983: 101), bearing in at least one case a red *dipinto* (LCP vessel 34964).

As to the origin of these cargoes, beyond speculating on the possible route the ships were following, detailed chemical and petrographic analyses can, in some cases, point to specific production centers or regions. Wavelength-dispersive X-ray fluorescence conducted on a selection of LRA1s from the Plaka wreck suggested that some of them were products of the Arsuz workshop, based on similarities with data from samples collected by Empereur and Picon (Waksman et al. 2014: 922). The results of petrographic analysis on one amphora from the Ma'agan Mikhael B ship point to a possible Cypriot origin (Creisher et al. 2019: 106); the LRA1s aboard the Burgaz wreck align with west Cilician fabrics (Leidwanger, Greene, and Tuna 2015: 305).

As a brief note about contents, we should mention that pitch-lining is reported on vessels from Burgaz (Leidwanger, Green, and Tuna 2015: 304) and at least one amphora from Marmaris B (Brennan et al. 2020: 303), while a "black tarry deposit" was observed at the time (1954) of the first survey on the Chios Site 9, Agios Stefanos Islet east (Theodoulou et al. 2015a). However, the most remarkable evidence comes from the Ma'agan Mikhael B ship, where a single rescued LRA1, marked with a graffito on the upper shoulder, still preserved part of its original content, some eight kilograms of raisins/grapes.

The chronological range of the wrecks encompasses almost the complete time span of production and diffusion of LRA1s, while the geographical distribution is centered around the northeast Mediterranean, specifically the southern coast of Turkey. The very detailed dating of wrecks off the Asia Minor shores provides a good glimpse at the traffic along what has been convincingly called the "*quaestor* corridor," to which also the Chios ships contribute.

§7.3. Beyond the Imperial Frontiers. Appendix to Consumption and Distribution: O. India

Literature on LRA1s often offers the evocative image of the amphora being attested "from Britain to India." But while the North Atlantic connection has been thoroughly examined and discussed (see §7.1.M), it is easy to lose track of LRA1s when moving from the Red Sea/Gulf of Aden regions, where evidence is scanty, toward the Indian subcontinent. While distribution of the amphora "beyond the imperial frontiers" likely represents a derivative and even peripheral aspect of the vessel's circulation, long-distance trade connecting the Mediterranean, the Red Sea and Gulf regions, the eastern African coasts, and the Indian subcontinent was an essential component of late antique economies.[17]

An assessment of the presence of LRA1s in Indian sites is briefly reported here for the sake of completeness; we are aware, however, that a more robust review of the available evidence is needed. Roberta Tomber (2010: 48–50; cf. Autiero 2015) has underlined how in her own survey of Roman imported amphoras in India, sherds of Mesopotamian torpedo jars had been frequently misinterpreted as LRA1s—a confusion, it seems, that can arise quite easily, and be resolved only through close study, as recently demonstrated by the case of a group of presumed LRA1 sherds from Adulis.[18]

At present, we can report the ascertained presence of LRA1s in a few sites, as seen in the map below (based on Krishnan and Balvally 2015: 237; Tomber 2008: 166, table 3).

---

17. The famous episode recalled by Procopius, according to whom Justinian would have pushed the Ethiopian to bypass the Sasanian merchantmen involved in the silk trade to shorten (and have control over) the long journey of the fabric to the Mediterranean cities is indicative in this regard (Schneider 2014: 196); also cf. the Constantinopolitan interests in Lower Nubia discussed above.

18. See Zerai et al. 2022; pitching residuals were analyzed, and the results pointed out the inner lining of the amphora was made with bitumen, common in Mesopotamia, rather than resin, thence the reconsideration of the class of vessel to which the sherds pertain.

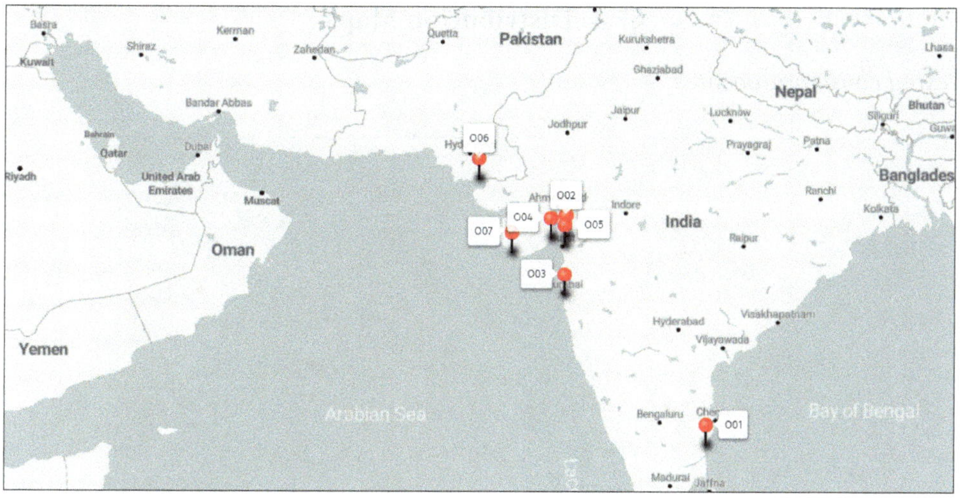

Figure 45. Map showing LRA1 consumption sites in our region O, including: O01 Arikamedu; O02 Bharuch (?); O03 Elephanta; O04 Hathab; O05 Kamrej; O06 Kateshwar (?); O07 Somnath.

§7.4. Distribution Maps

7.4.1. Attested consumption sites

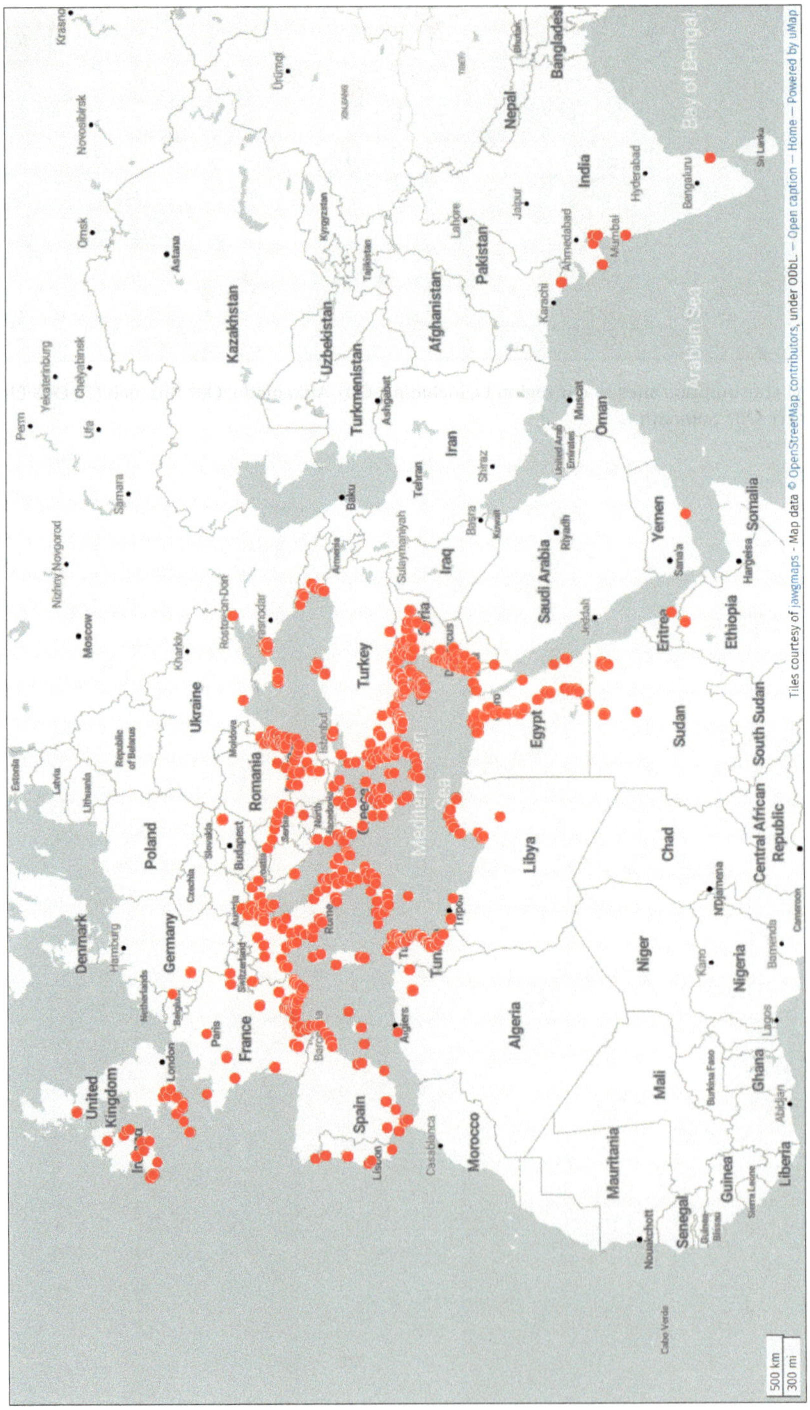

Figure 46. A map of known LRA1 consumption sites, as reported in the handbook.

7.4.2. Distribution of LRA1s according to typology

Fig. 47.1

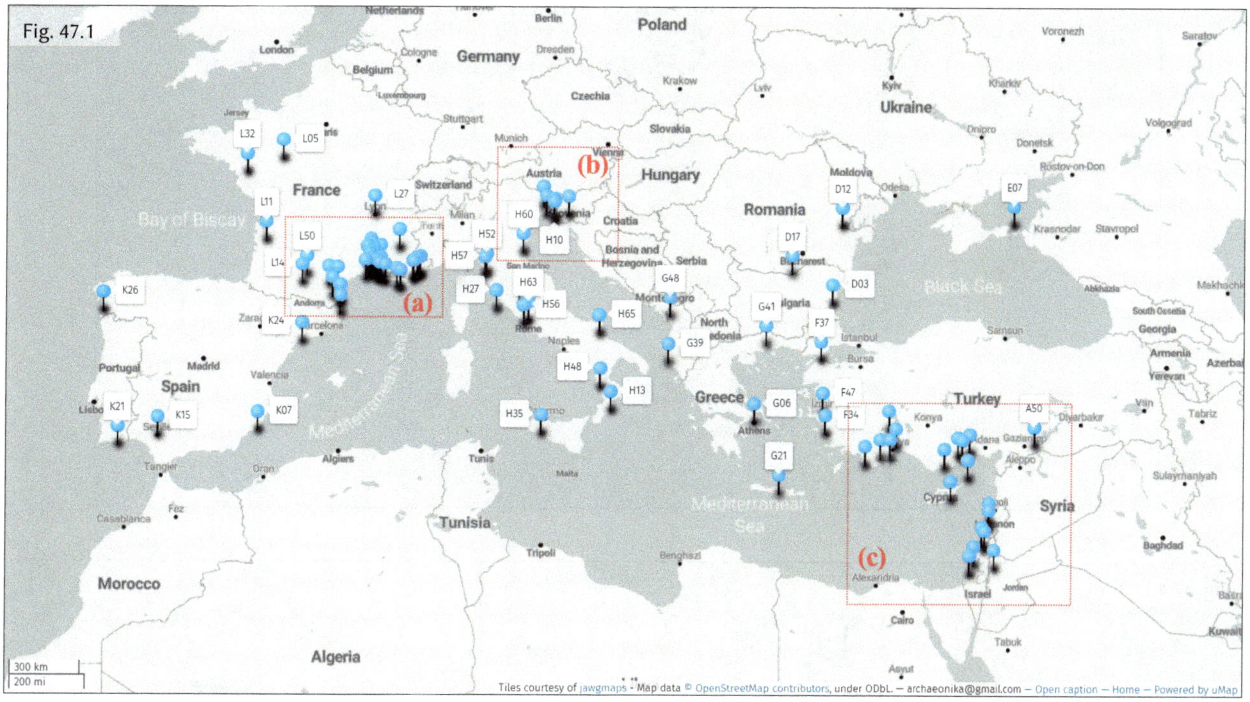

Fig. 47.2

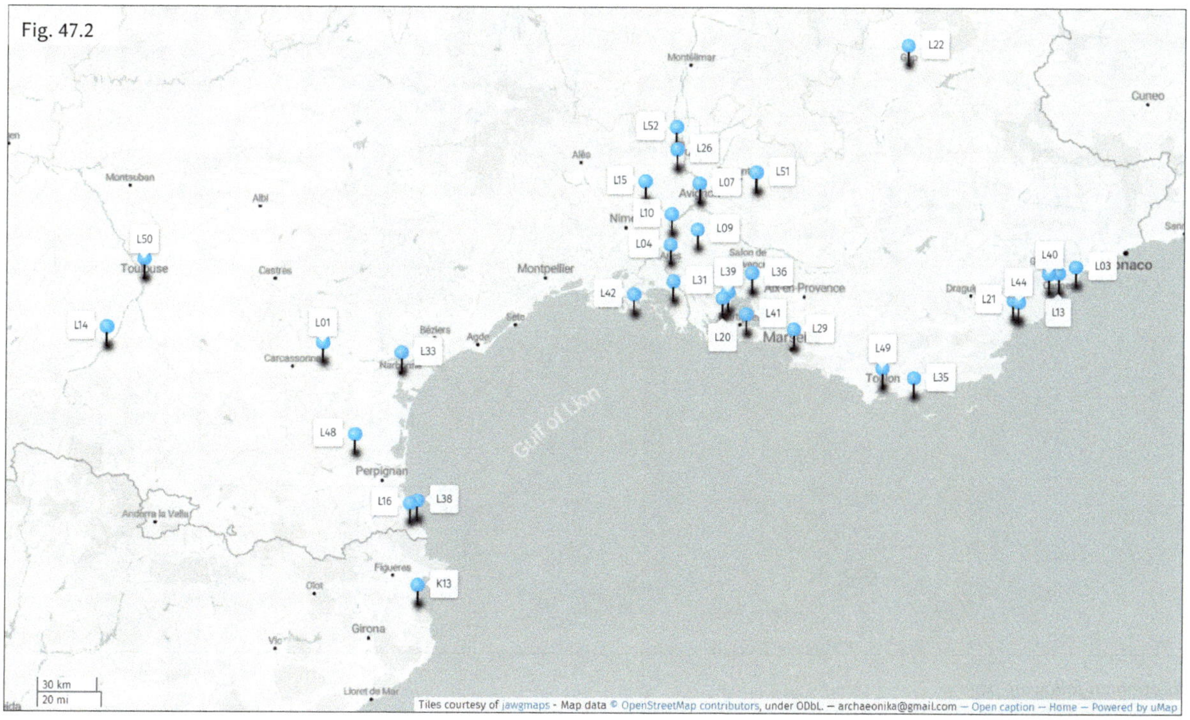

See caption on page 105

Fig. 47.3

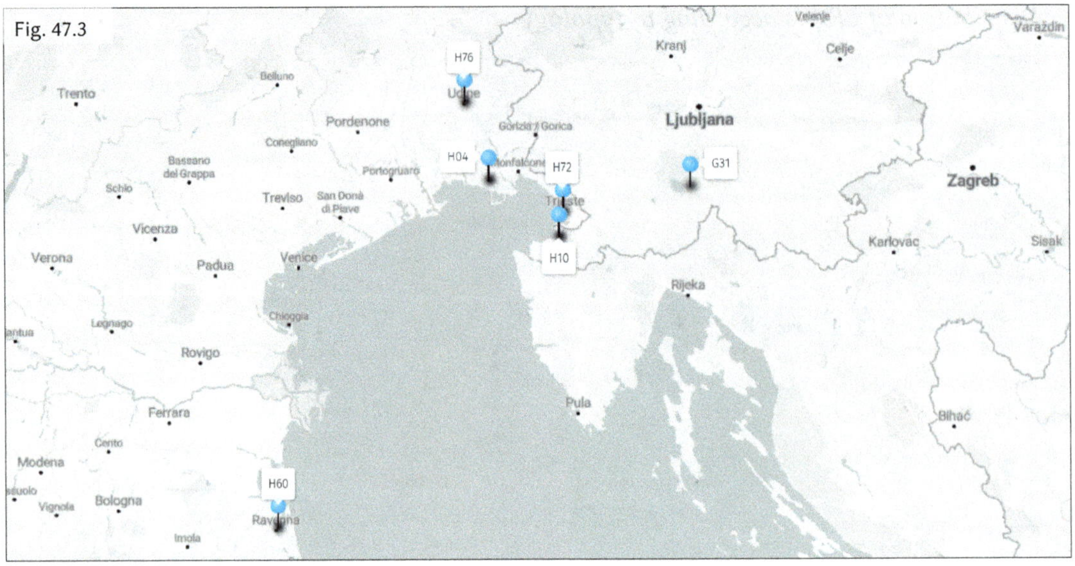

Fig. 47.4

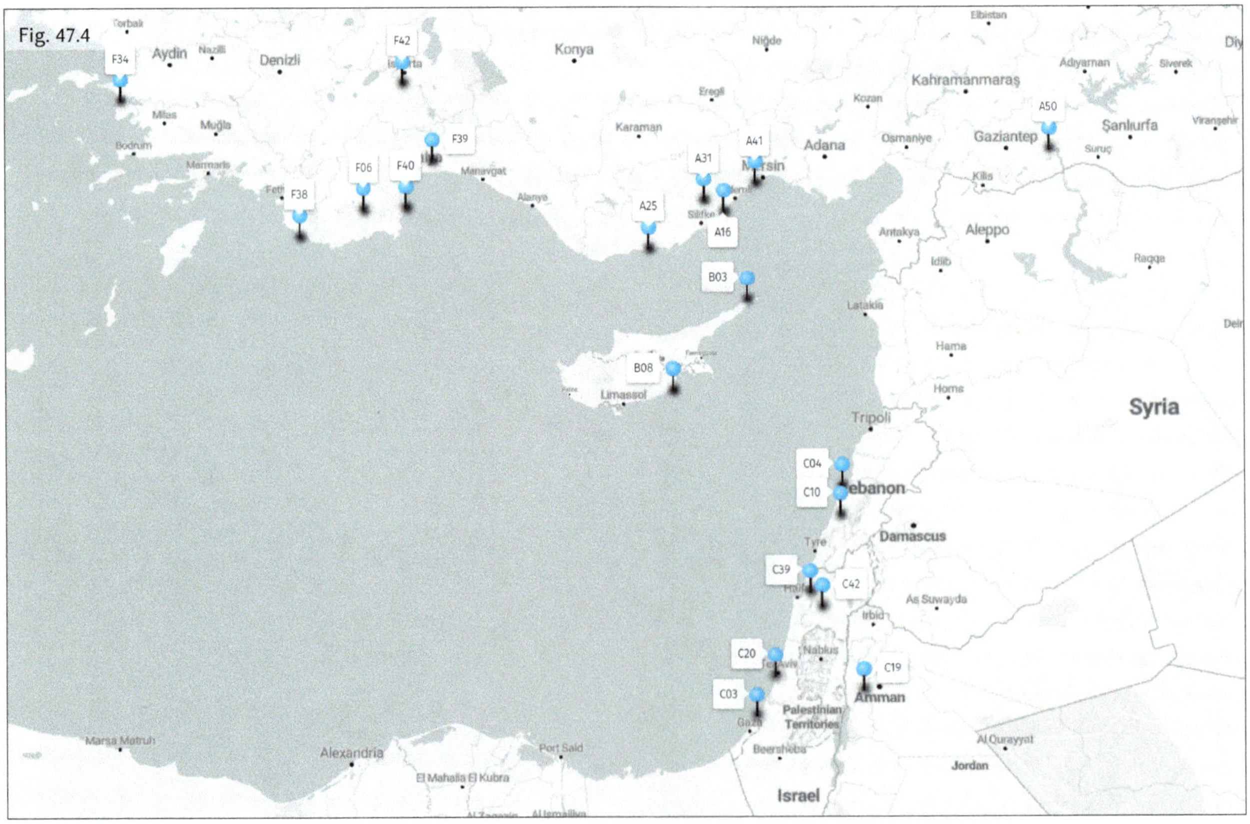

See caption on following page

Figure 47.1–4 (*see previous pages*). Distribution maps of LRA1s type A in our catalog, including: A16 Elaiussa Sebaste; A25 Kelenderis; A31 Olba; A41 Soli-Pomepiopolis; A50 Zeugma; B03 Aphendrika; B08 Cape Kiti/Kition; C03 Ashkelon; C04 Beirut; C10 Chhim; C19 Iraq al-Amir; C20 Jaffa; C39 Tell Keisan; C42 Zippori; D03 Anchialos; D12 Dinogetia; D17 Iatrus; E07 Il'ich; F06 Arykanda; F34 Miletos; F37 Parion; F38 Patara; F39 Perge; F40 Phaselis; F42 Sagalassos; F47 Smyrne; G06 Athens; G21 Gortyn; G31 Križna gora; G39 Orikos; G41 Philippi; G48 Scodra; H04 Aquileia; H10 Capris, Iustinopolis; H13 Caulon-Stilida; H27 Giglio Island; H35 loc. Carabollace; H48 Paola; H52 Pisa; H56 Portus; H57 Portus Pisanus; H60 Ravenna; H63 Roma; H65 Salapia; H72 Tergeste; H76 Udine; K07 Carthago Nova, Karthago Spartaria; K13 Emporiae/Emporion; K15 Hispalis/Seville; K21 Ossonoba; K24 Tarraco; K26 Vigo/Vicus Spacorum; L01 Aigues-Vives; L03 Antibes/Antipolis; L04 Arelatum/Arles; L05 Aubigné-Racan; L07 Avignon; L09 Baux-de-Provence; L10 Beaucaire; L11 Bordeaux; L13 Cannes; L14 Carbonne; L15 Collias; L16 Collioure; L20 Fossae Marianae; L21 Frejús; L22 Gap; L26 Laudun; L27 Lugdunum; L29 Massalia/Marseille; L31 Montille d'Ulmet; L32 Nantes; L33 Narbo; L35 Olbia/Hyères; L36 Oppidum de Constantine; L38 Port-Vendres; L39 Saint-Blaise; L40 Saint-Cassien/ad horrea (Cannes); L41 Saint-Julien-les-Martigues; L42 Saintes-Maries de la Mer; L44 Saint-Raphaël; L48 Tautavel; L49 Telo Martius/Toulon; L50 Toulouse/Tolosa; L51 Venasque; L52 Vénéjan.

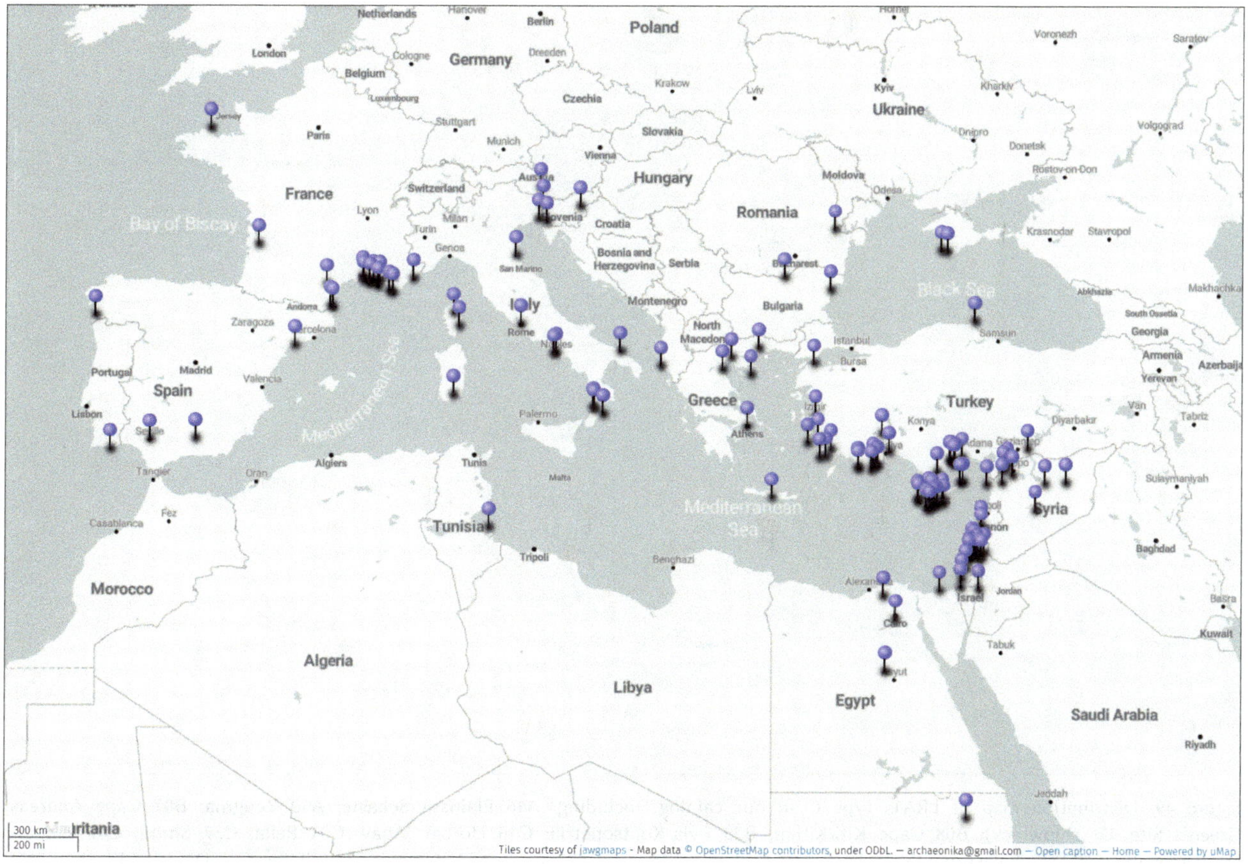

Figure 48. Distribution map of LRA1s type B in our catalog, including: A12 Dehes; A15 Diocaesarea; A16 Elaiussa Sebaste; A18 Hadir; A19 Halabiye/Zenobia; A22 Kanytelis; A25 Kelenderis; A28 Korykos; A31 Olba; A32 Palmyra; A33 Qal'at Sem'an; A36 Ras Ibn Hani; A37 Resafa/Sergiopolis; A40 Sergilla; A41 Soli-Pomepiopolis; A50 Zeugma; B02 Amathus; B03 Aphendrika; B04 Ayia Marina-Mavrovouni; B06 Avdimou Bay (shipwreck); B07 Cape Andreas, Green's Site 17 (shipwreck); B08 Cape Kiti/Kition; B10 Cape Zevgari (shipwreck); B14 Keratidhi; B22 Panayia Ematousa; B27 Skouriotissa-Vouppes; B28 Thalassines-Spilies; B29 Zygi-Petrini; C03 Ashkelon; C04 Beirut; C05 Beisan/Scythopolis; C08 Caesarea; C10 Chhim; C12 Dor; C14 Ein Boqeq; C15 Hippos-Sussita; C16 Horbat 'Aqav; C20 Jaffa; C23 Jezreel/Esdraela; C30 Ostrakine; C36 Shavei Zion; C38 Tell Fara; C39 Tell Keisan; C42 Zippori; D12 Dinogetia; D17 Iatrus; D25 Odessos; E02 Chersonesus; E10 Mangup; E20 Sinop; F02 Andriake; F06 Arykanda; F08 Burgaz (shipwreck); F17 Kambos (Lipsi); F20 Keramos; F27 Knidos; F31 Limyra; F34 Miletos; F37 Parion; F38 Patara; F39 Perge; F41 Rhodiapolis; F42 Sagalassos; F47 Smyrne; F50 Xanthos; G06 Athens; G18 Dion; G21 Gortyn; G39 Orikos; G41 Philippi; G44 Rifnik; G52 Thessaloniki; G56 Tonovcov grad; G57 Torone; H04 Aquileia; H05 Bivona;

H11 Carales/Cagliari; H13 Caulon-Stilida; H22 Egnatia; H41 Misenum; H42 Neapolis/Naples; H53 Piscino di Piscopio; H60 Ravenna; H63 Roma; H72 Tergeste; H74 Teurnia; I07 Baouît/Abba Apollotos; I28 Naukratis; I29 Saint Jeremiah's Monastery, Saqqara; J05 Djerba; K02 Benalùa; K15 Hispalis/Seville; K21 Ossonoba; K24 Tarraco; K26 Vigo/Vicus Spacorum; L02 Aix-en-Provence/Aquae Sextae; L03 Antibes/ Antipolis; L04 Arelatum/Arles; L11 Bordeaux; L12 Bréhat; L17 Corte; L18 Elne; L20 Fossae Marianae; L29 Massalia/Marseille; L30 Menerbes; L31 Montille d'Ulmet; L35 Olbia/Hyères; L36 Oppidum de Constantine; L38 Port-Vendres; L39 Saint-Blaise; L47 Solenzara; L49 Telo Martius/Toulon; N12 Sudanese Mine R45.

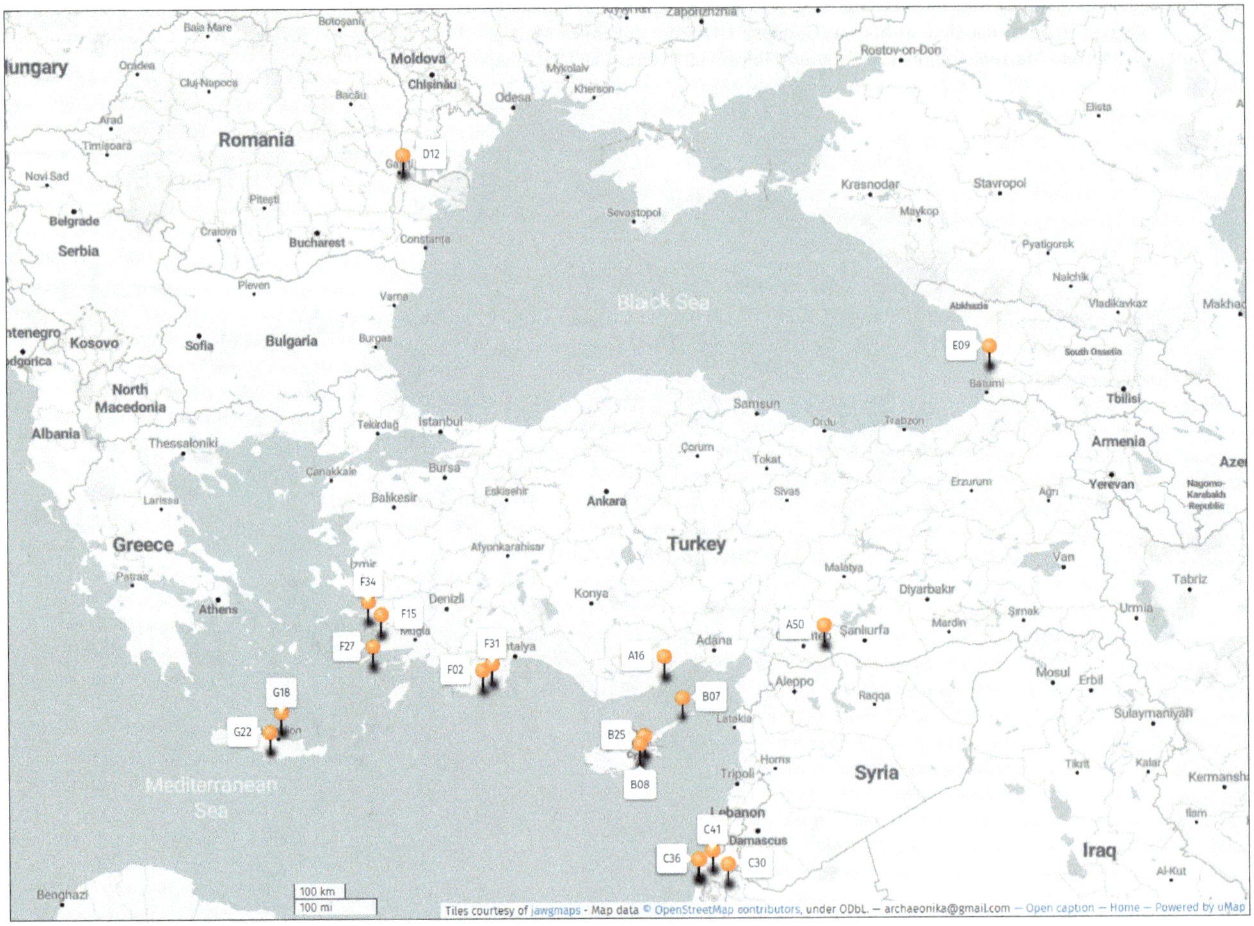

Figure 49. Distribution map of LRA1s type C in our catalog, including: A16 Elaiussa Sebaste; A50 Zeugma; B07 Cape Andreas, Green's Site 17 (shipwreck); B08 Cape Kiti/Kition; B25 Pyla-Koutsopetria; C16 Horbat 'Aqav; C31 Pella; C37 Shuni; C42 Zippori; D12 Dinogetia; E09 Lake Palastiomi (Natechebi); F02 Andriake; F15 Iasos; F27 Knidos; F31 Limyra; F34 Miletos; G17 Dia Island (shipwreck); G21 Gortyn.

Figure 50. Distribution map of LRA1s "transitional" (brown) and "*survival*" (magenta) in our catalog, including: A03 Antiocheia ad Cragum; A13 Delice kiln site; A28 Korykos; C10 Chhim; C25 Ma'agan Mikhael B (shipwreck); D03 Anchialos; E04 Demirci; F17 Kambos (Lipsi); F19 Kephalos; F30 Leukos.

7.4.3. Diachronic maps of LRA1 consumption

Fig. 51.1

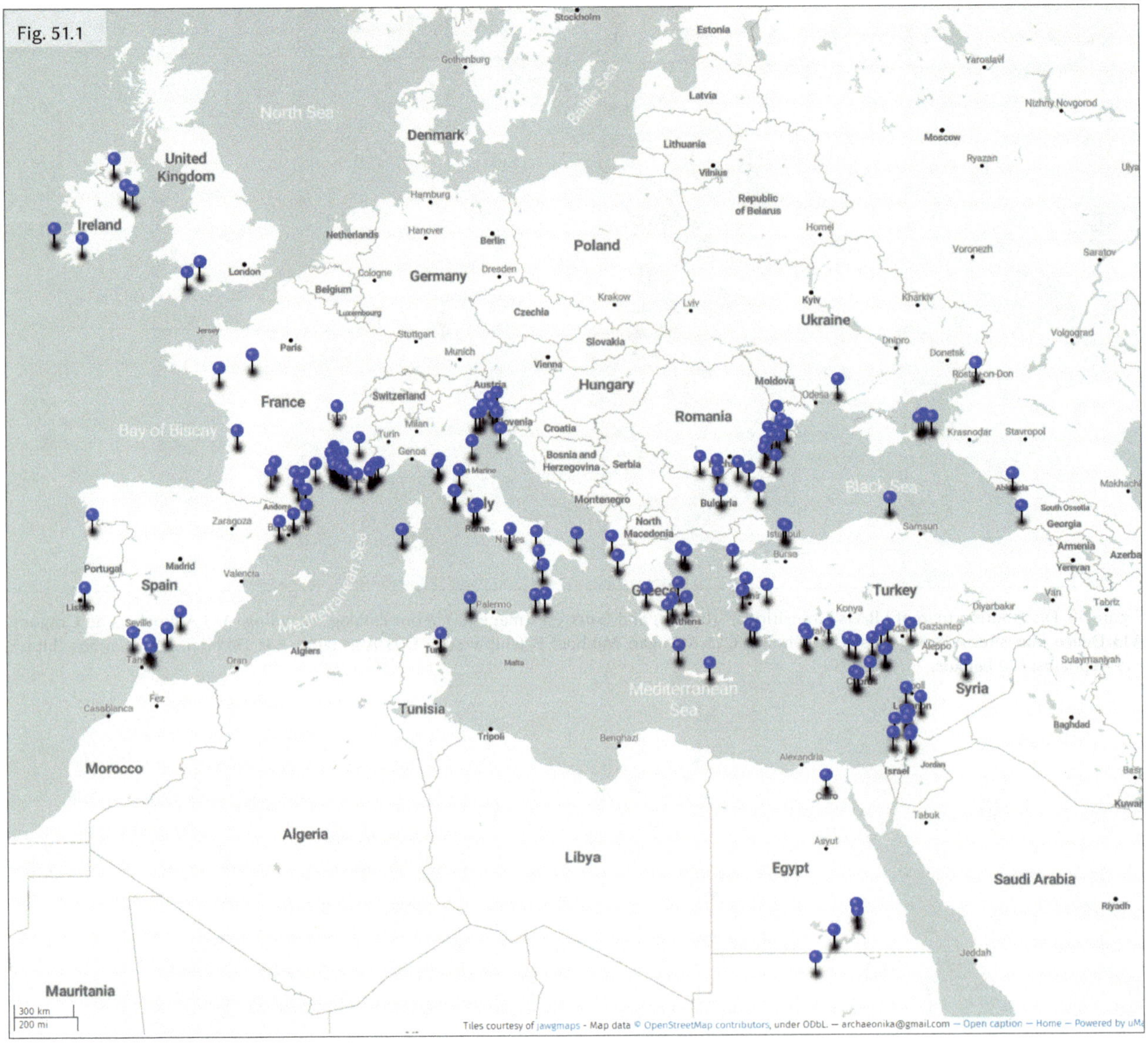

See caption on following page

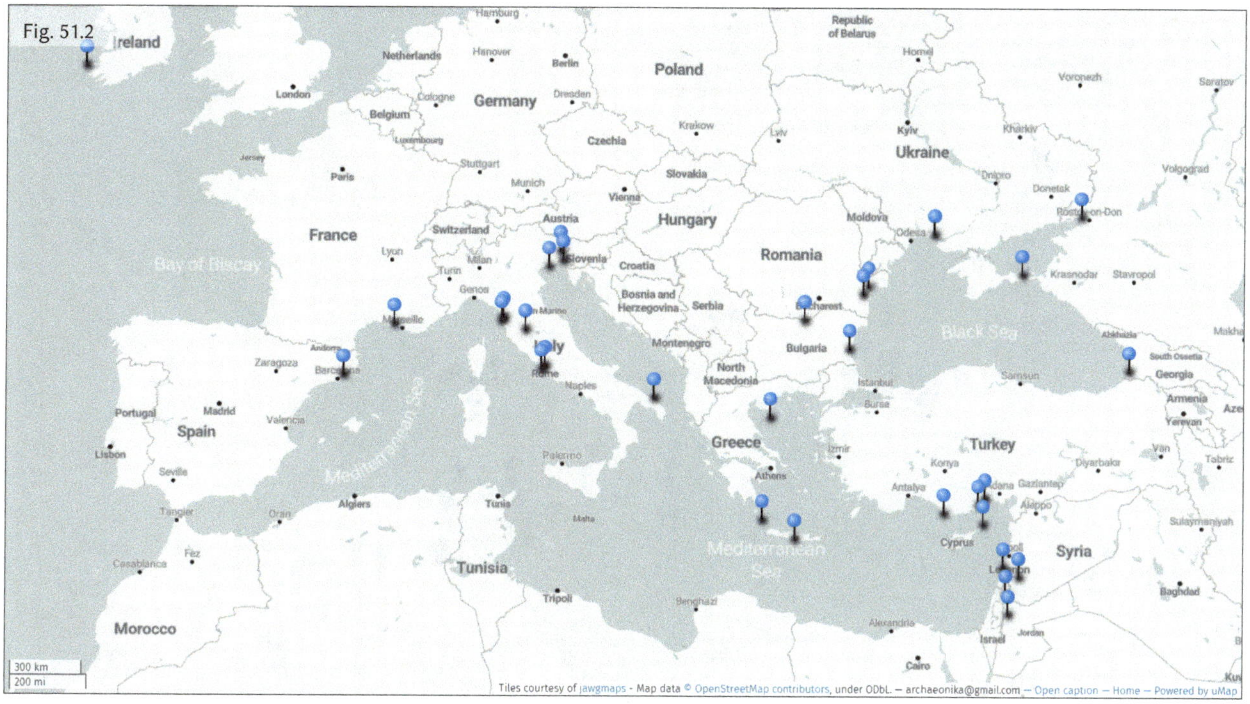

Figure 51.1–3. Distribution maps of LRA1s between the mid-/late 4th to the early 6th century (blue) in our catalog, including: from the mid-/late 4th century (light blue): A03 Antiocheia ad Cragum; A16 Elaiussa Sebaste; A41 Soli-Pomepiopolis; B03 Aphendrika; C04 Beirut; C11 Damascus; C15 Hippos-Sussita; C19 Iraq al-Amir; D03 Anchialos; D22 (L)ibida; D24 Novae; D41 Ulmetum; E13 Olbia Pontica, Borysthenes; E15 Petra/Tsikhisdziri; E23 Tanais; E24 Tyritake; G02 Antikythera; G21 Gortyn; G27 Kanistro; H04 Aquileia; H26 Giancola; H33 Jesolo; H45 Ostia; H50 Pievina; H52 Pisa; H57 Portus Pisanus; H63 Roma; H76 Udine; K17 Iluro; L20 Fossae Marianae; M22 Reask (conjectural); N14 Wadi Qitna; from the 5th century (purple): A02 Anemurium; A06 Aphrodisias/Ovacık; A46 Umm el-Tlel; A48 Yumurtalik/Aigai (Cilicia); B05 Ayios Philon; B06 Avdimou Bay (shipwreck); B10 Cape Zevgari (shipwreck); B22 Panayia Ematousa; C05 Beisan/Scythopolis; C08 Caesarea; C09 Capernaum; C18 Huqoq; C27 Mount Nebo; C34 Rehovot-in-the-Negev; D01 Aegyssus; D04 Bjolgrad; D05 Callatis; D08 Cernavodă/Axiopolis; D10 Constantinople; D11 Dichin; D14 Halmyris/Murighiol; D16 Histria; D21 Küçükyalı; D23 Madara; D29 Piatra Frecăţei/Beroe; D30 Razgrad; D34 Stara Zagora; D35 Sucidava/Corabia; D39 Tropaeum Traiani; E03 Cibilium/Tsebelda; E08 Kytaion; E11 Myrmekion; E16 Phanagoria; E21 Sinop B (shipwreck); F06 Arykanda; F13 Halasarna; F22 Klazomenai; F27 Knidos; F28 Kyme in Aeolis; F31 Limyra; F44 Sardis; F45 Side; F49 Troy/Ilion; G04 Argos; G06 Athens; G10 Brijuni Island; G11 Butrint; G12 Byllis; G16 Corinth; G26 Kallithea; G28 Kastri/Larymna; G32 Kryoneri; G40 Pefkochori; G55 Tonovcov grad; H06 Blanda Julia; H12 Casignana Roman Villa; H16 Classe; H18 Concordia Sagittaria; H20 Cosa; H38 Marettimo Island; H42 Neapolis/Naples; H44 Orbetello; H48 Paola; H51 Piran; H55 Porto Torres; H61 Rhegion; H75 Torcello; H81 Villa S. Giovanni di Ruoti; I29 Saint Jeremiah's Monastery, Saqqara; J33 Sidi Jdidi/Aradi; K02 Benalùa; K03 Braga/Bracara Augusta; K05 Cadiz/Gades; K06 Carteia; K08 Cetobriga; K11 Cubelles; K18 Iulia Traducta/Algeciras; K19 Málaga; K22 Puig Rodon villa (Corça); K23 Septem/Ceuta; L01 Aigues-Vives; L03 Antibes/Antipolis; L04 Arelatum/Arles; L05 Aubigné-Racan; L07 Avignon; L09 Baux-de-Provence; L10 Beaucaire; L11 Bordeaux; L14 Carbonne; L15 Collias; L16 Collioure; L21 Frejús; L22 Gap; L25 La Reille; L26 Laudun; L27 Lugdunum; L29 Massalia/Marseille; L31 Montille d'Ulmet; L32 Nantes; L33 Narbo; L36 Oppidum de Constantine; L38 Port-Vendres; L40 Saint-Cassien/ad horrea (Cannes); L41 Saint-Julien-les-Martigues; L44 Saint-Raphaël; L45 Saint-Tropez/Athenopolis; L48 Tautavel; L49 Telo Martius/Toulon; L50 Toulouse/Tolosa; L51 Venasque; L52 Vénéjan; M05 Cadbury Castle; M10 Clogher; M11 Collierstown; M14 Garranesn (Lisnacaheragh); M17 High Peak, Sidmouth; M21 Portmarnock; N03 Ballana; N05 Firka; N06 Kalabsha/Talmis.

Fig. 51.3

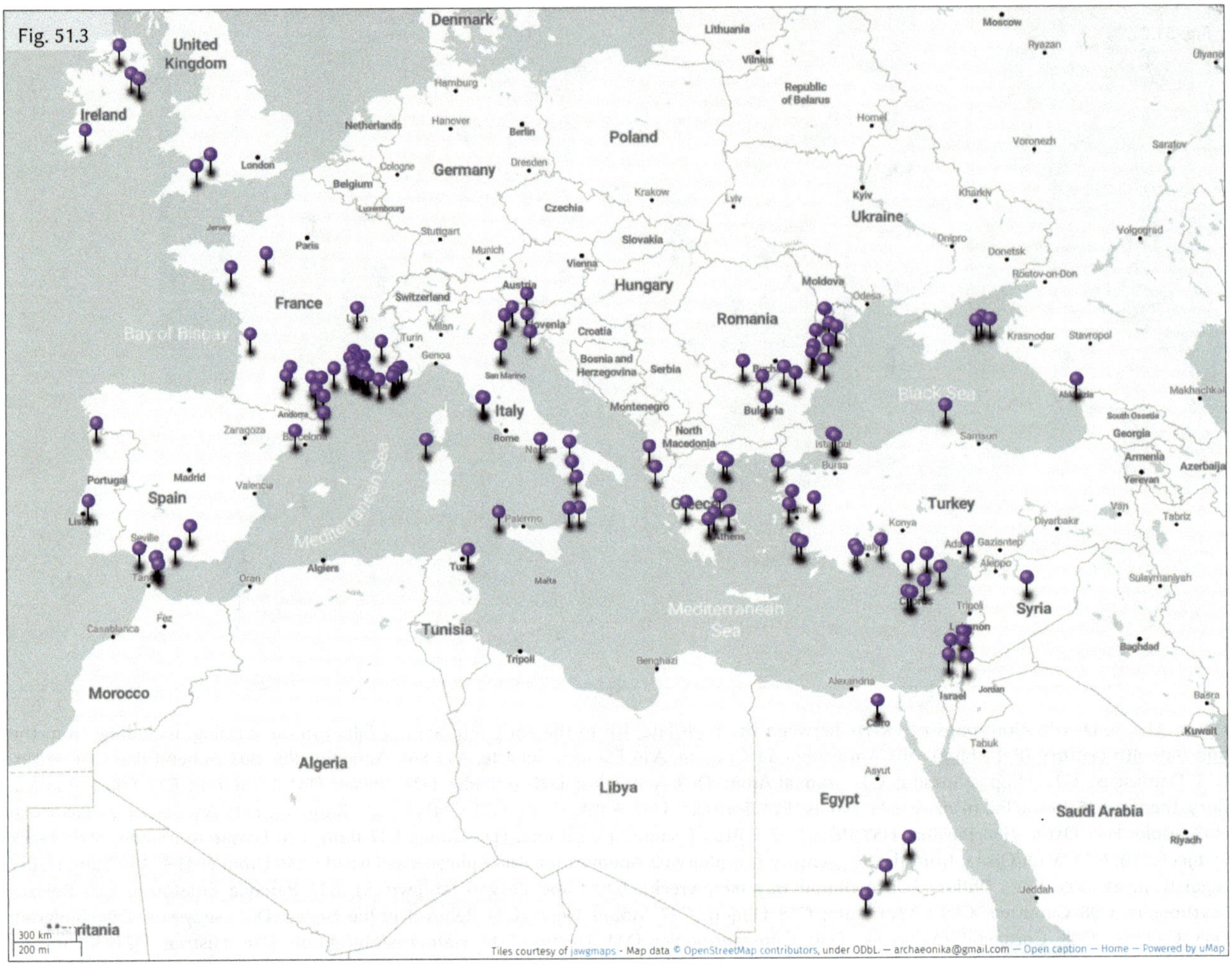

See caption on previous page

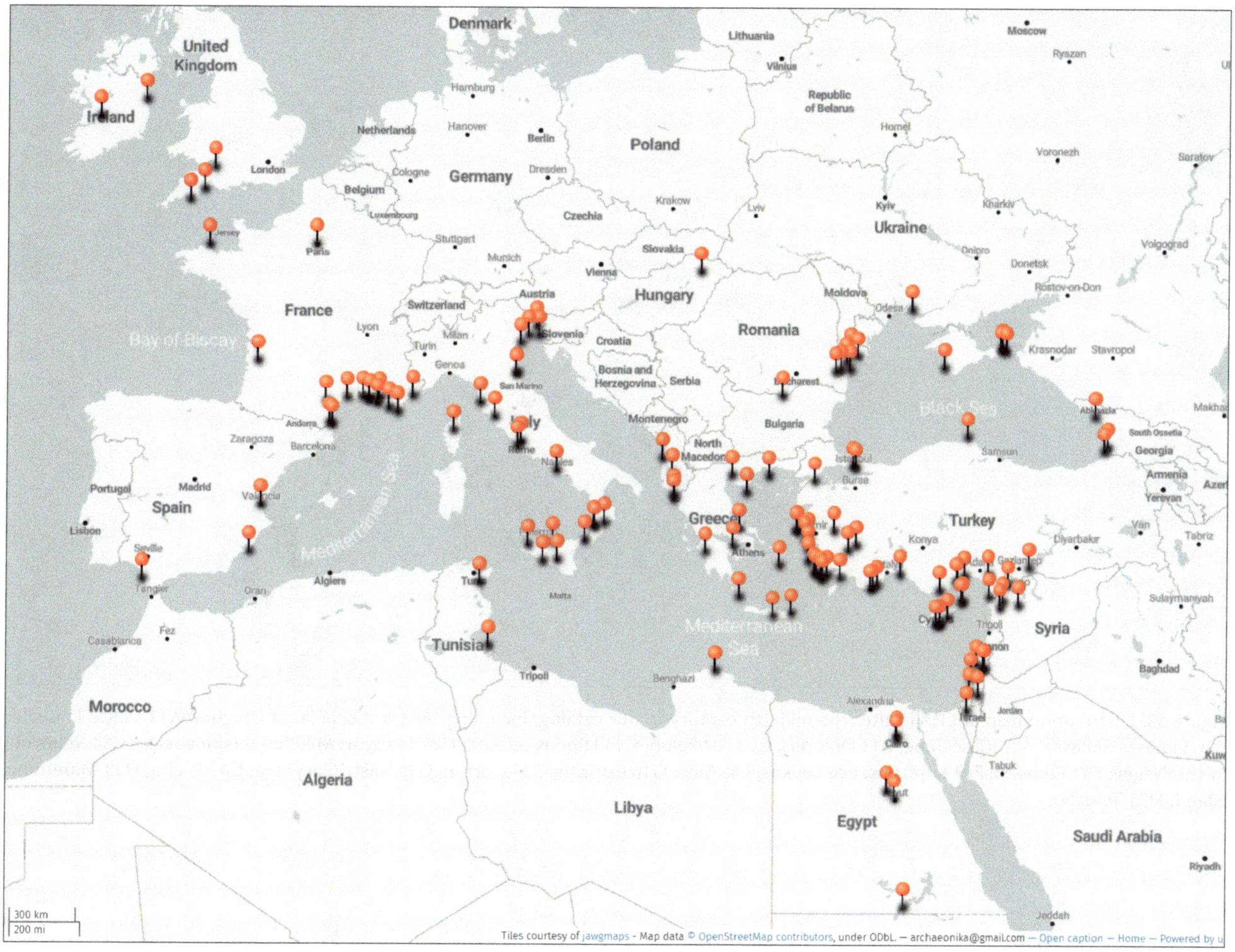

Figure 52. Distribution map of LRA1s from the early 6th to the mid-7th century in our catalog, including: A01 Androna; A05 Apamea; A16 Elaiussa Sebaste; A25 Kelenderis; A28 Korykos; A33 Qal'at Sem'an; A35 Ras el Bassit; A40 Sergilla; A41 Soli-Pomepiopolis; A48 Yumurtalik/Aigai (Cilicia); A50 Zeugma; B02 Amathus; B03 Aphendrika; B05 Ayios Philon; B13 Dodekaskala; B25 Pyla-Koutsopetria; B29 Zygi-Petrini; C08 Caesarea; C09 Capernaum; C13 Elusa; C18 Huqoq; C22 Jerusalem; C34 Rehovot-in-the-Negev; C35 Shelomi; D01 Aegyssus; D06 Capidava Fortress; D10 Constantinople; D14 Halmyris/Murighiol; D16 Histria; D21 Küçükyalı; D22 (L)ibida; D24 Novae; D41 Ulmetum; E01 Apsaros/Gonio; E02 Chersonesus; E05 Dranda; E06 Hermonassa; E13 Olbia Pontica, Borysthenes; E14 Pantikapaion, Bosporos/Kerch; E15 Petra/Tsikhisdziri; E21 Sinop B (shipwreck); E24 Tyritake; F02 Andriake; F03 Aphrodisias; F08 Burgaz (shipwreck); F09 Chios Site 9, Agios Stefanos Islet east (shipwreck); F10 Chios Site 10, South Prasonisi Islet south (shipwreck); F13 Halasarna; F14 Hierapolis/Pamukkale; F17 Kambos (Lipsi); F18 Kekova Island (shipwreck); F21 Kizilburun (shipwreck); F22 Klazomenai; F24 Knidos C (shipwreck); F27 Knidos; F29 Laggeri; F31 Limyra; F32 Marmaris B (shipwreck); F33 Mastichari; F37 Parion; F43 Samos; F44 Sardis; F45 Side; G01 Aliki (Thasos); G02 Antikythera; G08 Berat; G11 Butrint; G16 Corinth; G19 Dyrrachium, Epidamnos; G21 Gortyn; G28 Kastri/Larymna; G37 Olympia; G40 Pefkochori; G42 Phoinike; G43 Pseira; G52 Thessaloniki; G54 Tiszavasvári; H02 Akragas/Agrigento; H04 Aquileia; H15 Cefalù (shipwreck); H16 Classe; H18 Concordia Sagittaria; H42 Neapolis/Naples; H45 Ostia; H49 Philosophiana; H53 Piscino di Piscopio; H60 Ravenna; H61 Rhegion; H63 Roma; H64 Roselle/Rusellae; H68 Scolacium; H69 Segesta; H75 Torcello; H76 Udine; H78 Vada Volaterrana; H80 Vibo Valentia; I07 Baouît/Abba Apollotos; I21 Lamluda; I24 Manqabad; I26 Old Cairo; I29 Saint Jeremiah's Monastery, Saqqara; J04 Djerba; J32 Sidi Jdidi/Aradi; K05 Cadiz/Gades; K07 Carthago Nova, Karthago Spartaria; K25 Valentia/Valencia; L02 Aix-en-Provence/Aquae Sextae; L03 Antibes/Antipolis; L11 Bordeaux; L12 Bréhat; L17 Corte; L18 Elne; L20 Fossae Marianae; L23 La Capelière; L24 La Palud (shipwreck); L28 Maguelone; L29 Massalia/Marseille; L30 Menerbes; L37 Paris; L38 Port-Vendres; L39 Saint-Blaise; L49 Telo Martius/Toulon; M15 Glastonbury Tor; M17 High Peak, Sidmouth; M18 Inis Cealtra; M20 Mothecombe; M21 Portmarnock; N03 Ballana.

Figure 53. Distribution map of LRA1s after the mid-7th century in our catalog, including: A03 Antiocheia ad Cragum; A13 Delice kiln site; A16 Elaiussa Sebaste; A27 Kilise Tepe; B11 Dhiorios; C03 Ashkelon; C15 Hippos-Sussita; C25 Ma'agan Mikhael B (shipwreck); C34 Rehovot-in-the-Negev; F11 Emporio; F19 Kephalos; F30 Leukos; F45 Side; G16 Corinth; G21 Gortyn; G28 Kastri/Larymna; G43 Pseira; H38 Marettimo Island; H75 Torcello.

Chapter 8. Final Considerations: LRA1s as Transport Amphoras in a Changing World

Let us end as we began, by asking: What is a Late Roman Amphora 1? We have analyzed this form through multiple lenses, including typology, production, petro-fabric characterization, inscriptions, contents, and distribution patterns. Are we able to define it, at last? A technical answer is readily available: the LRA1 is the most common transport container in the Mediterranean from the end of the 4th to the mid-7th century, though it may be found before and after this stretch. It was used primarily by various actors on behalf of the state to fulfill the imperial *annona* wine requirements and for the commercial wine trade. Vessels were reused for a wide variety of purposes, chief among them the shipping of oil.

The earliest known evidence for LRA1 *production* may be found in a late 4th century kiln at Elaiussa-Sebaste (§3.6), and the latest at the Aegean workshops like Kambos (§3.9) and Laggeri (§3.12) which likely continued into the late 7th or 8th centuries. The LRA1 was produced in at least 21 different workshops in the eastern Mediterranean, and its morphology and volumetrics vary accordingly; it can be cylindrical, or slightly globular, or have a "pinched waist," and it is always covered in raised ribs. Volumes varied from at least 6–27 l, and probably more. The identification of LRA1s at a site means that the site was inhabited or at least visited at some point during the 4th–7th centuries and, further, that it was a node in long-distance wine trade routes or dynamic regional networks that reused amphoras for medium- to short-distance commodity shipping. Depending on the specific context and regional milieu in which an LRA1 is excavated, it may provide insights into: the growing influence of church estates on imperial and local society; burial practices of elites navigating their relationship with the vestiges of the old Roman lifeways; subsistence strategies in fortified settlements along the Byzantine Danubian frontier; and/or diplomatic conversations between polities looking to bolster their defenses or economic ties.

To, let us say, a successful small-scale merchant living in an eastern Mediterranean port city during the early 6th century, an LRA1 was a commonplace and useful shipping container (though perhaps more generic than other amphora types) that contained quality wine to buy or sell. For a devout Christian residing in a semi-remote monastic complex in the Iberian Peninsula, the amphora carried an intrinsic value alongside its wine: a sense of connection with the heartland of the devotee's faith. When petrographic analysis is feasible, an LRA1 can show discrete and multicomponent trade routes from a ceramic production facility all the way to these imaginary consumer's residences or workplaces.

There are also more open-ended, and therefore exciting, "big picture" answers to our query. The LRA1 phenomenon represents a tangible step in the evolution of maritime shipping from the earliest origins of ceramics to the present day. It is one of the best-known markers of the shift from content-specific vessels in the Hellenistic and Roman periods (think branding) to the generic and multifunctional koine of the Byzantine period. Narrowing this transition to a particular point in space and time is not possible (at least, at the moment) but the macro-trend is nevertheless well-attested over the second half of the LRA1's lifespan. Sometimes, this simple question may be better addressed through its negation—What is an LRA1 *not*? It is not, and perhaps never will be, a high-resolution temporal marker that will aid in dating a site to the level of a half-century. The creation of our synchronic and diachronic distribution maps illustrates the intrinsic difficulties in narrowing down the broad LRA1 chronology, which is too often based on typology. Unfortunately, attempts at constructing meticulous, clear-cut typologies that would enable high-confidence chronological inferences clash with the high variability of vessel forms, volumes, and capacities. This diversity is a natural product of massive popularity and scale of production. Thus, the LRA1 is probably *not* a ceramic type for which scholars in the future will hone a rigorously tested morphological sequence that can be universally applied to any instance of the amphora.

We hope that this handbook will prove to be just the first section of a new chapter in the broad study of transport amphoras like the LRA1. The earliest stages of the research on many of these types of vessels, and certainly on the LRA1, were marked by the countless names under which the vessel was originally recorded, rendering it impossible to perceive, much less examine, the wider frame. The creation of the Late Roman Amphora nomenclature, and subsequent awareness of the broad implications that targeted analysis of the LRA1s would bring, opened a second, more dynamic phase that saw, among other things, the acquisition of instrumental knowledge on the areas of production. This second phase concluded with the development of assessed typologies, chronologies, local and regional distribution patterns (Pacetti 1995; Opaiţ 2004; Pieri 2005a). In the past twenty years or so, archaeological investigations and significant discoveries—most importantly, of actual kilns and workshops—opened the door to an entirely new realm of possibilities. It is our hope that this volume and the LCP will enable the study of novel challenges, such as mapping the directionality and intensity of LRA1 exchange routes, and compiling and studying discrete corpora of LRA1 *tituli* and graffiti as products of the now-visible trading sphere in which they operated. The first step in the pursuit of collectively attaining such ambitious achievements is clear. We should use the growing array of new digital tools to make our discoveries and studies readily available to the broader archaeological community. The LCP offers everyone the opportunity to democratize data access, which will in turn facilitate more robust research.

After revising such a comprehensive body of evidence, we humbly offer some words of advice on best practices when excavating, interpreting, and publishing LRA1s. First, it is not advisable to use an LRA1 to date a site, stratum, or locus more narrowly than the scale of a century to a century and a half. On the same note, caution should be taken when assigning a subtype to small fragments. The boundaries between LRA1 subtypes are fluid, and a single characteristic such as rim curvature or handle profile is usually not enough to distinguish between them. Macroscopic fabric descriptions, relatively cheap and able to be done in the field, should be given when possible, but on their own cannot support conclusions concerning a vessel's origin. For this, petrographic or other archaeometric analyses are necessary, as many of the clays used to make these amphoras share many geological attributes. Next, it is imperative to include stamps and inscriptions when publishing an LRA1 assemblage. Though these markings may not be decipherable in the moment, they can be invaluable for future scholars. Finally ... sign up to become a contributor on the LCP!

Chapter 9. Relevant Online Databases, Repositories, Discussion Forums, Webliography

§9.1. Roman Open Data, CEIPAC Database on Inscribed Roman Pottery

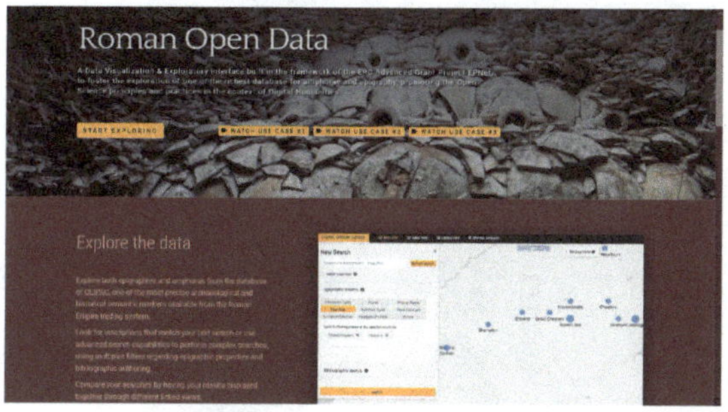

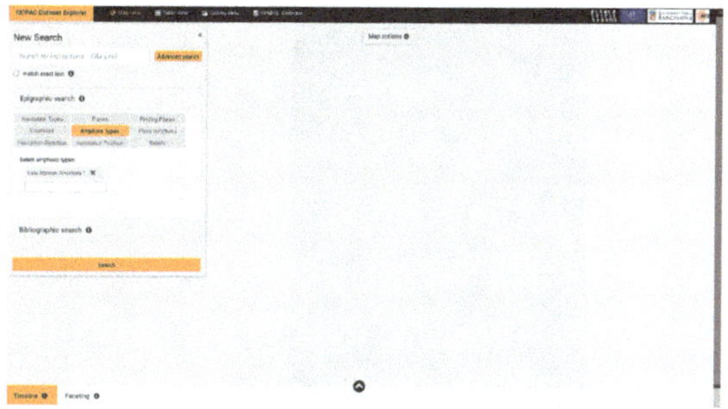

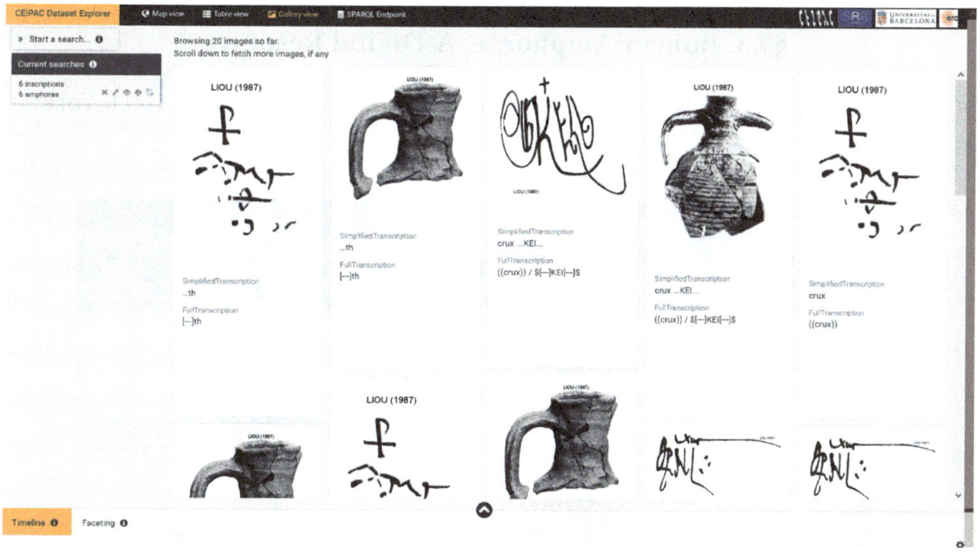

§9.2. FACEM Database on Greek, Punic, and Roman Pottery and Fabrics

The original time-span covered in the *Fabrics of the Central Mediterranean* database was the 6th to 2nd century BCE, but it has been announced that the platform would expand to include data from the 7th century BCE through the 7th century CE; the new release was expected in 2024 but has not been launched as of July 2025.

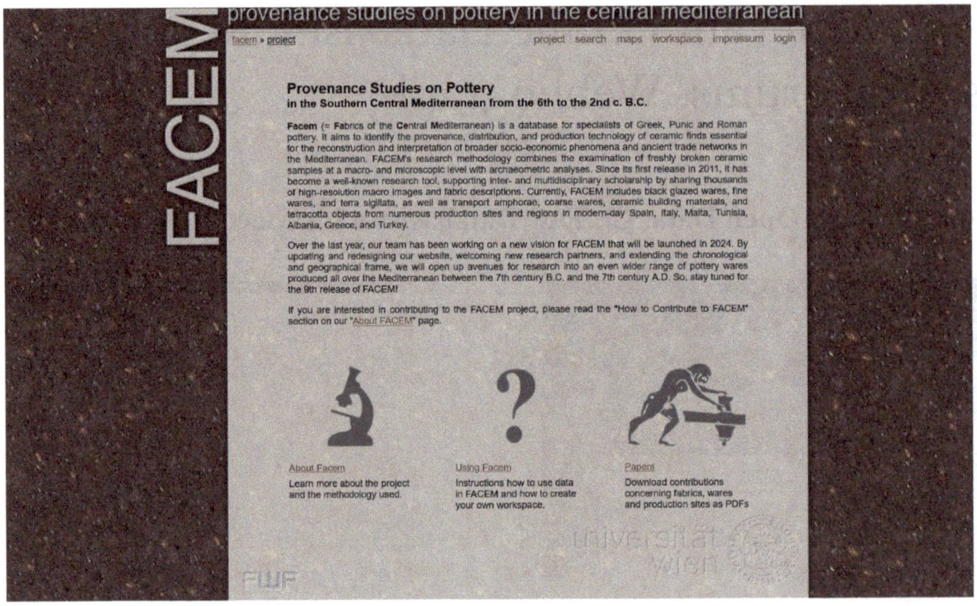

§9.3. Roman Amphorae: A Digital Resource

University of Southampton (2014) Roman Amphorae: A Digital Resource [dataset]. York: Archaeology Data Service [distributor] https://doi.org/10.5284/1028192.

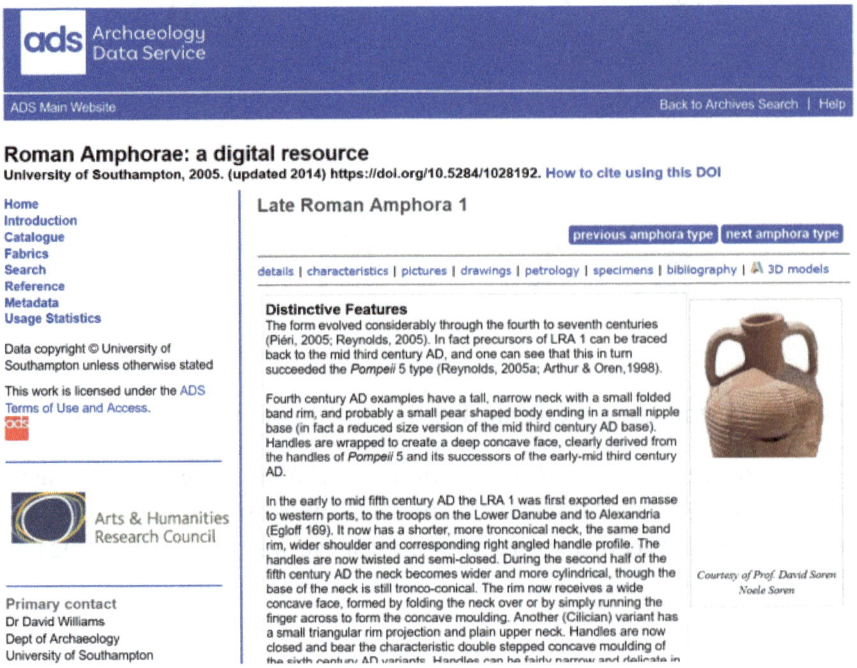

§9.4. Study Group for Roman Pottery

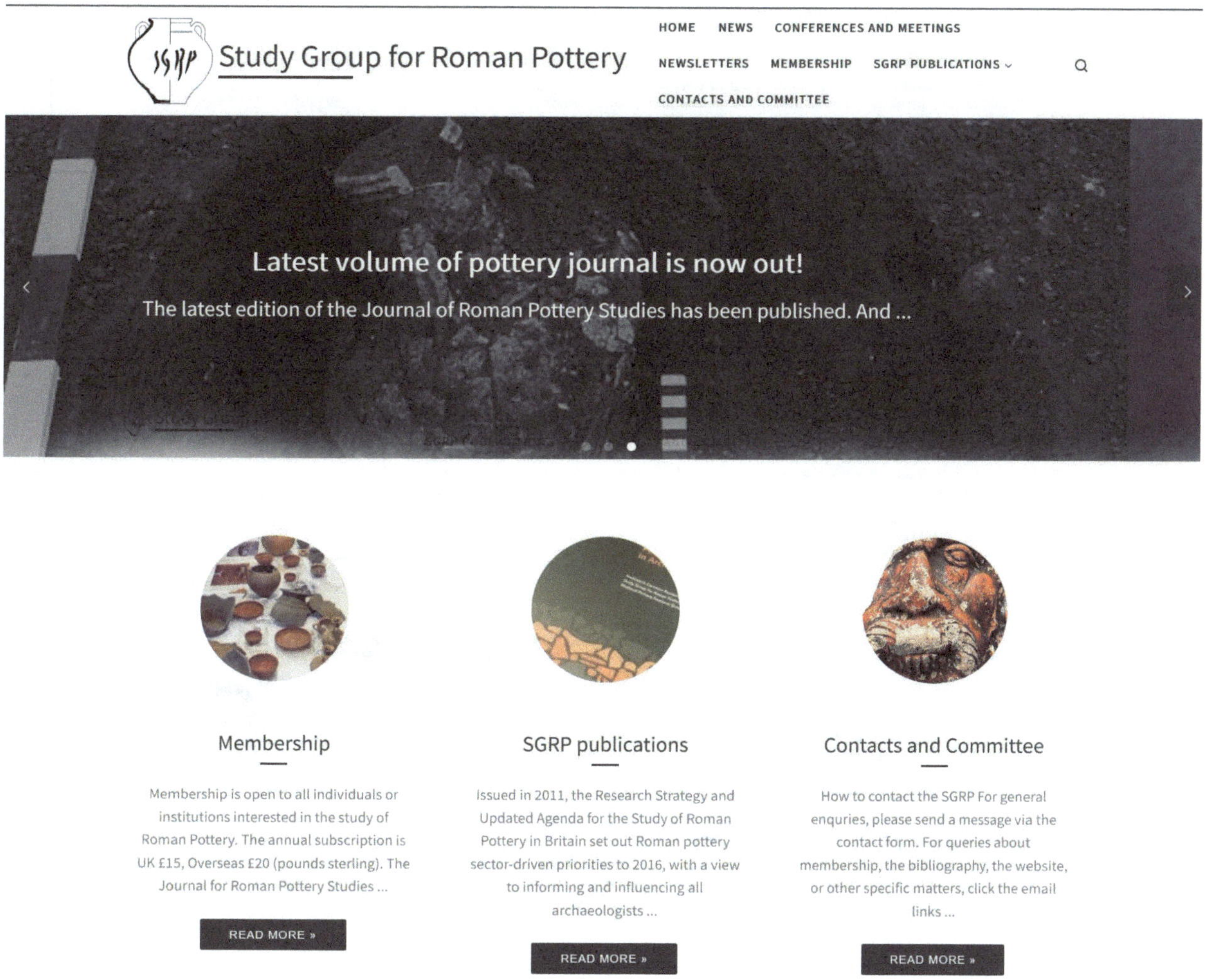

§9.5. Potsherd: Atlas of Roman Pottery

POTSHERD: ATLAS OF ROMAN POTTERY

Home » Atlas » Ware » B2

INTRODUCTION
- Atlas
- Publications

WARES
- All wares

CLASSES
- All classes
- Amphoras
- Terra Sigillata
- Coarse wares
- Fine wares
- Mortaria

SOURCES
- All sources
- Britain
- Gaul
- Germania
- Iberia
- Italy
- Africa
- Eastern Empire

MAPPING & DATABASES
- Terra sigillata forms
- National Roman fabric reference collection

OTHER TOPICS
- Tools
- Sherd scans

B2 AMPHORAS

An **ovoid two-handled amphora with a ribbed body** in sandy light-coloured fabrics. Produced at several locations in the north-east Mediterranean (Syria, Cyprus and south-east Turkey) from the 5th to 7th centuries AD, and widely distributed around the Mediterranean but more rarely in the north-west provinces.

ROMAN AMPHORAE: A DIGITAL RESOURCE
(University of Southampton, 2005. doi:10.5284/1028192)

Late Roman Amphora 1 (form)
LRA 1 fabric

Pages include details of typology, chronology, distribution, epigraphy and hi-resolution images of thin-sections. Access to this resource requires agreement to terms and conditions.

Fabric and technology

Hard sandy cream or yellow fabric with white limestone inclusions visible in the surface.

Forms

Two handled ovoid vessels with ribbed bodies, cylindrical necks and beaded or thicked lips.

Chronology

From 5th to 7th c. AD.

Source

Several productions sites around the north-east Mediterranean, including the Rhodes, Cyprus, but perhaps principally from the south-east corner of Asia Minor (Cilicia) and the Antioch area.

Distribution

Wide distribution around Eastern Mediterranean; rarer in west, but examples from Italy, Spain, southern Gaul, Switzerland, Brittany and post-Roman sites in western Britain.

Aliases

Augst class 58. *Keay* fabric 18. *Keay* class LIII. *Peacock and Williams* class 44 (Kuzmanov XIII, Scorpan 8B, Carthage LR1, Benghazi LR1, Keay LIII).

Bibliography

For sources: Empereur and Picon 1989. Distribution: Thomas 1981; Giot and Querré 1985; Bonifay and Villedieu 1989; Pieri 1998; Riley 1979. General: Tomber and Williams 1986; Fulford 1989; Reynolds 1995, 71-83.

References

Bonifay and Villedieu 1989. Bonifay, M. and Villedieu, F., 'Importations d'amphores orientales en Gaule (Ve-VIIe siècles)' in *Recherches sur la céramique Byzantine*, ed. V. Déroche and J.-M. Spieser, BCHsuppl, **18**, (1989), pp. 17-46.

Empereur and Picon 1989. Empereur, J.-Y. and Picon, M., 'Les régions de production d'amphores impériales en Méditerranée orientale' in *Amphores romaines et histoire économique: dix ans de recherche*, Collection de l'cole Française de Rome, **114**, École Française de Rome, Rome, (1989), pp. 223-48.

Fulford 1989. Fulford, M. G., 'Byzantium and Britain: a Mediterranean perspective on Post-Roman Mediterranean imports in western Britain and Ireland', *MedArch*, **33**, (1989), pp. 1-6.

Giot and Querré 1985. Giot, P. R. and Querré, G., 'Le tesson d'amphore B 2 de l'le Lavret (Bréhat, Côtes-du-Nord)', *Revue Arch. Ouest*, **2**, (1985), pp. 95-100.

Pieri 1998. Pieri, D., 'les importations d'amphores oreintales en Gaule méridionale durant l'Antiquité tardive et le Haut Moyen Age (IVe-VIIe siècles après J.-C.). Typologie, chronologie et contenu' in *Actes du Congrès d'Istres. 21-24 mai 1998. Société Française d'tude de la Céramique Antique*, ed. L. Rivet, SFECAG, Marseille, (1998), pp. 97-106.

Reynolds 1995. Reynolds, P., *Trade in the Western Mediterranean, AD 400-700: The ceramic aevidence*, BAR International Series, **604**, Tempvs Reparatvm, Oxford, (1995).

Riley 1979. Riley, J. A., 'The coarse pottery from Benghazi' in *Excavations at Sidi Khrebish, Benghazi (Berenice). II*, ed. J. A. Lloyd, Supplements to Libya Antiqua, **5**, Department of Antiquities, Tripoli, (1979), pp. 91-497.

Thomas 1981. Thomas, C., *A provisional list of imported pottery in Post-Roman Britain and Ireland*, Special report, **7**, Institute of Cornish Studies, Redruth, (1981).

Tomber and Williams 1986. Tomber, R. and Williams, D. F., 'Late Roman amphorae in Britain', *Journal of Roman Pottery Studies*, **1**, (1986), pp. 42-54.

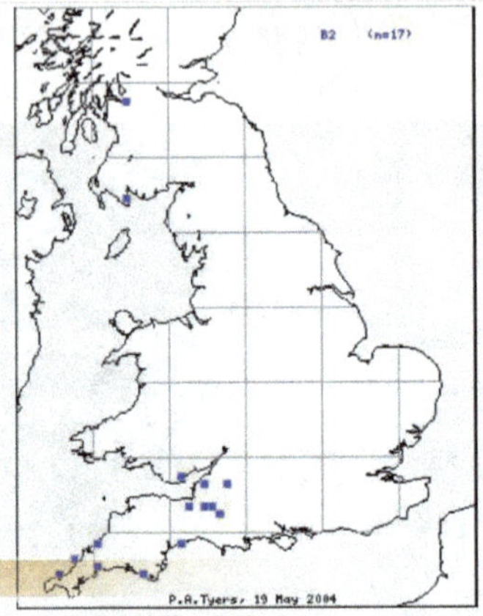

Distribution of B2 amphoras in Britain

NATIONAL ROMAN FABRIC REFERENCE COLLECTION
(Dore & Tomber 1998, Museum of London Archaeology Service Monograph **2**)

Fabric code: P&W AM 44 (Peacock & Williams Class 44 amphorae, p.108).

Thumbnail images

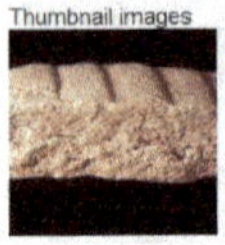

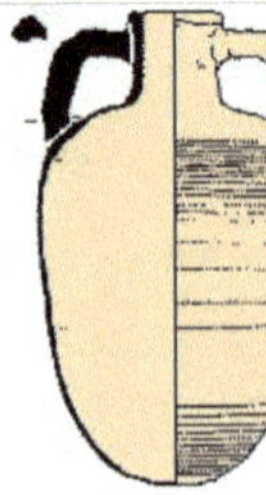

B2 amphoras

URL: http://potsherd.net/atlas/Ware/B2 • Author: P A Tyers © Text 1996, 2014: Layout 2012, 2014. Some images may be linked to other web sites.

§9.6. Regional and Local Databases: A Work in Progress

A preliminary list of online databases and repositories related to regional and/or local projects.

9.6.1. A. Cilicia and Northern Levant: Rough Cilicia Archaeological Survey Project (RCSP)

https://docs.lib.purdue.edu/rcas/
https://purr.purdue.edu/publications/3152/2

9.6.2. B. Cyprus: Sydney Cyprus Survey Project (SCSP) and Troodos Archaeological and Environmental Survey Project (TAESP)

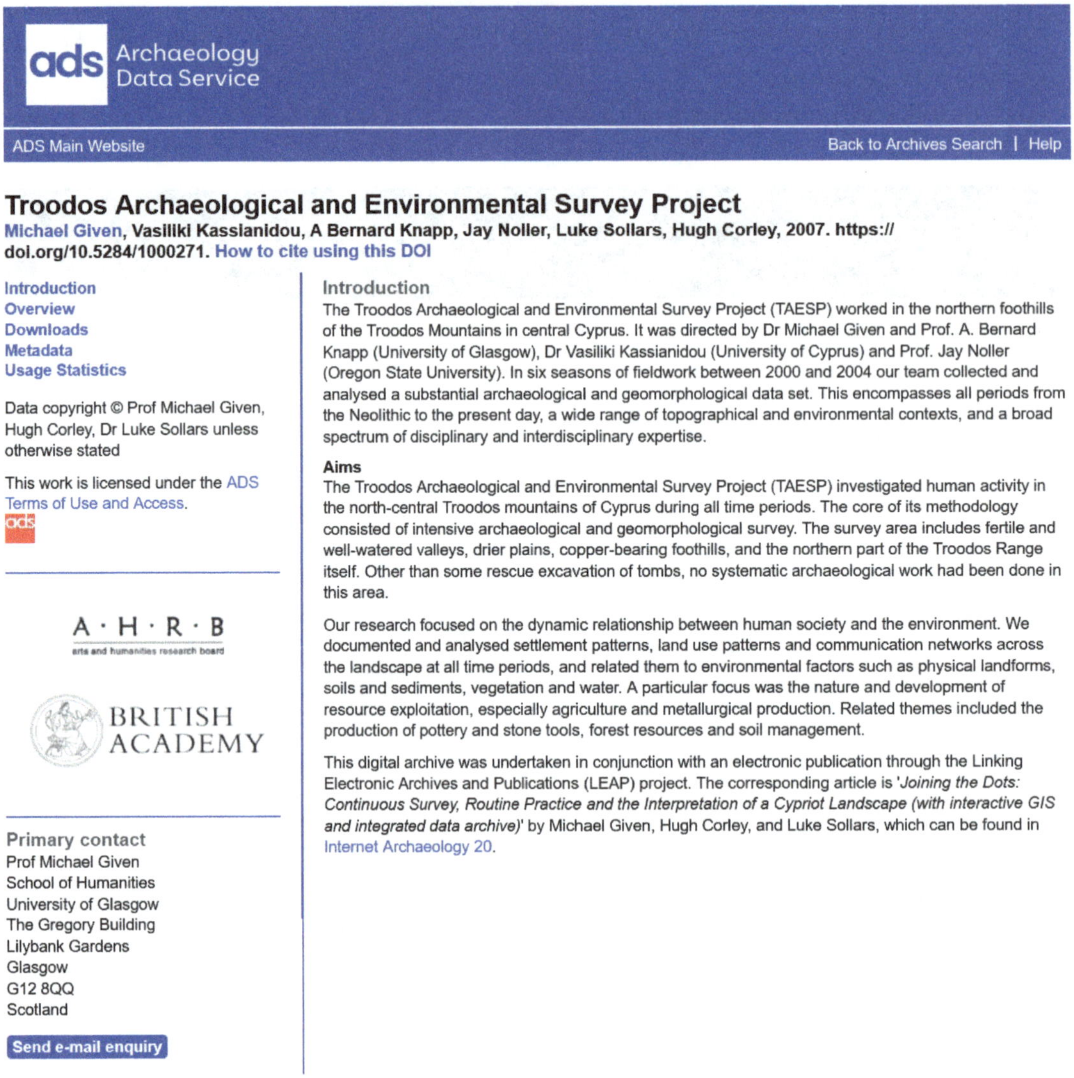

ads Archaeology Data Service

ADS Main Website

Back to Archives Search | Help

Troodos Archaeological and Environmental Survey Project

Michael Given, Vasiliki Kassianidou, A Bernard Knapp, Jay Noller, Luke Sollars, Hugh Corley, 2007. https://doi.org/10.5284/1000271. How to cite using this DOI

Introduction
Overview
Downloads
Metadata
Usage Statistics

Data copyright © Prof Michael Given, Hugh Corley, Dr Luke Sollars unless otherwise stated

This work is licensed under the ADS Terms of Use and Access.

A · H · R · B
arts and humanities research board

BRITISH ACADEMY

Primary contact
Prof Michael Given
School of Humanities
University of Glasgow
The Gregory Building
Lilybank Gardens
Glasgow
G12 8QQ
Scotland

Send e-mail enquiry

Introduction

The Troodos Archaeological and Environmental Survey Project (TAESP) worked in the northern foothills of the Troodos Mountains in central Cyprus. It was directed by Dr Michael Given and Prof. A. Bernard Knapp (University of Glasgow), Dr Vasiliki Kassianidou (University of Cyprus) and Prof. Jay Noller (Oregon State University). In six seasons of fieldwork between 2000 and 2004 our team collected and analysed a substantial archaeological and geomorphological data set. This encompasses all periods from the Neolithic to the present day, a wide range of topographical and environmental contexts, and a broad spectrum of disciplinary and interdisciplinary expertise.

Aims

The Troodos Archaeological and Environmental Survey Project (TAESP) investigated human activity in the north-central Troodos mountains of Cyprus during all time periods. The core of its methodology consisted of intensive archaeological and geomorphological survey. The survey area includes fertile and well-watered valleys, drier plains, copper-bearing foothills, and the northern part of the Troodos Range itself. Other than some rescue excavation of tombs, no systematic archaeological work had been done in this area.

Our research focused on the dynamic relationship between human society and the environment. We documented and analysed settlement patterns, land use patterns and communication networks across the landscape at all time periods, and related them to environmental factors such as physical landforms, soils and sediments, vegetation and water. A particular focus was the nature and development of resource exploitation, especially agriculture and metallurgical production. Related themes included the production of pottery and stone tools, forest resources and soil management.

This digital archive was undertaken in conjunction with an electronic publication through the Linking Electronic Archives and Publications (LEAP) project. The corresponding article is '*Joining the Dots: Continuous Survey, Routine Practice and the Interpretation of a Cypriot Landscape (with interactive GIS and integrated data archive)*' by Michael Given, Hugh Corley, and Luke Sollars, which can be found in Internet Archaeology 20.

Michael Given et al. 2013. *Landscape and Interaction. The Troodos Archaeological and Environmental Survey Project, Cyprus.* Volume 1: *Methodology, Analysis and Interpretation.* Council for British Research in the Levant and Oxbow Books. https://www.jstor.org/stable/j.ctv2xqng7r.

9.6.3. B. Cyprus: Pyla-Koutsopetria Archaeological Project I: Pedestrian Survey (PKAP)

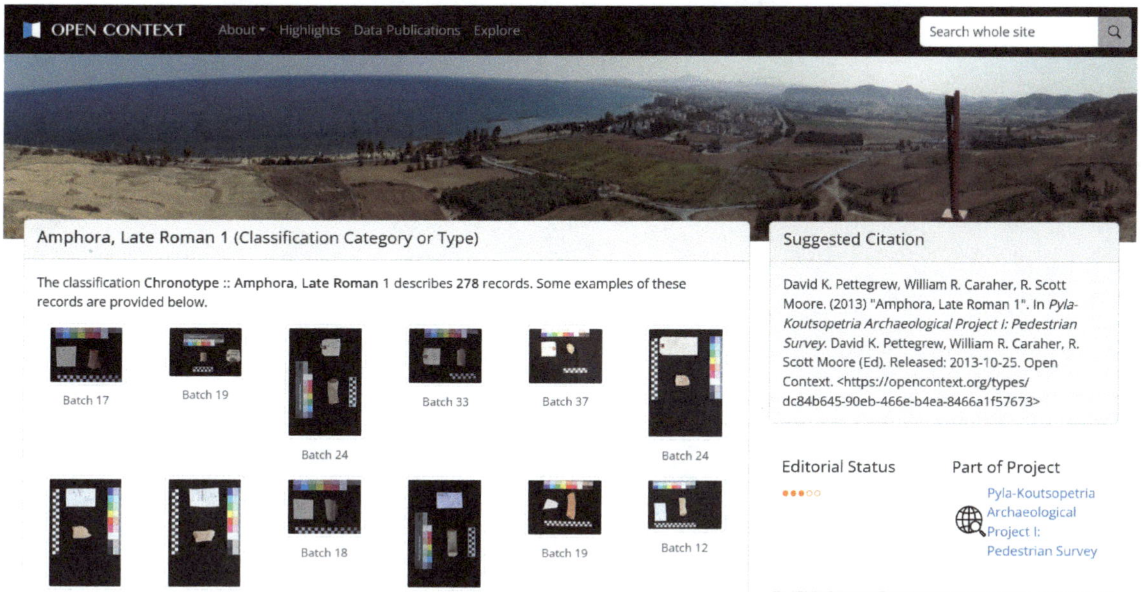

9.6.4. G. Greece: The Kenchreai Archaeological Archive (KAA)

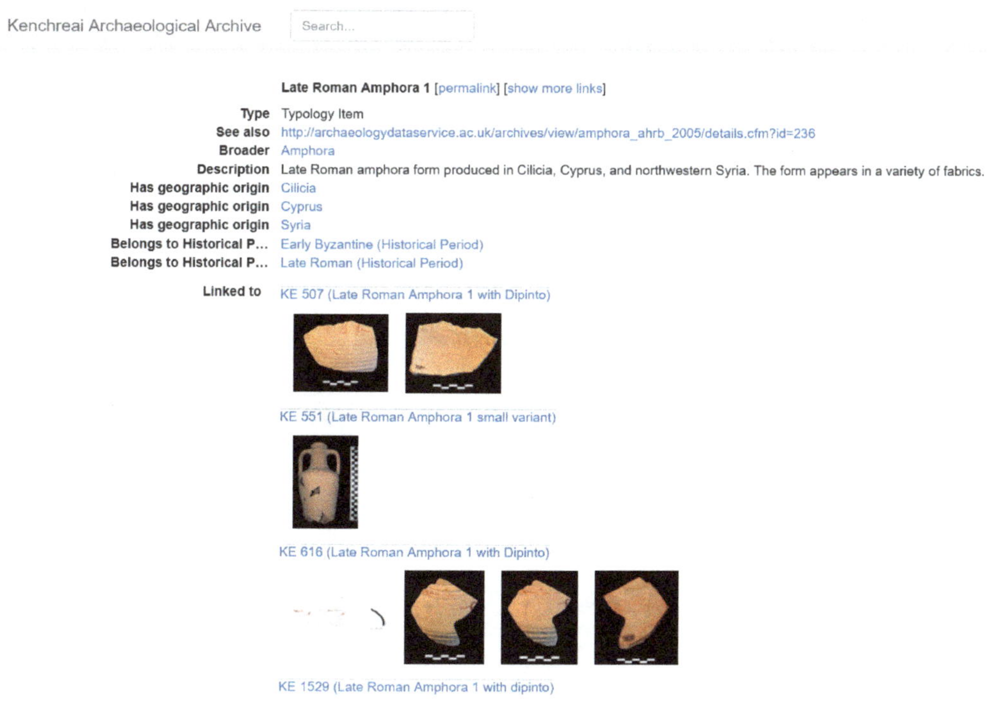

Chapter 10. Tables

§10.1. Production

10.1.1. Diachronic map of LRA1 production showing each workshop's output

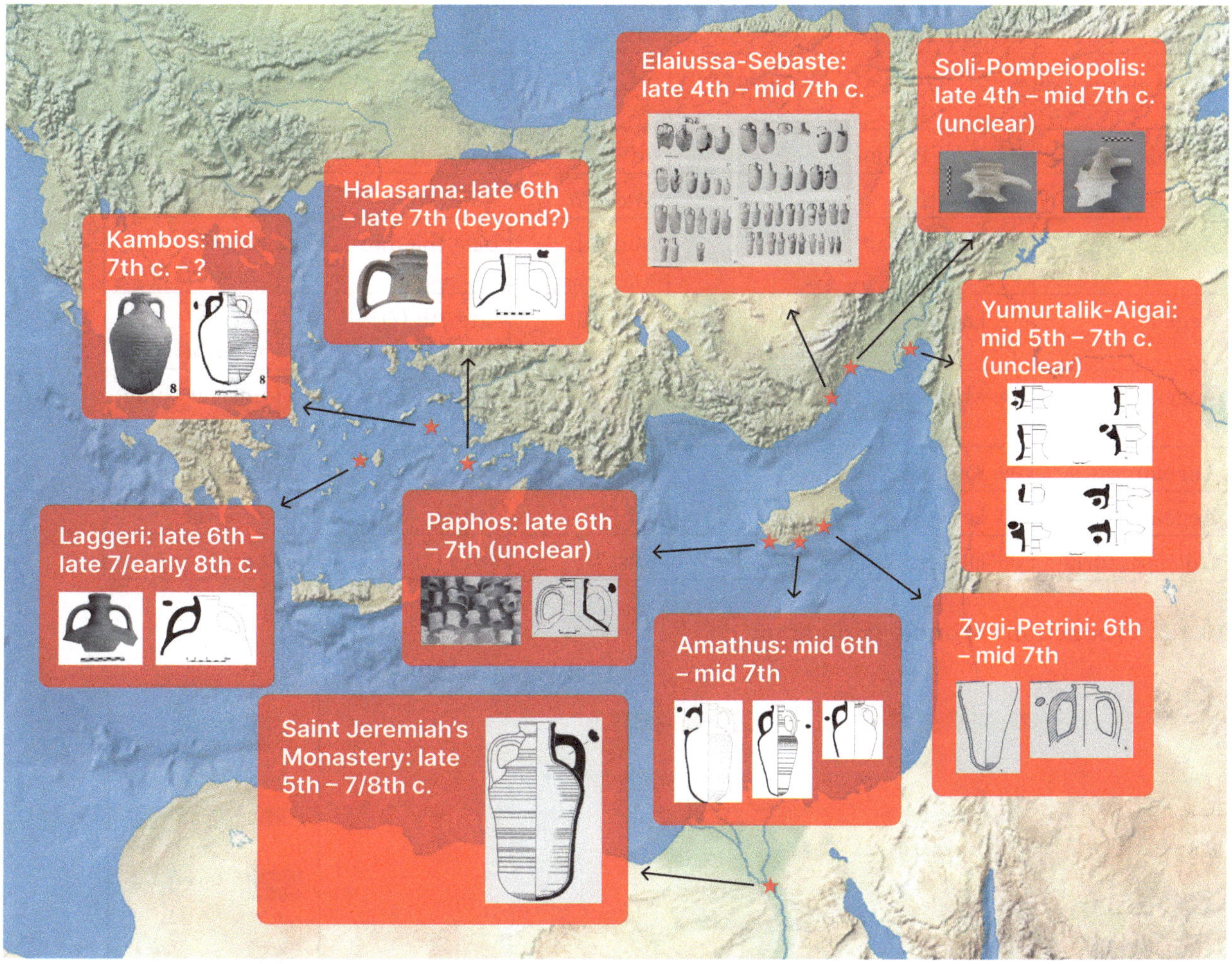

Note that only workshops that have preserved locally produced LRA1s are included. Unfortunately, many workshops have not been excavated and there are no published images of their products (graphics by G. Gillett).

10.1.2. Chronology of production centers' activities

Region	Production Center	Start	End	Type(s)
Cilicia/Isauria	02. Antiocheia ad Cragum	4th	8th	*survival*
Cilicia	06. Elaiussa Sebaste	Late 4th	second third of 7th	A, B, C
Cilicia	18. Soli-Pompeiopolis	Late 4th	early 7th	A, B
Cilicia	20. Yumurtalik	Mid-5th	7th	B
Egypt	16. St. Jeremiah's Monastery	6th	7th (?)	Egyptian type B
Cyprus	21. Zygi-Petrini	6th	mid-7th	B
Cyprus	01. Amathus	Mid-6th	mid-7th	B
Aegean	07. Halasarna	Mid-6th	past the mid-7th	B (and *survivals* ?)
Aegean	12. Laggeri	Late 6th	late 7th (?)	Parian *survival*
Aegean	14. Mastichari	?	early 7th (?)	unclear (type B?)
Aegean	09. Kambos (Lipsi)	Mid-7th (?)	?	B, *survival*
Aegean	13. Leukos	1st (?)	9th	*survival*
Cilicia/Isauria	05. Delice Kiln	8th (?)	10th (?)	*survival*

10.1.3. Production chronology diagram

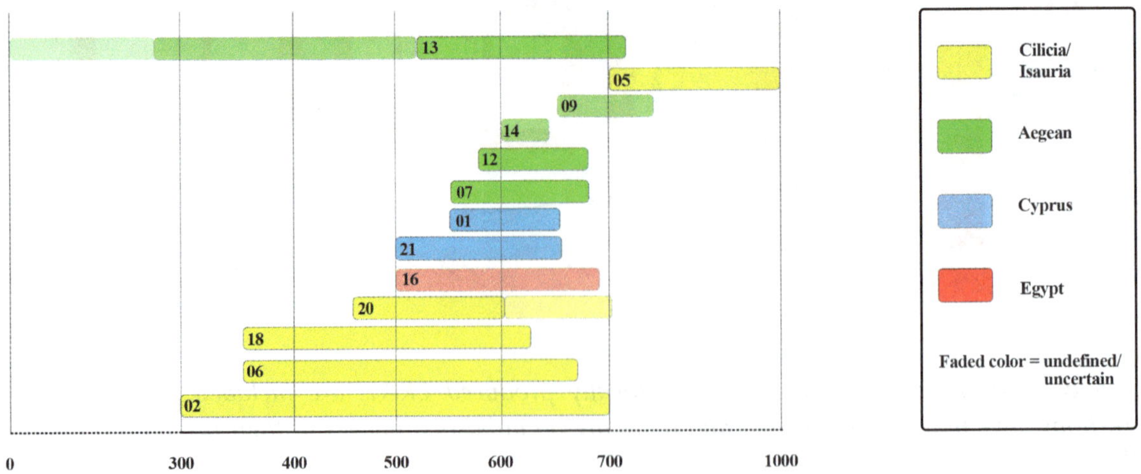

(graphics by V. Iacomi)

§10.2. Inscriptions: *Dipinti* Occurrences

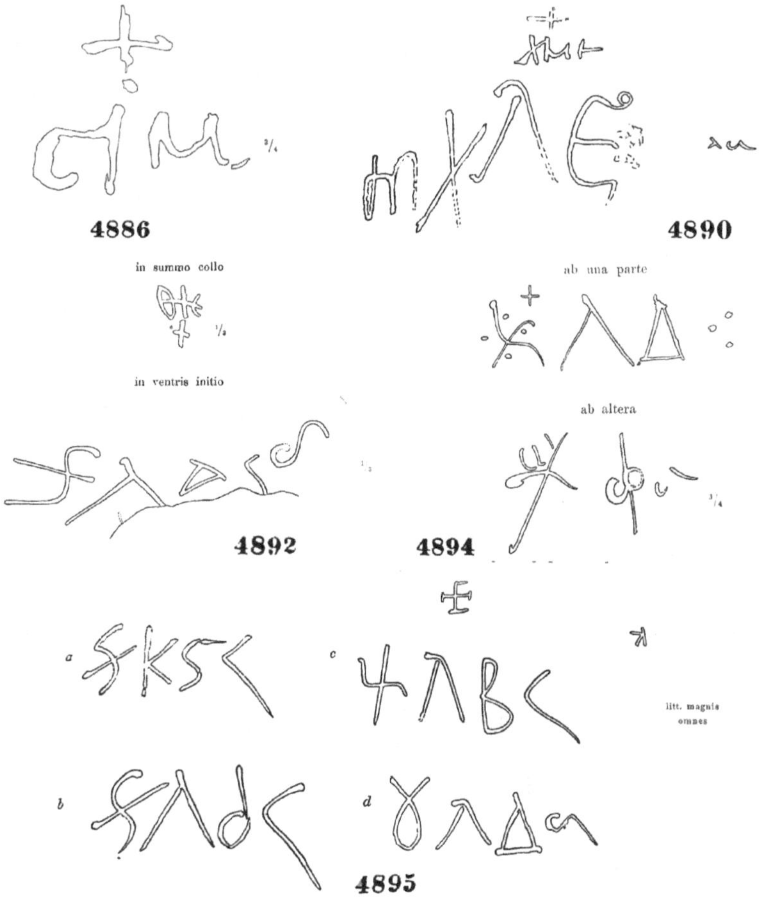

Figure 54. *Tituli picti* on LRA1s from late 1800s excavations in Rome, as reported in *CIL* 15 (graphics V. Iacomi).

We summarize here the type and occurrences of *dipinti* available in the existing literature. The table is not exhaustive, but we hope that it will be a first step towards building a more comprehensive catalog using digital tools like the LCP.

Table 10.2

No.	Site	Type of inscription	Notes	Reference	LCP vessel ID
A05	Apamea	-	Illustration only	Vokaer 2017: fig. 1.7	33726
A32	Palmyra	(c)	Reported presence of *dipinti*, deemed unreadable, in a few sherds; illustration only for one of them.	Majcherek 2019: fig. 4.7	33413
A33	Qal'at Sem'an	(a)	Illustration only	Pieri 2005b: figs. 7.42 and 7.50	33414, 33417
A40	Sergilla	-	Illustration only	Pieri 2005b: fig. 7.47	33389
B11	Dhiorios	-	3 or 4 lines of text, one tentatvely read as παλ, maybe for παλ(αιοῦ)?, written in faded reddish brown ink. Other marks and single letters might be referring to prices or number of vessels.	Catling 1972: 266, fig. 27	33449
B27	Skouriotissa-Vouppes	-	-	Given et al. 2013: 164, TCP554	33461
C02	Ashdod	-	The dipinto may be a Hebrew or Aramaic inscription, including the letters "א ח ה ת."	Freedman 1967: fig. 14.2	33473
C09	Capernaum	-	Reported	Schindler 2017: 408, cat. no. 56:46	-
C16	Horbat 'Aqav	-	Unintelligible	Calderon 2000: 134, fig. 25	33512
C25	Ma'agan Mikhael B (shipwreck)	-	The inscription has four Greek letters. Illustration only.	Creisher et al. 2019: 108	33519
C34	Rehovot-in-the-Negev	-	-	Rosenthal-Heginbottom 1988: 83, pl. II.125, fig. 70, ill. 282; 89, pl. III.126, fig. 69, ill. 271	33527, 33528
C41	Upper Zohar	-	Reported, not published	Harper 1995: 31, no. 146	-

No.	Site	Type of inscription	Notes	Reference	LCP vessel ID
D01	Aegyssus	-	Faint red dipinto on amphora AEG78/00029, but seemingly not readable	Stănescu 2018: 219	-
D05	Callatis	traces of (a)?; cross	Amphora KP 8 features a dipinto and painted cross above it, on the neck of the vessel.	Opaiț and Ionescu 2016	33949, 33950
D10	Constantinople, Saraçhane	-	Reported	Hayes 1992: 78	-
D12	Dinogetia	-	Extensive catalog fully published and discussed in Opaiț et al. 2022. Notable the *titulus* reporting the name and origin of the wine producer, and the type of vineyard.	Patabs IV; http://patabs.ge/7003/; Opaiț et al. 2022: pl. 49 nos. 1022 and 2001; pl. 50 no. 1080; pl. 52 no. 1283	34202, 34212, 34221, 34226,
D14	Halmyris / Murighiol	(a)	Read as ΧΛΓ...Πρ(εσβυτέρυ) (?), '33 *sextarii*...priest (?)'	Opaiț 1991: 146, pl. 17.103	34189
D16	Histria	(e) ?	One example published, bearing a single letter read as Σ	Bădescu and Cliante 2014 Derda 1992: 147, II.3, II.4	33557
D17	Iatrus	(a), (b)	Fully published and studied[1]	Conrad 1999, 2007: Pl. 4.1075, 1077, Pl. 15.1305, Pl. 16.1310	33894, 33896, 33898, 33899
D24	Novae	(a)	Interpreted as "tax notations or trade marks" (Biernacki and Klenina 2015: 108)	Biernacki and Klenina 2015: fig. 11.2 and 11.3	33930, 33931
D27	Orgame / Argamum	(e) ?[2]	Mentioned.	Paraschiv 2006: 89; Bădescu and Cliante 2014: 174	-
D31	Sacidava	-	Fully published and studied	Scorpan 1975: Pl. 3.7, Pl. 3.8 Derda 1992: II.1	33938, 33939

1. The abbreviations *chi + mu* (for *Christon Maria*?) and *iota + chi-rho* (for *Iesous Christos*?) are frequently attested; *dipinti* of the (a) type include the *sextarii* formula.
2. It is the red painted circle possibly to be interpreted as a control mark; see ch. 5.

No.	Site	Type of inscription	Notes	Reference	LCP vessel ID
D35	Sucidava / Corabia	-	Fully published and studied	Derda 1992: II.6	-
D37	Toprachioi	(a) and (d)	Illustration only	Opaiț 2004: 8, fig. 2	33943
D39	Tropaeum Traiani	(a)	Two *dipinti* and a graffito are visible, probably inscribed by a different hand, though whether they are all part of the original lifecycle of the vessel is unclear.	Grigoraș and Panaite 2021: pl. 8.43	34150
E14	Pantikapaion, Bosporos/Kerch	(1) Type (a) ? (2) (b), (c)	(1) Partially published. (2) Illustration only	(1) Fedoseev et al. 2010: 77, fig. 18.2 (2) Smokotina 2015: 126 (15.K09.305.16a, fig. 4.15; 16. K09.354.2161, fig. 4.16; 17. K09.354.2162, fig. 4.17; 18.K08.97.34a, fig. 4.18)	33619, 33621, 33620, 34786, 34787
E24	Tyritake	(a), (b), (c)	Illustration only	Smokotina 2020: fig. 32 no. A39, fig. 33 no. A40	33661, 33662
F03	Aphrodisias		Reported	Hudson 2008: 339, fig. 16 (cat. no. 3.32)	33682
F06	Arykanda		Reported	Yaman 2018: 295, Pl. 72 no. 476 and no. 478	33677, 33679
F12	Ephesus	(a), (b), (c)	Fully published	Sänger and Cesteros 2019: fig. 1–5	35185, 35186, 35187, 35188, 35189
F13	Halasarna	(a), (e) ?		Diamanti 2023: fig. 13 Diamanti 2010	30553
F28	Kyme in Aeolis	(a)	Reported, not published	Di Giovanni 2012: 161 and fig. 21a–d	33811, 33822, 33823, 33824
F38	Patara	(a)	Read as γλυκε	Dündar 2018: 171 and fig. 11	33698

No.	Site	Type of inscription	Notes	Reference	LCP vessel ID
F42	Sagalassos	(c)	Reported, not published	Bes 2022: 184, fig. 5, cat. no. SA-2004-DA-15.21	33845
F44	Sardis	-	Reported, not published	Rautman 1995: 49, no. 1.33 and fig. 9 no. 3.30 and fig. 26	33692, 33694
F49	Troy / Ilion	(a), (b), and (c)	-	Heath and Tekkök 2006–2009: no. 27	28289
G06	Athens, Agora	-	Full catalog, interpretative models	Lang 1976: Hc23, I45	35026
G16	Corinth	(1) (a) (2) various (Kenchreai)[3]	(1) On four lines, the complete set of (a) inscriptions. Fully published (2) drawings and photographs published	(1) Slane and Sanders 2005: 274, fig. 13, 4–8 (2) Kenchreai 2013–2024	34478
G18	Dion	(b) or (c)?	Briefly mentioned ("...traces of *dipinti* on their shoulders").	Fragoulis, Minasidis, and Mentzos 2014: 298 and 304, fig. 12.1	34829
G21	Gortyn	(b) or (c)	Briefly discussed	Portale and Romeo 2001: 330, pl. 83a–c	34469, 34470, 34471
G24	Itanos	-	Just mentioned	Greco et al. 1999: 528	-
G52	Thessaloniki	-	Just mentioned	Akrivopoulou and Slampeas 2014	-
G56	Torone	-	Visible in illustration	Papadopoulos 1989: 87, fig. 12	34057
H15	Cefalù (shipwreck)	(a)	Partially read (figure caption)	Purpura 1983: 102, fig. 11	34964
H16	Classe	-	One case of mention of honey	Cirelli and Lasi 2003: 55	-
H40	Milan	-	The inscription would refer to Chios (non vidi)	Mentioned in Auriemma 2007: 148	-

3. Note that Kenchreai is included here under Corinth, but the harbor is located several kilometers southeast of Corinth proper.

No.	Site	Type of inscription	Notes	Reference	LCP vessel ID
H42	Naples / Napoli	(a), (b), (c)	Fully published, it reads as Σεργί(ου) on the first line, ψ..ε... : ... on the second, and μ: 40 on the third.	Carsana and Del Vecchio 2023: 79, and 81 figs. 3.24	34939
H60	Ravenna	-	Some of the photographs published by Fiaccadori may pertain to LRA1s (body sherds); Cirelli mentions some inscriptions in Latin and at least one in Hebrew[4]	Fiaccadori 1983; Cirelli 2014: 543 and 551, fig. 8	34988
H61	Rhegion	(a)	acrostic χμγ	Racheli 1991: 711	-
H63 (HR01)	Roma: Schola Praeconum, Palatine Hill	(a), (d)	Published (not singularly) with analysis	Whitehouse et al. 1985: 200, no. 32	35175
H63 (HR02)	Roma: Temple of Cybele, Palatine Hill	(a), (d)	Published, with long analysis	Pensabene 1981: 190–195, no. 1, 2, 21, 22, 24 ; Whitehouse et al. 1985: 191–192, no. 7, 25–27	35176, 35177, 35178, 35179, 35180, 35181, 35182, 35183, 35184
H63 HR05)	Roma: Caelian Hill Houses	(a), (b)	-	De Rossi 1890; CIL 15: 4893; reported in Pieri 2005a: 83, fig. 40, with references	35174
H63 (HR11)	Roma: Crypta Balbi	(a)	-	Roman Amphorae: a digital resource, ADS collection 463	-
H63	Roma: Other various provenance	(a), (b)	-	De Rossi 1890 and CIL 15: 4886, 4890, 4892, 4895c–d, 4897; see below, figure 54	-

4. We could not ascertain whether the inscription *JIWE* 1, 10 (see Lacerenza 2003: 83 n. 56) was actually painted on an LRA1; cf. Dukan, Sirat and Zerdoun 1984 (non vidi). According to Rutgers (2020: 264 n. 11), the authors would have claimed the inscription to be proof of kosher wine.

No.	Site	Type of inscription	Notes	Reference	LCP vessel ID
H63 (HR14)	Roma: Vicus Caprarius archaeological area	(a)	-	Personal observation of one of the authors (V. I., March 2024)	-
I04	Alexandria	(a), (c)	-	Empereur and Picon 1989[5]	-
I05	Antinoupolis	(a), (b), (c), (d), (e)	See above, §5.1	Fournet 2021: 64, 67; Fournet and Pieri 2008; Fournet 2012: 253, fig. 6, 10 (right), 11	34794, 34822, 34823, 34824
I08	Berenice/ Benghazi	-	Just mentioned in the text	Riley 1979: 215–16	-
I12	Deir el-Naqlun	-	(1) Complete analysis and commentary; reference to high quality "sacred olive oil"; (2) mentioned	(1) Derda 1992: 141, no. I.1; (2) Danys-Lasek 2014: 566	34768
I13	Dime/ Soknopaious Nesos	(a), (c)	Only mentioned	Caputo and Davoli 2023	-
I20	Kellia	(a), (b), (c),	Complete analysis and/or illustration and transcription	Fournet 2012: fig. 2, 5, 8, 9; 2021: 65–66	35167, 35168, 35169, 35170
I27	Oxyrhynchus	(d)	Illustration	Fournet 2012: 255, fig. 10 (left)	34821
I29	Saqqara	(a)	(1) Just mentioned, brief notes; (2) illustration and transcription; (3) illustration and transcription	(1) Gascou 1987; (2) Fournet 2012: 253, fig. 7; (3) Fournet 2021: 64, with references	35171, 35172
I30	Taposiris Magna	(b) in black, (c) in red	-	Le Bomin 2016: 44, fig. 6.17–19	34817, 34818, 34819
J02	Carthago	(a), (b), (c)	At least 44 inscriptions are reported,	Davies 1984	-
J34	Tipasa	?	Indecipherable	Bonifay 2015: 534; Quevedo et al. 2023: fig. 13.13, table 7	35190

5. Empereur and Picon 1989, fig. 15: the amphora is preserved at the Graeco-Roman Museum of Alexandria (cat. 23025), but its provenance is not reported.

No.	Site	Type of inscription	Notes	Reference	LCP vessel ID
K24	Tarraco	(a), (b)	Reported and discussed	Remolà Vallverdú 2000: fig. 77.1, 77.4, 77.5, 78.3, 80.5, 80.6	34669, 34672, 34673, 34676, 34701, 34702
L04	Arelatum (Arles)	-	Fully published	Liou 1987: 122–23, A7	35019
L07	Avignon	-	Just mentioned	Pieri 2005a: 79	-
L29	Massalia/ Marseille	-	Only in black ink	Bonifay and Pieri 1995: 108; cf. Pieri 2005a: 259, pl. 19, no.3; Liou 1987	35020
L39	Saint-Blaise	(a), (c)	Fully published	Liou 1987: 125–28, SB1–SB2; Pieri 2012; cf. CEIPAC database https://romanopendata.eu	35021
L43	Saint-Martin-de-Crau	(a)	Partially read	Liou 1987: 128, fig. 38 CEIPAC database https://romanopendata.eu; cf. Pieri 2005a: 262, pl. 22 no.1	34595
N03	Ballana	(c)	Reference to the "high-trained vines"	Emery and Kirwan 1938: pl. 118 no. 40 (non vidi); cf. Fournet 2021: 66; mentioned in Pensabene 1981: 194; Hautumm 1981	35173
N05	Firka	-	Illustration only	Kirwan 1935: fig. 2 (top left)	34865
N06	Kalabsha	-	Illustration only	Strouhal 1984: 181–89, fig. 124 and Pl. 65	34180
N15	Wadi Qitna	(a), (b)	Brief description	Strouhal 1984: 181–89, fig. 141, no. P970	34181

§10.3. Consumption and Distribution Patterns

In the reference column we cite the relevant plates and/or figures of LRA1s from the bibliographical resources we consulted; unless stated differently in the notes, these vessels may also be found on the LCP through their unique vessel ID, cited in the last column. When the presence of LRA1s is included in excavation/survey reports or other forms of published pottery assemblages but *without images*, we use the phrase "reported in" before the reference; when the presence of LRA1s is indicated from to cross-references, we use the formula "mentioned in" before the reference; these vessels are not registered on the LCP. Finally, in the tables we use the following abbreviations:

LR=Late Roman
EB=Early Byzantine

10.3.A. Cilicia[6] and northern Levant

No.	Site	LCP region	Details (chronology, type, and notes)	Reference	LCP vessel ID
A01	Androna	Syria/Homes Desert	Mid-6th to mid-7th c.; more frequent than North Syrian amphoras	Reported in Mango 2002: 314	-
A02	Anemurium	Turkey/eastern Mediterranean	Beginning of 5th to 6th c.; type B, Cilician type C, potentially some LRA1 *survivals* (?); "by far the most common Late Antique to EB amphora at Anemurium"	Williams 1989: 95–97, figs. 56–58	33717, 33718, 33719
A03	Antiocheia ad Cragum	Turkey/eastern Mediterranean	Production center 02	Rauh 2023: 21–22; Dillon et al. 2019d (online repository with images)	35022
A04	Antioch	Turkey/eastern Mediterranean	-	Fisher et al. 2025	35023
A05	Apamea	Syria/Orontes Valley	ca. 6 to mid-7th c.; transitional type and type B; 11.6% MNI of all amphoras in presented contexts (4th most frequent type)	Vokaer 2017: 781, fig. 1.1–7, table 2	33720, 33721, 33722, 33723, 33724, 33725, 33726
A06	Aphrodisias / Ovacık	Turkey/eastern Mediterranean	LRA1s are the most common amphora from the LR period, representing almost half of all LR pottery	Varinlioğlu et al. 2023 (online repository with images)	33727, 33728, 33729, 33730, 33731, 33732, 33733, 33734
A07	Arsuz	Turkey/eastern Mediterranean	Production center 04	Reported in Empereur and Picon 1989	-
A08	Asar Tepe	Turkey/eastern Mediterranean	Sherds collected from field survey	Kızılarslanoğlu, Pejša and Rauh 2020 (online repository with images)	33735

6. See the open-access and extensive Rough Cilicia Archaeological Survey Project (RCSP) for high-resolution data on ceramics, including LRA1s, in Western Rough Cilicia (https://doi.org/10.4231/9SKX-FD80).

No.	Site	LCP region	Details (chronology, type, and notes)	Reference	LCP vessel ID
A09	Boğsak Island	Turkey/eastern Mediterranean	Sherds collected from field survey; 67% of all amphoras analyzed by survey team (the most frequent type)	Wohmann, Rauh and Varinlioğlu 2023: fig. 5.2–5.8	33736, 33737, 33738, 33739, 33740, 33741, 33742
A10	Charadros	Turkey/eastern Mediterranean	Sherds collected from field survey	Autret et al. 2019: charadros-2004-t2-u4-194 (online repository with images)	33743
A11	Dana Island	Turkey/eastern Mediterranean	Sherds collected from field survey	Varinlioğlu et al. 2020 (online repository with images)	33744, 33745, 33746, 33747, 33748
A12	Dehes	Syria/Orontes Valley	Type B	Majcherek 2019; Orssaud 1992: fig. B/2 no. 12	33749
A13	Delice kiln site	Turkey/eastern Mediterranean	Production center 05	Rauh 2023: fig. 30	30597
A14	Dibsi Faraj	Syria/Homs Desert	Fortified Christian town/citadel and possible garrison town	Mentioned in Pieri 2005a: 182, appendix 1; mentioned in Majcherek 2019: 402 n. 38; Leone and Sarantis 2020	-
A15	Diocaesarea	Turkey/eastern Mediterranean	Type B; most common amphora type in presented contexts	Kramer 2012: pl. 49 nos. 390-92	34096, 34113, 34142

No.	Site	LCP region	Details (chronology, type, and notes)	Reference	LCP vessel ID
A16	Elaiussa Sebaste	Turkey/eastern Mediterranean	Production center 06	Burragato et al. 2007; Ferrazzoli and Ricci 2010; Borgia and Iacomi 2010; Kızılarslanoğlu and Aytek 2018	30575, 30576, 30577, 30578, 30579, 30580, 30581, 30582, 30583, 30584, 30585, 30586 30587, 30588, 30589, 30590, 30591, 33102 33104, 33105, 33106, 33107, 33108, 33110, 33112, 33113, 33114, 33115, 33116, 33117 33118, 33119, 33120, 33121, 33122, 33123, 34579
A17	Gocuk Asari	Turkey/eastern Mediterranean	Sherds collected from field survey	Dillon et al. 2019a (online repository with images)	33765
A18	Hadir	Syria/Homs Desert	Type B; less than 1.05% of total ceramic assemblage in presented contexts	Rousset 2012: fig. 1.2–3	31426, 31427, 34137, 34138
A19	Halabiye / Zenobia	Syria/eastern mountains	Type B; less than 1.3% of all amphoras in presented contexts	Reported in Haidar Vela 2015: 187–88	-
A20	Hawarte	Syria/Homs Desert	Unpublished personal observation of G. Majcherek	Mentioned in Majcherek 2019: 402 n. 39	-
A21	Iotape	Turkey/eastern Mediterranean	Sherds collected from field survey	Autret et al. 2019 (online repository with images)	34094, 34095, 34097, 34098, 34099

No.	Site	LCP region	Details (chronology, type, and notes)	Reference	LCP vessel ID
A22	Kanytelis	Turkey/eastern Mediterranean	Mainly type B, but one instance of type A	Alkaç 2015: 149–50, figs. 1–3 (maps), 4–13 (vessels) and 14 (ceramic stopper)	34100, 34101, 34102, 34103, 34104, 34105, 34106, 34107, 34108, 34109, 34110
A23	Karataş	Turkey/eastern Mediterranean	Production center 10	Reported in Empereur and Picon 1989	-
A24	Kazanli	Turkey/eastern Mediterranean	-	Only mentioned (with no further reference) in Durukan 2015: 242.	-
A25	Kelenderis	Turkey/eastern Mediterranean	6th–7th c.; types A and B (from Elaiussa?); most common amphora type in presented contexts	Tekocak and Zoroğlu 2013: cat. nos. 10–32 and figs. 12–34; Zoroğlu 2020: fig. 7	34111, 34112, 34114, 34115, 34116, 34117 34118, 34119, 34120, 34121, 34122, 34123 34124, 34125, 34126, 34127, 34128, 34129 34130, 34131, 34132, 34133, 34134, 34135 34136
A26	Kestros	Turkey/eastern Mediterranean	Sherds collected from field survey	Dillon et al. 2019b (online repository with images)	34139, 34140, 34141
A27	Kilise Tepe	Turkey/eastern Mediterranean	ca. late 7th to early 8th c.	Jackson 2015: 360–68, fig. 7 no. J15/037	34011
A28	Korykos	Turkey/eastern Mediterranean	6th–7th c.; type B or transitional type	Alkaç 2012: figs. 1–14	33390, 33391, 33392, 33393, 33394, 33395, 33396, 33397, 33398, 33399

No.	Site	LCP region	Details (chronology, type, and notes)	Reference	LCP vessel ID
A29	Naula	Turkey/eastern Mediterranean	Believed to have worked as the harbor of Laertes. Sherds collected from field survey	Çaylak Türker 2014: 273, 277, fig. 2.3–4	33400, 33401
A30	Nephelion	Turkey/eastern Mediterranean	Sherds collected from field survey	Autret et al. 2019: nos. Sc_179a–f (online repository with images)	33402, 33403, 33404, 33405, 33406
A31	Olba	Turkey/eastern Mediterranean	Mainly type B, but some type A from contexts in the city's theater and monastery	Aydın et al. 2021: 143, pls. 2.1–10; 3.11–15	33750, 33751, 33752, 33753, 33754, 33755, 33756, 33757, 33758, 33759, 33760, 33761, 33762, 33763, 33764
A32	Palmyra	Syria/eastern mountains	Mainly type B, but some type A; 5.7% of all amphoras in presented context, predominant among the imports	Majcherek 2019: fig. 4, 399–402	33407
A33	Qal'at Sem'an	Syria/Homs Desert	ca. 7th c.; type B	Pieri 2005b: fig. 7.42–43, 48, 50	33414, 33415, 33416, 33417
A34	Qusair al-Saila	Syria/Homes Desert	Note that Reynolds contests that LRA1s were found at the desert *lime* site (2013: 105)	Konrad 2001: pl. 85.1, 3–4	33418, 33419, 33420
A35	Ras el Bassit	Syria/coast/An-Nusayriah Mountains	Second quarter of the 6th to early 7th c.	Mills and Beaudry 2010: 863 fig. A32.1 A1.2	31424
A36	Ras Ibn Hani	Syria/coast/ An-Nusayriah Mountains	Type B; LRA1s are purportedly the most common amphora type at the port city, with other forms including LRA4s, type D Snp I and North Syrian amphoras	Bounni et al. 1981: fig. 7; mentioned in Vokaer 2013: 489	33421

No.	Site	LCP region	Details (chronology, type, and notes)	Reference	LCP vessel ID
A37	Resafa / Sergiopolis	Syria/Homs Desert	Unknown types, but maybe B; note that Reynolds contests that LRA1s are found at the desert *lime* site (2013: 105)	Mentioned in Pieri 2005a: 183	-
A38	Seleucia Pieria	Turkey/eastern Mediterranean	Production center 17	Reported in Empereur and Picon 1989. Mentioned in Williams 2005a	-
A39	Selinus	Turkey/eastern Mediterranean	Sherds collected from field survey	Dillon et al. 2019c (online repository with images)	33422, 33423, 33424, 33425
A40	Sergilla	Syria/Homs Desert	ca. 7th c.; type B	Pieri 2005b: fig. 7.39–41, 44–47, 49	33389, 33426, 33427, 33428, 33429, 33430, 33431, 33432
A41	Soli-Pompeiopolis	Turkey/eastern Mediterranean	Production center 18	Autret, Yağci, and Rauh 2010: figs. 6–8	20497, 20498
A42	Syedra	Turkey/eastern Mediterranean	Collected from the surface of several agricultural installations in the hills around Syedra	Reported in Can et al. 2017: 245	-
A43	Tahta Limani	Turkey/eastern Mediterranean	Sherds collected from field survey	Varinlioğlu et al. 2020 (online repository with images)	33433, 33434
A44	Tarsus	Turkey/eastern Mediterranean	Production center 19	Reported in Empereur and Picon 1989: 241; Alkaç and Adibelli 2024: fig. 9	33435
A45	Terimini	Turkey/eastern Mediterranean	Sherds collected from field survey	Varinlioğlu et al. 2020 (online repository with images)	33436
A46	Umm el-Tlel	Syria/Al-Jazira	5th–6th c.; LRA3s were also found at the desert *lime*	Reported in Majcherek and Taha 2004: 232–33	-
A47	Yılanlı Island (shipwreck)	Turkey/eastern Mediterranean	See table 10.3.S2	Reported in Bilir 2017	-

No.	Site	LCP region	Details (chronology, type, and notes)	Reference	LCP vessel ID
A48	Yumurtalik / Aigai (Cilicia)	Turkey/eastern Mediterranean	Production center 20	Şenol and Alkaç 2017: figs. 7–16	30564, 30565, 30566, 30567, 30568, 30569, 30570, 30571, 30572, 30573
A49	Zephyrion/ Mersin	Turkey/eastern Mediterranean	-	Only mentioned (with no further reference) in Durukan 2015: 242.	-
A50	Zeugma	Turkey/central Euphrates	Mid 6th to early 7th c.; types A, B, C	Reynolds 2013: 102, table 1, fig. 12	28290

10.3.B. Cyprus[7]

No.	Site	LCP region	Details (chronology, type, and notes)	Reference	LCP vessel ID
B01	Alassa	Cyprus/western south coast	-	Mentioned in Demesticha and Michaelides 2001: 292	-
B02	Amathus	Cyprus/eastern south coast	Production center 01	Empereur 2018: 181–185, fig. 1 and 3	30556, 30557, 30558, 30559, 30560
B03	Aphendrika	Cyprus/Karpass Peninsula	Probably the harbor of the still unidentified Urania. LRA1s (possibly types A and B) represent 76–82% of the amphora assemblage between the 4th and the 7th c.	Kiessel, Saymanlier, and Taluğ 2024: 150, 152, and 169, fig. 12–13	33437, 33438
B04	Ayia Marina-Mavrovouni	Cyprus/Troodos Mountains	Type B (?); sherds collected from field survey	Given and Sollars 2013: 14; Given et al. 2013: TCP591	33439

7. Detailed and high-resolution data on ceramics, including LRA1s, in Cyprus are available in open access online repositories of local and/or regional projects; see above, §9.6.2 (https://doi.org/10.5284/1000271 and https://www.jstor.org/stable/j.ctv2xqng7r) for the Sydney Cyprus Survey Project (SCSP) and Troodos Archaeological and Environmental Survey Project (TAESP); and §9.6.3 (https://opencontext.org/types/dc84b645-90eb-466e-b4ea-8466a1f57673) for the Pyla-Koutsopetria Archaeological Project I: Pedestrian Survey (PKAP).

No.	Site	LCP region	Details (chronology, type, and notes)	Reference	LCP vessel ID
B05	Ayios Philon	Cyprus/Karpass Peninsula	Early 5th to the mid-7th c.; LRA2s appear to be more common at the church complex that featured many *opus sectile* mosaic floors	Plat Taylor and Megaw 1981: fig. 42.362	33465
B06	Avdimou Bay (shipwreck)	Cyprus/western south coast	Type B; likely a secondary component to the main LRA4 cargo; see table 10.3.S1	Reported in Leidwanger 2007: 312	-
B07	Cape Andreas, Green's "Site 17" (shipwreck)	Cyprus/Karpass Peninsula	Types B and C, probably representing the majority of amphora types at Site 17; sherds coll., see table 10.3.S1	Green 1973: figs. 21–22	30595
B08	Cape Kiti/Kition	Cyprus/eastern south coast	Types A and B, and Cypriot type C, of which type B is the most frequent; LRA1s are together the predominant type in the assemblages around Cape Kiti	Envig and Astrom 1975: figs. 24, 27, 28; Demesticha 2015: figs. 3, 6, 7, table 2	33440, 33441, 33442, 33443, 33444, 33445
B09	Cape Petounda	Cyprus/eastern south coast	Unknown types found alongside LRA4s, near an early Christian baptistery	Reported in Papakosta 2020	-
B10	Cape Zevgari (shipwreck)	Cyprus/eastern south coast	Type B made up the entire ship's amphora cargo (just over 150 amphoras see table 10.3.S1	Leidwanger 2007: figs. 3–4	33446, 33447
B11	Dhiorios	Cyprus/Kyrenia Mountains and north coast	Ca. second half of 7th c., but likely not a part of the ceramic workshop's output	Catling 1972: figs. 20.P 319, 27.P 266	33448, 33449
B12	Dodekaskala	Cyprus/Troodos Mountains	Four of the five LR amphora sherds collected from field surveys at Dodekaskala were LRA1s	Reported in Boutin and Given 2013: table 3.8	-

No.	Site	LCP region	Details (chronology, type, and notes)	Reference	LCP vessel ID
B13	Kalavassos-Kopetra	Cyprus/eastern south coast	6th–7th c.; representing ⅔ of all amphora sherds, ca. 13% of which might be Cypriot products	Rautman et al. 1999: 379; Caraher, Moore, and Pettegrew 2014: 126	-
B14	Keratidhi	Cyprus/western south coast	Type B (Yassi Ada type I); only one LRA1 sherd among at least four LRA2s and many nondiagnostic Byzantine amphora; collected from underwater survey	Reported in Morris and Peatfield 1987: catalog no. K 109	-
B15	Kourion	Cyprus/western south coast	Production center 11	Reported in Empereur and Picon 1989; Williams 2005a: 159 fig. 2, 164 pl. 2	33451, 33450, 34825
B16	Laonarka	Cyprus/Troodos Mountains	The single LR amphora sherd collected from field surveys at Laonarka was an LRA1	Reported in Boutin and Given 2013: table 3.11	-
B17	Lapithos	Cyprus/Kyrenia Mountains and north coast	Non vidi	Catling and Dikigoropoulos 1970: 47 (non vidi)	17010
B18	Litharkies	Cyprus/Troodos Mountains	A small number of sherds were collected from field surveys at the mining site, less than locally made types	Reported in Graham 2013: table 4.7	-
B19	Mandres	Cyprus/western Mesoria	Sherds collected from field survey around modern Mandres, three of the four LR amphora sherds were LRA1s	Reported in Given and Sollars 2013: table 2.15	-
B20	Maroni-Petrera	Cyprus/eastern south coast	21% of all LR amphoras by weight	Rautman et al. 1999: 379; Reported in Caraher, Moore, and Pettegrew 2014: 126	-
B21	Nea Paphos	Cyprus/western south coast	Production center 15	Demesticha and Michaelides 2001: 290, fig. 9–10	35024

No.	Site	LCP region	Details (chronology, type, and notes)	Reference	LCP vessel ID
B22	Panayia Ematousa	Cyprus/eastern south coast	Second half of the 5th c.; type B	Winther-Jacobsen 2005: 310–11, fig. 160.A6.13, A6.15	33452, 33453
B23	Pano Limna	Cyprus/Troodos Mountains	The majority of LR amphora sherds collected from field surveys at Pano Limna were LRA1s (61.5%)	Reported in Boutin and Given 2013: table 3.13	-
B24	Phoukasa	Cyprus/Troodos Mountains	A single sherd was collected from a field survey at the farmstead site, the only LR amphora found	Reported in Given and Sollars 2013: 18	-
B25	Pyla-Koutsopetria	Cyprus	ca. 7th c.; mainly type C; LRA1s were 30% of all amphoras from the LR period, 58% of which might be Cypriot products	Caraher, Moore, and Pettegrew 2014: 126–40, fig. 4.23 nos. 13.32, 18.42, 31.22, 187.12B, and 73.27	33454, 33455, 33456, 33457, 33458
B26	Salamis	Cyprus/eastern coast	-	Mentioned in Pacetti 1995: 278. Mentioned in Pieri 2005a: 182, appendix 1	-
B27	Skouriotissa-Vouppes	Cyprus/Troodos Mountains	Type B (?); the most common LR amphora type found in the main Skouriotissa slag heap	Boutin and Given 2013: table 3.27–28; Given et al. 2013: TCP531, 546, 554	33459, 33460, 33461
B28	Thalassines-Spilies	Cyprus/western south coast	Type B (Yassi Ada type I); the most frequent amphora type collected from the underwater survey	Morris and Peatfield 1987: catalog nos. TS 114–115b (no images), 117–118; 120, 122, 129 (no images) and 130	33462, 33463, 33464
B29	Zygi-Petrini	Cyprus/eastern south coast	Production center 21	Manning et al. 2000: fig. 13	30600, 30601

10.3.C. Southern Levant

No.	Site	LCP region	Details (chronology, type, and notes)	Reference	LCP vessel ID
C01	Aila/Aqaba	Jordan/Wadi ʿArabah	-	Mentioned in Tomber 2004: 400	-
C02	Ashdod	Israel-Palestinian Authority/southern coastal plain	-	Freedman 1967: 34 and 69, fig. 14.2	33473
C03	Ashkelon	Israel-Palestinian Authority/southern coastal plain	7th–12th c.; type A (?) and B	Johnson 2008: nos. 486–489	28238, 28239, 28794, 28795
C04	Beirut	Lebanon/northern coast	Late 4th to the late 6th c.; types A and B; increased from 6.09% (late 4th c.) to 9.3% (early 5th) to 43% (late 6th) of amphora imports, frequently alongside LRA4, bag-shaped jars, and Sinopean amphoras	Reynolds 2010b: tables 2b–6, fig. 4e	33474
C05	Beisan / Scythopolis	Israel/Beth She'an Valley	Early 6th c.; type B; one of four imported amphoras found in the southern theater	Sandhaus and Balouka 2015: fig. 4.9.4	33475
C06	Bethany	Jordan/Jordan Valley	-	Mentioned in Pieri 2005a: 182	-
C07	Bosra	Syria/Hauran	-	Mentioned in Bes et al. 2020: 61 n. 60	-
C08	Caesarea	Israel/central coastal plain	5th–early 7th c.; type B; with examples from contexts around Caesarea	Ratzlaff et al. 2017: fig. 9	28117, 28118, 28119, 28121, 28122, 28237
C09	Capernaum	Israel/Galilee	Late 5th or early 6th to first half of 7th c.	Reported in Schindler 2017: 128, cat. nos. 56:46; 63:4	-

No.	Site	LCP region	Details (chronology, type, and notes)	Reference	LCP vessel ID
C10	Chhim	Lebanon/Lebanon Mountains	Mainly type B, but also type A and transitional; LRA1s were the largest group of non-Levantine amphoras, at 61.1%, with LRA2, LRA3, Tripolitanian, and Sinopean amphoras also present; hypothesized to be non-Cypriot products	Wicenciak 2019: 318–19; 2021a: 106, pls. 186–190	33476, 33477, 33478, 33479, 33480, 33481, 33482, 33483, 33484, 33485, 33486, 33487, 33488, 33489, 33490, 33491, 33492, 33493, 33494, 33495, 33496, 33497, 33498, 33499, 33500
C11	Damascus	Syria/central Syrian plateau	4th c. (?); the single LRA1 handle was found in a phase containing rare Agora M334, LRA3, LRA4, and spatheion sherds	Tréglia and Berthier 2010: 871, fig. 3.8	31425
C12	Dor	Israel/Carmel coastal plain	Type B (including Yassia Ada subtypes Ia and II); found alongside LRA4 and LRA5s	Shalev, Gambash, and Yasur-Landau 2019: fig. 10.4–5, 10	33502, 33503, 33504
C13	Elusa	Israel/Negev	Mid-6th–mid-7th c.	Bar-Oz et al. 2019: table S3; Holmqvist 2019: fig. 5.17	33505
C14	Ein Boqeq	Israel/Negev	Type B; at least one LRA5 sherd was also found at the desert fortress site	Gichon 1993: tables 47: 4–6; 51:4	33506, 33507, 33508, 33509
C15	Hippos-Sussita	Israel/Golan	4th–early 8th c.; type B; found alongside LRA4s in a residential-industrial structure in the city	Kapitaikan 2018: 103, pl. 25.38	33510
C16	Horbat ‘Aqav	Israel/Carmel Mountains	Types B and C (?)	Calderon 2000: pl. XIX:20–22	33511, 33512, 33513

No.	Site	LCP region	Details (chronology, type, and notes)	Reference	LCP vessel ID
C17	Horbat Castra	Israel/Carmel Mountains	Type B	Haddad 2009: 79–91, fig. 3:2–3; Van den Brink et al. 2013: fig. 17.5	31223, 31224, 31225
C18	Huqoq	Israel/Galilee	Late 5th to mid-to-late 6th c.; found alongside an LRA3 in a domestic area of the village	Reported in Schindler 2017: 150	-
C19	Iraq al-Amir	Jordan/central highlands	ca. 363–450; type A; the only import besides the more frequent bag-shaped jars found in a large rectangular building (qasr) in the village	Hudson and Hartman 2020: fig. 5.14.82	28954
C20	Jaffa	Israel/central coastal plain	Types A (?) and B; LRA1s were the only imported Byzantine amphoras found at the Rabbi Yehuda Me-Raguza excavation in Jaffa	de Vincenz 2020: fig. 2.7–8; Gendelman 2020: fig. 8.4	33514, 33515, 33516
C21	Jerash	Jordan/northern highlands	-	Reported in Romanowska, Lichtenberger, and Raja 2021: table 1; Sodini and Villeneuve 1992: fig. 2.2	34779
C22	Jerusalem	Israel-Palestinian Authority/central highlands	(1) Two LRA1 sherds found in an early 6th c. stratum and one in a stratum dating to the very end of the 6th c.; the former stratum also contained LRA4s. (2) Tyropoeon Valley, 6th–7th c. contexts	(1) Fleitman and Mazar 2015: fig. I.5.1.179–180.[8] (2) Crowfoot and Fitzgerald 1929: 81, pl. 14.29 (non vidi)	33517, 33518

8. The identification of no. 179 as an LRA1 is questionable on the basis of its concave neck.

No.	Site	LCP region	Details (chronology, type, and notes)	Reference	LCP vessel ID
C23	Jezreel / Esdraela	Israel/Jezreel Valley	One LRA1 type B is published from the wine-producing village; seemingly less common at the site than bag-shaped jars	Grey 2014: table 5, table 5, fig. 18.2	31105
C24	Khirbet el-Mukhayyat	Jordan/central highlands		Mentioned in Pieri 2005a: 183	-
C25	Ma'agan Mikhael B (shipwreck)	Israel/Carmel coastal plain	Mid-7th to mid-8th c.; a few LRA1 *survival* (?) sherds (potentially produced in Paphos), found alongside the more common LRA2s and LRA5s, and LRA4s as well as African types	Creisher et al. 2019: fig. 2.1	33519
C26	Mezad Yerouham	Israel/Negev	-	Taxel 2018: fig. 2.13	21032
C27	Mount Nebo	Jordan/central highlands	5th–6th c. context	Saller 1941: pl. 145:13–14, 18 (?)	33521, 33522, 33523
C28	Nahal Beqa'	Israel/Negev	-	Mentioned in Pieri 2005a: 183	-
C29	Neapolis / Nablus	Israel/central highlands	LRA3s and LRA4s were also found, and possibly Agora M334s and spatheia	Mentioned in Bes et al. 2020: 72 n. 351	-
C30	Ostrakine	Egypt/Sinai	Type B; also found at the Christian port city were LRA2 or BGA, LRA4, LRA5, LRA7, spatheia and other African amphoras	Arthur and Oren 1998: fig. 6.5	33524
C31	Pella	Jordan/Jordan Valley	Cypriot type C (?); also found at the Decapolis city were LRA3 and Sinopean amphoras	McNicoll et al. 1992: pl. 112.5, 113.1	33525,[9] 33526
C32	Porphyreon	Lebanon/southern coast	-	Wicenciak 2021b: 15, 24	-

9. This LRA1 specimen might be a Sinopean "carrot" amphora, which is very hard to distinguish from later, smaller LRA1s, particularly those produced in Cyprus. It is included here because several other scholars have interpreted it as an LRA1 (e.g., Pieri 2005a: appendix 1).

No.	Site	LCP region	Details (chronology, type, and notes)	Reference	LCP vessel ID
C33	Qasrawet	Egypt/Sinai	Before the end of the 4th c.; multiple LRA1s were found at the fortified garrison, along with Africana I and II, Africana III/ Keay 25, LRA3, LRA4, BGA, and San Lorenzo 7 amphoras	Reported in Arthur and Oren 1998: 198–203	-
C34	Rehovot-in-the-Negev	Israel/Negev	Second half of 5th to late 7th or early 8th c.; six type B sherds; also found in the desert city were LRA4s (22 sherds), various LRA5s (44 sherds)	Rosenthal-Heginbottom 1988: 83, pl. II.125; 89 pl. III.126–130	33527, 33528, 33529, 33530, 33531, 33532
C35	Shelomi	Israel/Galilee	ca. 610–614/617; LRA1s represented 26.3% of the amphora assemblage from this phase at the ecclesiastic estate, while LRA5s were 73.7%	Reported in Dauphin and Kingsley 2003: 68	-
C36	Shavei Zion	Israel/northern coastal plain	Type B (?); at least two LRA1 sherds were found at the site, alongside LRA5s and spatheia	Prausnitz 1967: fig. 11.6–7	33533, 33534
C37	Shuni	Israel/central coastal plain	Cypriot LRA1 type C (but also very similar to type D Snp I)	Gendelman 2022: fig. 3.aa	33535
C38	Tell Fara	Israel/southern coastal plain	Type B (and possibly type C); the three LRA1 sherds from the small Byzantine site at Tell Fara were all of the exact same fabric, and LRA4s and LRA5s were much more common	Tubb 1986: fig. 2.4–5, 5.4	33536, 33537, 33538

No.	Site	LCP region	Details (chronology, type, and notes)	Reference	LCP vessel ID
C39	Tell Keisan	Israel/northern coastal plain	Types A and B; ranging from 1.61–4.3% of the amphora assemblage by total number and weight (respectively), compared to 91–97% for the LRA5 and its local subtype the LRA6	Landgraf 1980: fig. 26.2–4, table 5	33539, 33540, 33541
C40	Tyre	Lebanon/southern coast	Found alongside Reynolds' Amphora 339 (Reynolds 2005: 572)	Bikai, Fulco, and Marchand 1996: fig. 103.15, 19; Gatier et al. 2010: pl. 8.6	33542
C41	Upper Zohar	Israel/Negev	An LRA2 was also found at the fort site	Reported in Harper 1995: 31	-
C42	Zippori/ Sepphoris	Israel/Galilee	Types A, B, and C (and Snp type D I); other types in the amphora assemblage in the city's eastern church were LRA2s, LRA3s, Samos jars, LRA2/13s, Africana I–III types, Agora M334s, Almagro 51cs, and others	de Vincenz 2024	26898, 27977, 27979, 27980, 27981, 27983, 27985, 27986, 27988, 27989, 27991, 27992, 27993, 27994, 27995, 27997, 27999, 27998, 28000, 28955

10.3.D. Late Roman Thrace

No.	Site	LCP region	Details (chronology, type, and notes)	Reference	LCP vessel ID
D01	Aegyssus	Romania/Black Sea coast	LRA1s and LRA2s are the most attested vessels in the 5th–7th c., in almost equal percentage (cf. Stănescu 2018: 222, graphic 1)	Stănescu 2018: 219–20, fig. 8.1–4	33944, 33945, 33946, 33947
D02	Apollonia Pontica	Bulgaria/Danube lowlands	LRA1s are the most common amphora find for the period of the late antique fortress	Reported in Baralis et al. 2012: 178	-
D03	Anchialos	Bulgaria/Danube lowlands	End of 4th to mid-6th c.; type A or transitional	Gyurdzhiyska and Ivanov 2019: fig. 10.4	33948
D04	Bjolgrad	Ukraine/western Black Sea coast	5th–6th c. contexts	Mentioned in Pacetti 1995: 278	-
D05	Callatis	Romania/Black Sea coast	5th–6th c. contexts	Opaiţ and Ionescu 2016: 71, pls. XVIII, 110; XIX, 111	33949, 33950
D06	Capidava Fortress	Romania/Black Sea coast	Amphoras deposit sealed by the collapsed roof; the last phase of use of this *horreum*-type building is dated to the end of the 6th. c.	Opriş and Ratiu 2016: 26–27 fig. 5 (cat. no. 2), fig. 8 (cat. no. 1), fig. 17 nos. 1, 2, 5; reported in Opriş and Ratiu 2019: 142–43	33951, 33952, 33953
D07	Carsium/Harsova	Romania/Black Sea coast	-	Mentioned in Pieri 2005a: 184, appendix 1	-
D08	Axiopolis/Cernavodă	Romania/Black Sea coast	Late 5th to late 6th c. contexts	Mentioned in Pacetti 1995: 279	-
D09	Cetatea	Romania/Danubian Plain	-	Mentioned in Pieri 2005a: 183, appendix 1	-
D10	Constantinople	Turkey/Marmara	5th–7th c.	Hayes 1992: 63–64; Kara 2015: 5a, 6a, 7a; Öncü and Çölmekçi 2018: 18, fig. 1 and drawing 1	33954, 33955, 33956, 33957, 33958, 33959, 33960, 33961, 34795, 34796, 34797

No.	Site	LCP region	Details (chronology, type, and notes)	Reference	LCP vessel ID
D11	Dichin	Bulgaria/Danube lowlands	LRA1s represent, together with LRA2s, the most common amphoras of the first phase (ending in the last quarter of the 5th c.), ca. 75% of the amphora assemblage. They are absent in the second phase (6th c.)	Reported in Swan 2010: 108–9; Poulter 2019 (non vidi)	-
D12	Dinogetia	Romania/Black Sea coast	Types A, B, and C	Opaiț et al. 2022: 85–89	34201, 34202, 34203, 34204, 34205, 34206, 34207, 34208, 34209, 34210, 34211, 34212, 34213, 34214, 34215, 34216, 34217, 34218, 34219, 34220, 34221, 34222, 34223, 34224, 34225, 34226, 34227, 34228, 34229, 34230, 34231, 34232, 34233, 34234, 34235
D13	Gradiste	North Macedonia	Type B	Georgiev 1989: fig. 4.1	33962
D14	Halmyris/ Murighiol	Romania/Black Sea coast	Formerly, Independența. Beginning of the 5th to early 7th c.; LRA1s count for the 26.7% of the amphora assemblage, possibly up to 45% in the last occupational phase (see also table 10.2)	Opaiț 1991; Topoleanu 2000: 134–36, cat. nos. 336–343, pls. XLI–XLII. Mentioned in Opriș and Ratiu 2019: 144	33963, 33964, 33965, 33966, 33967, 33968, 33969, 33970, 34189

No.	Site	LCP region	Details (chronology, type, and notes)	Reference	LCP vessel ID
D15	Haskovo	Bulgaria/southeastern lowlands	-	Mentioned in Pieri 2005a: 184, appendix 1	-
D16	Histria	Romania/Black Sea coast	5th–7th c.	Bădescu 2012: 312–316, pl. 1.1–5; Bădescu and Cliante 2014: 173–76, fig. 3 nos. 1–14; Bădescu and Bivolaru 2015: 193–95, figs. 3.1–12; 4.1–18	33543, 33544, 33545, 33546, 33547, 33548, 33549, 33550, 33551, 33552, 33553, 33554, 33555, 33556, 33557, 33558, 33559, 33560, 33561, 33562, 33563, 33564, 33565, 33566, 33567, 33568, 33569, 33570, 33571, 33572, 33573, 33574, 33575, 33576, 33577, 33578, 33579, 33580, 33581, 33582, 33583, 33584, 33585, 33586, 33587, 33588, 33589, 33590, 33591
D17	Iatrus	Bulgaria/Danube lowlands	Types A and B	Reported in Conrad 1999: 183; 2007: cat. nos. 1075–1078, pl. 4; cat. nos. 1304–1311 (*dipinti*), pls. 15–16	33894, 33895, 33896, 33897, 33898, 33899
D18	Kaliakra	Bulgaria/Black Sea coast	-	Mentioned in Pieri 2005a: 184, appendix 1	-

No.	Site	LCP region	Details (chronology, type, and notes)	Reference	LCP vessel ID
D19	Kavarna	Bulgaria/Black Sea coast	-	Mentioned in Pieri 2005a: 184, appendix 1	-
D20	Küçükçekmece / Lake Bathonea	Turkey/Marmara	-	Reported in Kaya and Aslan 2017	-
D21	Küçükyalı	Turkey/Marmara	5th–7th c.; 14.34% of the amphora assemblage	Wohmann 2016: 68–70, pls. 1.10; 12.1–7	33900, 33901, 33902, 33903, 33904, 33905, 33906, 33907
D22	(L)ibida	Romania/Black Sea coast	4th–7th c.; 25.87% of the amphora assemblage	Reported in Paraschiv 2014: 425. Mentioned in Opriş and Ratiu 2019: 145	-
D23	Madara	Bulgaria/Black Sea coast	5th–6th c. contexts	Mentioned in Pacetti 1995: 278	-
D24	Novae	Bulgaria/Danube lowlands	Attested from the late 4th to the early 7th c., with a peak during the 6th c.	Reported in Klenina 2014: 931–32; Biernacki and Klenina 2015: 109, figs. 10.1–21; 11.1–5; reported in Dyczek 2017: 689	33908, 33909, 33910, 33911, 33912, 33913, 33914, 33915, 33916, 33917, 33918, 33919, 33920, 33921, 33922, 33923, 33924, 33925, 33926, 33927, 33928, 33929, 33930, 33931, 33932, 33933
D25	Odessos	Bulgaria/Danube lowlands	Type B	Kouzov and Christov 2018: 22–23, pl. 1.2	33934, 33935
D26	Oltina	Romania/Black Sea coast	-	Mentioned in Pieri 2005a: 184, appendix 1	-
D27	Orgame / Argamum	Romania/Black Sea coast	LRA2s are much more common at the coastal town	Mentioned in Paraschiv 2006: 89	-

No.	Site	LCP region	Details (chronology, type, and notes)	Reference	LCP vessel ID
D28	Ovech Fortress (Provadia)	Bulgaria/Black Sea coast	-	Mentioned in Pieri 2005a: 184, appendix 1	-
D29	Piatra Frecăţei / Beroe	Romania/Black Sea coast	Attested in contexts from the end of 5th to the end of 6th c.	Mentioned in Pacetti 1995: 279	-
D30	Razgrad	Bulgaria/Black Sea coast	Attested between the 5th and the 6th c.	Mentioned in Pacetti 1995: 278	-
D31	Sacidava	Romania/Black Sea coast	Types B and C (Cypriot?); LRA2s and LRA3s were also found at the fortress site	Scorpan 1975: pl. 3	33936, 33937, 33938, 33939
D32	Sadovec	Bulgaria/Danube lowlands	-	Mentioned in Pieri 2005a: 184, appendix 1	-
D33	Sliven	Bulgaria/Danube lowlands	-	Mentioned in Pacetti 1995: 278	-
D34	Stara Zagora	Bulgaria/Danube lowlands	Attested in contexts from the turn of the 5th c.	Mentioned in Pacetti 1995: 278	-
D35	Sucidava/Corabia	Romania/Dobrogea	Stamped LRA1s are dated to the end of the 4th–5th c.	Gherge and Amon 2011 (non vidi). Mentioned in Karagiorgou 2001: 135–36	-
D36	Tomis	Romania/Black Sea coast	-	Mentioned in Pieri 2005a: 184, appendix 1; Opaiţ 2004: 9 (with illustration)	33940, 33941
D37	Topraichioi	Romania/Black Sea coast	LRA1s represent 18.2% of LR amphora assemblage	Mentioned in Paraschiv 2006: 91; Opaiţ 2004: 8 (with illustration)	33942, 33943
D38	Troesmis	Romania/Black Sea coast	-	Mentioned in Pieri 2005a: 184, appendix 1; Opaiţ 2004: 8 (with illustration)	34148

No.	Site	LCP region	Details (chronology, type, and notes)	Reference	LCP vessel ID
D39	Tropeum Traiani	Romania/Black Sea coast	5th–6th c.; type A, LRA1s represent 38% of the amphora assemblage	Mentioned in Opriş and Ratiu 2019: 145; Grigoraş and Panaite 2021: 92–93, pls. VIII–X	34149, 34150, 34151, 34152, 34153, 34154 , 34155, 34156, 34157, 34158, 34159, 34160, 34161, 34162, 34163, 34164
D40	Tulcea, Villa Telita	Romania/Black Sea coast	One type A LRA1 was found at this 4th c. villa site, likely dating to the final quarter of the 4th c.	Baumann 1984: pl. 14.4	34147
D41	Ulmetum	Romania/Black Sea coast	Specimens found in 4th–late 5th c. and mid- to late 6th c. contexts; Zeest 99, Zeest 100, Antonova 5, and LRA2 type amphoras were also found in strata dating to this period at the fort site	Gamureac 2017: 252 cat. nos. 45–47, 263 pl. VIII; 2018: pls. 4.6; 5.22; 6.29–30; Bajenaru 2023: fig. 5.65–66 and 75–76	34143, 34144, 34145, 34146, 34165, 34166, 34167, 34168, 34169, 34170, 34171

10.3.E. Late Roman Pontica, eastern and northern Black Sea

No.	Site	LCP region	Details (chronology, type, and notes)	Reference	LCP vessel ID
E01	Apsaros / Gonio	Georgia/Black Sea coast	Represents 1.44% of the amphora assemblage in 1st–7th c. contexts	Komar, Rogava, and Motskobili 2024: 84–86, fig. 9 (top left, top right, mid-left, mid-right, bottom right)	33625, 33626, 33627, 33628, 34042
E02	Chersonesus	Crimea/Black Sea coast	From a deposit with TPQ from Justinian's reign; type B; LRA1s are 27.1% of amphoras	Sazanov 2017: figs. 1.1–1.9	33592, 33593, 33594, 33595, 33597, 33596, 33598, 33599, 33629

No.	Site	LCP region	Details (chronology, type, and notes)	Reference	LCP vessel ID
E03	Cibilium / Tsebelda	Georgia/Black Sea coast	First half of the 6th c.	Sazanov 1999: 269, figs. 7.6; 8.3, 5–6; 11.1, 9; 12.1–12.4	33600, 33601, 33602, 33603, 33604, 33605, 33606, 33607, 33608, 33609
E04	Demirci	Turkey/western Black Sea	LRA1 transitional	Kassab Tezgör 2010: 152, no. 25 (Pls. 23 and 36); 158, no. 50 (pls. 24 and 39); and 185, no. 155 (Pl. 48)	35198, 35199, 35200
E05	Dranda	Georgia/Black Sea coast	Third quarter of the 6th c.	Mentioned in Sazanov 1999: 270	-
E06	Hermonassa	Russia/southwest	Third quarter of the 6th c.	Mentioned in Sazanov 1999: 270	-
E07	Il'ich	Russia/southwest	Type A; usually the predominant amphora in the limited contexts presented in the article.	Sazanov 2023: figs. 5.1; 11.1; 17.1–2	33610, 33611, 33612, 33624
E08	Kytaion	Crimea/Black Sea coast	First half of the 6th c.	Sazanov 1999: 270 and fig. 11.7	34785
E09	Paliastomi (Natechebi)	Georgia/Black Sea coast	Type C (?); identified during underwater surveys of the settlement	Gamkrelidze 1992: fig. 7a–c	33613, 33614, 33615
E10	Mangup	Crimea/Black Sea coast	Type B	Reported in Ivanova/Yashnaya 2019: 51; reported in Naumenko 2023: 225	-
E11	Myrmekion	Crimea/Black Sea coast	First half of the 6th c.	Mentioned in Sazanov 1999: 270	-
E12	Nokalakevi / Archaiopolis	Georgia/Black Sea coast	-	Personal observation by one of the authors (V. I., 2013)	33616 (fig. 55)
E13	Olbia Pontica, Borysthenes	Ukraine/western Black Sea coast	4th–7th c.; context related to the Cherniakhov culture	Twardecki and Buiskikh 2021: 266, fig. 10.C	33617

No.	Site	LCP region	Details (chronology, type, and notes)	Reference	LCP vessel ID
E14	Pantikapaion, Bosporos/Kerch	Crimea/Black Sea coast	Material from a dump pit, end of the 6th to beginning of the 7th c.; LRA1s second most common group of transport amphoras (four) after Cretan vessels (six, including a TRC9)	Fedoseev et al. 2010: 73–77, pl. I 18.1, figs. 18.1a–1b and 18.2; Smokotina 2015: figs. 4.15–4.18	33618, 33619, 33620, 33621, 34786, 34787
E15	Petra/Tsikhisdziri	Georgia/Black Sea coast	4th–6th c.	Inaishvili and Vashakidze 2010: 152, pl. 86.4–5	33622, 33623
E16	Phanagoria	Russia/southwest	First half of the 6th c.	Mentioned in Sazanov 1999: 270; mentioned in Pacetti 1995: 278	-
E17	Pitiunt / Bichvinta	Georgia/Black Sea coast	-	Mentioned in Sazanov 1999: 265	-

Figure 55. LRA1 rim and handle in Nokalakevi Antiquarium (Georgia); LCP vessel ID 33616. Photograph by V. Iacomi (June 2013).

No.	Site	LCP region	Details (chronology, type, and notes)	Reference	LCP vessel ID
E18	Plaka (shipwreck)	Crimea/Black Sea coast	See table 10.3.S1	Waksman et al. 2014, fig. 4–5	33630, 33631, 33632, 33633, 33634, 33635, 33636, 33637, 33638, 33639, 33640, 33641, 33642, 33643, 33644, 33645, 33646, 33647, 33648, 33649, 33650, 33651
E19	Pompeiopolis	Turkey/western Black Sea	LRA1s represent 13% of an amphora assemblage where LRA4s are distinctly predominant (39%)	Mentioned in Opaiţ 2021: 82; cf. Opaiţ 2018: 707, fig. 27	33652
E20	Sinop	Turkey/western Black Sea	Type B (among the imported LRA1s); underwater finds; the major port city of Sinop was the center of production of "carrot amphoras," the type D Snp I subtype of which is considered a sort of local hybrid with the LRA1; see introduction for further discussion on Sinop	Kassab Tezgör 2020: 40–43, pls. XV, XVI, XVIII.1, XVIII.3, XVIII.5–6	33653, 33654, 33655, 33656, 33657
E21	Sinop B (shipwreck)	Turkey/western Black Sea	See table 10.3.S1	Mentioned in Ballard et al. 2001: 616–18; mentioned in Ward and Ballard 2004: 5–6	-
E22	Sivag-Kerman	Crimea	36% of the pottery assemblage	Reported in Naumenko 2018: 67	-
E23	Tanais	Russia/southwest	From late 4th–beginning of the 5th c.	Sazanov 1999: 269, figs. 8.1–2; 11.4	33658, 33659, 33660

No.	Site	LCP region	Details (chronology, type, and notes)	Reference	LCP vessel ID
E24	Tyritake	Crimea/Black Sea coast	Quite rare in the 4th–5th c. (1–3%), LRA1 presence steadily increases through the 6th c. (from 12–13% to 25%)	Smokotina 2016: 716 and fig. 5.1–2; 2020: 571, fig. 32–33	33661, 33662

10.3.F. Asia Minor and Aegean Islands

No.	Site	LCP region	Details (chronology, type, and notes)	Reference	LCP vessel ID
F01	Agios Ioannis	Greece/central Aegean	Cave complex; surface pottery sherds	Kormazopoulou and Diamanti 2021: 900 and figs. 7, 10, and 12	33688, 33689, 33690
F02	Andriake	Turkey/southwest	Late 6th–mid 7th c.; types B and possibly C; LRA2/13s, LRA4s, and LRA5/6s were also found in the basilica of the port site, though no quantification is presented	Çömezoğlu 2023: fig. 4.a–4.e	33683, 33684, 33685, 33686, 33687
F03	Aphrodisias	Turkey/Aegean	Late 6th c.; residential areas; amphoras in general poorly represented	Hudson 2008: 330, fig. 16.3.32	33682
F04	Apolakkia	Greece/Rhodes	Production center 03	Reported in Empereur and Picon 1989	-
F05	Arap Island (shipwreck ?)	Turkey/Aegean	See table 10.3.S2	Pulak 1989: 78, fig. 2 (cat. no. 2.8/E/2)	33681
F06	Arykanda	Turkey/Aegean	Ca. 425–525/550; types A and B; LRA1s were the most common amphora in late antique strata in the city, with other types including LRA2s (the second most prevalent), LRA3s, Agora M273, and Samos Cistern type amphoras	Yaman 2018: 295–99, catalog nos. 470–483, pl. 72	33677, 33678, 33679, 33680

No.	Site	LCP region	Details (chronology, type, and notes)	Reference	LCP vessel ID
F07	Assos	Turkey/Marmara	The most common amphora in the Early Byzantine levels of the northern Stoa	Ayaz 2021: 102; cat. no., pls. 4.41; 7.41; 8.41	33676
F08	Burgaz (shipwreck)	Turkey/Aegean	See table 10.3.S1	Leidwanger, Green, and Tuna 2015: cat. BZ.11.L4.A.2, BZ.12.L4.wreck.1, BZ.12.L4.wreck.2, BZ.12.L4.wreck.3, BZ.12.L4.wreck.4	33671, 33672, 33673, 33674, 33675
F09	Chios Site 9, Agios Stefanos Islet east (shipwreck)	Greece/central Aegean	See table 10.3.S1	Reported in Theodoulou et al. 2015a	-
F10	Chios Site 10, South Prasonisi Islet south (shipwreck)	Greece/central Aegean	See table 10.3.S1	Theodoulou et al. 2015a: figs. 6a–c, 7d, 8e; and pl. 2	33666, 33667, 33668, 33669, 33670
F11	Emporio	Greece/Cyclades	8th–9th c.; LRA1 *survival*; another probable LRA1-inspired globular amphora was found in the same context in the fortress	Ballance et al. 1989: fig. 43.280; Poulou-Papadimitriou 2018: 34, fig. 5c	33664, 35197
F12	Ephesus	Turkey/Aegean	Rare occurrence (Agora, Terrace House 2)	Bezeczky 2013: 153–60; Sänger and Cesteros 2019	29796, 29797, 29798, 29799, 29800, 29801, 29802, 35185, 35186, 35187, 35188, 35189
F13	Halasarna	Greece/central Aegean	Production center 07	Diamanti 2010: figs. 1a; 2a; Poulou-Papadimitriou and Didioumi 2010; Diamanti 2023: figs. 4–6, 13–14	30435, 30544, 30545, 30546, 30547, 30548, 30549, 30550, 30551, 30552, 30553, 30554

No.	Site	LCP region	Details (chronology, type, and notes)	Reference	LCP vessel ID
F14	Hierapolis / Pamukkale	Turkey/inner west	End of the 6th to beginning of the 7th c.; domestic context.	Ruggiu and Cottica 2007: 164, fig. 4d	33843
F15	Iasos	Turkey/Aegean	Type C	Baldoni 2010–2011: 291–92 and fig. 12.23–24	33841, 33842
F16	İçmeler, Ismeler	Turkey/Aegean	Production center 08	Reported in Empereur and Picon 1989	-
F17	Kambos (Lipsi)	Greece/central Aegean	Production center 09	Papavassiliou, Sarantidis, and Papanikolaou 2014: fig. 9, table 1.8, 1.17–20	29807, 29808, 29809, 29810, 30119
F18	Kekova Island (shipwreck)	Turkey/southwest	See table 10.3.S2	Aslan and Orhan 2020: 302–4 fig. 4 (cat. nos. 1–2)	33839, 33840
F19	Kephalos	Greece/Kos	8th–early 9th c.; LRA1 *survival*; it has been proposed that the LRA1s at the Christian coastal site were locally made, but there is little evidence to support this hypothesis	Didioumi 2014: 171, fig. 17a–b	33837, 33838
F20	Keramos	Turkey/Aegean	Type B; from a general survey of the territory; the LRA1 presented here comes from an otherwise unknown underwater deposit	Kizil and Yaman 2017: 21, 28 pl. 4.8	33836
F21	Kizilburun (shipwreck)	Turkey/Aegean	See table 10.3.S1	Pulak and Rogers 1994: fig. 2	33835
F22	Klazomenai	Turkey/Aegean	Late 5th–early 7th c.; type B; the most common amphora in the farmstead site	Gürbüzer 2018: 144–46, fig. 15.59–61	33832, 33833, 33834
F23	Knidos A (shipwreck)	Turkey/Aegean	See table 10.3.S1	Reported in Brennan et al. 2020	-
F24	Knidos C (shipwreck)	Turkey/Aegean	See table 10.3.S1	Reported in Brennan et al. 2020	-

No.	Site	LCP region	Details (chronology, type, and notes)	Reference	LCP vessel ID
F25	Knidos O (shipwreck)	Turkey/Aegean	See table 10.3.S1	Brennan et al. 2020: fig. 28, 30a	30593
F26	Knidos T (shipwreck)	Turkey/Aegean	See table 10.3.S1	Brennan et al. 2020: figs. 17–18	30561, 30562
F27	Knidos	Turkey/Aegean	First quarter of the 5th c. to the mid 7th c.; types B and C (?); LRA2s, LRA3s, and spatheia were also recovered from the heating and cooling structure/workshop	Doksanalti 2020: 394, fig. 8.45–51	33825, 33826, 33827, 33828, 33829, 33830, 33831
F28	Kyme in Aeolis	Turkey/Aegean	5th to the first half of the 6th c. contexts; LRA1s predominant in the amphora assemblage (over 30%)	Reported in Di Giovanni 2014; 2012: 161, fig. 21a–d	33811, 33822, 33823, 33824
F29	Laggeri	Greece/central Aegean	Production center 12	Diamanti 2016: figs. 2.1–2, 2.8–9; 2023	29803, 29804, 29805, 29806
F30	Leukos	Greece/Cyclades	Production center 13	Mentioned in Nelson et al. 2015	-
F31	Limyra	Turkey/southwest	ca. 450–650; types B and C	Vroom 2007: 281–82, fig. 10a; Bes 2020: table 3, fig. 13	31716, 31717
F32	Marmaris B (shipwreck)	Turkey/Aegean	See table 10.3.S1	Brennan et al. 2020: fig. 12–15 (cf. fig. 13b for an image of a single vessel)	30592
F33	Mastichari	Greece/central Aegean	Production center 14	Poulou-Papadimitriou and Didioumi 2015: 401–18	-

No.	Site	LCP region	Details (chronology, type, and notes)	Reference	LCP vessel ID
F34	Miletos	Turkey/Aegean	Types A, B, and C (?) and possibly Elaiussa-specific variations; LRA1s are the most common LR to EB amphora type at Miletos, but LRA2s, LRA4s, LRA7s, Keay 62, and other types were also recovered at the major port city	Berndt 2003: 61–64, 243–51, tables 80–90	33848, 33849, 33850, 33851, 33852, 33853, 33854, 33855, 33856, 33857, 33858, 33859, 33860, 33861, 33862, 33863, 33864, 33865, 33866, 33867, 33868, 33869, 33870, 33871
F35	Myndos	Turkey/Aegean	10 LRA1 sherds, as well as LRA2, LRA3, LRA5, LRA13, Samos cistern, and agora M273 sherds in mainly LB but some EB contexts at the coastal Christian town	Reported in Gulsefa 2016: 64–65	-
F36	Olympos	Turkey/southwest	Predominant (20%) in the amphora assemblage (ecclesiastical contexts)	Reported in Olcay Uçkan et al. 2022: 424–25	-
F37	Parion	Turkey/Marmara	5th–7th c.; types A and B; LRA1s are predominant in the amphora assemblages of those stratigraphic contexts	Akkaş 2020: 193–96, fig. 10.26–34; Ergürer and Akkaş 2023: 190–92, figs. 10.1–2	33810, 33812, 33813, 33814, 33815, 33816, 33817, 33818, 33819, 33820, 33821
F38	Patara	Turkey/southwest	Types A and B	Dündar 2018: 170–71, figs. 7 and 11	33697, 33698
F39	Perge	Turkey/southwest	Types A and B; southern basilica	Buluç 2022: 230, fig. 44 cat. nos. 129–130	33695, 33696

No.	Site	LCP region	Details (chronology, type, and notes)	Reference	LCP vessel ID
F40	Phaselis	Turkey/southwest	Type A; underwater survey of the southern harbor (no wreck or recognized jettison area)	Aslan and Orhan 2019: 90–91, fig. 6	33847
F41	Rhodiapolis	Turkey/southwest	Type B (?); early Byzantine church on the acropolis; most common transport amphora	Çömezoğlu 2014: 667; 674 fig. 8a	33846
F42	Sagalassos	Turkey/southwest	Types A and B; the site might have produced an imitative form since late 4th c. (Poblome et al. 2008). From various urban contexts at variable percentage (from ca. 4.5% up to over 66%)	Poblome et al. 2008; Bes 2022: 147, 149 tab. 1, figs. 4–5	33845
F43	Samos	Greece/Samos	Second half of the 6th to the early 7th c.; LRA1s found at the ecclesiastical bath complex (in association with LRA2s) and in the Eupalinos tunnel	Reported in Steckner 1989: 57–62	-
F44	Sardis	Turkey/Aegean	Late 5th to early 7th c.; recovered from wells in the residential sector; LRA1s and LRA2s combined predominant in the amphora assemblage	Rautman 1995: 42, cat. 1.33 fig. 9; 2.91 fig. 21; 3.30 fig. 26	33692, 33693, 33694
F45	Side	Turkey/southwest	Beginning of the 5th to the end of the 7th c.	Dündar 2012: 45–46 and fig. 5; Alanyali 2016: 146	33844
F46	Skyros	Greece/central Aegean	LRA1s ca. 4% of the total amphora assemblage between the 4th and the mid-9th c. in this extensive survey	Reported in Karambinis 2015: 222, table 11.3	-
F47	Smyrne	Turkey/Aegean	Types A and B; second most predominant amphora after LRA3s	Reported in Şenol 2015: 249; reported in Taşlıalan and Drew-Bear 2005: 408	-

No.	Site	LCP region	Details (chronology, type, and notes)	Reference	LCP vessel ID
F48	TK05-AD Bozburun peninsula (shipwreck)	Turkey/Aegean	See table 10.3.S2	Mentioned in Leidwanger 2017; Royal 2006	-
F49	Troy / Ilion	Turkey/Marmara	Postearthquake deposit of the early 6th c.	Heath and Tekkök 2006–2009, nos. 27–28	28289, 35196
F50	Xanthos	Turkey/southwest	Type B; recovered from the acropolis of the city	Pellegrino 2002: 246, fig. 1.3; 2003: 220, fig. 6.8	33663, 33691
F51	Yassi Ada (shipwreck)	Turkey/Aegean	Ca. 630; ca. 100 LRA1s	See appendix to table S1	30594, 34564, 34565, 34566, 34567, 34568, 34569, 34570, 34571, 34572, 34573, 34574, 34575, 34576, 34577

10.3.G. Western Balkans and central Mediterranean

No.	Site	LCP region	Details (chronology, type, and notes)	Reference	LCP vessel ID
G01	Aliki (Thasos)	Greece/Macedonia	6th c.	Blondé, Gros, and Pétridis 2011: 197, fig. 2l, 2r	34460, 34461
G02	Antikythera	Greece/Cyclades	Partially based on surveys. LRA1s second most common import (after LRA2s) in the late 4th to early 7th c. (ca. 10%)	Quercia et al. 2011: 59–60 and table 3, cat. nos. 72–73	34459
G03	Aquae/Prahovo	Serbia/Balkan Mountains east	-	Jeremic 2022: 34	-

No.	Site	LCP region	Details (chronology, type, and notes)	Reference	LCP vessel ID
G04	Argos	Greece/Peloponnese	ca. 20% of 5th–6th c. amphora assemblages	Mentioned in Oikonomou-Laniado 2003: 46 (with references)	-
G05	Askra	Greece/central Greece	Large *kome*; presence of LRA1s and LRA2s point to a late antique occupation of the site.	Mentioned in Vionis 2017: 152	-
G06	Athens	Greece/Attica	Makrygianni plot (new Acropolis Museum), domestic context: well deposit of the 5th–6th c.; ca. 17%; types A and B	Robinson 1959: M333, pl. 32 (= Lang 1976: Hc23) ; Lang 1976: I45; Kouveli and Manoli 2021: 115–16, fig. 3.50–51	34493, 34494, 34495, 35026
G07	Belgrad	Serbia/northern lowlands	-	Mentioned in Pieri 2005a: 183, appendix 1	-
G08	Berat	Albania/southern highlands	Rebuilding of the fortification, 6th c.	Spahiu 2011: 64, pl. II.13	34092
G09	Bosman / *ad scrufolas*	Serbia/Balkan Mountains east	-	Mentioned in Pieri 2005a: 183, appendix 1	-
G10	Brijuni Island	Croatia/Istria	*Castrum* villa, 5th c. context. LRA1s count for over 65% of the amphora assemblage	Bezeczky, Berni Millet and Cesteros 2015: 193–95, fig. 3.6	34091
G11	Butrint	Albania/coastal lowlands	Mid-5th to mid-6th. 34.5% of the imports in the period 525–550, percentage that drops to 4.8% in the late 6th c.	Reynolds 2004: fig. 13.174–185; 2017: fig. 2.13	34480, 34481, 34482, 34483, 34484, 34485, 34486, 34487, 34488, 34489, 34490, 34491, 34492
G12	Byllis	Albania/coastal lowlands	Episcopal complex by basilica B, 5th to the second half of the 6th c.; type B	Reported in Beaudry et al. 2002: 676, 678, 681; reported in Bonifay and Cerova 2006: 858 n. 19.	-
G13	Cezava/Novae	Serbia/Balkan Mountains east	-	Mentioned in Pieri 2005a: 183, appendix 1	-

No.	Site	LCP region	Details (chronology, type, and notes)	Reference	LCP vessel ID
G14	Chinitsa	Greece/Peloponnese	Although Megaw and Jones identify these sherds as globular amphoras (i.e., LRA2s), we agree with Pieri that they better match LRA1 morphology	Mentioned in Pieri 2005a: 181, appendix 1; Megaw and Jones 1983: pl. 24.1–3	34826, 34827, 34828
G15	Cibalae	Croatia/Pannonia	-	Nagy and Szakmany 2019: 220, fig. 6A (thin section photo)	34479
G16	Corinth	Greece/Peloponnese	Kenchreai: ca 10% of the amphora assemblage (late 6th to early 7th c. context).[10] Urban context (Panayia field): second half of the 5th to the mid-/late 7th c.	Heath et al. 2015: 13 (Kenchreai); Slane and Sanders 2005: 274, fig. 13 no. 4–8 (with *titulus*)	34478
G17	Dia Island (shipwreck)	Greece/Crete	See table 10.3.S2	Theodoulou et al. 2015b: 620, fig. 8	34090
G18	Dion	Greece/Thessaly	Ecclesiastical context; LRA1s most common amphora find. Type B	Fragoulis, Minasidis and Mentzos 2014: 298, figs. 5.1–5.4, 12.1	34474, 34475, 34476, 34477, 34829
G19	Dyrrachium, Epidamnos	Albania/coastal lowlands	Eastern imports grew during the 6th c.	Shkodra-Rugria 2007: 313, fig. 2.4	34089
G20	Gajtan	Albania/coastal lowlands	One sherd identified via survey, compared to eight LRA2s	Shkodra-Rugria 2023: 216, table 12.6, pl. 12.2a (break photo)	34578
G21	Gortyn	Greece/Crete	Type A already attested in late 4th c.; type B attested throughout the mid-6th to mid-/late 7th; type C. LRA1s became predominant among the eastern imports in ca. 600–670 (25–30%)	Portale and Romeo 2001: 328–31, figs. 156–158; 398–399; pl. 65a–b, 83a–c; Portale 2014: fig. 16.10–11	34466, 34467, 34468, 34469, 34470, 34471, 34472, 34473

10. See the open-access Kenchreai Archaeological Archive (KAA; http://kenchreai.org/kaa/typology/p-lra-1) for high-resolution data on ceramics, including LRA1s, at Corinth's harbor. Note that Kenchreai is included here under Corinth, but the harbor is located several kilometers southeast of Corinth proper.

No.	Site	LCP region	Details (chronology, type, and notes)	Reference	LCP vessel ID
G22	Gumenicë	Albania/southern highlands	Unexplored area, but late antique settlement identified thanks to LRA1	Reported in Xhyheri et al. 2012	-
G23	Hadrianopolis	Albania/southern highlands	"Late levels" related to the rearrangement of the bath complex	Perna et al. 2014: 504 and fig. 6; Perna 2014: 240 and fig. 51	34464, 34465
G24	Itanos	Greece/Crete	LRA1s and LRA2s predominant among the imports	Reported in Greco et al. 1999: 528	
G25	Iustiniana Prima	Serbia/Kosovo and south	From investigations in the Lower Town. LRA1s represent a mere 1%, whereas *spatheia* and LRA2s predominate.	Bikić and Ivanišević 2012: 44, fig. 5.5	34088
G26	Kallithea	Greece/Macedonia	Water mill built by the temple of Zeus Ammon, 5th or 6th c. LRA1s and LRA2s predominant among the amphoras.	Vasiliou and Tsigarida 2014: 723 and fig. 9.1	34087
G27	Kanistro	Greece/Macedonia	Domestic/residential context of the second third 4th–beginning of the 5th c.; together with LRA2s	Vasiliou and Tsigarida 2014: 724 and figs. figs. 5.1–3; 10.8	34083, 34084, 34085, 34086
G28	Kastri / Larymna	Greece/Attica	5th–6th c. to at least mid- or late 7th c. LRA1s associated with LRA2s in "overwhelming" quantity	Mentioned in Vionis 2017: 153	-
G29	Knossos	Greece/Crete	See the discussion at §7.1G	Hayes 2001: 450, fig. 10 no. B61	34082
G30	Kostolac	Serbia/northern lowlands	-	Mentioned in Pieri 2005a: 183, appendix 1	-
G31	Križna gora	Slovenia/Adriatic coastal lowlands	Type A	Modrijan 2014: 54, pl. 4.4–5	34462, 34463

No.	Site	LCP region	Details (chronology, type, and notes)	Reference	LCP vessel ID
G32	Kryoneri	Greece/central Greece	5th–6th c.	Chamilaki 2023: 591, figs. 5a–b; 6b–f; 7g	34074, 34075, 34076, 34077, 34078, 34079, 34080, 34081
G33	Kula	Bulgaria/Danube lowlands	-	Mentioned in Pacetti 1995: 278	-
G34	Kythera	Greece/Peloponnese	-	Mentioned in Pieri 2005a; Coldstream and Huxley 1972: fig. 52, pl. 49.47	34055
G35	Marathon	Greece/Attica	-	Mentioned in Pieri 2005a: 181, appendix 1	-
G36	Nikopolis	Greece/Epirus	Excavation of the "Bishop's House": LRA1s count for the 20.2% of the amphora assemblage. Pottery deposit by Basilica A: LRA1s ca. 10.2% of the amphora assemblage; the context is dated to the first half of the 5th on the ground of LRA1 typology	Reynolds and Pavlidis 2014: 452 and fig. 6.2–7; 2017: 653 and fig. 6.5, 9.1–2	34050, 34051, 34052, 34053, 34054, 34070, 34071, 34072, 34073
G37	Olympia	Greece/Peloponnese	Garbage disposal, several varied vessels mostly for wine transport/consumption; 6th c. context.	Reported in Martin 2014: 761–62	-
G38	Onchesmos/ Saranda	Albania/southern highlands	-	Muçaj et al. 2014: 321–23	-
G39	Orikos	Albania/coastal lowlands	Attested in various investigated contexts. Types A and B	De Mitri and Loprieno 2018: 101, pl. 5.3; 2020: 110, pl. 13.1	34049, 34093
G40	Pefkochori	Greece/Macedonia	Oil press installation, 5th–7th c. LRA1s attested as a scarce occurrence	Mentioned in Vasiliou and Tsigarida 2014: 726	-

No.	Site	LCP region	Details (chronology, type, and notes)	Reference	LCP vessel ID
G41	Philippi	Greece/Thrace	Context of the "Workshop building" (6th to early 7th c.). Types A and B	Zachariadis 2014: 706, fig. 9	34048
G42	Phoinike	Albania/southern highlands	The most common amphora in 6th–7th c. contexts	Cirelli 2021: fig. 4. 1–2	34046, 34047
G43	Pseira	Greece/Crete	Rural complex of possible monastic nature, late 6th–middle to second half of the 7th	Poulou-Papadimitriou and Nodarou 2014: fig. 10 (petrographic sample) and 19	34069
G44	Rifnik	Slovenia/Pannonian lowlands	Late antique hilltop settlement (end of the 3rd–late 6th/early 7th c.). Type B, at least three different fabrics recognized.	Bausovac 2010: 695–96, fig. 3.15	34064, 34065, 34066, 34067, 34068
G45	Romuliana / Gamzigrad	Serbia/Balkan Mountains east	-	Reported in Conrad 2020: 136; 148 kat. 3; 153–154 kat. 41	-
G46	Ruginium	Croatia/Istria	-	Mentioned in Starac 2006: 101	-
G47	Salona	Croatia/Dalmatia	-	Chevalier et al. 2005: 391, fig. 83.14	34063
G48	Scodra	Albania/coastal lowlands	Type A (Egloff/Kellia 169)	Reported in Hoxha 1994: 237	-
G49	Sikyon	Greece/Peloponnese	Two LRA1 sherds, far fewer than LRA2s	Tzavella, Trainor and Maher 2014: cat. SP 97.05, fig. 7	34062
G50	Sirmium	Serbia/northern lowlands	-	Mentioned in Hárshegyi and Ottományi 2013: 485	-
G51	Thespiai	Greece/central Greece	5.7% of imports (inferred from Bes and Poblome 2017: 333, table 12.7)	Mentioned in Bes and Poblome 2017: 330	-
G52	Thessaloniki	Greece/Macedonia	7th c., type B. *Dipinti* mentioned, no photographs nor comments	Akrivopoulou and Slampeas 2014: 288, and fig. 10	34061

No.	Site	LCP region	Details (chronology, type, and notes)	Reference	LCP vessel ID
G53	Thorikos	Greece/Attica	LRA1s are defined as "predominant" both in the mines and in the living quarters	Reported in Konstantinidou, Monsieur, and Hasenzagl 2018: 53–54; Docter, Monsieur, and van de Put 2013: fig. 31 nos. 75, 76, 77	34045, 34056, 34060
G54	Tiszavasvári	Hungary/ Great Hungarian Plain	ca. first half of 7th c.; type B (small) the grave good from an Avar period burial of a male	Csiky and Magyar-Harshegyi 2015: fig. 3	34059
G55	Tonovcov grad	Slovenia/Julian Alps and center	Type B. Large increase in LRA1s occurrence from the mid-5th c.	Modrijan 2011: 141–50, pl. 69.4	34058
G56	Torone	Greece/Macedonia	LRA1s count for 6.61% of the amphora assemblage, 36.90% of the minimum number of "recognized amphora types" (Papadopoulos 1989: 82, table 3). Type B	Papadopoulos 1989: 87, fig. 12	34057
G57	Velika	Greece/Thessaly	-	Reported in Sdrolia, Didioumi, and Koutsoyiannis 2018: 198	-
G58	Viminacium	Serbia/northern lowlands	LRA1s are the most common amphora (Popović 1987: 36 states they represent 54.3% of the total collected amphoras) with LRA2s (called "Pontic amphoras of the types Riley LR1 and LR2")	Reported in Raičković 2012: 154; Popović 1987: 16, fig. 13.1–5	34830, 34831, 34832, 34833, 34834
G59	Zagreb	Croatia/Pannonian plan	-	Mentioned in Pieri 2005a: 184, appendix 1	-

10.3.H. Late Roman Italy

No.	Site	LCP region	Details (chronology, type, and notes)	Reference	LCP vessel ID
H01	Agnuli	Italy/southern Adriatic coast	-	Casavola 1999: pl. 3.30; mentioned in Totten, De Mitri, and Loprieno 2023: 107	34967
H02	Akragas / Agrigento	Italy/Sicily	Agrigentum's harbor, 6th–7th c. occupational phase. Rare occurrence of eastern imports (LRA1s, LRA2s, and LRA3s)	Mentioned in Caminneci 2015: 482	-
H03	Albenga	Italy/northern Apennines	Reused as building material in the construction of the dome of the Baptistry (erected by the end of the 5th–beginning of the 6th c.)	Mentioned in Pieri 2005a: 186, appendix 1; Lamboglia 1956 (non vidi)	-
H04	Aquileia	Italy/Po Plain	Types A and B. In general, LRA1s are attested as early as the end of the 4th c. and throughout the 6th in various contexts of the city	Mentioned in Auriemma and Quiri 2007: 38–40; Bueno, Novello, and Mantovani 2012: 163–64, fig. 7.1; Dobreva and Riccato 2015: 115–17, pl. 1.9, 1.10–11; Dobreva and Zago 2021: 328 and fig. 15.4, 16.1	34968, 34969, 34970, 34971, 34972, 35011
H05	Bivona	Italy/southern Tyrrhenian coast	Harbor of Vibo Valentia. Type B ("Kellia 164"). Attested in copious amounts (unspecified)	Reported in Cuteri et al. 2014: 67	-
H06	Blanda Julia	Italy/southern Tyrrhenian coast	5th–6th (one vessel only; scarcity of East/Levantine imports in general)	Reported in Sangineto 2006: 319	-
H07	Brixia / Brescia	Italy/Po Plain	-	Mentioned in Pacetti 1995: 276	-
H08	Canusium	Italy/southern Adriatic coast	-	Laganara and Volpe 1985: fig. 3.9; mentioned in Volpe 1989: 632	34966

No.	Site	LCP region	Details (chronology, type, and notes)	Reference	LCP vessel ID
H09	Capo Rizzuto	Italy/Ionian coast	In general, eastern imports prevail over African imports (amphoras and tableware)	Mentioned in Cuteri and Salamida 2010: 509	-
H10	Capris, Iustinopolis	Slovenia/Adriatic coastal lowlands	Type A	Mentioned in Modrijan 2014: 54	-
H11	Carales / Cagliari	Italy/Sardinia	Type B	Sanna, Soro, and Nervi 2021: 472 and fig. 3.12	34965
H12	Casignana Roman Villa	Italy/Ionian coast	Rare occurrence, with larger diffusion from mid-5th c.	Mentioned in Cuteri and Salamida 2010: 509	-
H13	Caulon / Stilida	Italy/Ionian coast	LRA1s are the only eastern import; attested in the hinterland as well. Types A and B	Mentioned in Cuteri and Salamida 2010: 509	-
H14	Cazzanello Roman Villa	Italy/central Tyrrhenian coast	-	Mentioned in Pieri 2005a: 186, appendix 1	-
H15	Cefalù (shipwreck)	Italy/Sicily	See table 10.3.S1	Purpura 1983: fig. 11	34694
H16	Classe	Italy/Po Plain	5th–7th (after the Justinianic conquest, increase from 8% to 14%)	Cirelli 2014: 543 and 552, fig. 7.1–2, 9 (table on pottery frequency)	34989, 34990
H17	Comacchio	Italy/Po Plain	Attested "in scarce quantities"	Mentioned in Negrelli 2021: 208; Corti 2023: fig. 2, table 2.1	34962, 34963
H18	Concordia Sagittaria	Italy/Po Plain	LRA1s attested in a 5th–7th c. context.	Mentioned in Auriemma and Quiri 2007: 38	-
H19	Contrada Cignana	Italy/Sicily	Late antique village composed by seven buildings. LRA1s and LRA2s are the most representative amphoras (ca. 20%)	Rizzo and Zambito 2010: fig. 1.15	34961
H20	Cosa	Italy/northern Tyrrhenian coast	Attested in context of the first half of the 5th c.	Mentioned in Pacetti 1995: 275	-

No.	Site	LCP region	Details (chronology, type, and notes)	Reference	LCP vessel ID
H21	Crecchio	Italy/central Adriatic coast	LRA1s account for the 14.8% of the amphora assemblage	Mentioned in Pieri 2005a: 186, appendix 1; mentioned in Auriemma and Quiri 2007: 40; Staffa and Pellegrini 1993: fig. 44.8–11	35012, 35013, 35014, 35015
H22	Egnatia	Italy/southern Adriatic coast	Type B; LRA1s are just under 15% of the amphora assemblage; one vessel reused for an *enchytrismos*	Cassano et al. 2008: figs. 13 (pottery distribution table), 14.5, 16	34959, 34960
H23	Finale Ligure (S. Antonino di Perti)	Italy/northern Apennines	Fortress built during the Byzantine occupation. Just one LRA1 attested	Mentioned in Pacetti 1995: 275; mentioned in Remolà Vallverdú 2000: 278	-
H24	Florentia	Italy/northern Thyrrenian coast	See ch. 6	Pecci, Salvini, and Cantini 2010: fig. 1 nos. 16.79–16.84, 16.86	34952, 34953, 34954, 34955, 34956, 34957, 34958
H25	Genoa	Italy/northern Apennines	One LRA1 reused for an infant burial	Bellatalla, Bertino, and Gardini 1989: 395	-
H26	Giancola	Italy/southern Adriatic coast	End of 4th–beginning of the 6th c.; late antique deposit in the abandonment levels of a former Roman villa with *fundus*	Cocchiaro et al. 2005: 428 and fig. 20.5–6	34950, 34951
H27	Giglio Island	Italy/northern Tyrrhenian coast	Jettison area in front of the harbor (Giglio Porto); type A ("Kellia 169")	De Tommaso et al. 1992: 115–16, fig. 85 and pl. 4 (cat. nos. 125–128)	34946, 34947, 34948, 34949
H28	Giurdignano	Italy/southern Adriatic coast	-	Mentioned in Totten, De Mitri, and Loprieno 2023: 107	-
H29	Grumentum	Italy/southern Apennines	Urban settlement abruptly ended during the first half of the 5th c.; LRA1s attested in low frequency	Reported in Giardino 1991: 832	-

No.	Site	LCP region	Details (chronology, type, and notes)	Reference	LCP vessel ID
H30	Hala Milieri	Malta	-	Mentioned in Pieri 2005a: 187, appendix 1	-
H31	Imola	Italy/Po Plain	-	Mentioned in Pacetti 1995: 276; mentioned in Pieri 2005a: 187, appendix 1	-
H32	Invilino-Ibligo	Italy/Alps	-	Mentioned in Pieri 2005a: 187, appendix 1	-
H33	Jesolo	Italy/Po Plain	Settlement occupied from the late 4th c. to the end of the 5th/beginning of the 6th c. Eastern imports in general prevail as a whole, LRA1s are as common as African transport vessels (cf. Gelichi et al. 2017: 46, fig. 21)	Reported in Gelichi et al. 2017: 37–47	-
H34	Lipari	Italy/Sicily	-	Mentioned in Pacetti 1995: 276; mentioned in Pieri 2005a: 186, appendix 1	-
H35	loc. Carabollace	Italy/Sicily	Possible storage/stocking site near an ancient port/harbor (*statio Ad Aquas*?). Overall, prevailing African imports; LRA1s the most common eastern amphora (62%). Type A	Caminneci 2010: 7–8, fig. 17.22–23; Caminneci, Franco and Galioto 2010: 274–75, and 280 fig. 1.22–23	34944, 34945
H36	Loppio-S.Andrea	Italy/Alps	Fortified late antique settlement on a lake island. Sporadic occurrence of LRA1s (ca. 0.8% of the amphora assemblage)	Reported in Maurina and Capelli 2005: 413–14; 2007: 482	-
H37	Luna / Luni	Italy/northern Apennines	-	Mentioned in Pacetti 1995: 275; mentioned in Pieri 2005a: 187, appendix 1; cf. Costantini 2011: 415 n. 147	-

No.	Site	LCP region	Details (chronology, type, and notes)	Reference	LCP vessel ID
H38	Marettimo Island	Italy/Sicily	Monastic community, 5th–early 8th c.	Reported in Ardizzone et al. 2012: 176	-
H39	Metapontum	Italy/Ionian coast	Settlement abandoned in the course of the 6th c. LRA1s attested in low frequency	Giardino 1991: 844 and 846, fig. 8.1	34943
H40	Milan	Italy/Po Valley	-	Mentioned in Auriemma 2007	-
H41	Misenum	Italy/southern Tyrrhenian coast	Former imperial military harbor, occupational continuity up to the 9th c. LRA1s are attested in various contexts (Grotta di Dragonara, Cudemo Roman baths, theatre). Type B	Reported in De Rossi et al. 2010: 488–90	-
H42	Neapolis / Naples	Italy/southern Tyrrhenian coast	*Insula* and *domus* by S. Maria del Carmine ai Mannesi (5th–7th c.), 7.7% by the turn of the 7th c.; area of the harbor (6th–7th c.), 5.52% of the amphora assemblage. Type B	Arthur 1994: 251 (non vidi); cf. Reynolds 2010a: 224, table 20; Carsana and Del Vecchio 2023: 79, fig.3.24; Ebanista and Romano 2018: figs. 2–3, cat. nos. gnn0623, gnn0635, gnn0641	34939, 34940, 34941, 34942
H43	Nora	Italy/Sardinia	3rd–7th c. context; presence of LRA1s just mentioned	Mentioned in Nervi 2014: 846. Mentioned in Sanna, Soro, and Nervi 2021: 466	-
H44	Orbetello	Italy/northern Tyrrhenian coast	Mid-5th–6th c. contexts	Mentioned in Pacetti 1995: 275	-
H45	Ostia	Italy/central Tyrrhenian coast	Contexts dated from the end of the 4th/beginning of the 5th through the 6th c.	Reported in Martin and De Sena 2003: 47; 2005. Reported in Martin 2008	-
H46	Otranto	Italy/southern Adriatic coast	LRA1s are the dominant type of eastern amphora, far greater than LRA2, 3, 4, and others, counting up to the 25% of the amphora assemblage	De Mitri 2005: figs. 4.8–9; 6.1–3. Cf. Auriemma and Quiri 2007: 40	35004, 35005, 35006, 35007, 35008

No.	Site	LCP region	Details (chronology, type, and notes)	Reference	LCP vessel ID
H47	Palikè	Italy/Sicily	Overall eastern Mediterranean imports prevailing over African imports	Reported in Arcifa 2016: 22; 2023: figs. 3.9, 6.3.1–2, 6.3.4–7	34973, 34998, 34999, 35000, 35001, 35002, 35003
H48	Paola	Italy/southern Tyrrhenian coast	An LRA1 reused in a late antique necropolis, end of 5th–beginning of 6th c. Type A ("Kellia 169")	Reported in Tosti 2014: 27–28	-
H49	Philosophiana	Italy/Sicily	In mid-/late 6th to mid-7th c. contexts. Rare occurrence.	Vaccaro 2017: fig. 7	34997
H50	Pievina	Italy/northern Tyrrhenian coast	Farmstead, late 4th to the mid-/late 5th c. context.	Vaccaro 2014: 17 and fig. 9.11	34996
H51	Piran	Slovenia/Adriatic coastal lowlands	Increased eastern imports from the second half of the 5th c. (St. George Church)	Reported in Vidrih Perko and Župančič 2005: 522	-
H52	Pisa	Italy/northern Tyrrhenian coast	Piazza Duomo context (from Hellenistic to early Medieval periods). LRA1s attested in the 4th–5th c. contexts, but missing in the 6th–7th c. Type A	Costantini 2011: 413–15, figs. 12.7, 13; 2014: 986 and fig. 2.11	34994, 34995
H53	Piscino di Piscopio	Italy/southern Tyrrhenian coast	Ecclesiastical or martyrial context (6th–7th c.). Mostly type B, generally scarce occurrence	Reported in Cuteri et al. 2014: 67	-
H54	Pollena Trocchia	Italy/southern Tyrrhenian coast	LRA1 reused as infant burial	Castaldo, De Simone, and Russell 2023: fig. 3	34993
H55	Porto Torres	Italy/Sardinia	Public archaeology excavation by the new harbor terminal. LRA1s, attested in the early 5th c., become rarer in the second half of the 5th–first half of the 6th c.	Reported in Deriu 2015: 947–48	-

No.	Site	LCP region	Details (chronology, type, and notes)	Reference	LCP vessel ID
H56	Portus	Italy/central Tyrrhenian coast	Area nearby the bishopric, possible warehouses. Type A (Egloff/Kellia 169).	Reported in D'Ammassa, Manna, and Rosati 2023	-
H57	Portus Pisanus	Italy/northern Tyrrhenian coast	Commercial building erected by the ancient harbor ca. mid-3rd/mid-4th c. Type A	Ducci, Pasquinucci, and Genovesi 2011: 45, fig. 4.15–16; mentioned in Menchelli 2020: 220	34991, 34992
H58	Predloka	Slovenia/Adriatic coastal lowlands	-	Reported in Vidrih Perko and Župančič 2005: 522	-
H59	Punta del Serrone (shipwreck)	Italy/southern Adriatic coast	See below, table 10.3.S2	Reported in Carta Beni Culturali Regione Puglia, cod. BRBIU000506, http://cartapulia.it/dettaglio?id=123547	-
H60	Ravenna	Italy/Po Plain	LRA1 are three times more common than LRA2s in the 6th–7th c. (predominant eastern import being LRA4s). Types A, B	Cirelli and Lasi 2003: 55 (top image); Cirelli 2007: 46–47; 2014: fig. 8	34988
H61	Rhegion	Italy/southern Tyrrhenian coast	5th–7th c. contexts	Mentioned in Racheli 1991: 710	-
H62	Rimini	Italy/central Adriatic coast	Attested in a necropolis context	Mentioned in Auriemma and Quiri 2007: 40	-
H63	Rome / Roma	Italy/central Tyrrhenian coast	LRA1s are usually attested in all the investigated late Roman contexts, but never in preponderant amounts (African imports are predominant)	See below, appendix to table H	34190, 34191, 34192, 34193, 34194, 34195, 34196, 34197, 34198, 35174, 35175, 35176, 35177, 35178, 35179, 35180, 35181, 35182, 35183, 35184

No.	Site	LCP region	Details (chronology, type, and notes)	Reference	LCP vessel ID
H64	Roselle / Rusellae	Italy/northern Tyrrhenian coast	Only one vessel from a limited context dated to the end of 6th–early 7th c.	Reported in Vaccaro 2014: 14	-
H65	Salapia	Italy/southern Adriatic coast	Domestic waste deposit, 6th c., from a "city block near the center of the town." Type A	Totten, De Mitri, and Loprieno 2023: 107, fig. 4.1–4.5	34983, 34984, 34985, 34986, 34987
H66	S. Giacomo degli Schiavoni	Italy/central Adriatic coast	The only eastern import, covering up to 18% of the amphora assemblage	Mentioned in Auriemma and Quiri 2007: 40	-
H67	San Giusto	Italy/southern Adriatic coast	LRA1s represent the most common eastern import	Reported in Lapadula 1998: 269	-
H68	Scolacium	Italy/Ionian coast	Above all during the 6th c.; among the most common imports from the east (8%)	Racheli 1991: 719, and figs. 22–23; mentioned in Cuteri and Salamida 2010: 509	34981, 34982
H69	Segesta	Italy/Sicily	African transport amphoras are triple that of the rare eastern imports (LRA1s and LRA2s) in the 6th and 7th c.	Facella, Minniti, and Capelli 2014: 543 and fig. 7.5	34980
H70	Sibari	Italy/Ionian coast	-	Mentioned in Pacetti 1995: 276	-
H71	Supersano	Italy/Ionian coast	-	Mentioned in Totten, De Mitri, and Loprieno 2023: 107	-
H72	Tergeste	Italy/Po Plain	LRA1s are the most common amphoras among the eastern imports. Types A and B	Reported in Auriemma 2007; Degrassi et al. 2010: fig. 5.16–17	34978, 34979
H73	Terrasini	Italy/Sicily	-	Purpura 1977: 64, fig. 21a	34977
H74	Teurnia	Austria/Tyrolean Alps	Type B	Ramstetter 2018: 409, fig. 6.4–5	34975, 34976
H75	Torcello	Italy/Po Plain	Coastal settlement from the 5th to the end of the 7th c. (when ecclesiastical buildings are erected)	Reported in Gelichi et al. 2017: 27–37	-

No.	Site	LCP region	Details (chronology, type, and notes)	Reference	LCP vessel ID
H76	Udine	Italy/Po Plain	In a 4th to 7th c. context. Reportedly, type A	Mentioned in Modrijan 2014: 54; mentioned in Auriemma and Quiri 2007: 38	-
H77	Ugento	Italy/Ionian coast	-	Mentioned in Totten, De Mitri, and Loprieno 2023: 107	-
H78	Vada Volaterrana	Italy/northern Tyrrhenian coast	Port system of Volaterrae; investigation of a quarter occupied 1st to the 7th c., with *horrea*. LRA1s represent the bulk of the eastern imports	Reported in Menchelli 2020: 220	-
H79	Vagnari	Italy/southern Apennines	General low incidence of eastern imports (ca. 12% of the amphora assemblage) in the period from the 3rd to the 7th c. LRA1s are the most attested type	Disantarosa 2011: 397–98, fig. 5.16	34974
H80	Vibo Valentia	Italy/southern Tyrrhenian coast	Various urban contexts. Generally scarce occurrence, attested in 6th and 7th c. contexts	Reported in Cuteri et al. 2014: 66	-
H81	Villa S. Giovanni di Ruoti	Italy/southern Apennines	Second half of the 5th to early 6th c. contexts (460–535)	Mentioned in Pacetti 1995: 276. Cf. Reynolds 2010a: 227, table 20.	-

Appendix to Table H: LRA1s in Rome

No.	Location	Notes	Reference	LCP vessel ID
HR01	Palatine Hill: Schola Praeconum	*Dipinti.* According to Reynolds 2010a: 201, table 2c, LRA1s and Keay 52 might have been confused, thus making any statistics unreliable	Whitehouse et al. 1985; see table 10.2	35175

No.	Location	Notes	Reference	LCP vessel ID
HR02	Palatine Hill: temple of Cybele (Magna Mater)	*Dipinti*. Second half of the 5th c.; LRA1s represent 22% of the amphora assemblage, the most common wine transport amphora of the context (both types A and B)	Pensabene 1981; Whitehouse et al. 1985; see table 10.2. See also Panella et al. 2010: 67	35176, 35177, 35178, 35179, 35180, 35181, 35182, 35183, 35184
HR03	Palatine Hill: northeastern slope	Eastern imports became more relevant in the 5th c. and prevailing in the 6th c. (LRA4s, LRA1s, Agora M334, and LRA3s)	Casalini 2015: 543, 545 and pl. 3.11	34198
HR04	Roman Forum, *Lacus Juturnae*	Attested in contexts from mid-5th to early 6th c., 1–4.5%	Mentioned in Pacetti 1995: 275	-
HR05	Caelian Hill houses	*Dipinti*	Reported in De Rossi 1890: 36–41	35174
HR06	Caelian Hill, *Basilica Hilariana*	First half of the 6th c. 4% of the amphora assemblage (at least one type A); second half of the 6th–early 7th c. 3%	Reported in Vatta and Bertoldi 2004: 477	-
HR07	Caelian Hill, S. Stefano Rotondo	Attested "in limited quantities"	Reported in Martin 1991: 161–63	-
HR08	Caelian Hill, *Domus Gaudentii*	End of the 5th–first half of the 6th c.; 11% (unclear whether of the whole amphora assemblage or of the imports)	Mentioned in Pacetti 1995: 274	-
HR09	Aventine Hill	4.4% of the amphora assemblage	Fontana et al. 2004: 558, pl. VI no. 53	34195
HR10	Aventine Hill, mitreum by S. Prisca Church	Beginning of the 5th c., rare occurrence	Mentioned in Pacetti 1995: 275	-
HR11	Campus Martius, Crypta Balbi	Area of the Mitreum: mid-5th c. context, LRA1s the most common eastern transport amphora; around the second half of the 6th c., ca. 10% of the amphora assemblage. Area of the exedra: well into the 7th c.; African imports prevail among the transport amphoras.	Reported in Saguì, Ricci, and Romei 1997: 36; Saguì and Coletti 2004; Saguì 2002: 14–15 and fig. 6.3	34197

No.	Location	Notes	Reference	LCP vessel ID
HR12	Campus Martius, temple of Matidia	LRA1s attested in several stratigraphic units, from sporadic sherds to between 2–4% of the whole assemblage	Reported in Brando 2015	-
HR13	Campus Martius, Palazzo della Cancelleria	-	Mentioned in Pacetti 1995: 275	-
HR14	Quirinal, *Vicus Caprarius* archaeological area	-	Personal observation of one of the authors (V. I., March 2024)	-
HR15	Oppian Hill, *Porticus Liviae*	2.5% of imported amphoras	Mentioned in Pacetti 1995: 274	-
HR16	Trastevere, San Francesco a Ripa	Late antique works on a mid-Imperial age *horreum* implied the creation of a terracing system (probably against the Tiber's floods) entirely made out of dumped/recycled amphoras—including LRA1 type A. African amphoras predominant.	Filippi, Dell'Era, and Ferrazzoli 2014	-
HR17	Via Marmorata (by Testaccio and the Emporium)	Of the total amphora assemblage (where African imports prevail) LRA1s represent 7.7% from the mid-4th to mid-5th c. and 9% from the mid-5th to mid-6th c. (types A and B attested)	Bertoldi 2011: 162, fig. 9.21; 164, fig.14.15–17, 16.1	34190, 34191, 34192, 34193, 34194
HR18	Lungotevere Testaccio (by Testaccio and the Emporium)	-	Pacetti 1995: 274	-
HR19–24	Other, various provenance	All with *dipinti*	De Rossi 1890 and *CIL* 15.4886, 4890, 4892, 4895c–d, 4897	-
HR25	Capitoline Hill, St. Maria in Aracoeli	Few fragments, possibly one belonging to type A	Martin, Cuyler, and Banducci 2020: 57–58, pl. 33.3	34196

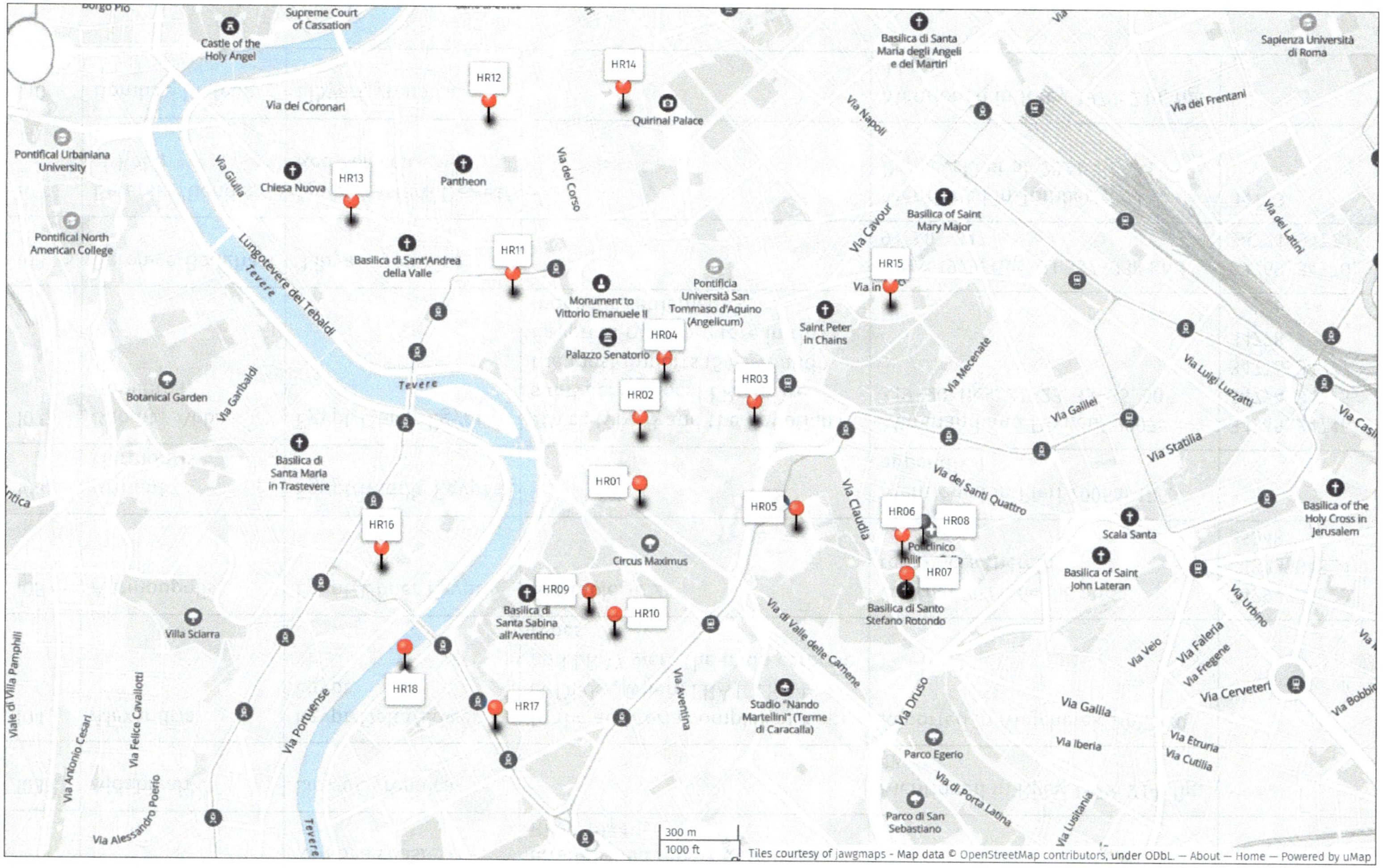

Figure 56. Map showing LRA1s consumption sites in the city of Rome, including: HR01 Palatine Hill: Schola Praeconum, HR02 Palatine Hill: temple of Cybele (Magna Mater), HR03 Palatine Hill: Northeastern slope, HR04 Roman Forum: *Lacus Juturnae*, HR05 Caelian Hill houses, HR06 Caelian Hill: Basilica Hilariana, HR07 Caelian Hill: S. Stefano Rotondo, HR08 Caelian Hill: *Domus Gaudentii*, HR09 Aventine Hill, HR10 Aventine Hill: mitreum by S. Prisca Church, HR11 Campus Martius: Crypta Balbi, HR12 Campus Martius: temple of Matidia, HR13 Campus Martius: Palazzo della Cancelleria, HR14 Quirinal: *Vicus Caprarius* archaeological area, HR15 Oppian Hill: *Porticus Liviae*, HR16 Trastevere: San Francesco a Ripa, HR17 Via Marmorata (by Testaccio and the Emporium), HR18 Lungotevere Testaccio (by Testaccio and the Emporium), HR 25 Capitoline Hill, St. Maria in Aracoeli.

10.3.I. Late Roman Egypt

No.	Site	LCP region	Details (chronology, type, and notes)	Reference	LCP vessel ID
I01	Abu Mina	Egypt/Delta/Lower Egypt	-	Mentioned in Pieri 2005a: 69; 185, appendix 1	-
I02	Abu Sha'ar	Egypt/Eastern Desert/ Red Sea coast	LRA1s mentioned in the unpublished report of pottery Riley 1984	Mentioned in Jørgensen 2020: 51	-
I03	Ajdabiyah	Libya/Cyrenaica	-	Mentioned in Riley 1979: 214, fig. 42	-
I04	Alexandria	Egypt/Delta/Lower Egypt	In the auditoria complex at Kom el-Dikka, where LRA1, LRA4, and LRA7 were the main ceramic types	Reported in Majcherek 2007: 30	-
I05	Antinoupolis	Egypt/Upper Egypt	See table 10.2	Fournet 2021: 64–68 and references therein	34794, 34822, 34823, 34824, 35048
I06	Armant / Hermontis	Egypt/middle Egypt	-	Mentioned in Pieri 2005a: 185, appendix 1	-
I07	Baouît / Abba Apollotos	Egypt/Upper Egypt	7th c.; type B and the Egyptian subtype; nonlocal LRA1s are the most imports (54.1%) and Egyptian types are rare in this monastic settlement	Marchand and Dixneuf 2007: 319–20, figs. 21–23, 33–35, 50	34745, 34746, 34774, 34775, 34776, 34777, 34778
I08	Berenice/Benghazi	Libya/Cyrenaica	-	Riley 1979: figs. 91.337–338 and 91.346–347	34769, 34770, 34771, 34772
I09	Berenike/Bender el-Kebir	Egypt/Eastern Desert/ Red Sea coast	-	Mentioned in Tomber 2004 Popławski et al. 2021: fig. 8a	34773
I10	Bomba / Plateia	Libya/Cyrenaica	-	Mentioned in Riley 1979: 214, fig. 42 (map)	-

No.	Site	LCP region	Details (chronology, type, and notes)	Reference	LCP vessel ID
I11	Boreum	Libya/Cyrenaica	-	Mentioned in Riley 1979: 214, fig. 42 (map)	-
I12	Deir el-Naqlun	Egypt/Fayoum	Egyptian type B; monastic settlement	Derda 1992: table 5.I.1 (inv. no. 265/86); Danys-Lasek 2014: figs. 10c:Nd.11.245; 11g: Nd.11.069, Nd.11.094	34767, 34768, 35193, 35194
I13	Dime/Soknopaiou Nesos	Egypt/Fayoum	See table 10.2	Caputo and Davoli 2023: fig. 6.g–j	16126, 16125
I14	Elephantine	Egypt/Upper Egypt	-	Mentioned in Pieri 2005a: 185, appendix 1	-
I15	Esna / Latopolis	Egypt/Upper Egypt	-	Mentioned in Pieri 2005a: 185, appendix 1	-
I16	Gasr el-Atallat	Libya/Cyrenaica	-	Mentioned in Riley 1979: 214, fig. 42 (map)	-
I17	Giza	Egypt/Delta/Lower Egypt	LRA1s are the most common amphora; traces of resin lining inside some vessels. A fragment must have been used as an ostrakon.	Malykh 2007: 50–52, 59, fig. 1–7	34760, 34761, 34762, 34763, 34764, 34765, 34766
I18	Hermopolis / El-Ashmunein	Egypt/middle Egypt	-	Mentioned in Pieri 2005a: 185, appendix 1	-
I19	Jalu	Libya/Cyrenaica	-	Mentioned in Riley 1979: 214, fig. 42 (map)	-
I20	Kellia	Egypt/Delta/Lower Egypt	-	Egloff 1977: pls. 57.4; 19.1–2, 19.5–6, 19.7c–d, 62.5; Fournet 2012: fig. 2, 5, 8–9	34753, 34754, 34755, 34756, 34757, 34758, 34759, 35167, 35168, 35169, 35170
I21	Lamluda	Libya/Cyrenaica	Mid-6th c.	Reported in Antonelli and Menozzi 2014: 887–88	-

No.	Site	LCP region	Details (chronology, type, and notes)	Reference	LCP vessel ID
122	Marea	Egypt/Delta/Lower Egypt	Excavations of the Byzantine and Early Islamic House H1. Sherds of LRA1s found together with LRA3 and LRA4	Gwiazda and Wielgosz-Rondolino 2019: 265, fig. 4.1–2	34751, 34752
123	Marina el-Alamein	Egypt/Delta/Lower Egypt	-	Mentioned in Pieri 2005a: 186, appendix 1; Majcherek 1993: fig. 1.20	34750
124	Manqabad	Egypt/middle Egypt	6th–7th c.	Incordino 2020: 75, 90, cat. nos.110, 116	34748, 34749
125	Marsa Nakari/ Nechesia(?)	Egypt/Eastern Desert/ Red Sea coast	Just mentioned after personal communications of the author (Reddy 2013) with excavators	Mentioned in Reddy 2013: 152	-
126	Old Cairo	Egypt/Delta/Lower Egypt	6th–7th c.; with *dipinti*	Gascoigne 2007: fig. 4–6	34743, 34744, 34747
127	Oxyrhynchos / Bahnasa	Egypt/middle Egypt	See table 10.2	Fournet 2012: fig. 10	34821
128	Naukratis	Egypt/Delta/Lower Egypt	Especially type B; "particularly prevalent" in the British Museum excavations	Thomas 2018: 16–17, fig. 38	34820
129	Saqqara, Saint Jeremiah's Monastery	Egypt/Delta/Lower Egypt	Production center 16	Ghaly 1992: fig. 16	30652
130	Schedia	Egypt/Delta/Lower Egypt		Reported in Martin 2010: 946	

No.	Site	LCP region	Details (chronology, type, and notes)	Reference	LCP vessel ID
131	Taposiris Magna	Egypt/Delta/Lower Egypt		Le Bomin 2016: figs. 2.10, 6.1–19	34800, 34801, 34802, 34803, 34804, 34805, 34806, 34807, 34808, 34809, 34810, 34811, 34812, 34813, 34814, 34815, 34816, 34817, 34818, 34819
132	Tebtynis	Egypt/Fayoum	-	Mention in Pieri 2005a: 186, appendix 1; cf. Incordino 2020	-
133	Tocra	Libya/Cyrenaica	-	Mentioned in Cosentino 2023: 5	-
134	Tolmeta / Ptolemais	Libya/Cyrenaica	-	Mentioned in Riley 1979: 214, fig. 42 (map)	-
135	Umm el Qa'ab	Egypt/middle Egypt	-	Mentioned in Pieri 2005a: 186, appendix 1	-
136	Wadi Natrun	Egypt/Delta/Lower Egypt	Types A and B; also identified at the monastic site were LRA4s, LRA7s, Egyptian 5/6 and North African amphoras	Konstantinidou 2010: 951–52, figs. 4.15, 8.32	34790, 34791, 34792, 34793, 34798, 34799
137	Zaviet Hammama	Libya/Cyrenaica	-	Mentioned in Riley 1979: 214, fig. 42	-

10.3.J. Late Roman Africa

No.	Site	LCP region	Details (chronology, type, and notes)	Reference	LCP vessel ID
J01	Bir Flaguess	Tunisia/eastern coast	A spatheion fragment was also identified from field surveys at the port town	Reported in Slim et al. 2004: 116	-
J02	Carthage	Tunisia/northern coast	-	Riley 1981; cf. Bonifay 2015: 533 and n. 18, with reference to publications after Riley 1981; Williams 2005a: 163 pl. 1; 165 pl. 3 (left and right)	34496, 34502, 34503
J03	Clupea	Tunisia/northern coast	-	Mentioned in Bonifay 2015: 534; Piton 2010 (non vidi)	-
J04	Djerba	Tunisia/eastern coast	6th c.; type B	Fontana 2000: 108, fig. 6.1	34501
J05	El Aouabed, Koudiat Jaber	Tunisia/eastern coast	LRA2s and Keay 25, 34, 35B, 62Q (?) type amphora sherds were also identified during field surveys at the anchorage site	Reported in Slim et al. 2004: 134	-
J06	En Nadour	Tunisia/eastern coast	Africana III/Keay 25 amphora sherds were also identified during field surveys at the agricultural-fishing village site	Reported in Slim et al. 2004: 114	-
J07	Gourine est	Tunisia/eastern coast	Spatheia, Keay 35B, and Tripolitana III amphora sherds were also identified during field surveys at the town site	Reported in Slim et al. 2004: 108	-
J08	Henchir Chougaf	Tunisia/eastern coast	Keay 35B amphora sherds were also identified during field surveys at the site, which might have been a town	Reported in Slim et al. 2004: 110	-

No.	Site	LCP region	Details (chronology, type, and notes)	Reference	LCP vessel ID
J09	Henchir El Flouss	Tunisia/eastern coast	Keay 34 and 62 type amphoras as well as LRA2s were also identified during field surveys at the small site, composed of a cistern and many ceramic sherds	Reported in Slim et al. 2004: 135	-
J10	Henchir El Hefair	Tunisia/eastern coast	Keay 61 and 62 type amphoras as well as other cylindrical African types and LRA2s were also identified during field surveys at the coastal tell site	Reported in Slim et al. 2004: 165	-
J11	Henchir El Kebir	Tunisia/eastern coast	Cylindrical African amphoras and LRA2s were also identified at the coastal town, identified as such by its necropolis	Reported in Slim et al. 2004: 164	-
J12	Henchir Ferchatt	Tunisia/eastern coast	Keay 25 amphora sherds were also identified during field surveys at the necropolis site	Reported in Slim et al. 2004: 116	-
J13	Henchir Ech Cheggaf, Sidi Mansour	Tunisia/eastern coast	LRA2s were also identified during field surveys at the coastal fishing town	Reported in Slim et al. 2004: 133	-
J14	Henchir Leich	Tunisia/eastern coast	Africana IID, Keay 25, 35, and LRA2s were also identified during field surveys at the coastal site	Reported in Slim et al. 2004: 123	-
J15	Horrea Caelia	Tunisia/eastern coast	Keay 62 type amphoras were also identified during field surveys at the coastal town, featuring a sizeable warehouse complex	Reported in Slim et al. 2004: 160	-
J16	Khechad	Tunisia/northern coast	LRA2s, spatheia, and other African amphoras were also identified during field surveys at the coastal site (perhaps a fishing village)	Reported in Slim et al. 2004: 212	-
J17	Leptiminus / Lamta	Tunisia/eastern coast	Keay 61 or 62 type amphoras and LRA2s were also identified at the coastal city	Reported in Slim et al. 2004: 154	-

No.	Site	LCP region	Details (chronology, type, and notes)	Reference	LCP vessel ID
J18	Leptis Magna	Libya/Tripolitania	End of the 4th or beginning of the 5th c.; type A; LRA1s were a minor component in the imported amphora assemblage from presented contexts, ca. 4.43%, with Agora M235/M327, Kapitan II, LRA3, and Middle Roman 1 amphoras all more prevalent at the eastern bath complex of the port city	Bonifay et al. 2013: 106 and figs. 14.15, 19.16–17	34498, 34499, 34500
J19	Maamoura	Tunisia/northern coast	Keay 61 and 62, spatheia, and LRA2s were also identified at this probable port town	Reported in Slim et al. 2004: 170	-
J20	Macomades Minores, Iunci	Tunisia/eastern coast	Keay 25, 61, and 62 amphoras; spatheia; and LRA3s, LRA4s, and LRA7s were also identified during field surveys at the fortified coastal town	Reported in Slim et al. 2004: 122	-
J21	Missua/Sidi Daoud	Tunisia/northern coast	Nondiagnostic African, Hispanic, and Greek or Italian amphora types were also identified during field and underwater surveys at the port city	Reported in Slim et al. 2004: 186; Trabelsi 2019: 13	-
J22	Nabeul/Neapolis	Tunisia/northern coast	According to personal observations by Bonifay	Mentioned in Bonifay 2015: 534 n. 18	-
J23	Naoura	Tunisia/eastern coast	Spatheia were also identified during field surveys at the small ruins	Reported in Slim et al. 2004: 98	-
J24	Oued Maltine	Tunisia/eastern coast	A single LRA1 sherd was identified during field surveys at the small site, potentially a monastery	Reported in Slim et al. 2004: 118	-
J25	Ras el Ain	Tunisia/eastern coast	Nondiagnostic African amphoras were identified alongside LRA1s during field surveys at the coastal ruins	Reported in Slim et al. 2004: 153	-
J26	Ras el Koran	Tunisia/northern coast	Africana IIC, Keay 25.3/35B and Keay 52, and spatheia type amphoras were also identified during field surveys at the coastal ruins (fortified settlement?)	Reported in Slim et al. 2004: 212	-

No.	Site	LCP region	Details (chronology, type, and notes)	Reference	LCP vessel ID
J27	Rass Enghela	Tunisia/northern coast	Nondiagnostic African amphoras and LRA2s were also identified during field surveys at this coastal fishing village	Reported in Slim et al. 2004: 210	-
J28	Rass Jezira	Tunisia/eastern coast	Keay 34 (?), 62, spatheia, and LRA2s were also identified during field surveys at the coastal town	Reported in Slim et al. 2004: 140	-
J29	Sabratha	Libya/Tripolitania	-	Mentioned in Riley 1979: 214	-
J30	Sidi Aamer	Algeria/ Mediterranean coast	-	Mentioned in Riley 1979: 214, fig. 42	-
J31	Sidi Ali Moujehed Sud	Tunisia/northern coast	Keay 35B type amphoras were also identified during field surveys at the coastal ruins	Reported in Slim et al. 2004: 176	-
J32	Sidi Jdidi/Aradi	Tunisia/northern coast	Few non-African imported amphoras, including LRA4 and Almagro 51C, but LRA1s seem to be the most common in type from the second half of the 5th to the early 7th c. in the ancient town	Reported in Mukai 2016: tables 1, 51, 56, 106–107, 109, 133–134	-
J33	Sullecthum	Tunisia/eastern coast	Africanan IA, IIA, and IIC; spatheia; Keay 41C; and LRA2s were also identified during field surveys at the port city	Reported in Slim et al. 2004: 146; Bonifay et al. 2002: 171, fig. 20.281	34497
J34	Tipasa	Algeria/ Mediterranean coast	LRA1 with undecipherable red *tituli picti*; Keay 25.3, Tripolitana III, and nondiagnostic Nabeul type amphoras were also identified during field surveys in the city's hinterland	Mentioned in Bonifay 2015: 534; Quevedo et al. 2023: fig.13.13, table 7	35190
J35	Themetra	Tunisia/eastern coast	Africana I type amphoras were also identified during field surveys at the coastal city	Reported in Slim et al. 2004: 159	-
J36	Utica	Tunisia/northern coast	-	Mentioned in Pieri 2005a: 182, appendix 1	-

10.3.K. Iberian Peninsula and Morocco

No.	Site	LCP region	Details (chronology, type, and notes)	Reference	LCP vessel ID
K01	Barcino/Barcelona	Spain/Catalan coastal range	Visigothic court under Ataulf (early 5th c.). LRA1s attested at several urban excavation sites, ranging 0.71 to 8.28%, alongside LRA4s (only relevant eastern imports)	Reported in Carreras Monfort and Berni Millet 2005	-
K02	Benalùa	Spain/Baetic range	First half of the 6th c. context. Type B ("Kellia 164")	Mentioned in Remolà Vallverdú 2000: 287; cf. Reynolds 2010a: 227, table 22	-
K03	Braga/Bracara Augusta	Portugal/central–northern highlands	LRA1s attested in mid-5th to 6th c. contexts	Mentioned in Reynolds 2010a: 221, table 19	-
K04	Cabrera/Capraria	Spain/Balearic Islands	-	Mentioned in Alvarez et al. 2011: 64	-
K05	Cádiz/Gades	Spain/Baetic range	From the late 5th to the late 6th or early 7th c.	Mentioned in Reynolds 2010a: 98–99	-
K06	Carteia	Spain/Baetic range	Second half of the 5th c.	Mentioned in Reynolds 2010a: 98	-
K07	Carthago Nova, Karthago Spartaria	Spain/Baetic range	Presence of Byzantine army after the 550s reconquest. Area of the Roman theater, late antique commercial building (*tabernae*): LRA1s the most common (21.5%) among the eastern amphora; type A. "Shaft fill" of the 7th c.: LRA1s predominant among the imports from the east.	Murcia Muñoz et al. 2005: 12, 17, fig. 8.8–9; Mentioned in Reynolds 2011: 109	34535, 34536
K08	Cetobriga / Tróia	Portugal/central plains	Large *garum* installment. 5th c. context: LRA1s count for the 0.9% of the imported amphoras	Vaz Pinto, Magalhães, and Brum 2012: 402–5, fig. 8 (pottery distribution table), 9.37	34534

No.	Site	LCP region	Details (chronology, type, and notes)	Reference	LCP vessel ID
K09	Coimbra	Portugal/central–northern highlands	-	Mentioned in Pacetti 1995: 276	-
K10	Conimbriga	Portugal/	-	Mentioned in Pieri 2005a: 185, appendix 1	-
K11	Cubelles	Spain/Catalan coastal range	5th c.	Mentioned in Reynolds 2010a: 87	-
K12	Cullera Island	Spain/Baetic range	-	Mentioned in Pieri 2005a: 185, appendix 1	-
K13	Emporiae, Emporion	Spain/Catalan coastal range	Chemical analyses point to a possible provenance from Arsuz (comparison with samples by Empereur and Picon). Type A	Remolà Vallverdú 2000: 269; Fantuzzi, Ontiveros, and Reynolds 2017: 96; 106, and 95 fig. 2 (EMP 306, EMP 309–310, EMP 326, EMP 351); Cf. Pieri 2005a: 72, 185	34521, 34522, 34523, 34524, 34525
K14	Favatrix (shipwreck)	Spain/Balearic Islands	See below, table 10.3.S2	Reported in Fundación Juan March 1977: 95–102	-
K15	Hispalis/Seville	Spain/Guadalquivir River Valley	Late antique domestic contexts. Types A and B	de Amores Carredano, García Vargas, and González Acuña 2007: 135; figs. 3.12, 6.43, 45	34531, 34532, 34533
K16	Ibiza	Spain/Balearic Islands	-	Mentioned in Pieri 2005a: 185, appendix 1	-
K17	Iluro	Spain/Catalan coastal range	Contexts from the end of the 4th to the beginning/first half of the 6th c.	Remolà Vallverdú 2000: 269; Fantuzzi, Ontiveros, and Reynolds 2017: 96, 95 fig. 2	34519, 34520, 35017, 35018

No.	Site	LCP region	Details (chronology, type, and notes)	Reference	LCP vessel ID
K18	Iulia Traducta / Algeciras	Spain/Baetic range	Second half of the 5th c.	Mentioned in Reynolds 2010a: 98	-
K19	Málaga	Spain/Baetic range	Mid-5th c.	Mentioned in Reynolds 2010a: 98	-
K20	Olisipo	Portugal/central plains	Excavation of a "cesspit" by the castle's hill.	Reported in Banha da Silva and de Man 2015: 399	-
K21	Ossonoba/Faro	Portugal/Algarve and southern highlands	LRA1s together with LRA4s the most representative eastern imports. Types A and B ("Kellia 169 e 164")	de Almeida et al. 2014: 155; 158, fig. 5	34528, 34529, 34530
K22	Puig Rodon villa (Corça)	Spain/Catalan coastal range	Mid-5th c. context	Mentioned in Reynolds 2010a: 87	-
K23	Septem/Ceuta	Spain/Ceuta and Melilla	LRA1s most representative eastern amphora in the late 5th–early 6th c. contexts	Bernal Casasola, Bustamante Alvarez, and Sáez Romero 2014: 822; 832, fig. 7.7–8	34526, 34527

No.	Site	LCP region	Details (chronology, type, and notes)	Reference	LCP vessel ID
K24	Tarraco	Spain/Catalan coastal range	Type A (6–12% of the amphora assemblages in 5th c. contexts) and type B	Fantuzzi, Ontiveros, and Reynolds 2017: 96 fig. 2 (cat. no. 202, 206, 233, 241); Remolà Vallverdú 2000: 215–25, figs. 77.1–5, 78.1–10, 79.1–13, 80.1–6, 81–82	34665, 34666, 34667, 34668, 34669, 34670, 34671, 34672, 34673, 34674, 34675, 34676, 34677, 34678, 34679, 34680, 34681, 34682, 34683, 34684, 34685, 34686, 34687, 34688 34689, 34690, 34691, 34692, 34693, 34694, 34695, 34696, 34697, 34698, 34699, 34700, 34701, 34702
K25	Valentia/Valencia	Spain/Catalan coastal range	7th c. contexts.	Rosselló Mesquida and Ribera I Lacomba 2005: 156 and fig. 2.13	34664
K26	Vigo/Vicus Spacorum	Spain/Iberian Massif	LRA1s are the predominant eastern amphora in late antique contexts (up to 76% by the end of the 6th–beginning of the 7th c.). Types A and B	Fernández 2012: 357 and figs. 2.1–11; cf. Fernández 2016: 122	34652, 34653, 34654, 34655, 34656, 34657, 34658, 34659, 34660, 34661, 34662, 34663

10.3.L. Late Roman Gaul

No.	Site	LCP region	Details (chronology, type, and notes)	Reference	LCP vessel ID
L01	Aigues-Vives	France/ Mediterranean coast	5th to the beginning of the 6th c.; type A	Mentioned in Pieri 2005a: 74	-
L02	Aix-en-Provence/ Aquae Sextae	France/ Mediterranean coast	6th to first half of the 7th c.; type B	Mentioned in Pieri 2005a: 76	-
L03	Antibes/Antipolis	France/ Mediterranean coast	5th to the first half of the 7th c.; types A and B	Pieri 2005a: 74, 76 and pl. 18 no. 5	34874
L04	Arelatum/Arles	France/ Mediterranean coast	5th to the beginning of the 6th c.; types A and B; LRA4s prevailing among the eastern imports	Reported in Bonifay, Conges, and Leguilloux 1989: 661. Reported in Congès, Leguilloux, and Brien-Poitevin 1991: 207–9, 216, 220. Reported in Richarté 2011: 6. Cp. Liou 1987: 122–23, A7	35019
L05	Aubigné-Racan	France/Loire Valley central	5th to the beginning of the 6th c.; type A	Mentioned in Pieri 2005a: 74	-
L06	Augst / Augusta Raurica	Switzerland/Jura Mountains	-	Mentioned in Pieri 2005a: 187, appendix 1; Martin-Kilcher 1994: 441, no. 5542, Pl. 244	34873
L07	Avignon	France/ Mediterranean coast	5th to the beginning of the 6th c.; type A	Mentioned in Pieri 2005a: 74	-
L08	Bad Kreuznach	Germany/Rhineland	Villa site, at which LRA1s were very rare, as were Kapitan II amphoras	Reported in Ehmig 2005: 191	-
L09	Baux-de-Provence	France/ Mediterranean coast	5th to the beginning of the 6th c.; type A	Mentioned in Pieri 2005a: 74	-
L10	Beaucaire	France/ Mediterranean coast	5th to the beginning of the 6th c.; type A	Mentioned in Bonifay 1986: 276; mentioned in Pieri 2005a: 74	-

No.	Site	LCP region	Details (chronology, type, and notes)	Reference	LCP vessel ID
L11	Bordeaux	France/Midi and southwest	5th–first half of the 7th c.; types A and B	Mentioned in Pieri 2005a: 74, 76	-
L12	Bréhat	France/Brittany and west	6th–first half of the 7th c.; type B	Mentioned in Pieri 2005a: 76	-
L13	Cannes	France/ Mediterranean coast	Type A	Mentioned in Pieri 2005a: 74	-
L14	Carbonne	France/ Mediterranean coast	5th to the beginning of the 6th c.; type A	Mentioned in Pieri 2005a: 74	-
L15	Collias	France/ Mediterranean coast	5th to the beginning of the 6th c.; type A	Mentioned in Pieri 2005a: 74	-
L16	Collioure	France/ Mediterranean coast	5th to the beginning of the 6th c.; type A	Mentioned in Pieri 2005a: 74	-
L17	Corte	France/Corse	6th to the first half of the 7th c.; type B	Mentioned in Pieri 2005a: 76	-
L18	Elne	France/ Mediterranean coast	6th to the first half of the 7th c.; type B	Mentioned in Pieri 2005a: 76	-
L19	Epomanduodurum	France/Rhone and Alps	-	Reported in Kuhnle et al. 2007: 423	-
L20	Fossae Marianae	France/ Mediterranean coast	Attested from mid-4th to the 7th c.; types A and B	Rodriguez Lopez 2016: 243, fig. 142, pls. XI.1–5, XI bis.1–6	34635, 34636, 34637, 34638, 34639, 34640, 34641, 34642, 34643, 34871, 34872
L21	Frejús	France/ Mediterranean coast	5th to the beginning of the 6th c.; type A	Mentioned in Pieri 2005a: 74	-
L22	Gap	France/ Mediterranean coast	5th to the beginning of the 6th c.; type A	Mentioned in Pieri 2005a: 74	-
L23	La Capelière	France/ Mediterranean coast	Ca. mid-6th c. context.	Duperron 2019: 238, fig. 199	34634

No.	Site	LCP region	Details (chronology, type, and notes)	Reference	LCP vessel ID
L24	La Palud (shipwreck)	France/ Mediterranean coast	See below, table 10.3.S2	Long and Volpe 1998: 335, fig. 298 nos. 81–82	34632, 34633
L25	La Reille	France/ Mediterranean coast	Single LRA1 in a 5th c. context; rural settlement related to wine production	Reported in Duperron, Bourgaut, and Leger 2019: 227	-
L26	Laudun	France/ Mediterranean coast	6th to the first half of the 7th c.; type B	Mentioned in Pieri 2005a: 76	-
L27	Lugdunum	France/Rhone and Alps	5th to the beginning of the 6th c.; type A	Reported in Becker, Constantin, and Villedieu 1989: 657; mentioned in Pieri 2005a: 74	-
L28	Maguelone	France/ Mediterranean coast	Episcopal seat of a diocese related to Nîmes, by a harbor. Funerary context (end of the 6th–early 7th c.)	Reported in Garnotel and Raynaud 2014: 56	-
L29	Massalia/Marseille	France/ Mediterranean coast	5th–beginning of the 6th c.: 15–28% of the amphora assemblage. 6th–first half of the 7th c.: most common amphora of the phase. Type A (the most common amphora 5th–beginning 6th c.), type B	Bonifay 1986: 279 and fig. 7.20–21; 290 and fig. 13.56; Bonifay and Pieri 1995: 107, figs. 6.41–48; 108–9 and fig. 7.49–51; Pieri 2005a: 74 and pls. 14, 15.1–8, 17.1–4, 19.3	34606, 34607, 34608, 34609, 34610, 34611, 34612, 34613, 34614, 34615, 34616, 34617, 34618, 34619, 34620, 34621, 34622, 34623, 34624, 34625, 34626, 34627, 34628, 34629, 34630, 34631, 35020
L30	Menerbes	France/ Mediterranean coast	6th–first half of the 7th c.; type B	Mentioned in Pieri 2005a: 76	-

No.	Site	LCP region	Details (chronology, type, and notes)	Reference	LCP vessel ID
L31	Montille d'Ulmet	France/ Mediterranean coast	Harbor settlement, beginning of the 5th to the mid-6th c.; types A and B	Duperron and Landuré 2019: 574 and fig. 6.6–7; Duperron 2021: 563, fig. 16 (frequency table); and 564, fig. 17.7	34603, 34604, 34605
L32	Nantes	France/Brittany and west	5th to the beginning of the 6th c.; type A	Mentioned in Pieri 2005a: 74	-
L33	Narbo	France/Midi and southwest	5th to the beginning of the 6th c.; type A	Alessandri, Pieri, and Sanchez 1998: fig. 4.8	34602
L34	Nîmes	France/ Mediterranean coast	5th to the beginning of the 6th c.; type A	Mentioned in Pieri 2005a: 74	-
L35	Olbia/Hyères	France/ Mediterranean coast	Types A and B; eastern imports are predominant in the amphora assemblage; LRA1s became the most common amphora in the second half of the 5th c.	Bats 2006: 74, fig. 8.1–2; 81, fig. 12.8; cf. Pieri 2005a: 74, 76	34600, 34601, 35192
L36	*Oppidum* de Constantine	France/ Mediterranean coast	5th to the first half of the 6th c. phase; types A and B; LRA1s the most common amphora at the hilltop *oppidum*	Duperron 2013: 256, 257, 271, 273, 288, 319, 358, figs. 33 (frequency table), 35.13, 52.9; and 298, fig. 66.9; figs. 90.7; 132.4	34598, 34599, 34644, 34867, 34868, 34869, 34870
L37	Paris	France/Normandy and north	6th to the first half of the 7th c.; type B	Mentioned in Pieri 2005a: 76	-
L38	Port-Vendres	France/ Mediterranean coast	5th–first half of the 7th c.; types A and B	Pieri 2005a: 74, 76 and pl. 16.7	34597
L39	Saint-Blaise	France/ Mediterranean coast	6th to the first half of the 7th c.; types A, B	Mentioned in Bonifay 1986: 279; cf. Pieri 2005a: 72–74, 76; 2012: fig. 2.11a; Liou 1987: SB1	34596, 35021
L40	Saint-Cassien/*ad horrea* (Cannes)	France/ Mediterranean coast	5th to the beginning of the 6th c.; type A	Mentioned in Pieri 2005a: 74. Reported in Pellegrino 2011: 115, 134	-

No.	Site	LCP region	Details (chronology, type, and notes)	Reference	LCP vessel ID
L41	Saint-Julien-les-Martigues	France/ Mediterranean coast	5th to the beginning of the 6th c.; type A	Mentioned in Pieri 2005a: 74	-
L42	Saintes-Maries de la Mer	France/ Mediterranean coast	Type A	Mentioned in Pieri 2005a: 74	-
L43	Saint-Martin-de-Crau	France/ Mediterranean coast	-	Mentioned in Bonifay 1986: 279; cf. Pieri 2005a: 262, pl. 22 no. 1 (*dipinti*) = Liou 1987: fig. 38 (SMC)	34595
L44	Saint-Raphaël	France/ Mediterranean coast	5th to the beginning of the 6th c.; type A	Mentioned in Bonifay 1986: 290; mentioned in Pieri 2005a: 74	-
L45	Saint-Tropez/ Athenopolis	France/ Mediterranean coast	Roman villa *des Platanes*, occupied up to the 5th c. LRA1s attested in the postoccupational phases, first half of the 6th c.	Reported in Brun et al. 1997: 214	-
L46	Sion-sous-le-Scex	Switzerland/Alps	-	Mentioned in Pieri 2005a: 187, appendix 1	-
L47	Solenzara	France/Corse	Type B	Mentioned in Pieri 2005a: 76	-
L48	Tautavel	France/ Mediterranean coast	5th–beginning of the 6th c.; type A	Mentioned in Pieri 2005a: 74	-
L49	Telo Martius/ Toulon	France/ Mediterranean coast	5th–first half of the 7th c.; types A and B	Reported in Brun, Lecacheur, and Pasqualini 1992: 127; mentioned in Pieri 2005a: 74, 76	-
L50	Toulouse/Tolosa	France/ Mediterranean coast	5th–beginning of the 6th c.; type A	Mentioned in Pieri 2005a: 74	-
L51	Venasque	France/ Mediterranean coast	5th–beginning of the 6th c.; type A	Mentioned in Pieri 2005a: 74	-
L52	Vénéjan	France/ Mediterranean coast	5th–beginning of the 6th c.; type A	Mentioned in Pieri 2005a: 74	-

No.	Site	LCP region	Details (chronology, type, and notes)	Reference	LCP vessel ID
L53	Voerendaal Ten Hove	Netherlands/central lowlands south	LRA1s are attested in the postbuilding settlement following the Roman villa, and are defined as an absolute rarity; late antique frequentation confirmed by coins.	Van den Berg 2023: 589, 603–4, fig. 24.9	34594

10.3.M. British Isles

No.	Site	LCP region	Details (chronology, type, and notes)	Reference	LCP vessel ID
M01	Alt Glut, Dumbarton Castle	Scotland/lowlands		Alcock and Alcock 1991: illus. 13 nos. 39, 41, 47–48	34333, 34334, 34335, 34336
M02	Ballygarran	Ireland/southwestern highlands	From a church site at Ballygarran	Weadick n.d.: 1940:811	34349
M03	Bantham	England/southwest	Late 5 to late 6th or early 7th c.; type B and LRA1 *survivals*; LRA1s are ca. 82.76%, while LRA4s are 2.18% at of the amphora assemblage (by MNV) from the port site, hypothesized to have been a major entry point for Mediterranean imports	Snyder 1996: 19; Reed, Bidwell, and Allan 2010: figs. 14.1, 14.3–4, 14.6–7, 16.12, 17.21–22, 18; Duggan 2020	34337, 34338, 34339, 34340, 34341, 34342, 34343, 34344, 34345, 34346
M04	Blanchfieldsland	Ireland/midlands east	The only type of imported Mediterranean amphora recorded from the ringfort site; from an enclosure ditch	Mentioned in Doyle 2009: 27, 40	-
M05	Cadbury Castle	England/southwest	5th–6th c.; LRA2s are more common than LRA1s at the fortified hilltop settlement	Alcock 1995: illus. 6.4.1–7	34297, 34327, 34328, 34329, 34330, 34331, 34332

No.	Site	LCP region	Details (chronology, type, and notes)	Reference	LCP vessel ID
M06	Caherlehillan	Ireland/southwestern highlands	LRA1s identified in a cemetery context at the site	Doyle 2009: fig. 13.2; Kelly 2010: 60–61	34316
M07	Cannington	England/southwest	Two sherds; petrographic analysis showed relatively little limestone	Rahtz, Hirst, and Wright 2000: 295, fig. 199.171	34326
M08	Rock of Cashel in Tipperary	Ireland/midlands east	Three total sherds from three different loci	Doyle 2009: 41–42, fig. 14 nos. 5:148, 5:172, 5:174	34296, 34314, 34315
M09	Cawsand	England/southwest	Type B; residue analysis on the single LRA1 specimen (which was recovered by a diver and amateur collector with no stratigraphic data) suggested it last transported red wine	Duggan 2013: fig. 1, 3	34325
M10	Clogher	Northern Ireland	5th–6th c.; one LRA2 sherd was found in addition to the two LRA1 sherds at the fortified royal/elite complex, made up of a ringfort within a ditch enclosure	Doyle 2009: 43–44, fig. 16 nos. 15.9 and 15.12; Kelly 2010: 61	34347, 34348
M11	Collierstown	Ireland/midlands east	Late 5th to early 6th c.; a Phocaean red slipped ware (PRSW) bowl sherd was found alongside nine LRA1 sherds at this small cemetery	Mentioned in Doyle 2009: 44; Kelly 2010: 49, 85–88, fig. 4 nos. A008/015:286:1, A008/015:247:1, and A008/015:4:79	34323, 34324
M12	Dalkey Island	Ireland/midlands east	One Africana II sherd and one LRA2 sherd were found in addition to the one LRA1 sherd at the coastal fort and trade *entrepôt* (?)	Doyle 1998: fig. 3.1	34322
M13	Dinas Powys	Wales	Some PRSW and ARS sherds were also found at the elite hilltop settlement	Mentioned in Kelly 2010: 40	

No.	Site	LCP region	Details (chronology, type, and notes)	Reference	LCP vessel ID
M14	Garranes (Lisnacaheragh)	Ireland/southwestern highlands	5th–6th c. (including one hearth context C^{14}-dated to 396–539); LRA1s are the most common imported amphora, with eight type B sherds identified at the royal ringfort site, compared to one LRA2	O'Brien and Hogan 2021: figs. 7.21 no. E629:114, 7.23 (pottery frequency table), 7.28 (LRA1s and LRA2s distribution chart), 10.7	34320, 34321, 34350
M15	Glastonbury Tor	England/southwest	6th–7th c.; multiple LRA1 sherds were found at the monastic (?) site, though the type was notably absent from the nearby abbey complex	Rahtz 1970: 5, 65–67, fig. 28.4–5; mentioned in Williams 1980; mentioned in Snyder 1996: 23–24	34318, 34319
M16	Gwithian	England/southwest	Nine LRA2 sherds were found alongside 54 LRA1 sherds at the domestic site	Mentioned in Thomas 1959: 92	-
M17	High Peak, Sidmouth	England/southwest	5th–7th c., with two radiocarbon dates from wood charcoal yielding ranges of 380–540 and 550–640; excavators at the bivallate hillfort site separated LRA1s and a "Bantham-type" subclass of LRA1s based on the distinct buff fabric; samples were recovered in Areas A, B, G	Rainbird and Hughes 2014: 17–20, fig. 6b	34317
M18	Inis Cealtra	Ireland/midlands west	6th c. or later; from a context north of St. Caimín's Church at the ecclesiastical trade hub	Mentioned in McCarthy 2017: 70; Doyle 2009: fig. 24 no. 38 (left)	34313

No.	Site	LCP region	Details (chronology, type, and notes)	Reference	LCP vessel ID
M19	Llandough	Wales	LRA1s were identified in five burials at the large monastic cemetery, possibly as a part of funerary rituals, and it is notable that a Roman-style villa (2nd–early 4th c.) overlaps with a part of the site	Holbrook and Thomas 2005: table 5.31; fig. 40.1 cat 5, 40.2 cat. 8, 40.3 cat. 4, 40.4 cat. 9	34309, 34310, 34311, 34312
M20	Mothecombe	England/southwest	Likely before the late-6th to early 7th c.; LRA1s are, by sherd count and MNV, the most common imported amphora at the small port settlement, with far less frequent LRA2 and north African amphoras also present	Agate et al. 2012: table 6, ills. 12–13 cat. P5a, P6a, P7, P8a-b	34305, 34306, 34307, 34308
M21	Portmarnock	Ireland/midlands east	LRA1 sherds were identified in the fill of ditch surrounding an enclosure, the context being radiocarbon dated to 416–623	Mentioned in O'Brien and Hogan 2021: 259	-
M22	Reask	Ireland/Atlantic coast, south	The main occupation at the site has been radiocarbon dated to 395±90; four LRA1 sherds found in funerary contexts or their related fills, one was from an occupation layer, and one from the fill above a slab shrine at the ringfort site	Fanning 1981: 68, 114, fig. 17.133, 144, 175, 176, and 276	34300, 34301, 34302, 34303, 34304
M23	Sillina	England/southwest	LRA1s and LRA4s were the two amphora types imported from the eastern Mediterranean and found at this religious site (non-Christian to Christian over 4th–7th c.)	Mentioned in Snyder 1996: 26	-

No.	Site	LCP region	Details (chronology, type, and notes)	Reference	LCP vessel ID
M24	Tintagel	England/southwest	Tintagel represents the largest deposit of imported ceramics from the eastern Mediterranean, including amphoras, in Britain; an estimated 29 LRA1 vessels, alongside 34 LRA2s and three LRA3s have been found at the elite site (by MNV); mainly from midden contexts (pers. comm. M. Duggan)	Campbell 2011: table 12; Barrowman, Batey, and Morris 2007: fig. 129.3650 and 3863	34298, 34299

10.3.N. Nubia and Red Sea Region

No.	Site	LCP region	Details (chronology, type, and notes)	Reference	LCP vessel ID
N01	Adoulis	Eritrea	-	Mentioned in Tomber 2004; cf. Zerai et al. 2022	-
N02	Aksum	Ethiopia/Tigray	-	Reported in Williams 2000: 496 and fig. 420, nos. 35, 36, and 47; Philipson 2000: fig. 283c	34866
N03	Ballana	Egypt/Upper Egypt	Burial context (grave offerings), cemetery 219 and 220. Reportedly, LRA1s contained animal bones; they often showed pitch-lining. Mid-5th to the late 6th c.	Emery and Kirwan 1938: 401–5 (non vidi); cf. Fournet 2021: 66 (with image of the *titulus*)	35173
N04	Faras / Pachora	Egypt/Upper Egypt	-	Mentioned in Pieri 2005a: 69; 185, appendix 1. Cf. Strouhal 1984: 156, with references; Griffith 1927: pl. 48.3	34864

No.	Site	LCP region	Details (chronology, type, and notes)	Reference	LCP vessel ID
N05	Firka	Sudan/north	Reportedly, to be dated to the 5th c., with inscription	Mentioned in Pieri 2005a: 185, appendix 1. Mentioned in Strouhal 1984: 156; Kirwan 1935: fig. 2	34865
N06	Kalabsha / Talmis	Egypt/Upper Egypt	Late 5th–early 6th c. ?	Strouhal 1984: 156, P776	34180
N07	Old Dongola	Sudan/north	-	Danys 2016: 776 and fig. 10 (cat. no. ADd.12.298)	34183
N08	Qana	Yemen/Northern Desert	-	Mentioned in Majcherek 2019: 400; Salles and Sedov 2010 (non vidi)	-
N09	Qustul	Egypt/Upper Egypt	Burial context (grave offerings)	Emery and Kirwan 1938 (non vidi)	-
N10	Sayala	Egypt/Upper Egypt	-	Hautumm 1981: ill. 18	34187
N11	Sudanese Mine R37	Sudan/Eastern Desert	Mining site. From a pedestrian survey	Massa 2020: 89, fig. 9.8	34186
N12	Sudanese Mine R45	Sudan/Eastern Desert	Mining site. From a pedestrian survey	Massa 2020: 89 and fig. 9.8	34185
N13	Sudanese Mine R57	Sudan/Eastern Desert	Mining site. From a pedestrian survey	Massa 2020: 89, fig. 9.7	34184
N14	Sudanese Mine R60	Sudan/Eastern Desert	Mining site. From a pedestrian survey	Massa 2020: 89, fig. 9.8C	34179
N15	Wadi Qitna	Egypt/Upper Egypt	Burial context; reported as a rare occurrence; called “Bf” type amphora. Probably attested as early as the late 4th c.	Strouhal 1984: 154–56, fig. 124 P 1244; fig. 141.P 970; pl. 65P 778	34181, 34182, 34863

10.3.S1. Major Shipwrecks

No.	Shipwreck	Ref. no.	Cargo	Date	LRA1 figures	Notes	Reference
S01	Avdimou Bay	B05	Mostly LRA4s (ca. 30)	Mid- to late 5th c.	Two LRA1s	3–4 m depth. LRA1s identified together with three millstones (ballast or cargo?). Maybe a modest merchant venture.	Leidwanger 2007: 311–13; 2013b: 187
S02	Burgaz	F08	LRA1s and LRA2s	Late 6th or 7th c.	LRA1s were ca. 60% of the cargo (estimated)	4–5 m depth. Type B (?); several vessels retain pitch on the interior, few on the exterior as well. Fabrics seem compatible with a (western?) Cilician origin. Authors suggest some of the amphoras were reused.	Leidwanger et al. 2015
S03	Cape Andreas	B06	Ceramics found in close proximity to terracotta sarcophagi	-	Types B and (Cilician?) C attested. Pitched	-	Green 1973: figs. 20–22
S04	Cape Zevgari	B08	ca. 150 LRA1s	5th or early 6th c.	-	5–7 m depth; 35 × 15 m area. Some 100 m from a jettison deposition. Only one vessel collected, showing no traces of pitch lining. Small-scale commercial venture.	Leidwanger 2007: 308–11; 2013b: 186–87

No.	Shipwreck	Ref. no.	Cargo	Date	LRA1 figures	Notes	Reference
S05	Cefalù	H15	Tableware (*sigillata*), tools, amphoras (including LRA1s, predominant type).	Mid-6th	Not given, but defined as prevalent; reportedly, no pitched-lining.	2 m depth; 35 × (at least) 6 m. Not excavated (and unfortunately plundered: Purpura 2004a); the wreck was originally preserved in a sort of mound, covered by the ballast stones that partially consist of *spolia*, like high-quality architectural elements. Stone "cannon-balls" (to be used with a catapult) and some weapons reinforce the interpretation as a military ship. Probably sunk because of a fire.	Purpura 1983: 102, fig. 11; 2004a; 2004b
S06	Chios Site 9, Agios Stefanos Islet east	F09	LRA1s	6th–7th c.	-	Macroscopic analysis (1954) on some vessels: tarry black deposit inside.	Theodoulou et al. 2015a
S07	Chios Site 10, South Prasonisi Islet south	F10	LRA1s	6th–7th c.	Only five vessels collected, but LRA1s are said to represent the main cargo (type B, other types attested as well).	32 m depth; 13 × 10 m. Each collected LRA1 had minor differences in morphology.	Theodoulou et al. 2015a: 48–50, figs. 6 (A–C), 7 (D), 8 (E); and table 2
S08	Kekova Island (shallow reef eastern wreck)	F18	-	-	Types A and B	Between 10–22 m depth.	Aslan and Orhan 2020: 302–4 fig. 4.a, b (cat. nos. 1–2)

No.	Shipwreck	Ref. no.	Cargo	Date	LRA1 figures	Notes	Reference
S09	Kizilburun	F21	Marble columns	6th c. (?)	"15 to 20 amphoras of a single type" which appears to be Cypriot type C LRA1s.	The shipwreck measured ca. 14 × 4.8 m and was found at a depth of 39–40 m. The ship was transporting finished marble flutes, likely for a single monumental building (church?). The authors proposed a date of either the 6th or the 10–12th c., with them preferring the latter and we the former.	Pulak and Rogers 1994: 17–18, fig. 2
S10	Knidos A	F23	LRA1s; few tiles	Second quarter or middle of the 6th c.	Between 700–800 vessels, maybe up to 1200; different sizes (type C prevalent).	360 m depth; northeast–southwest-oriented wreck; 14× 8 m. "Either the cargo was picked up from multiple locations or … different batches of amphora arrived at the port of embarkation from various points in the countryside."	Brennan et al. 2020: 295–99
S11	Knidos C	F24	LRA1s	End of the 6th or very beginning of the 7th c.	550 visible amphoras, but probably the same cargo size as Knidos A. Presence of piriform examples of various sizes.	Ca. 435 m depth; northeast–southwest-oriented wreck, ca. 14× 8 m. About 40% of artifacts damaged by trawling. Galley wares attested (singleton LRA2 and a small jug).	Brennan et al. 2020: 299–303

No.	Shipwreck	Ref. no.	Cargo	Date	LRA1 figures	Notes	Reference
S12	Knidos O	F25	LRA2 (some 45 vessels)	Second quarter of the 7th c.	Single LRA1 (by the stern, alongside a small number of galley wares).	Ca. 430 m depth; northeast–southwest-oriented wreck covering at least 8 × 4 m. Small ship engaged in short trips, probably specialized in local or regional coastal trading.	Brennan et al. 2020: 317–20
S13	Knidos T	F26	No evidence of a large amphora cargo, possibly organic produce	Second or third quarter of the 6th c.	2 LRA1s together with ballast stones compose the E pile; 10 type B LRA1s in the W pile (with at least 4 LRA2s).	Ca. 455 m depth; wreck composed of two distinct piles, both oriented east–west: east pile ca. 4.5 × 2 m, west pile ca. 4.5 × 3 m (galley wares). Given the absence of a real (amphora) cargo and the position of the ballast, the ship was likely hauling a large organic cargo, perhaps grain.	Brennan et al. 2020: 307–17
S14	La Palud	L24	Large-sized African transport jars (Keay 55, Keay 62).	Mid-6th/ second half of the 6th c.	Few LRA1s	6 to 7 m depth; covered surface 60–80 m^2. LRA1s were part of the galley wares (with LRA2s and African *sigillata* D plates)	Long and Volpe 1998: 335, fig. 298 nos. 81–82; http://oxrep.classics.ox.ac.uk/databases/sites/france/la_palud/802_la_palud_1/

No.	Shipwreck	Ref. no.	Cargo	Date	LRA1 figures	Notes	Reference
S15	Ma'agan Mikhael B	C25	"More than a hundred amphoras." The actual cargo must have consisted of LRA2 and LRA5	mid-7th to mid-8th c.	LRA1 *survival*	2 m depth; 19.6 × 4.9 m, east–west oriented; well preserved remains of the hull. An assemblage of some 38 amphoras (LRA1, LRA2, LRA4, and LRA5) was uncovered. Chronology confirmed by C^{14} analysis. Petrographic analysis on one vessel indicated a possible Cypriot origin; it bore an inscription incised on the upper shoulder (not studied); it still contained almost 8 kg of raisins/grapes.	Cohen and Creisher 2020: fig. 2.1; Cohen and Cvikel 2019: 197
S16	Marmaris B	F32	LRA1s	Second half of the 6th c.	750 visible amphoras, but must have originally been similar to Knidos A	520 m depth; north–south oriented; 17 × 10 m. Ca. 60% of artifacts damaged by trawling. Galley wares: two amphoras Tezgör type D Snp I; a casserole. Macroscopic analysis: "some of the interiors are exposed and visible. One LRA1 jar appears to have a pitch-lined interior"	Brennan et al. 2020: 303–7
S17	Plaka	E18	Carrot amphoras and LRA1s	Second quarter of the 6th to third quarter of the 7th c.	-	Ten-meter depth. Chemical and petrographic analyses suggest some of the amphoras may have been produced in Arsuz/Rhosos. It also contained Sinopean carrot amphoras, but the two batches come from different areas of production.	Waksman et al. 2014: figs. 4–5

No.	Shipwreck	Ref. no.	Cargo	Date	LRA1 figures	Notes	Reference
S18	Sinop B	E21	Sinopean carrot amphoras	5th–7th c.	Some 10 LRA1s in the cargo	85 m depth; 24 × 12 m	Ballard et al. 2001: 616–18; Ward and Ballard 2004: five–six LRA1s mentioned in Opaiț et al. 2019: 77
S19	Yassi Ada	F49	Ca. 700 LRA2s	Third decade of the 7th c.	Ca. 100 LRA1s	21 m long; estimated cargo of 60 tons. "The ship appears to have been engaged in official imperial supply, having been organized and sailed under the supervision of the church to support Heraclius's military forces on campaign against the Persian armies in the east during the late 620s" (van Doornick et al. 2023: 250).	See below, appendix to table S1 (van Doornick et al. 2023)

Appendix to Table S1. Yassi Ada Quick Bibliography: The 7th Century Shipwreck

Reference	Main Topic	Notes
Bass and van Doornick 1982	Full report of the investigations and findings. LRA1s are defined "type 1," thus the definition of the "Yassi Ada 1" name common in later literature	LRA1s type C: pp. 155–57
van Doornick 1989	Stamps and graffiti; reuse of the amphoras	On LRA2s
van Alfen 1996	Study on typology and volumes of LRA1s	-
van Doornick 2002	Yassi Ada presented in the frame of other known shipwreck of the Early to Mid-Byzantine periods	Pp. 900–901
Leidwanger 2014	Archaeometric analysis on LRA1s; possible eastern Cilician origin for many of the vessels.	Figs. 3–4
van Doornick 2014	Amphora manufacturing process and considerations	On LRA2s

Reference	Main Topic	Notes
van Doornick 2015	State of the art of the research on the shipwreck; useful summaries of the main topics.	No direct reference to LRA1s
Ward 2015	Analyses on residuals of the original contents on both LRA1s and LRA2s; the large majority of the specimens related to grape vines. More than 80% of 1,413 identified seeds were from grapes (but: large number of grape seeds in a few containers); 30 olive stones (2%)	-
Beltrame 2015	Spatial analysis of the distribution of objects other than cargo aboard the ship. Reconstruction of the galley.	No direct reference to LRA1s
van Doornick et al. 2023	Archaeometric analysis and study on standardization	Mostly on LRA2s

10.3.S2. Other Shipwrecks

List of other known shipwrecks with LRA1s, either mentioned in previous literature but not revised herein, or insufficiently documented.

No.	Shipwreck	Ref. no.	Mention	Notes	Full reference
S20	Arap Island	F05	Leidwanger 2017: 602, table 2	Not clear if a wreck or a large seabed deposit.	Pulak 1989: 78, fig. 2 (cat. no 2,8/E72)
S21	Dia Island (Crete)	G18	-	Shipwreck 5 of the Crete Project 2011; identified not far from the southern shore of the island, "at the southwestern side of the cape diving Hagios Georgios and Kapari Bay." 27 m depth. Not investigated; two vessels collected from the original cargo, LRA1 type C and LRA2 (or LRA13?).	Theodoulou et al. 2015b: 620, fig. 8

No.	Shipwreck	Ref. no.	Mention	Notes	Full reference
S22	Elaiussa (?)	A16 Production center 06	-	Underwater survey and partial excavations (2012–2013) revealed a seabed deposit at a shallow depth (max. 7.9 m) along the eastern shore of the promontory. Preliminary analysis suggests that the deposit resulted from the sinking of at least two distinct mixed cargoes, one to be dated to the early Byzantine phase (presence of LRA1s, pers. comm. by Dr. Pipere to one of the authors [V. I.]).	Pipere 2018
S23	Favaritx (Menorca)	K14	-	22 m depth, northeast coast of Menorca. Repeatedly plundered, not excavated. Anonymous author of the report. Liturgical and domestic bronze decorative objects. At least one LRA1.	Fundación Juan March 1977: 95–102
S24	Gulf of Keramos	F20	-	A tile cargo (?), at least one LRA1 (galley ware?, see Frost 1963: 215, fig. 7). The report contains little specific data on the wreck.	Frost 1963
S25	Punta del Serrone (Brindisi)	H59	Auriemma and Quiri 2007: 40	One or more wrecks; the main cargo consisted of a set of bronze statues, possibly Greek (to be related to Herod Atticus; Delphi has been suggested). LRA1s and LRA2s were reportedly part of the galley wares.	Carta Beni Culturali Regione Puglia, cod. BRBIU000506; http://cartapulia.it/web/guest/dettaglio?id=126509
S26	TK05-AD (Bozburun peninsula)	F48	Leidwanger 2017: 602, table 2	85 m depth, ca. 2 km offshore. "The amphoras form a c. 9 × 3 m oval that narrows to a point at both ends" suggesting a merchant's hold. At least 9, possibly 11 anchors. LRA1 type B, LRA3b.	Royal 2006: 211–12
S27	Yılanlı Island	A47	Reported in Bilir 2017	By Kelenderis, maybe more an anchorage site than a wreck.	-

References

Abdelhamid, S.

2013 Against the *Throw-away-mentality*: The Reuse of Amphoras in Ancient Maritime Transport. Pp. 91–106 in *Mobility, Meaning and the Transformations of Things*, ed. H.P. Hahn and H. Weiss. Oxford: Oxbow Books.

Agate, A., Duggan, M., Roskams, S., Turner, S., Campbell, E., Hall, A., Kinnaird, T., Luke, Y., McIntosh, F., Neal, C., and Young, R.

2012 Early Medieval Settlement at Mothecombe, Devon: The Interaction of Local, Regional and Long-Distance Dynamics. *Archaeological Journal* 169: 343–94. https://doi.org/10.1080/00665983.2012.11020918.

Akkaş, I.

2020 Commercial Amphora Finds from Parion Slope Bath (From 1st Century BC to 7th Century AD). *Arkhaia Anatolika* 3: 178–243. https://doi.org/10.32949/Arkhaia.2020.21.

Akrivopoulou, S., and Slampeas, P.

2014 Late Roman Coarse Ware from a Rescue Excavation in Thessaloniki. Pp. 287–95 in *LRCW4: Late Roman Coarse Wares, Cooking Wares and Amphorae in the Mediterranean: Archaeology and Archaeometry. The Mediterranean: A Market without Frontiers*, ed. N. Poulou-Papadimitriou, E. Nodarou, and V. Kilikoglou, 2 vols. BAR International Series 2616. Oxford: Archaeopress.

Alanyali, H.S.

2016 Side 2015 Yılı Kazı ve Araştırmaları: Excavations and Research at Side in 2015. *Anadolu Akdenizi Arkeoloji Haberleri. News of Archaeology from Anatolia's Mediterranean Areas* 14: 114–30.

Alcock, L.

1995 *Cadbury Castle, Somerset, The Early Medieval Archaeology*. Cardiff: University of Wales Press.

Alcock, L., and Alcock, E.A.

1991 Reconnaissance Excavations on Early Historic Fortifications and Other Royal Sites in Scotland, 1974–84: 4, Excavations at Alt Glut, Clyde Rock, Strathclyde, 1974–75. *Proceedings of the Society of Antiquaries of Scotland* 120: 95–149. https://doi.org/10.9750/PSAS.120.95.149.

Alessandri, P., Pieri, D., and Sanchez, C.

1998 Note sur un lot d'amphores du Ve siècle de notre ère à Narbonne (Aude). Pp. 117–22 in *Importations d'amphores en Gaule du sud, du règne d'Auguste à l'antiquité tardive: Actes du Congrès d'Istres 21–24 mai 1998)*. Marseille: SFECAG.

van Alfen, P.G.

1996 New Light on the 7th-c. Yassi Ada Shipwreck: Capacities and Standard Sizes of LRA1. *Journal of Roman Archaeology* 9: 189–213. https://doi.org/10.1017/S1047759400016561.

Alkaç, E.

2012 Korykos (Kilikia) Yüzey Araştırmalarında Bulunan LR1 Amphoraları. *Olba* 20: 323–44.

2015 Kanytellis Kazisindan Late Roman 1 Amphoralari. Pp. 149–57 in *Kanytellis Kanlidivane, Dağlık Kilikia'da Bir Kırsal Yerleşimin Arkeolojisi*, ed. Ü. Aydınoğlu. Istanbul: Mersin.

Alkaç, E., and Adıbelli, I. A.

2024 Cilician Amphorae from the Tarsus Zeytin Pazarı Excavation. *Arkeoloji Dergisi* 32.1: 85–97. https://doi.org/10.51493/egearkeoloji.1456366.

Alvarez, A., Roda, I., Rullan, M., Garcia-Moreno, A., and Domenech A.

2011 Primers resultats dels estudis dels elements marmoris del jaciment de l'Antiguitat Tardana del Plan de ses Figueres de l'illa de Cabrera. *Bolletí de la Societat Arqueològica Lul·liana* 67: 55–71 (Catalan).

de Almeida, R., Viegas, C., Beja, N., and Teixeira, N.

2014 Ânforas do Mediterrâneo Oriental em Faro (Ossonoba): Novos dados para equacionar o comércio durante a Antiguidade Tardia. Pp. 151–60 in *As produções cerâmicas de imitação na Hispania: II Congreso*

Internacional da SECAH – Ex Officina Hispana. Braga, 3–6 April 2013, ed. R. Morais, A. Fernández, and M.J. Sousa. Monografías ex officina hispana 2. Porto: Faculdade de Letras da Universidade do Porto.

de Amores Carredano, F., García Vargas, E., and González Acuña, D.

2007 Ánforas tardoantiguas en Hispalis (Sevilla, España) y el comercio mediterráneo. Pp. 133–46 in *LRCW2: Late Roman Coarse Wares, Cooking Wares and Amphorae in the Mediterranean: Archaeology and Archaeometry*, ed. M. Bonifay and J.-C. Tréglia, 2 vols. BAR International Series 1662. Oxford: Archaeopress, 2007.

Antonelli, S., and Menozzi, O.

2014 Late Roman Coarse Ware and Amphorae from Cyrenaica (Libya): The Case of Lamluda. Pp. 885–95 in *LRCW4: Late Roman Coarse Wares, Cooking Wares and Amphorae in the Mediterranean: Archaeology and Archaeometry. The Mediterranean: A Market without Frontiers*, ed. N. Poulou-Papadimitriou, E. Nodarou, and V. Kilikoglou, 2 vols. BAR International Series 2616. Oxford: Archaeopress.

Arcifa, L.

2016 Rocchicella di Mineo: Il sito tra età protobizantina e età tematica. Pp. 17–28 in *Dopo l'Antico: Ricerche di archeologia medievale*, ed. L. Arcifa and L. Maniscalco. Palermo: Regione Siciliana, Assessorato dei beni culturali e dell'identità siciliana.

2023 The Making of the Frontier in the 9th Century: Rocchicella di Mineo (CT) and Rural Landscapes in Eastern Sicily. Pp. 211–27 in *Suburbia and Rural Landscapes in Medieval Sicily*, ed. A.C. Barba and G. Mandala. Archaeologies, Histories, Islands and Borders in the Mediterranean 14. Oxford: Archaeopress Archaeology.

Ardizzone, F., Pezzini, E., Agrò, F., and Pisciotta, F.

2012 Dati sulla circolazione della ceramica e sulle rotte del Mediterraneo occidentale attraverso i contesti tardoantichi e medievali di Marettimo. Pp. 173–77 in *Atti del IX Congresso Internazionale sulla Ceramica Medievale nel Mediterraneo, Venezia, Scuola grande dei Carmini, Auditorium Santa Margherita, 23–27 Novembre 2009*, ed. S. Gelichi. Florence: All'insegna del Giglio.

Arthur, P.

1994 *Il complesso archeologico di Carminiello ai Mannesi, Napoli (scavi 1983–1984)*. Collana del Dipartimento, Università degli studi di Lecce, Dipartimento di scienze dell'antichità. Settore storico-archeologico 7. Galatina: Congedo.

Arthur, P., and Oren, E.D.

1998 The North Sinai Survey and the Evidence of Transport Amphorae for Roman and Byzantine Trading Patterns. *Journal of Roman Archaeology* 11: 193–212. https://doi.org/10.1017/S1047759400017256.

Aslan, E., and Orhan, U.

2019 Phaselis Amphoras Detected in Underwater Surveys in South Harbor Area in 2019. *Phaselis* 5: 85–99. https://doi.org/10.18367/Pha.19004.

2020 Evaluation of the Finds Recovered from the Underwater Rescue Excavation of the Kekova Island Shallow Reef Eastern Wreck/Kekova Adasi Sığ Resif Doğu Batığı Sualtı Kurtarma Kazısında Ele Geçen Buluntularin Değerlendirilmesi, *Cedrus* 8: 299–323.

Aşkın, E.

2022 Eirenopolis (Isauria) Kırsalından Bir Şarap Atölyesi ve Bir Üzüm Presi. *Seleucia* 12: 199–214.

Auriemma, R.

2007 Produzioni orientali. Pp. 136–54 in *Trieste antica: Lo scavo di Crosada**. I materiali*, ed. C. Morselli with R. Auriemma and P. Maggi, 2 vols. Fonti e studi per la storia della Venezia Giulia. Trieste: Editreg.

Auriemma, R., and Quiri, E.

2007 La Circolazione delle Anfore in Adriatico tra V e VIII sec d.C. Pp. 31–64 in *La Circolazione delle Ceramiche nell'Adriatico tra Tarda Antichità ed Altomedioevo. Venezia, 24–25 Giugno 2004*, ed. S. Gelichi and C. Negrelli. Documenti di Archeologia 43. Mantova: Società Archeologica.

Autiero, S.

2015 Indian Ocean Trade: A Reassessment of the Pottery Finds from a Multidisciplinary Point of View (3rd Century BC–5th Century AD). *Vicino Oriente* 19: 113–25. https://doi.org/10.53131/VO2724-587X2015_8.

Autret, C.

2022 LRA1 Manufactured at Soli-Pompeiopolis: Production and Distribution. Pp. 159–71 in *Amphorae from the Eastern Mediterranean and Beyond: Production and Distribution from the Early to the Late Roman Period*, ed. A. Kaldeli. Studies in Mediterranean Archaeology and Literature 191. Nicosia: Astrom.

Autret, C., Black, M., Dillon, M., Kızılarslanoğlu, H.A., Pejša, S., and Rauh, N.K.

2019 *Rough Cilicia Archaeological Survey Project Context Collection.* Purdue University Research Repository. https://doi.org/10.4231/1RAM-JR22.

Autret, C., Yağci, R., and Rauh, N.K.

2010 An LRA1 Amphora Kiln Site at Soli/Pompeiopolis. *ANMED* 8: 203–7.

Ayaz, M.

2021 Stratified Early Byzantine Pottery from the Assos North Stoa: Observations on Pottery Groups. Pp. 91–116 in *Veränderungen von Stadtbild und urbaner Lebenswelt in spätantiker und frühbyzantinischer Zeit: Assos im Spiegel städtischer Zentren Westkleinasiens*, ed. B. Böhlendorf-Arslan. Byzanz zwischen Orient und Okzident 23. Mainz: Römisch-Germanischen Zentralmuseums.

Aydın, S., Alkaç, E., Eroğlu, M., and Kadıoğlu, Y.K.

2021 Olba Kazıları Late Roman 1 Amphoraları ve Arkeometri Sonuçlarının Değerlendirilmesi. *Seleucia* 11: 137–74.

Bădescu, A.

2010 Roman-Byzantine Pottery in Scythia (End of 4th–Beginning of the 7th c.): The Study of Pottery as a Source of Knowledge for the Social and Economic Dynamics. Pp. 551–60 in *Antiquitas Istro-pontica: Mélanges d'archéologie et d'Histoire Ancienne Offerts À Alexandru Suceveanu*, ed. M.V. Angelescu, I. Achim, A. Bâltâc, V. Rusu-Bolindeț, and V. Bottez. Cluj-Napoca: Mega.

2012 Oriental Amphorae Type LRA 1 and LRA 2 Discovered at Histria (Basilica Extra Muros Sector). *Materiale Şi Cercetări Arheologice Serie Nouă* 8: 311–28.

Bădescu, A., and Bivolaru, A.

2015 Oriental Amphorae Discovered at Histria in the Acropolis Centre-South Sector (2014). *Materiale Şi Cercetări Arheologice Serie Nouă* 11: 193–208. https://doi.org/10.3406/mcarh.2015.1000.

Bădescu, A., and Cliante, L.

2014 Oriental Amphorae Discovered at Histria in the Central-north Sector (Campaign 2012). *Materiale Şi Cercetări Arheologice Serie Nouă* 10: 173–93. https://doi.org/10.3406/mcarh.2014.979.

Bajenaru, C.

2023 Amphorae from Late 4th and 5th Century Contexts in the Late Roman Fort at Ulmetum, Province of Scythia. Pp. 675–81 in *LRCW6: Late Roman Coarse Wares, Cooking Wares and Amphorae in the Mediterranean: Archaeology and Archaeometry. Land and Sea: Pottery Routes*, ed. V. Caminneci, E. Giannitrapani, M.C. Parello, and M.S. Rizzo, 2 vols. Roman and Late Antique Mediterranean Pottery 19. Oxford: Archaeopress.

Baldoni, D.

2010–2011 Materiali dallo scavo della torre del porto occidentale di Iasos. *Atti dell'Accademia delle Scienze di Ferrara* 88: 285–318.

Ballance, M., Boardman, J., Corbett, S., and Hood, S.

1989 *Excavation in Chios 1952–1955: Byzantine Emporio.* British School of Archaeology in Athens Supplementary Volume 20. Oxford.

Ballard, R.D., Hiebert, F.T., Coleman, D.F., Ward, C., Smith, J.S., Willis, K., Foley, B., Croff, K., Major, C., and Torre, F.

2001 Deepwater Archaeology of the Black Sea: The 2000 Season at Sinop, Turkey. *American Journal of Archaeology* 105: 607–23. https://doi.org/10.2307/507409.

Banha da Silva, R., and de Man, A.
2015 Palácio dos Condes de Penafiel: A Significant Late-Antique Context from Lisbon. Pp. 397–402 in *A cerâmica medieval no Mediterrâneo: Actas do X Congresso Internacional, Silves, 22 a 27 outubro*, ed. M.J. Gonçalves and S. Silves Gómez Martínez, 2 vols. Mértola: Câmara municipal Campo Arqueológico de Mértola.

Bar-Oz, G., Weissbrod, L., Erickson-Gini, T., Tepper, Y., Malkinson, D., Benzaquen, M., Langgut, D., Dunseth, Z.C., Butler, D.H., Shahack-Gross, R., Roskin, J., Fuks, D., Weiss, E., Marom, N., Ktalav, I., Blevis, R., Zohar, I., Yoav, F., Filatova, A., Gorin-Rosen, Y., Yan, X., and Boaretto, E.
2019 Ancient Trash Mounds Unravel Urban Collapse a Century before the End of Byzantine Hegemony in the Southern Levant. *Proceedings of the National Academy of Sciences* 116: 8239–48. https://doi.org/10.1073/pnas.1900233116.

Baralis, A., Lungu, V., Panayotova, K., Blanco, T., Bony, G., Comfort, A., Claquin, L., Delfieu, R., Dolea, A., Dupont, P., Flaux, C., Guy, M., Musat, A., Nedev, D., Riapov, A., Rossignol, I., Slavova, I., Streinu, M., and Thiriot, J.
2012 Le programme ANR Pont-Euxin: bilan des campagnes 2012 à Apollonia du Pont (Sozopol, dpt. de Bourgas, Bulgarie) et Orgamè / Argamum (Jurilovca, dpt. de Tulcea, Roumanie). *Dialogues d'histoire ancienne* 38: 165–87. https://doi.org/10.3406/dha.2012.3447.

Baratta, G.
1999 Gli impianti di produzione. Pp. 129–40 in *Elaiussa Sebaste: Campagne di scavo 1995–1997*, ed. E. Equini Schneider. Bibliotheca archaeologica 24. Rome: "L'Erma" di Bretschneider.

Barrowman, R.C., Batey, C.E., and Morris, C.D.
2007 *Excavations at Tintagel Castle, Cornwall, 1990–1999.* Reports of the Research Committee of the Society of Antiquaries of London 74. London: Society of Antiquaries of London.

Bass, G.F., and van Doornick, F.H., Jr.
1982 *Yassı Ada I: A Seventh-Century Byzantine Shipwreck.* Nautical Archaeology Series 1. College Station: Texas A&M University Press.

Bats, M.
2006 L'Antiquité tardive. Pp. 69–113 in *Olbia de Provence (Hyères, Var) à l'époque romaine (Ier s. av. J.-C. – VIIe s. ap. J.-C.)*, ed. M. Bats. Études massaliètes 9. Aix-en-Provence: Édisud.

Baumann, V.H.
1984 Raport asupra cercetărilor arheologice efectuate în ferma romană de la Teliţa, punctul la Pod (judeţul Tulcea), în anul 1980. *Peuce* 9: 51–65, 51–65.

Bausovac, M.
2010 Late Roman Amphorae from Rifnik near Celje (Slovenia). Pp. 695–701 in *LRCW3: Late Roman Coarse Wares, Cooking Wares and Amphorae in the Mediterranean: Archaeology and Archaeometry. Comparison between Western and Eastern Mediterranean*, ed. S. Menchelli, S. Santoro, M. Pasquinucci, and G. Guiducci, 2 vols. BAR International Series 2185. Oxford: Archaeopress, 2010.

Beaudry, N., Blanc, P., Bonifay, M., Cerova, Y., Chevalier, P., Haxhimihali, M., Hobdari, E., Islami, A., Kozelj, T., Muçaj, S., Nallbani, E., Raynaud, M.-P., Savard, M., Sodini, J.-P., Tassignon, I., Vanderheyde, C., Wurch-Kozelj, M.
2002 Byllis (Albanie). *Bulletin de Correspondance Hellénique* 126.2: 659–84. https://doi.org/10.3406/bch.2002.7116.

Becker, C., Constantin, C., and Villedieu, F.
1989 Types d'amphores en usage à Lugdunum du Ier au VIe siècle. Pp. 656–59 in *Amphores romaines et histoire économique: Dix ans de recherche. Actes du colloque de Sienne (22–24 mai 1986).* Publications de l'École française de Rome 114. Rome: École Française de Rome.

Bellatalla, E., Bertino, A., and Gardini, A.
1989 Lo scavo dell'area urbana di via S. Vincenzo a Genova. *Archeologia Medievale* 16: 357–410.

Beltrame, C.
2015 The Contribution of the Yassıada Shipwreck Excavation to the Knowledge of Life Aboard Ancient Ships. Pp. 63–71 in *Maritime Studies in the Wake of the Byzantine Shipwreck at Yassıada, Turkey*, ed. D. N. Carlson, J. Leidwanger, and S.M. Kampbell. College Station: Texas A&M University Press.

Bernal Casasola, D., Bustamante Alvarez, M., and Sáez Romero, A.M.
2014 Contextos cerámicos tardorromanos de un ambiente haliéutico de la ciudad de *Septem* (*Mauretania Tingitana*). Pp. 819–832 in *LRCW4: Late Roman Coarse Wares, Cooking Wares and Amphorae in the Mediterranean: Archaeology and Archaeometry. The Mediterranean: A Market without Frontiers*, ed. by V. Kilikoglou, E. Nodarou, and N. Polou-Papadimitrou. BAR international series 2116. Oxford: Archaeopress.

Berndt, M.
2003 *Funde aus dem Survey auf der Halbinsel von Milet (1992–1999): Kaiserzeitliche und frühbyzantinische Keramik.* Internationale Archäologie 79. Rahden: Leidorf.

Bertoldi, T.
2011 Le anfore. Pp. 148–70 in *Alle pendici dell'Aventino: Gli Scavi di via Marmorata 2*, ed. A. Capodiferro and P. Quaranta. Milan: Electa.

Bes, P.
2020 Early Byzantine Pottery from Limyra's West and East Gate Excavations. *Adalya* 23: 377–409. https://doi.org/10.47589/adalya.838038.
2022 The "Bright" Side of the Mountain ... Imported Amphorae at Sagalassos, Turkey. Pp. 143–58 in *Amphorae from the Eastern Mediterranean and Beyond: Production and Distribution from the Early to the Late Roman Period*, ed. A. Kaldeli. Studies in Mediterranean Archaeology and Literature 191. Nicosia: Astrom.

Bes, P., and Poblome, J.
2017 Urban Thespiai: The Late Hellenistic to Late Roman Pottery. Pp. 317–49 in *Boeotia Project*, vol. 2: *The City of Thespiai, Survey at a Complex Urban Site.* McDonald Institute Monographs. Cambridge: McDonald Institute for Archaeological Research.

Bes, P., Diamanti, C., and Dolea, A.
2023 A Rare Stamp in the Collection: A Late Roman Amphora 1 Stamp Found in Limyra (Lycia, Turkey). *Rei Cretariæ Romanæ Favtorvm Acta* 47: 132–41.

Bes, P., Brughmans, T., Lichtenberger, A., Raja, R., and Romanowska, I.
2020 Ceramics in Cities in Context: An Overview of Published Roman Imperial to Umayyad Pottery in the Southern Levant. Pp. 55–128 in *Hellenistic and Roman Gerasa: The Archaeology and History of a Decapolis City*, ed. A. Lichtenberger and R. Raja. Jerash Papers 5. Turnhout: Brepols. https://doi.org/10.1484/M.JPEB.5.120807.

Betina, L. 2019. Contemporary Pottery-Making In Rhodes: Approaching Ancient through Modern Craft Traditions. *Journal of Archaeological Science: Reports* 27: 1-10.

Bezeczky, T.
2013 *The Amphorae of Roman Ephesus.* Forschungen in Ephesos 15.1. Vienna: Österreichischen Akademie der Wissenschaften.

Bezeczky, T., Berni Millet, P., and Cesteros, H.G.
2015 New Research on the Castrum Villa, on the Island of Brijuni (Croatia): Preliminary Report. Pp. 189–98 in *Per terram, per mare: Seaborne Trade and the Distribution of Roman Amphorae in the Mediterranean*, ed. S. Demesticha. Studies in Mediterranean Archaeology and Literature Pocket-book 180. Uppsala: Åströms.

Biernacki, A.B., and Klenina, E.
2015 Amphorae of the 4th–6th Centuries AD from Novae (Moesia Secunda): Typology and Chronology. Pp. 99–120 in *Per terram, per mare: Seaborne Trade and the Distribution of Roman Amphorae in the Mediterranean*, ed. S. Demesticha. Studies in Mediterranean Archaeology and Literature Pocket-book 180. Uppsala: Åströms.

Bikai, P.M., Fulco, W.J., and Marchand, J.
1996 *Tyre: The Shrine of Apollo.* Amman: National Press.
Bikić, V., and Ivanišević, V.
2012 Imported Pottery in Central Illyricum – a Case Study: Caričin Grad (Iustiniana Prima). *Rei Cretariæ Romanæ Favtorvm Acta* 42: 41–49.
Bilir, A.
2017 Roma İmparatorluk Dönemi ve Geç Antik Çağ'da Kilikya Bölgesi'nde Amphora Üretimi. Pp. 219–55 in *Prof. Dr. Recep Yildirim'a Armağan*, ed. P. Pinarcik, B. Gökce, M.S. Erkek, and S. Coşğun Kandal. Ankara: Bilgin Kültür Sanat Şti.
Blondé, F., Gros, J., and Pétridis, P.
2011 La céramique au quotidien à Thasos de l'époque archaïque à l'époque protobyzantine. *Revue des Études Grecques* 124: 193–204.
Bonifay, M.
1986 Observations sur les amphores tardives à Marseille d'après les fouilles de la Bourse (1980–1984). *Revue archéologique de Narbonnaise* 19: 269–301. https://doi.org/10.3406/ran.1986.1293.
2004 *Études sur la céramique romaine tardive d'Afrique.* BAR International Series 1301. Oxford: Archaeopress.
2015 Africa: Patterns of Consumption in Coastal Regions versus Inland Regions: The Ceramic Evidence (300–700 A.D.). *Late Antiquity Archaeology* 10: 529–66. https://doi.org/10.1163/22134522-12340041.
Bonifay, M., Capelli, C., Franco, C., Leitch, V., Riccardi, L., and Berni Millet, P.
2013 Les Thermes du Levant à Leptis Magna: Quatre contextes céramiques des IIIe et IVe siècles. *Antiquités africaines* 49: 67–150. https://doi.org/10.3406/antaf.2013.1544.
Bonifay, M., Capelli, C., Martin, T., Picon, M., and Vallauri, L.
2002 Le littoral de la Tunisie, étude géoarchéologique et historique (1987–1997): La céramique. *Antiquités africaines* 38–39: 125–202. https://doi.org/10.3406/antaf.2002.1355.
Bonifay, M., and Cerova, Y.
2006 La céramique – Rapport intermédiaire. *Bulletin de Correspondance Hellénique* 130: 858–61.
Bonifay, M., Conges, G., and Leguilloux, M.
1989 Amphores tardives (Ve– VIIe siècle) à Arles et à Marseille. Pp. 660–63 in *Amphores romaines et histoire économique: Dix ans de recherche. Actes du colloque de Sienne (22–24 mai 1986).* Publications de l'École française de Rome 114. Rome: École Française de Rome.
Bonifay, M., and Pieri, D.
1995 Amphores du Ve au VIIes. à Marseille: Nouvelles données sur la typologie et le contenu. *Journal of Roman Archaeology* 8: 94–120.
Borgia, E.
2003 La cisterna Occidentale (VIT). Pp. 32–35 in *Elaiussa Sebaste II: Un porto tra Oriente e Occidente*, ed. E. Equini Schneider. Bibliotheca Archaeologica 37. Rome: "L'Erma" Di Bretschneider.
Borgia, E., and Iacomi, V.
2010 Note preliminari su un complesso industriale per la produzione di anfore Late Roman 1 a Elaiussa Sebaste (Cilicia). *L'Africa Romana* 18: 1029–53.
Bounni, A., Lagarce, J., Lagrace, E., Saliby, E., Badre, L., Leriche, P., and Touma, M.
1981 Rapport préliminaire sur la quatrième campagne de fouilles (1978) à Ibn Hani (Syrie). *Syria* 58: 215–97. https://doi.org/10.3406/syria.1981.6736.
Boutin, A., and Given, M.
2013 The Karkotis Valley. Pp. 51–151 in *Landscape and Interaction: The Troodos Archaeological and Environmental Survey Project, Cyprus*, vol. 2: *The TAESP Landscape*, ed. M. Given, A.B. Knapp, J. Noller, L. Sollars, and V. Kassianidou. Levant Supplementary Series 15. Oxford: Oxbow.
Brando, M.
2015 Tempio di Matidia: Consistenza e cronologia di contesti stratigrafici antichi significativi. Pp. 295–311

in *Campo Marzio: Nuove Ricerche. Atti del Seminario di Studi sul Campo Marzio. Roma, Museo Nazionale Romano a Palazzo Altemps, 18–19 marzo 2013*, ed. F. Filippi. Rome: Quasar.

Brennan, M.L., Davis, D., Opaiţ, A., and Stay, M.

2020 Deep-water Shipwrecks in the East Mediterranean: A Microcosm of Late Roman Exchange. *Journal of Roman Archaeology* 33: 291–329. https://doi.org/10.1017/S1047759420001026.

Brun, J.-P., Aycard, P., Cazalas, G., Lecacheur, P., Leguilloux, M., and Pálfi, G.

1997 La *villa* romaine des Platanes à Saint-Tropez (Var). *Revue archéologique de Narbonnaise* 30: 203–17. https://doi.org/10.3406/ran.1997.1492.

Brun, J.-P., Lecacheur, P., and Pasqualini, M.

1992 Les amphores du port antique de Toulon (Telo Martius). Pp. 123–32 in *Les amphores en Gaule: Production et circulation. Table ronde internationale, Metz, 4–6 octobre 1990. CNRS, Ministère de la Culture et de la Communication, Service Régional de l'Archéologie de Lorraine*. Annales littéraires de l'Université de Besançon 474. Besançon: Université de Franche-Comté.

Bueno, M., Novello, M., and Mantovani, V.

2012 Progetto Aquileia: Casa delle Bestie Ferite. Commercio e consumo ad Aquileia. Analisi delle anfore tardoantiche alla luce di alcuni contesti. *Rei Cretariæ Romanæ Favtorvm Acta* 42: 159–68.

Buluç, N.

2022 Perge Güney Bazilika Kazıları Seramik ve Diğer Buluntular. Ph.D. dissertation, T. C. İstanbul Üniversitesi Sosyal Bilimler Enstitüsü Sanat Tarihi Anabilim Dali.

Burragato, F., di Nezza, M., Ferrazzoli, A.F., and Ricci, M.

2007 Late Roman 1 Amphora Types Produced at Elaiussa Sebaste. Pp. 689–700 in *LRCW2: Late Roman Coarse Wares, Cooking Wares and Amphorae in the Mediterranean: Archaeology and Archaeometry*, ed. M. Bonifay and J.-C. Tréglia, 2 vols. BAR International Series 1662. Oxford: Archaeopress.

Calderon, R.

2000 Roman and Byzantine Pottery. Pp. 91–165 in *Ramat Hanadiv Excavations: Final Report of the 1984–1998 Seasons*, ed. Y. Hirschfeld. Jerusalem: Israel Exploration Society.

Caminneci, V.

2010 Tra il mare ed il fiume. Dinamiche insediative nella Sicilia occidentale in età tardoantica: il villaggio in contrada Carabollace (Sciacca, Agrigento, Sicilia, Italia). *Fasti Online*. https://www.fastionline.org/folder/FOLDER-it-2010-213.

2015 Sulle sponde del Mediterraneo. Il porto di *Agrigentum* in età tardo antica e bizantina. Pp. 481–90 in *Isole e terraferma nel primo Cristianesimo: Identità locale ed interscambi culturali, religiosi e produttivi. Atti XI Congresso Nazionale di Archeologia Cristiana, Cagliari 23–27 settembre 2014*, ed. R. Martorelli, A. Piras, and P.G. Spanu. Studi e Ricerche di Cultura Religiosa, Nuova Serie 8. Cagliari: PFTS University Press.

Caminneci, V., Franco, C., and Galioto, G.

2010 L'insediamento tardoantico di Contrada Carabollace (Sciacca-Agrigento, Sicilia, Italia): Primi dati sui rinvenimenti ceramici. Pp. 273–82 in *LRCW3: Late Roman Coarse Wares, Cooking Wares and Amphorae in the Mediterranean: Archaeology and Archaeometry. Comparison between Western and Eastern Mediterranean*, ed. S. Menchelli, S. Santoro, M. Pasquinucci, and G. Guiducci, 2 vols. BAR International Series 2185. Oxford: Archaeopress, 2010.

Campbell, E.

2011 *Early Medieval Imported Pottery and Glass in the Atlantic Province AD 400–800, Digital Archive*. https://www.gla.ac.uk/schools/humanities/research/archaeologyresearch/projectarchive/earlymedievalimports/.

Campbell, J.

2010 The Romans to the Norman Conquest, 500 BC–AD 1066. Pp. 3–111 in *A World by Itself: A History of the British Isles*, ed. J. Clark. London: Random House.

Can, B., Çakir, A., Cannon, B., Murphy, D., and Kızılarslangoğlu, H.A.

2017 Surveys at Syedra 2016 (Second Season). *ANMED* 15: 242–50.

Caputo, C., and Davoli, P.

2023 Byzantine Pottery from Soknopaiou Nesos (Fayyum, Egypt). Pp. 735–48 in *LRCW6: Late Roman Coarse Wares, Cooking Wares and Amphorae in the Mediterranean: Archaeology and Archaeometry. Land and Sea: Pottery Routes*, ed. V. Caminneci, E. Giannitrapani, M.C. Parello, and M.S. Rizzo, 2 vols. Roman and Late Antique Mediterranean Pottery 19. Oxford: Archaeopress.

Caraher, W., Moore, R.S., and Pettegrew, D.K.

2014 *Pyla-Koutsopetria I: Archaeological Survey of an Ancient Coastal Town.* American Schools of Oriental Research Archeological Reports 21. Boston: American Schools of Oriental Research.

Carreras Monfort, C., and Berni Millet, P.

2005 Late Roman Amphorae in the City of Barcino (Barcelona). Pp. 165–78 in *LRCW1: Late Roman Coarse Wares, Cooking Wares, and Amphorae in the Mediterranean: Archaeology and Archaeometry*, ed. J.M. Gurt i Esparraguera, J. Buxeda i Garrigos, and M.A. Cau Ontiveros. BAR International Series 1340 Oxford: Archaeopress.

Carsana, V., and Del Vecchio, F.

2023 Contesti ceramici da un edificio di VI–VII secolo d.C. nell'area portuale di Neapolis. Pp. 77–89 in *LRCW6: Late Roman Coarse Wares, Cooking Wares and Amphorae in the Mediterranean: Archaeology and Archaeometry. Land and Sea: Pottery Routes*, ed. V. Caminneci, E. Giannitrapani, M.C. Parello, and M.S. Rizzo, 2 vols. Roman and Late Antique Mediterranean Pottery 19. Oxford: Archaeopress.

Carta Beni Culturali Regione Puglia

n.d. Official Online Repository of Puglia (Italy) Archaeological Heritage. http://cartapulia.it/.

Casalini, M.

2015 Roma e il Mediterraneo dal IV al VI secolo. Pp. 535–46 in *Le forme della crisi: Produzioni ceramiche e commerci nell'Italia centrale tra Romani e Longobardi (III–VIII sec. d.C.). Atti del Convegno, Spoleto-Campello sul Clitunno, 5–7 Ottobre 2012*, ed. E. Cirelli, F. Diosono, and H. Patterson. Bologna: Ante Quem.

Casavola, L.

1999 Le anfore della villa romana di Agnuli. Pp. 261–75 in *Atti del 17° Convegno Nazionale sulla Preistoria, Protostoria e Storia della Daunia, San Severo, 6–8 Dicembre, 1996*, ed. A. Gravina. San Severo: Archeoclub d'Italia.

Casana, J., Goodman, D.D., and Ferweda, C.

2023 A Wall or a Road? A Remote Sensing-based Investigation of Fortifications on Rome's Eastern Frontier. *Antiquity* 97.396: 1516–33. https://doi.org/10.15184/aqy.2023.153.

Cassano, R., Annese, C., Conte, R., D'Eredità, A., de Filippis, M.D., and Fioriello, S.

2008 Forme della Circolazione e della Produzione delle Merci ad Egnatia in Età Tardoantica. *Rei Cretariæ Romanæ Favtorvm Acta* 40: 417–41.

Castaldo, V., De Simone, G.F., and Russell, B.

2023 Sea or Land? Trade from the Coast to the Fringes of Campania. Pp. 90–102 in *LRCW6: Late Roman Coarse Wares, Cooking Wares and Amphorae in the Mediterranean: Archaeology and Archaeometry. Land and Sea: Pottery Routes*, ed. V. Caminneci, E. Giannitrapani, M.C. Parello, and M.S. Rizzo, 2 vols. Roman and Late Antique Mediterranean Pottery 19. Oxford: Archaeopress.

Catling, H.W.

1972 An Early Byzantine Pottery Factory at Dhiorios in Cyprus. *Levant* 4: 1–82. https://doi.org/10.1179/lev.1972.4.1.1.

Catling, H.W., and Dikigoropoulos, A. I.

1970 The Kornos Cave: An Early Byzantine Site in Cyprus. *Levant* 2: 37–62. https://doi.org/10.1179/lev.1970.2.1.37.

Çaylak Türker, A.

2014 Roman and Early Byzantine Amphorae from the Archaeological Survey in Pamphylia and Tracheia Cilicia. Pp. 271–79 in *LRCW4: Late Roman Coarse Wares, Cooking Wares and Amphorae in the Mediterranean: Archaeology and Archaeometry. The Mediterranean: A Market without Frontiers*, ed. N. Poulou-Papadimitriou, E. Nodarou, and V. Kilikoglou, 2 vols. BAR International Series 2616. Oxford: Archaeopress.

Chamilaki, K.

2023 A Late Roman Pottery Assemblage from a Port on the South Coast of Aetolia (Kryoneri): Preliminary Remarks on Pottery Circulation in Western Central Greece. Pp. 168–80 in *LRCW6: Late Roman Coarse Wares, Cooking Wares and Amphorae in the Mediterranean: Archaeology and Archaeometry. Land and Sea: Pottery Routes*, ed. V. Caminneci, E. Giannitrapani, M.C. Parello, and M.S. Rizzo, 2 vols. Roman and Late Antique Mediterranean Pottery 19. Oxford: Archaeopress.

Chevalier, P., Mardesic, J., Čaušević, M., Gauthier, M., Gioanni, S., Goddard, C.J., Morvillez, É., Penđer, B., and Topić, M.

2005 Salone (Croatie): Les fouilles du quartier annexe nord-ouest du groupe épiscopal (autour des "petits thermes nord" et de l'"oratoire A"). *Mélanges de l'École française de Rome. Antiquité* 117.1: 385–400. https://doi.org/10.3406/mefr.2004.10785.

Christidou-Stylianou, E.

2013 Uncovering an Early Christian Center on Karpathos, Greece. *Biblical Archaeology Society*. https://www.biblicalarchaeology.org/daily/biblical-topics/post-biblical-period/uncovering-an-early-christian-center-on-karpathos-greece/.

Choat, M.

2019 Egypt's Role in the Rise of Christianity, Monasticism, and Regional Schisms. Pp. 449–71 in *A Companion to Greco-Roman and Late Antique Egypt*, ed. K. Vandorpe. Blackwell Companions to the Ancient World. Hoboken, NJ: Wiley & Sons. https://doi.org/10.1002/9781118428429.ch29.

Cibecchini, F.

2021 Shipwrecks, Amphorae and Contents. Pp. 41–49 in *Roman Amphora Contents: Reflecting on the Maritime Trade of Foodstuff in Antiquity. In Honour of Miguel Beltrán Lloris. Proceedings of the Roman Amphora Contents International Interactive Conference (RACIIC) (Cadiz, 5–7 October 2015)*, ed. D. Bernal Casasola, M. Bonifay, A. Pecci, and V. Leitch. Roman and Late Antique Mediterranean Pottery 17. Oxford: Archaeopress.

Cirelli, E.

2007 Ravenna e il commercio nell'Adriatico in età tardoantica. Pp. 45–50 in *Felix Ravenna. La croce, la spada, la vela: l'alto adriatico fra V e VI secolo*, ed. A. Augenti and C. Bertelli. Milan: Skira.

2014 Typology and Diffusion of Amphorae in Ravenna and Classe between the 5th and the 8th Centuries. Pp. 541–52 in *LRCW4: Late Roman Coarse Wares, Cooking Wares and Amphorae in the Mediterranean: Archaeology and Archaeometry. The Mediterranean: A Market without Frontiers*, ed. N. Poulou-Papadimitriou, E. Nodarou, and V. Kilikoglou, 2 vols. BAR International Series 2616. Oxford: Archaeopress.

2021 Late Antique and Medieval Pottery from Phoinike (Albania). Pp. 719–28 in *Association Internationale pour l'Étude des Céramiques Médiévales et Modernes en Méditerranée: AIECM3. 12th Congress AIECM3 On Medieval and Modern Period Mediterranean Ceramics*, ed. P. Petridis, A. G. Yangaki, N. Liaros, and E.E. Via. Athens: National Hellenic Research Foundation (NHRF).

Cirelli, E., and Lasi, R.

2003 Schede. Pp. 49–59 in *Palatia – Palazzi Imperiali tra Ravenna e Bisanzio: Catalogo della mostra*, ed. A. Augenti. Ravenna: Istituzione Biblioteca Classense.

Cocchiaro, A., Palazzo, P., Annese, C., Disantarosa, G., and Leone, D.

2005 La ricerca archeologica nell'ager Brundisinus: Lo scavo della villa di Giancola. Pp. 405–41 in *Paesaggi ed insediamenti rurali in Italia meridionale fra Tardoantico e Altomedioevo*, ed. G. Volpe and M. Turchiano. Insulae Diomedeae 4. Bari: Edipuglia.

Cohen, M., and Creisher, M.

2020 The Ma'agan Mikhael B Shipwreck: Preliminary Report. In *"Under the Mediterranean": The Honor Frost*

Foundation Conference on Mediterranean Maritime Archaeology 20th–23rd October 2017 Short Report Series. https://doi.org/10.33583/utm2020.02.

Cohen, M., and Cvikel, D.

2019 Ma'agan Mikhael B, Israel: A Preliminary Report of a Late Byzantine–Early Islamic Period Shipwreck. *International Journal of Nautical Archaeology* 48.1: 189–207. https://doi.org/10.1111/1095-9270.12331.

Coldstream, J.N., and Huxley, G.L.

1972 *Kythera: Excavations and Studies Conducted by the University of Pennsylvania Museum and the British School at Athens.* London: Faber & Faber.

Çömezoğlu, Ö.

2014 Coarse Wares from the Early Byzantine Episcopal Church of Rhodiapolis: Cooking Wares and Amphorae. Pp. 665–75 in *LRCW4: Late Roman Coarse Wares, Cooking Wares and Amphorae in the Mediterranean: Archaeology and Archaeometry. The Mediterranean: A Market without Frontiers*, ed. N. Poulou-Papadimitriou, E. Nodarou, and V. Kilikoglou, 2 vols. BAR International Series 2616. Oxford: Archaeopress.

2023 Amphorae and Utility Vessels from Basilica B, Andriake (Antalya, Turkey). Pp. 661–74 in *LRCW6: Late Roman Coarse Wares, Cooking Wares and Amphorae in the Mediterranean: Archaeology and Archaeometry. Land and Sea: Pottery Routes*, ed. V. Caminneci, E. Giannitrapani, M.C. Parello, and M.S. Rizzo, 2 vols. Roman and Late Antique Mediterranean Pottery 19. Oxford: Archaeopress.

Congès, G., Leguilloux, M., and Brien-Poitevin, F.

1991 Un dépotoir de l'Antiquité tardive dans le quartier de l'Esplanade à Arles. *Revue archéologique de Narbonnaise* 24: 201–34. https://doi.org/10.3406/ran.1991.1385.

Conrad, S.

1999 Zu Typologie und Funktionsbestimmung der Amphoren aus dem Kastell Iatrus. Pp. 175–88 in *Der Limes an der unteren Donau von Diokletian bis Heraklios: Vorträge der internationalen Konferenz, Svištov 1.–5. September 1998*, ed. G. von Bülow and A. Milčeva. Sofia: Nous.

2007 Kommentierter Katalog der gefäßkeramischen Funde. Pp. 1–74 in *Iatrus-Krivina: Spätantike Befestigung und frühmittelalterliche Siedlung an der unteren Donau. 6, Ergebnisse der Ausgrabungen 1992–2000*, ed. G. von Bülow and N. Benecke. Limesforschungen 28. Mainz am Rhein: von Zabern.

2020 *Felix Romuliana*: Die Gefäßkeramik aus den Grabungen *extra muros* 2006–2008. Pp. 117–70 in *Gamzigrad-Studien. I: Ergebnisse der deutsch-serbischen Forschungen im Umfeld des Palastes "Romuliana,"* ed. G. von Bülow and S. Petković. Römisch-Germanische Forschungen 75. Wiesbaden: Reichert.

Corti, C.

2023 Importazioni e circolazione lungo il corso del Po tra IV e VII secolo: Un aggiornamento. Pp. 40–48 in *LRCW6: Late Roman Coarse Wares, Cooking Wares and Amphorae in the Mediterranean: Archaeology and Archaeometry. Land and Sea: Pottery Routes*, ed. V. Caminneci, E. Giannitrapani, M.C. Parello, and M.S. Rizzo, 2 vols. Roman and Late Antique Mediterranean Pottery 19. Oxford: Archaeopress.

Cosentino, S.

2023 Goods on the Move across the Late Antique Mediterranean: Some Remarks on Shipping, the Management of Ports and Trading Places. Pp. 1–14 in *LRCW6: Late Roman Coarse Wares, Cooking Wares and Amphorae in the Mediterranean: Archaeology and Archaeometry. Land and Sea: Pottery Routes*, ed. V. Caminneci, E. Giannitrapani, M.C. Parello, and M.S. Rizzo, 2 vols. Roman and Late Antique Mediterranean Pottery 19. Oxford: Archaeopress.

Costantini, A.

2011 Le anfore. Pp. 393–430 in *Archeologia in Piazza dei Miracoli. Gli scavi 2003–2009*, ed. A. Alberti and E. Paribeni. Pisa: Felici.

2014 Pisa: Importazioni tra tarda antichità e altomedioevo da Piazza Duomo. Pp. 985–92 in *LRCW4: Late Roman Coarse Wares, Cooking Wares and Amphorae in the Mediterranean: Archaeology and Archaeometry.*

The Mediterranean: A Market without Frontiers, ed. N. Poulou-Papadimitriou, E. Nodarou, and V. Kilikoglou, 2 vols. BAR International Series 2616. Oxford: Archaeopress.

Costello, B.

2011 An Analysis of the Architecture and Material Culture from the Earthquake House at Kourion, Cyprus. Ph.D. dissertation, University of Buffalo.

Crowfoot, J.W., and Fitzgerald, G.M.

1929 *Excavations in the Tyropoeon Valley, Jerusalem 1927.* Palestine Exploration Fund Annual 5. London: Harrison.

Creisher, M., Goren, Y., Artzy, M., and Cvikel, D.

2019 The Amphorae of the Ma'agan Mikhael B Shipwreck: Preliminary Report. *Levant* 51: 105–20. https://doi.org/10.1080/00758914.2020.1723355.

Csiky, G., and Magyar-Harshegyi, P.

2015 Wine for the Avar Elite? Amphorae from Avar Period Burials in the Carpathian Basin. Pp. 175–82 in *The Danubian Lands between the Black, Aegean and Adriatic Seas (7th Century BC–10th Century AD): Proceedings of the Fifth International Congress on Black Sea Antiquites (Belgrade 17–21 September 2013)*, ed. G.R. Tsetskhladze, A. Avram, and J. Hargrave. Oxford: Archaeopress Archaeology.

Curta, F.

2017 Coins, Forts and Commercial Exchanges in the Sixth- and Early Seventh-Century Balkans. *Oxford Journal of Archaeology* 36: 439–54. https://doi.org/10.1111/ojoa.12123.

Cuteri, F., and Salamida, P.

2010 Il litorale jonico calabrese da Crotone a Reggio (Calabria, Italia): Circolazione di manufatti ceramici tra V e VII secolo. Pp. 507–13 in *LRCW3: Late Roman Coarse Wares, Cooking Wares and Amphorae in the Mediterranean: Archaeology and Archaeometry. Comparison between Western and Eastern Mediterranean*, ed. S. Menchelli, S. Santoro, M. Pasquinucci, and G. Guiducci, 2 vols. BAR International Series 2185. Oxford: Archaeopress.

Cuteri, F., Iannelli, M.T., Vivacqua, P., and Cafaro, T.

2014 Da Vibo Valentia a Nicotera: La ceramica tardo romana nella Calabria tirrenica (Italia). Pp. 63–80 in *LRCW4: Late Roman Coarse Wares, Cooking Wares and Amphorae in the Mediterranean: Archaeology and Archaeometry. The Mediterranean: A Market without Frontiers*, ed. N. Poulou-Papadimitriou, E. Nodarou, and V. Kilikoglou, 2 vols. BAR International Series 2616. Oxford: Archaeopress.

D'Ammassa, C., Manna, P.A., and Rosati, P.

2023 Portus: Lo scavo di un isolato presso la fossa Traiana: Continuità, cesura e occupazione sporadica tra età imperiale, tardoantica e altomedioevale (II–VIII secolo d.C.). Pp. 353–78 in *Ostia e Portus dalla Repubblica alla Tarda Antichità: Studi di archeologia e di storia urbana sui porti di Roma. Atti del Sesto Seminario Ostiense (Ostia Antica-Roma, 10–11 aprile 2019)*, ed. M.L. Caldelli, N. Laubry, and F. Zevi. Collection de l'École française de Rome 612. Rome: Publications de l'École française de Rome.

Danys, K.

2016 Pottery from Dongola: A Stratigraphic Assemblage from Unit B.I.41. *PAM Polish Archaeology in the Mediterranean* 25: 761–79. https://doi.org/10.5604/01.3001.0010.3014.

Danys-Lasek, K.

2014 Pottery from Deir el-Naqlun (6th–12th Century): Preliminary Report from Polish Excavations in 2010 and 2011. *Polish Archaeology in the Mediterranean* 23: 543–642.

Daryaee, T.

2003 The Persian Gulf Trade in Late Antiquity. *Journal of World History* 14.1: 1–16.

Dauphin, C., and Kingsley, S.A.

2003 Ceramic Evidence for the Rise and Fall of a Late Antique Ecclesiastical Estate at Shelomi in Phoenicia Maritima. Pp. 61–75 in *One Land—Many Cultures: Archaeological Studies in Honour of Stanislao Loffreda Ofm*, ed. G.C. Bottini, L. di Segni, and L.D. Chrupcała. Jerusalem: Franciscan Printing Press.

Davies, S.M.

1984 The Dipinti, Stamps and Graffiti. Pp. 141–54 in vol. 1.2 of *Excavations at Carthage: The British Mission*, ed. M.G. Fulford and D.P.S. Peacock. British Academy Monographs in Archaeology. Sheffield: University of Sheffield Department of Prehistory and Archaeology.

Decker, M.

2012 The End of the Holy Land Wine Trade. *Strata: Bulletin of the Anglo-Israel Archaeological Society* 31: 103–16.

Degrassi, V., Gaddi, D., Mandruzzato, L., and Maselli Scotti, F.

2010 Tergeste (Trieste – Italia): materiale ceramico dai livelli di costruzione delle mura tardo imperiali (prima metà V sec. d.C.). Pp. 579–84 in *LRCW3: Late Roman Coarse Wares, Cooking Wares and Amphorae in the Mediterranean: Archaeology and Archaeometry. Comparison between Western and Eastern Mediterranean*, ed. S. Menchelli, S. Santoro, M. Pasquinucci, and G. Guiducci, 2 vols. BAR International Series 2185. Oxford: Archaeopress.

Demesticha, S.

2003 Amphora Production on Cyprus during the Late Roman Period. Pp. 469–76 in *Actes du VIIe Congrès international sur la céramique médiévale en Méditerranée, Thessaloniki, 11–16 October 1999*, ed. Ch. Bakirtzis. Athens: Pré-acets.

2013 Amphora Typologies, Distribution, and Trade Patterns: The Case of the Cypriot LR1 Amphorae. Pp. 169–78 in *The Transport Amphorae and Trade of Cyprus*, ed. M. L. Lawall and J. Lund. Gösta Enbom Monographs 3. Aarhus: Aarhus University Press.

2014 Typology in the Context: The Case of Late Roman Amphora. Pp. 599–606 in *LRCW4: Late Roman Coarse Wares, Cooking Wares and Amphorae in the Mediterranean: Archaeology and Archaeometry. The Mediterranean: A Market without Frontiers*, ed. N. Poulou-Papadimitriou, E. Nodarou, and V. Kilikoglou, 2 vols. BAR International Series 2616. Oxford: Archaeopress.

2015 Gone with the Waves: Scattered Roman Amphorae in Shallow Waters around Cape Kiti, Cyprus. Pp. 55–76 in *Per terram, per mare: Seaborne Trade and the Distribution of Roman Amphorae in the Mediterranean*, ed. S. Demesticha. Studies in Mediterranean Archaeology and Literature Pocket-book 180. Uppsala: Åströms.

Demesticha, S., and Michaelides, D.

2001 The Excavation of a Late Roman 1 Amphora Kiln in Paphos. Pp. 289–96 in *La céramique Byzantine et proto-islamique en Syrie-Jordanie: IVe-VIIIe siècles apr. J.-C. Actes du colloque tenu à Amman les 3, 4 et 5 décembre 1994*, ed. E. Villeneuve and P.M. Watson. Bibliothèque archéologique et historique 159. Beirut: Institut français d'archéologie du Proche-Orient.

Derda, T.

1992 Inscriptions with the formula Θεοῦ χάρις κέρδος on Late Roman Amphorae. *Zeitschrift für Papyrologie und Epigraphik* 94: 135–52.

Deriu, D.

2015 Porto Torres (SS): Quotidianità e rapporti commerciali nella *Turris Libisonis* tardo antica. Un contesto di V–VI secolo d.C. dall'area portuale. Pp. 947–50 in *Isole e terraferma nel primo cristianesimo, Identità locale ed interscambi culturali, religiosi e produttivi: Atti XI Congresso Nazionale di Archeologia Cristiana*, ed. R. Martorelli, A. Piras, and P.G. Spanu. Studi e e Ricerche di Cultura Religiosa Nuova Serie 8. Cagliari: PFTS University Press.

De Mitri, C.

2005 Otranto: Anfore da trasporto di età tardoromana (IV–VI sec. d.C.). Pp. 413–24 in *LRCW1: Late Roman Coarse Wares, Cooking Wares, and Amphorae in the Mediterranean: Archaeology and Archaeometry*, ed. J.M. Gurt i Esparraguera, J. Buxeda i Garrigos, and M.A. Cau Ontiveros. BAR International Series 1340. Oxford: Archaeopress.

De Mitri, C., and Loprieno, S.

2018 Il materiale ceramico della campagna di scavo 2018 a Orikos: Nota preliminare. *SLSA Jahresbericht – Rapport annuel* 2018: 81–121.

2020 Il materiale ceramico della campagna di scavo 2020 a Orikos: Nota preliminare. *SLSA Jahresbericht – Rapport annuel* 2020: 87–112.

De Rossi, G.B.

1890 *Bullettino di Archeologia Cristiana.* Serie Quinta – Anno Primo. Rome: Tipografia della Reale Accademia dei Lincei.

De Rossi, G., Di Giovanni, V., Miniero, P., Salmieri, S., and Soricelli, G.

2010 Il porto di Miseno (Campania – Italia) in età tardoantica: Analisi dei contesti ceramici. Pp. 487–95 in *LRCW3: Late Roman Coarse Wares, Cooking Wares and Amphorae in the Mediterranean: Archaeology and Archaeometry. Comparison between Western and Eastern Mediterranean*, ed. S. Menchelli, S. Santoro, M. Pasquinucci, and G. Guiducci, 2 vols. BAR International Series 2185. Oxford: Archaeopress.

De Tommaso, G., Dell'Amico, P., Firmati, M., Poggesi, G., Rendini, P., and Shepherd, J.

1992 La documentazione subacquea: I relitti. Pp. 70–116 in *Relitti di Storia: Archeologia subacquea in Maremma*, ed. M. Celuzza and P. Rendini, Siena: Nuova Immagine Editrice.

Dillon, M., Kızılarslanoğlu, H.A., Pejša, S., and Rauh, N.K.

2019a *RCSP Ceramics Collections in the Adanda Region 2000–2004.* Purdue University Research Repository. https://doi.org/10.4231/37AB-W910.

2019b *RCSP Ceramics Collections at Kestros, 1997.* Purdue University Research Repository. https://doi.org/10.4231/R71J97ZB.

2019c *RCSP Ceramics Collections at Selinus, 1997–1998.* Purdue University Research Repository. https://doi.org/10.4231/R7DV1H3X.

2019d *RCSP Ceramics Collections at Antiochia ad Cragum, 1997 and 2004.* Purdue University Research Repository. https://doi.org/10.4231/R7930RCH.

Diamanti, C.

2010 *Local Production and Import of Amphoras at Halasarna of Kos Island (5th–7th c.).* Athens: National and Kapodistrian University of Athens.

2016 The Late Roman Amphora Workshops of Paros Island in the Aegean Sea. *Rei Cretariæ Romanæ Favtorvm Acta* 44: 691–97.

2023 Mass Production of Late Roman and Early Byzantine Amphorae in the Aegean: Case Studies from the Islands of Cos and Paros. Pp. 273–95 in *Regional Economies in Action: Standardization of Transport Amphorae in the Roman and Byzantine Mediterranean. Proceedings of the International Conference at the Austrian Archaeological Institute and the Danish Institute at Athens, 16–18 October 2017*, ed. H.G. Cesteros and J. Leidwanger. Sonderschriften 63. Vienna: Österreichische Akademie der Wissenschaften.

2024a *Late Antique Stamped Amphorae as Evidence for Imperial Policy. The Halasarna Workshop, Cos Island.* Oxford: Archaeopress.

2024b The Religious and Administrative Stamped Amphorae of Late Antiquity. *Rei Cretariæ Romanæ Favtorvm Acta* 48: 27–34.

Diamanti, C., Kouzeli, K., and Petridis, P.

2014 Archaeology and Archaeometry in Late Roman Greece: The Case of Mainland and Insular Settlements, Workshops and Imports. Pp. 181–92 in *LRCW4: Late Roman Coarse Wares, Cooking Wares and Amphorae in the Mediterranean: Archaeology and Archaeometry. The Mediterranean: A Market without Frontiers*, ed. N. Poulou-Papadimitriou, E. Nodarou, and V. Kilikoglou, 2 vols. BAR International Series 2616 I. Oxford: Archaeopress.

Didioumi, S.

2014 Local Pottery Production in the Island of Cos, Greece from the Early Byzantine Period: A Preliminary Report. Pp. 169–80 in *LRCW4: Late Roman Coarse Wares, Cooking Wares and Amphorae in the Mediter-*

ranean: Archaeology and Archaeometry. The Mediterranean: A Market without Frontiers, ed. N. Poulou-Papadimitriou, E. Nodarou, and V. Kilikoglou, 2 vols. BAR International Series 2616. Oxford: Archaeopress.

Di Giovanni, V.

2012 Kyme eolica romana e tardoantica: Tipologia e cronologia delle classi ceramiche. Pp. 115–85 in *Nuovi studi su Kyme eolica: Produzioni e rotte trasmarine*, ed. L.A. Scatozza Höricht. Saggi 10. Naples: ClioPress.

2014 Aspects of Fine Ware Consumption in Aeolic Kyme (I–VI AD). Pp. 71–80 in *Late Hellenistic to Mediaeval Fine Wares of the Aegean Coast of Anatolia: Their Production, Imitation and Use*, ed. H. Meyza. Travaux de l'institut des cultures méditerranéennes et orientales de l'académie polonaise des sciences 1. Warsaw: Neriton.

Disantarosa, G.

2011 Amphorae. Pp. 387–407 in *Vagnari: Il villaggio, l'artigianato, la proprietà imperiale*, ed. A.M. Small. Insulae Diomedeae 17. Bari: Edipuglia.

Dobreva, D., and Riccato, A.

2015 Aquileia e il Vicino Oriente: Il commercio di prodotti levantini in area adriatica. *Aquileia Nostra* 86: 111–39.

Dobreva, D., and Zago, S.

2021 Aquileia e l'alto Adriatico nell'età della transizione: Aspetti di continuità e cambiamento commerciale alla luce dei contesti ceramici tardoantichi e altomedievali. Pp. 307–68 in *Italia settentrionale e regioni dell'arco alpino tra V e VI secolo d.C. Atti del Convegno (15–17 aprile 2021)*, ed. M. Buora, S. Magnani, and L. Villa. Storia e Archeologia 1. Trieste: Edizioni Università di Trieste.

Docter, R.F., Monsieur, P., and van de Put, W.D.J.

2013 Late Archaic to Late Antique Finds from Cistern No. 1 at Thorikos (2010 Campaign). Pp. 75–128 in *Thorikos 10: Reports and Studies*, ed. R.F. Docter. Ghent: Department of Archaeology, Ghent University.

Dodd, K.E.

2020 *Roman and Late Antique Wine Production in the Eastern Mediterranean: A Comparative Archaeological Study at Antiochia ad Cragum (Turkey) and Delos (Greece)*. Archaeopress Roman Archaeology 63. Oxford: Archaeopress.

Doksanalti, E.M.

2020 Knidos "Liman Caddesi" Geç Antik Dönem Atölye/Dükkan ve Buluntuları. *Olba* 28: 377–420.

van Doornick, F.H., Jr.

1989 The Cargo Amphoras on the 7th Century Yassi Ada and 11th Century Serçe Limani Shipwrecks: Two Examples of a Reuse of Byzantine Amphoras as Transport Jars. Pp. 247–57 in *Recherches sur la Céramique Byzantine*, ed. V. Déroche and J.-M. Spieser. Bulletin de Correspondance Hellénique Supplément 18. Athens: École française d'Athènes.

2002 Byzantine Shipwrecks. Pp. 899–905 in *The Economic History of Byzantium: From the Seventh through the Fifteenth Century*, ed. A.E. Laiou, 2 vols. Dumbarton Oaks Studies 39. Washington, DC: Dumbarton Oaks Research Library and Collection.

2014 Byzantine Amphoras Made for War? *INA Quarterly* 41.1: 21–27.

2015 The Seventh-century Byzantine Ship at Yassıada and Her Final Voyage: Present Thoughts. Pp. 205–16 in *Maritime Studies in the Wake of the Byzantine Shipwreck at Yassıada, Turkey*, ed. D.N. Carlson, J. Leidwanger, and S.M. Kampbell. College Station: Texas A&M University Press.

van Doornick, F.H., Jr., Leidwanger, J., Vo-Phamhi, H., and Gross, J.

2023 Achieving Standard Volumes in Amphora Production: New Evidence from the 7th-century Yassıada Shipwreck. Pp. 249–72 in *Regional Economies in Action: Standardization of Transport Amphorae in the Roman and Byzantine Mediterranean. Proceedings of the International Conference at the Austrian Archaeological Institute and the Danish Institute at Athens, 16–18 October 2017*, ed. H.G. Cesteros and J. Leidwanger. Sonderschriften 63. Vienna: Österreichische Akademie der Wissenschaften.

Doyle, I.W.

1998 The Early Medieval Activity at Dalkey Island, Co Dublin: A Re-Assessment. *Journal of Irish Archaeology* 9: 89–103.

2009 Mediterranean and Frankish Pottery Imports in Early Medieval Ireland. *Journal of Irish Archaeology* 18: 17–62.

Ducci, S., Pasquinucci, M., and Genovesi, S.

2011 Portus Pisanus nella tarda età imperiale (III–VI secolo): Nuovi dati archeologici e fonti scritte a confronto. Pp. 29–56 in *I sistemi portuali della Toscana mediterranea. Infrastrutture, scambi, economie dall'antichità a oggi*, ed. M.L. Ceccarelli Lemut, G. Garzella, and O. Vaccari. Ospedaletto: Pacini.

Duggan, M.

2013 A Late Roman 1 Amphora Recovered Off Cawsand, Plymouth Sound. *Cornish Archaeology* 52: 239–45.

2020 Britain in the Atlantic: Late Antique Ceramics and Connections. Pp. 13–24 in *Ceramics and Atlantic Connections: Late Roman and Early Medieval Imported Pottery on the Atlantic Seaboard*, ed. M. Duggan, S. Turner, and M.P.C. Jackson. Roman and Late Antique Mediterranean Pottery 15. Oxford: Archaeopress.

Dukan, M., Sirat, C., and Zerdoun, M.

1984 Une inscription hébraïque sur amphore trouvée à Ravenne. *Revue des Études Juives* 143: 287–303.

Dündar, E.

2012 A Group of Amphorae from Side Museum and a New Type of Amphora: The Lycian Amphora? *Archäologischer Anzeiger* 2012.1: 43–61.

2018 The Maritime Trade of Roman Patara: Preliminary Remarks on the Amphorae. *Skyllis* 18: 166–73.

Duperron, G.

2013 Le mobilier céramique tardo-antique (Ve et VIe s.) de l'oppidum de Constantine (Lançon-Provence, Bouches-du-Rhône). Pp. 241–375 in *Du Rhône aux Pyrénées: Aspects de la Vie Matérielle en Gaule Narbonnaise II*, ed. S. Mauné, G. Duperron, and M. Mergoil. Collection Archéologie et Histoire Romaine 25. Montagnac: Mergoil.

2019 Mobiliers céramiques de l'Antiquité tardive (période 5). Pp. 231–37 in *Le village de la Capelière en Camargue: Du début du V e siècle av. n. è. à la période de l'Antiquité tardive*, ed. C. Landuré, P. Arcelin, and G. Arnaud-Fassetta. Bibliothèque d'Archéologie Méditerranéenne et Africaine 26. Aix-en-Provence: Presses Universitaires de Provence.

2021 Les céramiques d'un dépotoir du milieu du Ve siècle dans l'établissement portuaire de la Montille d'Ulmet. Pp. 555–69 in *Société française d'étude de la céramique antique de Gaule: Actes du congrès d'Auch, septembre 2021*, ed. L. Rivet. Marseille: SFECAG.

Duperron, G., Bourgaut, R., and Leger, C.

2019 Deux ensembles de mobiliers tardo-antiques (Ve s.) de l'établissement rural de la Reille à Montbazin (Hérault). Pp. 201–39 in *Du Rhône aux Pyrénées: Aspects de la Vie Matérielle en Gaule Narbonnaise II*, ed. S. Mauné and G. Duperron. Archéologie et Histoire Romaine 25. Montagnac: Mergoil.

Duperron, G., and Landuré, C.

2019 Premières données sur le faciès céramique et les échanges commerciaux dans l'établissement portuaire de la Montille d'Ulmet (Arles) durant la première moitié du VIe siècle. Pp. 569–91 in *Archéologie et histoire en territoire arlésien: Mélanges offerts à Jean Piton*, ed. D. Djaoui and M. Heijmans. Archéologie et Histoire Romaine 42. Drémil Lafage: Mergoil.

Durukan, M.

2015 Geç Antik Çağ'da Doğu Akdeniz'deki Ekonomik Gelişmenin Nedenleri: İpek Yolu ve Baharat Yolu'nun Rolü, LR1 Amphoraları ve Kilikia'daki Diğer Kanıtlar. *Adalya* 18: 241–57.

Dyczek, P.

2017 Amphorae from Late Roman Structures on the Site of the Legionary Barracks in Novae (Moesia Inferior). Pp. 683–91 in *LRCW5: Late Roman Coarse Wares, Cooking Wares and Amphorae in the Mediterranean: Archaeology and Archaeometry. La céramique commune, la céramique culinaire et les amphores de l'Antiquité tardive en Méditerranée*, ed. D. Dixneuf, 2 vols. Études alexandrines 42/43. Alexandrie: Centre d'Études Alexandrines.

Ebanista, C., and Romano, R.

2018 Le anfore dalla catacomba di S. Gennaro a Napoli: Nuovi dati sui traffici marittimi e gli interscambi nel Mediterraneo fra tarda antichità e alto medioevo. Pp. 63–84 in *Il Mediterraneo fra Tarda Antichità e Medioevo: Integrazione di culture, interscambi, pellegrinaggi. Atti del Convegno internazionale di studi Cimitile-Santa Maria Capua Vetere, 15–16 giugno 2017*, ed. C. Ebanista and M. Rotili. San Vitaliano (NA): Guida.

Egloff, M.

1977 *Kellia: La poterie copte. Quatre siècles d'artisanat et d'échanges en Basse-Égypte.* Recherches suisses d'archéologie copte 3. Geneva: Georg.

Ehmig, V.U.

2005 Der Besitzer der Bad Kreuznacher Peristylvilla – ein Händler "ostmediterraner Lebensmittel?" *Münstersche Beiträge zur antiken Handelsgeschichte* 24: 175–91.

Emery, W.B.

1948 *Nubian Treasure: An Account of the Discoveries at Ballana and Qustul.* London: Methuen.

Emery, W.B., and Kirwan, L.

1938 *The Royal Tombs of Ballana and Qustul,* Mission Archéologique de Nubie. Cairo: Service des antiquités de l'Égypte.

Empereur, J.-Y.

2018 The Late Roman Amphorae Found in Amathus Harbor. Pp. 181–90 in *The Hellenistic Harbour of Amathus Underwaters Excavations, 1984–1986*, vol. 2: *Artefacts Found during Excavation*, ed. J.-Y. Empereur. Études chypriotes 20. Athens: École française d'Athènes.

Empereur, J.-Y., and Picon, M.

1988 The Production of Aegean Amphorae: Field and Laboratory Studies. Pp. 33–38 in *New Aspects of Archaeological Science in Greece: Proceedings of a Meeting Held at the British School at Athens, January 1987*, ed. R.E. Jones and H.W. Catling. Fitch Laboratory Occasional Paper 3. Athens: British School at Athens.

1989 Les régions de production d'amphores impériales en Méditerranée orientale. Pp. 223–48 in *Amphores romaines et histoire économique: Dix ans de recherche. Actes du colloque de Sienne (22–24 mai 1986).* Publications de l'École française de Rome 114. Rome: École française de Rome.

Envig, O.T., and Åström, P.

1975 *Hala Sultan Tekke II: The Cape Kiti Survey, An Underwater Archaeological Survey.* Studies in Mediterranean Archaeology 45. Göteborg: Åström.

Ergürer, H.E., and Akkaş, İ.

2023 Parion: First Researches on Late Antique Coarse Wares, Cooking Wares and Amphorae. Pp. 181–209 in *LRCW6: Late Roman Coarse Wares, Cooking Wares and Amphorae in the Mediterranean: Archaeology and Archaeometry. Land and Sea: Pottery Routes*, ed. V. Caminneci, E. Giannitrapani, M.C. Parello, and M.S. Rizzo, 2 vols. Roman and Late Antique Mediterranean Pottery 19. Oxford: Archaeopress.

Erol, O., and Pirazzoli, P.A.

1992 Seleucia Pieria: An Ancient Harbour Submitted to Two Successive Uplifts. *International Journal of Nautical Archaeology* 21: 317–27. https://doi.org/10.1111/j.1095-9270.1992.tb00379.x.

Erten, H.N., Kassab Tezgör, D., Türkmen, I.R., and Zarasiz, A.

2004 The Typology and Trade of the Amphorae of Sinope: Archaeological Study and Scientific Analyses. Pp. 103–16 in *Transport Amphora and Trade in the Eastern Mediterranean*, ed. J. Eiring and J. Lund. Monographs of the Danish Institute at Athens 5. Athens: Danish Institute at Athens.

Everill, P., Lomitashvili, D., Murgulia, N., Colvin, I., and Lortkipanidze, B.

2017 Forty Seasons of Excavation: Nikalakevi-Tsikhegoji-Archaeopolis. *Iberia-Colchis* 13: 146–65.

Facella, A., Minniti, B., and Capelli, C.
2014 Ceramiche da un contesto tardoantico presso l'agorà di *Segesta* (TP). *Rei Cretariæ Romanæ Favtorvm Acta* 43: 539–46.
Fanning, T.
1981 Excavation of an Early Christian Cemetery and Settlement at Reask, County Kerry. *Proceedings of the Royal Irish Academy: Archaeology, Culture, History, Literature* 81C: 67–172.
Fantuzzi, L., Cau Ontiveros, M.A., and Reynolds, P.
2017 Archaeometric Characterisation of Late Roman Amphora 1 Imports in North-eastern Spain. Pp. 93–116 in *LRCW5: Late Roman Coarse Wares, Cooking Wares and Amphorae in the Mediterranean: Archaeology and Archaeometry. La céramique commune, la céramique culinaire et les amphores de l'Antiquité tardive en Méditerranée*, ed. D. Dixneuf, 2 vols. Études Alexandrines 42/43. Alexandria: Centre d'Études Alexandrines.
Fantuzzi, L., Cau Ontiveros, M.A., Solé, J.M., and Martorell, F.R.
2019 Eastern Mediterranean Amphorae from Late Antique Urban Centers of the Northeastern Iberian Peninsula: Archaeometric Characterization. *Archaeosciences* 43: 229–47. https://doi.org/10.4000/archeosciences.6897.
Fedoseev, N.F., Domżalski, K., Opaiţ, A., and Kulikov, A.V.
2010 Post-Justinian Pottery Deposit from Pantikapaion-Bosporos: Rescue Excavations at 12, Teatral'naja St. in Kerch, 2006. *Archeologia* 61: 63–94.
Fernández, A.F.
2012 Datos Preliminares Sobre las Ánforas Orientales Tardías de dos Yacimientos de Vigo (Galicia, Espana), con el Ejemplo de un Contexto de la Primera Mitad del S. VII. *Rei Cretariæ Romanæ Favtorvm Acta* 42: 355–62.
2016 Ánfora orientais tardoantigas (Late Roman Amphorae). Pp. 122–23 in *Emporium: Mil anos de comercio en Vigo*. Vigo: Concello de Vigo.
Ferrazzoli, A.F., and Ricci, M.
2007 Elaiussa Sebaste: Produzioni e consumi di una città della Cilicia tra V e VII secolo. Pp. 671–88 in *LRCW2: Late Roman Coarse Wares, Cooking Wares and Amphorae in the Mediterranean: Archaeology and Archaeometry* ed. M. Bonifay and J.-C. Tréglia, 2 vols. BAR International Series 1662. Oxford: Archaeopress.
2009 Cilician Ceramic Production from Roman to Byzantine Age: New Data from Elaiussa Sebaste. *Olba* 17: 33–44.
2010 Un Centro di Produzione delle Anfore LR 1: Elaiussa Sebaste in Cilicia. Gli Impianti, le Anfore. Pp. 815–26 in *LRCW3: Late Roman Coarse Wares, Cooking Wares and Amphorae in the Mediterranean: Archaeology and Archaeometry. Comparison between Western and Eastern Mediterranean*, ed. S. Menchelli, S. Santoro, M. Pasquinucci, and G. Guiducci, 2 vols. BAR International Series 2185. Oxford: Archaeopress.
Fiaccadori, G.
1983 I frammenti iscritti. Pp. 238–41 in *Ravenna e il porto di Classe: Venti anni di ricerche archeologiche a Ravenna e Classe*, ed. G. Bermond Montanari. Realtà regionale 7. Imola: University Press.
Filippi, F., Dell'Era, F., and Ferrazzoli, A.F.
2014 Roma, complesso di San Francesco a Ripa: Un esempio di uso secondario di anfore in età tardo antica. Pp. 1005–11 in *LRCW4: Late Roman Coarse Wares, Cooking Wares and Amphorae in the Mediterranean: Archaeology and Archaeometry. The Mediterranean: A Market without Frontiers*, ed. N. Poulou-Papadimitriou, E. Nodarou, and V. Kilikoglou, 2 vols. BAR International Series 2616. Oxford: Archaeopress.
Filipczak, P.
2015 *An introduction to the Byzantine Administration in Syro-Palestine on the eve of the Arab conquest*. Byzantina Lodziensia 26. Lodz: University of Lodz.

Finneran, N.
2006 Ethiopian Christian Material Culture: The International Context. Aksum, the Mediterranean and the Syriac Worlds in the Fifth to Seventh Centuries. *Reading Medieval Studies* 32: 75–89.
Fisher, C., Campbell, W.A., Lassus, J., and Elderkin, G.W.
2025 The Excavation of Antioch-on-the-Orontes Digital Resources 1932–1939. *OCHRE Data Service.* https://ochre.lib.uchicago.edu/antioch/.
Fleitman, Y.H., and Mazar, E.
2015 The Late Roman and Byzantine Pottery from 2012–2013 Excavation Seasons: Areas Upper A, B and C. Pp. 211–92 in *The Ophel Excavations to the South of the Temple Mount 2009–2013: Final Reports Volume I*, ed. E. Mazar. Jerusalem: Shoham Academic Research and Publication.
Fontana, S.
2000 Un "immondezzaio" di VI secolo da *Meninx*: La fine della produzione di porpora e la cultura materiale a Gerba nella prima età bizantina. Pp. 95–114 in *L'Africa romana: Atti del XIII convegno di studio Djerba, 10–13 dicembre 1998*, ed. M. Khanoussi, P. Ruggeri, and C. Vismara. Università degli studi di Sassari 6.1. Rome: Carocci.
Fontana, S., Munzi, M., Beolchini, V., de Luca, I., Del Vecchio, F.
2004 Un contesto di VII secolo dall'Aventino. Pp. 544–68 in *Roma dall'antichità al medioevo. II: Contesti tardo-antichi e altomedievali*, ed. L. Paroli and L. Vendittelli. Milan: Electa.
Fournet, J.-L.
2012 La "dipintologie" grecque: Une nouvelle discipline auxiliaire de la papyrologie? Pp. 249–58 in *Actes du 26e Congrès international de papyrologie Genève, 16–21 août 2010*, ed. P. Schubert. Recherches et rencontres 30. Geneva: Droz.
2021 How Late Antique *dipinti* Contribute to a Better Knowledge of Amphora Contents. Pp. 63–76 in *Roman Amphora Contents Reflecting on the Maritime Trade of Foodstuff in Antiquity. In Honour of Miguel Beltrán Lloris. Proceedings of the Roman Amphora Contents International Interactive Conference (RACIIC) (Cadiz, 5–7 October 2015)*, ed. D. Bernal Casasola, M. Bonifay, A. Pecci, and V. Leitch. Roman and Late Antique Mediterranean Pottery 17. Oxford: Archaeopress.
Fournet, J.-L., and Pieri, D.
2008 Les *dipinti* amphoriques d'Antinoopolis. Pp. 175–216 in *Antinoupolis I*, ed. R. Pintaudi. Scavi e materiali 1. Florence: Firenze University Press.
Fragoulis, K., Minasidis, D., and Mentzos, A.
2014 Pottery from the Cemetery Basilica in the Early Byzantine City of Dion. Pp. 297–304 in *LRCW4: Late Roman Coarse Wares, Cooking Wares and Amphorae in the Mediterranean: Archaeology and Archaeometry. The Mediterranean: A Market without Frontiers*, ed. N. Poulou-Papadimitriou, E. Nodarou, and V. Kiliko-glou, 2 vols. BAR International Series 2616. Oxford: Archaeopress.
Frechen, M., Neber, A., Tsatskin, A., Boenigk, W., and Ronen, A.
2004 Chronology of Pleistocene Sedimentary Cycles in the Carmel Coastal Plain of Israel. *Quaternary International* 121: 41–52. https://doi.org/10.1016/j.quaint.2004.01.022.
Freedman, D.N.
1967 Ashdod I: The First Season of Excavation 1962. *Atiqot* 7: 1–171.
Frost, H.
1963 *Under the Mediterranean: Marine Antiquities.* London: Routledge; Kegan Paul.
Fundación Juan March
1977 *Arqueologia submarina en Menorca.* Madrid: Fundación Juan March.
Gamkrelidze, G.
1992 Hydroarchaeology in the Georgian Republic (the Colchian Littoral). *International Journal of Nautical Archaeology* 21: 101–9. https://doi.org/10.1111/j.1095-9270.1992.tb00352.x.

Gamureac, Ş.-E.
2017 The Potsherds in Archaeological Context: Pottery from Late Roman Fort of Ulmetum (4th–6th Cent. AD). Report on the 2012 Archaeological Campaign at the North-west Gate (I). *Pontica* 50: 243–63.
2018 The Potsherds in Archaeological Context: The Common Pottery from Late Roman Fort of Ulmetum (4th–6th Century AD). Report on the 2010–2011 Archaeological Campaign at the North-west gate (II). *Pontica* 51: 319–41.
Gandila, A.
2021 Free Market, Black Market or No Market? Money and *annona* in the Northeastern Balkans (Sixth to Seventh Century). *Journal of Late Antiquity* 14: 294–334. https://doi.org/10.1353/jla.2021.0028.
Garnotel, A., and Raynaud, C.
2014 Villeneuve-les-Maguelone (Hérault): Maguelone. *Archéologie du Midi médiéval* 32: 52–57. https://doi.org/10.3406/amime.2014.2070.
Gascoigne, A.L.
2007 Amphorae from Old Cairo: A Preliminary Note. *Cahiers de la Céramique Égyptienne* 8: 161–73.
Gascou, J.
1987 Amphores byzantines à dipinti grecs de Saqqara. *Bulletin de liaison du Groupe international d'étude de la céramique Égyptienne*, 3: 24–27.
Gatier, P.-L., Baud, A., Cahu, D., Charpentier, G., Devillechaise, A., Duvette, C., Hachem, M.-E., Ferreira, P., Flammin, A., Haidar Vela, N., Husson, X., Kahwagi-Janho, H., Piaton, C., Pieri, D., and Schmitt, A.
2010 Mission archéologique de Tyr: Rapport préliminaire 2008–2009. *Bulletin d'Archéologie et d'Architecture Libanaises* 14: 135–239.
Gelichi, S., Negrelli, C., Ferri, M., Cadamuro, S., Cianciosi, A., and Grandi, E.
2017 Importare, produrre e consumare nella laguna di Venezia dal IV al XII secolo: Anfore, vetri e ceramiche. Pp. 23–113 in *Adriatico altomedievale (VI–XI secolo): Scambi, porti, produzioni*, ed. S. Gelichi, and C. Negrelli. Studi e ricerche. Venice: Ca' Foscari. http://doi.org/10.14277/6969-115-7/SR-4-1.
Gerousi, E.
2015 The Commercial Relations between Aegean and the Black Sea on the Basis of the Testimony of the Early Christian Amphoras. Pp. 127–36 in *Proceedings of the Symposium on City Ports from the Aegean to the Black Sea: Medieval–Modern Networks 22nd–29th August 2015*, ed. F. Karagianni and U. Kocabaş. Istanbul: Ege Yayınları.
Gendelman, P.
2020 Pottery Vessels and Stone Artifacts from the Persian, Roman and Byzantine Periods at the French Hospital Compound, Yafo (Jaffa). *Atiqot* 100: 157–88.
2022 Local Amphora Production and Seaborne Trade Patterns from the Province of Judaea/Syria-Palaestina: Evidence from Caesarea Maritima and Beyond. Pp. 79–96 in *Amphorae from the Eastern Mediterranean and Beyond: Production and Distribution from the Early to the Late Roman Period*, ed. A. Kaldeli. Studies in Mediterranean Archaeology and Literature 191. Nicosia: Astrom.
Georgiev, Z.
1989 Gradiste, a Late Antique and Early Byzantine Fortress near the Village of Pčinja. *Macedoniae acta archaeologica* 10: 199–214 (Macedonian).
Ghaly, H.
1992 Pottery Workshops of Saint-Jeremia (Saqqara). *Cahiers de la ceramique* Égyptienne 3: 161–72.
Gherge, P., and Amon, L.
2011 O Amforă Ştampilată, Descoperită În Cetatea Romano-bizantină De La Sucidava (Judeţul Olt). *Analele Universităţii din Craiova, Seria Istorie* 16: 23–26.
Giardino, L.
1991 Grumentum e Metaponto: Due esempi di passaggio dal tardoantico all'alto medioevo in Basilicata. *Mélanges de l'École française de Rome: Moyen-Age* 103: 827–58. https://doi.org/10.3406/mefr.1991.3202.

Gichon, M.
1993 *En Boqeq: Ausgrabungen in einer Oase am Toten Meer.* Mainz am Rhein: von Zabern.
Gillett, G.
2023 A Petrographic Network Analysis of the Distribution of Late Roman 1 Amphorae in the Eastern Mediterranean. M.A. thesis, Tel Aviv University Faculty of Humanities Sonia and Marco Nadler Institute of Archaeology.
Given, M., Knapp, A.B., Noller, J., Sollars, L., and Kassianidou, V.
2013 The Material Culture of the TAESP Landscape. Pp. 57–295 in *Landscape and Interaction: The Troodos Archaeological and Environmental Survey Project, Cyprus*, vol. 1: *Methodology, Analysis and Interpretation*, ed. M. Given, A.B. Knapp, J. Noller, L. Sollars, and V. Kassianidou. Levant Supplementary Series 14. Oxford: Oxbow Books.
Given, M., and Sollars, L.
2013 The Plains. Pp. 6–50 in *Landscape and Interaction: The Troodos Archaeological and Environmental Survey Project, Cyprus*, vol. 2: *The TAESP Landscape*, ed. M. Given, A.B. Knapp, J. Noller, L. Sollars, and V. Kassianidou. Levant Supplementary Series 15. Oxford: Oxford University Press.
Goodyear, M.
2019 North Africa's Place in the Mediterranean Economy of Late Antiquity. *World History Encyclopedia.* https://www.worldhistory.org/article/1331/north-africas-place-in-the-mediterranean-economy-o/.
Graham, M.
2013 The Upper Lagoudhera Valley. Pp. in 152–203 in *Landscape and Interaction: The Troodos Archaeological and Environmental Survey Project, Cyprus*, vol. 2: *The TAESP Landscape*, ed. M. Given, A.B. Knapp, J. Noller, L. Sollars, and V. Kassianidou. Levant Supplementary Series 15. Oxford: Oxford University Press.
Greco, E., Kalpaxis, T., Schnapp, A., Viviers, D.
1999 Itanos (Crète orientale). *Bulletin de Correspondance Hellénique* 123.2: 515–30. https://doi.org/10.3406/bch.1999.7246.
Green, J.N.
1973 An Underwater Archaeological Survey of Cape Andreas, Cyprus, 1969–70: A Preliminary Report. Pp. 141–78 in *Marine Archaeology: Proceedings of the Twenty-third Symposium of the Colston Research Society Held in the University of Bristol, April 4th to 8th, 1971*, ed. D.J. Blackman. Colston Papers 23. London: Butterworths.
Grey, T.
2014 Esdraela: The Ceramic Record from a Settlement of Hellenistic and Roman Times to Late Antiquity in Palestine. *Palestine Exploration Quarterly* 146: 105–34. https://doi.org/10.1179/0031032814Z.00000000094.
Griffith, F.L.
1927 Oxford Excavations in Nubia–continued. *Annals of Archaeology and Anthropology issued by the Institute of Archaeology* 14: 57–116.
Grigoraş, B., and Panaite, A.
2021 The Late Roman Amphorae from Tropaeum Traiani, Sector A (North of the Basilica A), 2005–2016. *Materiale şi cercetãri arheologice* New Series 17: 87–114. https://doi.org/10.3406/mcarh.2021.2152.
Gulsefa, G.
2016 2006–2013 Myndos Kazilarinda Bulunan Amphoralar ve Amphora Mühür Buluntulari/Amphora Finds and Its Stamps Which Were Found between 2006–2013 Myndos Excavation. Pp. 35–160 in *Myndos Excavations and Researches 2004–2013*, ed. D. Şahin. Myndos Araştırmaları 1. Ankara : Uludağ Üniversitesi Yayınıdır.
Gürbüzer, M.
2018 Late Roman Pottery from a Building in Klazomenai. *Olba* 26: 135–76.

Gwiazda, M., and Wielgosz-Rondolino, D.
2019 "Marea" on Lake Mareotis: A Roman Amphorae Dump, a Byzantine Period House, and Its Early Islamic Dwellers. *Journal of Egyptian Archaeology* 105: 259–73. https://doi.org/10.1177/0307513320905850.
Gyurdzhiyska, D., and Ivanov, S.
2019 Късноантичен Кладенец Extra Muros От Анхиало (Late Antique Extra Muros Stone Well from Anhialo). Pp. 94–113 in *Late Roman Fortress "Kovachevsko Kale" and the Bulgarian Lands (4th–6th c. AD)*, vol. 2, ed. O. Aleksandrov. Tărnovo: Faber.
Haidar Vela, N.
2015 Un lot de céramiques du VII siècle a Halabiya. Pp. 185–213 in *Zénobia-Halabiya, habitat urbain et nécropoles: Cinq années de recherches de la mission syro-française (2006–2010)*, ed. S. Blétry. Coruna: Sociedade Luso-Galega de Estudos Mesopotámicos.
Harper, R.P.
1995 *Upper Zohar, an Early Byzantine Fort in Palaestina Tertia: Final Report of Excavations in 1985–1986.* British Academy 9. Oxford: Oxford University Press.
Hárshegyi, P., and Ottományi, K.
2013 Imported and Local Pottery in Late Roman Pannonia. Pp. 471–528 in *Local Economies? Production and Exchange of Inland Regions in Late Antiquity*, ed. L. Lavan. Late Antique Archaeology 10. Leiden: Brill. https://doi.org/10.1163/22134522-12340040.
Hautumm, W.
1981 *Studien zu Amphoren der spätrömischen und frühbyzantinischen Zeit.* Fulda: Hautumm.
Hayes, J.W.
1992 *Excavations at Saraçhane in Istanbul, 2: The Pottery.* Princeton: Princeton University Press.
2001 Early Christian Pottery from Knossos: The 1978–1981 Finds from the Knossos Medical Faculty Site. *Annual of the British School at Athens* 96: 431–54. https://doi.org/10.1017/S0068245400005372.
Hayes, J.W, and Megaw, A.H.S.
2003 Hellenistc and Roman Pottery Deposits from the "Saranda Kolones" Castle Site at Paphos. *Annual of the British School at Athens* 98: 447–516. https://doi.org/10.1017/S0068245400016956.
Heath, S., Rife, J.L., Bravo III, J.J., and Blasdel, G.
2015 Preliminary Report on Early Byzantine Pottery from a Building Complex at Kenchreai (Greece). *ISAW Papers* 10. http://doi.org/2333.1/q83bk6k7.
Heath, S., and Tekkök, B.
2006–2009 Greek, Roman and Byzantine Pottery at Ilion (Troia). https://classics.uc.edu/troy/grbpottery/html/amphoras-r.html.
Hild, F., and Hellenkemper, H.
1990 *Tabula Imperii Byzantini 5, Kilikien und Isaurien.* Österreichische Akademie der Wissenschaften. Philosophisch-Historische Klasse. Denkschriften 215. Vienna: Österreichischen Akademie der Wissenschaften.
Hoff, M., Can, B., Townsend, R., Howe, T., Kızılarslanoğlu, H.A., and Dobos, G.
2018 Antiochia ad Cragum Excavations: 2016 and 2017 Seasons. *ANMED* 16: 1–14.
Holbrook, N., and Thomas, A.
2005 An Early-medieval Monastic Cemetery at Llandough, Glamorgan: Excavations in 1994. *Medieval Archaeology* 49: 1–92. https://doi.org/10.1179/007660905x54044.
Holmqvist, E.
2019 *Ceramics in Transition: Production and Exchange of Late Byzantine-Early Islamic Pottery in Southern Transjordan and the Negev.* Archaeopress Archaeology. Oxford: Archaeopress.
Hoxha, G.
1994 Muri rrethues i periudhës së vonë antike në qytetin e Shkodrës. *Iliria* 24: 231–47. https://doi.org/10.3406/iliri.1994.1640.

Hudson, N.
2008 Three Centuries of Late Roman Pottery. Pp. 319–45 in *Aphrodisias Papers 4: New Research on the City and Its Monuments*, ed. C. Ratté and R.R.R. Smith. Journal of Roman Archaeology Supplementary Series 70. Portsmouth, RI: Journal of Roman Archaeology.

Hudson, N., and Hartman, A.
2020 The Byzantine Pottery from the Qasr and Square Building. Pp. 229–60 in *The Excavations of 'Iraq al-Amir*, vol. 2, ed. N.L. Lapp. Annual of the American Society of Oriental Research 74. Boston: American Society of Oriental Research.

Iacomi, V.
2010 Some Notes on Late-Antique Oil and Wine Production in Rough Cilicia (Isauria) on the Light of Epigraphic Sources: Funerary Inscriptions from Korykos, LR 1 Amphorae Production in Elaiussa Sebaste and the Abydos Tariff. Pp. 19–32 in *Antik çağda Anadolu'da zeytinyağı ve şarap üretimi: Sempozyum bildirileri, 06–08 Kasım 2008, Mersin, Türkiye*, ed. Ü. Aydınoğlu and A. K. Şenol. Istanbul: KAAM Kilikia Arkeolojisini Araştırma Merkezi.
2020 Pottery Production in the Urbanscape and the Over Regional Commerce: LR1 Amphorae at Elaiussa and Beyond. Pp. 79–88 in *Men, Goods and Ideas Travelling over the Sea: Cilicia at the Crossroad of Eastern Mediterranean Trade Network. Archaeology and Economy in the Ancient World: Proceedings of the 19th International Congress of Classical Archaeology, Cologne/Bonn 2018*, ed. E. Equini Schneider. https://doi.org/10.11588/propylaeum.554.

Iacomi, V., and Cassiani, V.
2016 La Cilicia/Isauria tra IV e metà VII secolo: Insediamenti, produzioni e attività economiche. Nuove considerazioni alla luce dei più recenti studi sulla regione. In *LAC 2014 Proceedings, [S.l.], oct. 2016*. https://doi.org/10.5463/lac.2014.3.

Inaishvili, N., and Vashakidze, N.
2010 Typology and Chronology of Greek, Roman and Early Byzantine Amphorae from Petra-Tsikhisdziri. Pp. 151–52 in *Patabs I: Production and Trade of Amphorae in the Black Sea. Actes de la Table Ronde internationale de Batoumi et Trabzon, 27–29 avril 2006*. Varia Anatolica, 21. Istanbul: Institut Français d'Études Anatoliennes-Georges Dumézil.

Incordino, I.
2020 *Pottery of Manqabad: A Selected Catalogue of the Ceramic Assemblage from the Monastery of 'Abba Nefer' at Asuyt (Egypt)*. Access Archaeology. Oxford: Archaeopress.

Ivanova/Yashnaya, O.
2019 Торговельні контакти населення Мангуп-Кале в V ст. за матеріалами амфор та червонолакової кераміки. *EMINAK* 27: 47–59.

Jackson, M.
2015 2007–2011 Excavations at Kilise Tepe: A Byzantine Rural Settlement in Isauria. *Dumbarton Oaks Papers* 69: 355–80.

Jeremic, G.
2022 Прелиминарни резултати истраживања остатака касноантичког бедема у Прахову Кампање 2021. И 2022. Године. *Glasnik društva konzervatora Srbije* 46: 32–36.

Jiménez, J.M., and Narganes, J.M.M.
2015 Nunc autem a Gothis Subversa: The Province of Alicante and the Spanish Mediterranean Towns between the Byzantine and Visigothic Periods. *Early Medieval Europe* 23: 263–89. https://doi.org/10.1111/emed.12104.

Jørgensen, L.B.
2020 Textiles from a Late Roman/Byzantine Ecclesiastical Centre at Abu Sha'ar, Egypt. Pp. 49–59 in *Egyptian Textiles and Their Production: "Word" and "Object" 5 (Hellenistic, Roman, and Byzantine Periods)*, ed. M. Mossakowska-Gaubert. Lincoln, NE: Zea Books. https://doi.org/10.32873/unl.dc.zea.1082.

Johnson, B.

2008 *Ashkelon 2: Imported Pottery of the Roman and Late Roman Periods.* Final Reports of the Leon Levy Expedition to Ashkelon 2. Winona Lake, IN: Eisenbrauns.

Kaldeli, A.

2008 Roman Amphorae from Cyprus: Integrating Trade and Exchange in the Mediterranean, 2 vols. Ph.D. dissertation, University College London.

Kaldeli, A., Williams, D.F., and Michaelides, D.

2022 Early Roman Amphorae from Nea Paphos: Cypriot Production within an Empire Framework. Pp. 63–78 in *Amphorae from the Eastern Mediterranean and Beyond: Production and Distribution from the Early to the Late Roman Period,* ed. A. Kaldeli. Studies in Mediterranean Archaeology and Literature 191. Nicosia: Astrom.

Kapitaikan, L.-A.

2018 Final Pottery Report of the 2010–2011 Excavation Seasons. Pp. 88–209 in *Hippos-Sussita of the Decapolis: The First Twelve Seasons of Excavations 2000–2011,* vol. 2, ed. M. Eisenberg. Haifa: Zinman Institute of Archaeology.

Kara, Ü.

2015 Yenikapı Limanı'nda Ele Geçen Damgalı Amphoralar. Pp. 243–50 in *Antikçağ'da Doğu Akdeniz'de Zeytinyağı ve Şarap Üretimi: Uluslararası Sempozyum; 17–19 Kasım 2011 Urla, İzmir/Olive Oil and Wine Production in Eastern Mediterranean during Antiquity: International Symposium Proceedings; 17–19 November 2011 Urla, Turkey,* ed. A. Diler, K. Şenol, and Ü. Aydınoğlu. İzmir: Ege Üniversitesi.

2021 Geç Antik Çağ Amphoralarında Görülen Yazıt ve Mühürler Işığında *Annona* Sistemi: LRA 1, LRA 2, LRA 3 ve Zeest 80 [The *Annona* System from the Point of Amphoras, Inscriptions, and Stamps of Late Antique: LRA 1, LRA 2, LRA 3 and Zeest 80]. *Arkeologi Dergisi* 227.2: 65–78. https://doi.org/10.51493/egearkeoloji.840265.

Karagiorgou, O.

2001 LR2: A Container for the Military *annona* on the Danubian Border? Pp. 129–66 in *Economy and Exchange in the East Mediterranean during Late Antiquity: Proceedings of a Conference at Somerville College, Oxford, 29th May, 1999,* ed. S. Kingsley and M. Decker. Oxford: Oxbow.

2009 Mapping Trade by the Amphora. Pp. 37–58 in *Byzantine Trade, 4th–12th Centuries: The Archaeology of Local, Regional and International Exchange. Papers of the Thirty-eighth Spring Symposium of Byzantine Studies, St John's College, University of Oxford, March 2004,* ed. M. M. Mango. Farnham: Ashgate.

Karambinis, M.

2015 *The Island of Skyros from Late Roman to Early Modern Times: An Archaeological Survey.* Archaeological Studies Leiden University 28. Leiden: Leiden University Press.

Kassab Tezgör, D.

2010 Étude du matériel amphorique de la zone A et de la zone B. Pp. 141–86 in *Les fouilles et le matériel de l'atelier amphorique de Demirci près de Sinope. Recueil de travaux.* Varia Anatolica 22. Istanbul: Institut français d'Études Anatoliennes-Georges Dumézil.

2020 *Corpus des amphores romaines produites dans les centres de Mer Noire: Collections des muses de la côte turque de la Mer Noire (Ereli, Amasra, Sinop, Samsun, Giresun, Ordu, Trabzon et Amasya).* Archaeopress Roman Archaeology 74. Oxford: Archaeopress.

Katzjäger, D.

2014 Late Antiquity on Elephantine Island, Upper Egypt, Pottery as mirror of Roman Society. *Rei Cretariæ Romanæ Favtorvm Acta* 43: 597–601.

Kaya, D., and Aslan, A.

2017 Küçükçekmece Göl Havzasi (Bathonea?) Kazilari'nda Bulunan Amphora Tipalari. Pp. 323–32 in *İstanbul Küçükçekmece Göl Havzası Kazıları/Excavations of Küçükçekmece Lake Basin (Bathonea),* ed. Ş. G. Aydingün. Istanbul: Arkeoloji Sanat Yayınları.

Keay, S.J.

1984 *Late Roman Amphorae in the Western Mediterranean. A Typology and Economic Study: The Catalan Evidence*, 2 vols. BAR International Series 196. Oxford: British Archaeological Reports.

Kenchreai

2013–2023 Late Roman Amphora 1. In *Kenchreai Archaeological Archive*, edited by J. L. Rife and S. Heath. American Excavations at Kenchreai. http://kenchreai.org/kaa/typology/p-lra-1.

Kelly, A.

2010 The Discovery of Phocaean Red Slip Ware (PRSW) Form 3 and Bii Ware (LR1 amphorae) on Sites in Ireland: An Analysis within a Broader Framework. *Proceedings of the Royal Irish Academy: Archaeology, Culture, History, Literature* 110: 35–88. https://doi.org/10.1353/ria.2010.0009.

Kiessel, M., Saymanlier, A.M., and Taluğ, M.

2024 The Harbour at Aphendrika during the Early Byzantine Period and the Maritime Activity on the North-eastern Coast of Cyprus. *Olba* 32: 143–71.

Kirwan, L.P.

1935 The Oxford University Excavations in Nubia, 1934-1935. *The Journal of Egyptian Archaeology* 21.2: 191–198

1984 The Birth of Christian Nubia: Some Archaeological Problems. *Rivista degli studi orientali* 58: 119–34.

Kizil, A., and Yaman, A.

2017 A Group of Transport Amphorae from the Territorium of Ceramus: Typological Observations. *Anatolia Antiqua* 25: 17–32.

Kızılarslanoğlu, H.A., and Aytek, A.İ.

2018 Elaiussa Sebaste Üretimi "Geç Roma 1" Amphoralarının Geleneksel Tipoloji ve Geometrik Morfometrik Analizlerle Değerlendirilmesi. *MASROP E-Dergi* 12.2: 16–44.

Kızılarslanoğlu, H.A., Pejša, S., Rauh, N.K.

2020 *2019 Addendum and Erratum to the Rough Cilicia Archaeological Survey Project (RCSP) Context Collection.* Purdue University Research Repository. https://doi.org/10.4231/B6F2-9K09.

Klenina, E.Y.

2014 Trade Relations of Novae (Moesia Secunda) according to Ceramic Evidence from the Assemblage of the Late 5th–Early 6th Century. Pp. 931–41 in *LRCW4: Late Roman Coarse Wares, Cooking Wares and Amphorae in the Mediterranean: Archaeology and Archaeometry. The Mediterranean: A Market without Frontiers*, ed. N. Poulou-Papadimitriou, E. Nodarou, and V. Kilikoglou, 2 vols. BAR International Series 2616. Oxford: Archaeopress.

Kocabaş, U.

2015 The Yenikapı Byzantine-Era Shipwrecks, Istanbul, Turkey: A Preliminary Report and Inventory of the 27 Wrecks Studied by Istanbul University. *International Journal of Nautical Archaeology* 44: 5–38. https://doi.org/10.1111/1095-9270.12084.

Komar, P.

2016 Wines from Cyprus and Cilicia in Antiquity: Taste and Trade. *Electrum* 23: 155–85. https://doi.org/10.4467/20800909EL.16.008.5827.

Komar, P., Rogava, A., and Motskobili, T.

2024 Transport Containers from the Apsaros Fortress (Modern Gonio), Georgia (1st–7th Century AD): A Preliminary Overview of Forms and Fabrics. Pp. 71–90 in *Chrysomallos: Polish Archaeologists in the Black Sea Region*, ed. M. Matera and R. Karasiewicz-Szczypiorski. ŚWIATOWIT Supplement Series C: Pontica et Caucasica 4. Warsaw: Wydawnictwa Uniwersytetu Warszawskiego. https://doi.org/10.31338/uw.9788366210363.pp.71-92.

Konrad, M.

2001 *Der spätrömische Limes in Syrien: Archäologische Untersuchungen an den Grenzkastellen von Sura, Tetrapyrgium, Cholle und in Resafa.* Resafa 5. Mainz: von Zabern.

Konstantinidou, A

2010 Aspects of Everyday Life in a Monastic Settlement: Amphorae and Cooking Wares (4th–7th c.) from the Old Monastery of Baramus in the Wadi Natrun (Egypt): A First Glance. Pp. 951–61 in *LRCW3: Late Roman Coarse Wares, Cooking Wares and Amphorae in the Mediterranean: Archaeology and Archaeometry. Comparison between Western and Eastern Mediterranean*, ed. S. Menchelli, S. Santoro, M. Pasquinucci, and G. Guiducci, 2 vols. BAR International Series 2185. Oxford: Archaeopress.

Konstantinidou, A., Monsieur, P., and Hasenzagl, C.

2018 Ceramics from Roman and Byzantine Thorikos. Pp. 53–54 in *Exploring Thorikos*, ed. R. F. Docter and M. Webster. Ghent: Ghent University, Department of Archaeology.

Kormazopoulou, L., and Diamanti, C.

2021 Early Byzantine Pottery from the Caves of Agios Ioannis and Cyclops on the Island of Irakleia, Cyclades: Preliminary Results. Pp. 899–902 in *Association Internationale pour l'Étude des Céramiques Médiévales et Modernes en Méditerranée: AIECM3. 12th Congress AIECM3 On Medieval and Modern Period Mediterranean Ceramics*, ed. P. Petridis, A.G. Yangaki, N. Liaros, and E.-E. Bia, 2 vols. National Hellenic Research Foundation, Institute of Historical Research Series 10. Athens: Institute of Historical Research.

Kouveli, A., and Manoli, E.

2021 The Amphorae from the Wells of an Athenian House, 2nd–6th Centuries AD: Exploring Trends, Trading Routes, and Contacts. Pp. 104–27 in *Byzantine Athens: October 21–23, 2016*, ed. H. Saradi. Athens: Byzantine & Christian Museum.

Kouzov, C., and Christov, M.

2018 Rescue Archaeological Study in Ancient Odessos and Late Medieval Varna in 2017. *Journal of Historical and Archaeological Research* 2: 18–41 (Bulgarian).

Kramer, N.

2012 *Keramik und Kleinefunde aus Diokaisareia*. Diokaisareia in Kilikien, Ergebnisse des Surveys 2001–2006 Band 1. Berlin: de Gruyter.

Krishnan, K., and Balvally, R.

2015 Assessing the Early Historic Indian Ocean Trade through Ceramics. Pp. 231–67 in *Imperial Rome, Indian Ocean Regions and Muziris*, ed. K. S. Mathew. New Delhi: Manohar.

Kuhnle, G., Burgevin, A., Fort Bérangère, M. J.-P., Mouton-Venault, S., Dard, I., Gelot, J., and Mougin, P.

2007 La fortification du Bas-Empire. *Gallia* 64: 407–26. https://doi.org/10.3406/galia.2007.3322.

Külzer, A.

2022 The Harbour of Theodosius in Yenikapı, İstanbul: A Harbour Area through the Ages. Pp. 75–91 in *The Byzantine Harbours of Constantinople*, ed. F. Daim and E. Kislinger. Byzanz zwischen Orient und Okzident 24. Heidelberg: Propylaeum. https://doi.org/10.11588/propylaeum.911.c12066.

Kuzmanov, G.

1973 Tipologia i kronologia na rannozantiyskite amfori (IV–VI) [Typologie et chronologie des amphores de la haute époque byzantine]. *Archeologia* 10: 14–21.

Lacerenza, G.

2003 Le iscrizioni giudaiche in Italia dal I al VI secolo: Tipologie, origine, distribuzione. Pp. 71–92 in *I beni culturali ebraici in Italia: Situazione attuale, problemi, prospettive e progetti per il future. Atti del Convegno Internazionale Ravenna, 22–24 maggio 2001*, ed. M. Perani. Ravenna: Longo.

Laganara, C.A.M., and Volpe, G.

1985 Area del tempio di Giove Toro a Canosa: Relazione preliminare. *Archeologia Medievale* 12: 501–15.

Lamboglia, N.

1956 La questione della cupola nel Battistero di Albenga. Pp. 731–46 in *Studi in onore di Aristide Calderini e Roberto Paribeni*, III, ed. Milan: Ceschina.

Landgraf, J.

1980 Keisan's Byzantine Pottery. Pp. 51–99 in *Tell Keisan (1971–1976): Une cité phénicienne en Galilée*, ed. J.

Briend and J.-B. Humbert. Orbis Biblicus et Orientalis, Series Archaeologica 1. Fribourg: Éditions universitaires; Göttingen: Vandenhoeck & Ruprecht.

Lang, M.

1976 *Graffiti and Dipinti.* Athenian Agora 21. Princeton: American School of Classical Studies at Athens.

Lapadula, E.

1998 Le anfore. Pp. 268–69 in *San Giusto. La Villa, le Ecclesiae. Primi risultati dagli scavi nel sito rurale di San Giusto (Lucera): 1995–1997,* ed. G. Volpe. Scavi e ricerche 8. Bari: Edipuglia.

Le Bomin, J.

2016 Les thermes byzantins de Taposiris Magna: La céramique d'un dépotoir de la fin du VIe et du début VIIe s. Apr. J.-C. *Bulletin de Liaison de la Céramique Égyptienne* 26: 39–71.

Leidwanger, J.

2007 Two Late Roman Wrecks from Southern Cyprus. *International Journal of Nautical Archaeology* 36.2: 308–16. https://doi.org/10.1111/j.1095-9270.2007.00149.x.

2013a Opportunistic Ports and Spaces of Exchange in Late Roman Cyprus. *Journal of Maritime Archaeology* 8: 221–43. https://doi.org/10.1007/s11457-013-9118-0.

2013b Amphorae and Underwater Survey: Making Sense of Late Roman Trade from Scattered Sherds and Shipwrecks. Pp. 179–90 in *The Transport Amphorae and Trade of Cyprus,* ed. M.L. Lawall and J. Lund. Gösta Enbom Monographs 3. Aarhus: Aarhus University Press. https://doi.org/10.2307/jj.608268.19.

2014 A Preliminary Archaeometric Analysis of the Late Roman 1 Amphoras from the Cargo of the Seventh-Century Yassiada Shipwreck, Turkey. Pp. 897–906 in *LRCW4: Late Roman Coarse Wares, Cooking Wares and Amphorae in the Mediterranean: Archaeology and Archaeometry. The Mediterranean: A Market without Frontiers,* ed. N. Poulou-Papadimitriou, E. Nodarou, and V. Kilikoglou, 2 vols. BAR International Series 2616. Oxford: Archaeopress.

2017 From Time Capsules to Networks: New Light on Roman Shipwrecks in the Maritime Economy. *American Journal of Archaeology* 121: 595–619. https://doi.org/10.3764/aja.121.4.0595.

Leidwanger, J, Green, E.S., and Tuna, N.

2015 A Late Antique Ceramic Assemblage at Burgaz, Datça Peninsula, South-west Turkey, and the "Normality of the Mixed Cargo" in the Ancient Mediterranean. *International Journal of Nautical Archaeology* 44: 300–311. https://doi.org/10.1111/1095-9270.12110.

Leone, A., and Sarantis, A.

2020 The Middle Euphrates and Its Transformation from the Third to the Seventh Centuries: The Case of Dibsi Faraj. *Journal of Late Antiquity* 13: 308–51.

Lewit, T.

2015 The Second Sea: Exchange between the Mediterranean and the Black Sea in Late Antiquity. *Post-Classical Archaeologies* 5: 149–74.

2023 Wine and Oil Production in 4th–7th Century Monasteries of the Eastern Mediterranean. *Romula* 21: 7–27.

Liou, B.

1987 Inscriptions peintes sur amphores: Fos (suite), Marseille, Toulon, Port-la-Nautique, Arles, Saint-Blaise, Saint-Martin-de-Crau, Mâcon, Calvi. *Archaeonautica* 7: 55–139. https://doi.org/10.3406/nauti.1987.898.

Long, L., and Volpe, G.

1998 Le chargement de l'épave 1 de la Palud (VIe s.) à Port-Cros (Var): Note préliminaire. Pp. 317–42 in *Fouilles à Marseille: Les mobiliers (Ier–VIIe siècles ap. J.-C.),* ed. M. Bonifay, M.-B. Carre, and Y. Rigoir. Collection études massaliètes 5. Travaux du Centre Camille Jullian 22. Paris: Errance.

Lund, J.

2023 Speaking Volumes: On the Capacities of Transport Amphorae. Pp. 43–56 in *Regional Economies in Action: Standardization of Transport Amphorae in the Roman and Byzantine Mediterranean. Proceedings of the International Conference at the Austrian Archaeological Institute and the Danish Institute at Athens, 16–18*

October 2017, ed. H.G. Cesteros and J. Leidwanger. Sonderschriften 63. Vienna: Österreichische Akademie der Wissenschaften.

MacCoull, L.S.B.

2010 Why and How Was the Aphrodito Cadaster Made? *Greek, Roman, and Byzantine Studies* 50: 625–38.

Majcherek, G.

1993 Roman Amphora from Marina el-Alamein. *Mitteilungen des Deutschen Archäologischen Instituts: Abteilung Kairo* 49: 215–20.

2007 The Late Roman Auditoria of Alexandria: An Archaeological Overview. Pp. 11–50 in *Alexandria: Auditoria of Kom el-Dikka and Late Antique Education*, ed. T. Derda, T. Markiewicz, and E. Wipszycka. Journal of Juristic Papyrology Supplement 8. Warsaw: University of Warsaw.

2019 Filling the Gap: Mediterranean Amphorae in Late Antique Palmyra. *Syria* 96: 395–417. https://doi.org/10.4000/syria.10620.

Majcherek, G., and Taha, A.

2004 Roman and Byzantine Layers at Umm el-Tlel: Ceramics and Other Finds. *Syria* 81: 229–48.

Malykh, S.

2007 The Ceramic Import in Late Roman, Byzantine and Early Arabic Giza: On the External Contacts of the Memphite Area. *Cultural Heritage of Egypt and Christian Orient* 4: 45–60.

Mango, M.M.

2002 Excavation and Survey at Androna, Syria: The Oxford Team 1999. *Dumbarton Oaks Papers* 56: 307–15.

Manning, S., Monks, S.J., Sewell, D.A., and Demesticha, S.

2000 Late Roman Type 1a Amphora Production at the Late Roman Site of Zygi-Petrini, Cyprus. *Report of the Department of Antiquities of Cyprus* 2000: 233–57.

Marangou-Lerat, A.

1995 *Le vin et les amphores de Crète: De l'époque classique à l'époque impériale.* Études crétoises 30. Athens: École française.

Marchand, S., and Dixneuf, D.

2007 Amphores et conteneurs égyptiens et importés du VII siècle apr. J.-C. Sondages récents de Baouit (2003–2004). Pp. 309–43 in *Amphores d'Égypte de la Basse Époque à l'Époque Arabe*, vol. 1, ed. S. Marchand and A. Marangou. Cahiers de la Céramique Égyptienne 8. Cairo: Institut français d'archéologie orientale.

Marchand, J., Reynold, P., and Bomin, J.

2022 Proto-LRA 1 Amphorae from Taposiris Magna (Egypt): A Typological and Petrological Study. *Bulletin de Liaison de la Céramique Égyptienne* 31: 87–120.

Martin, A.

1991 Sondages under S. Stefano Rotondo (Rome): The Pottery and Other Finds. *Boreas* 14/15: 157–78.

2008 Imports at Ostia in the Imperial Period and Late Antiquity: The Amphora Evidence from the DAI-AAR Excavations. Pp. 105–18 in *The Maritime World of Ancient Rome*, ed. R.L. Hohlfelder. Memoirs of the American Academy in Rome Supplementary Volume 6. Ann Arbor: University of Michigan Press.

2010 The Pottery from a Late-Antique Settlement at Schedia (Western Delta, Egypt). Pp. 945–49 in *LRCW3: Late Roman Coarse Wares, Cooking Wares and Amphorae in the Mediterranean: Archaeology and Archaeometry. Comparison between Western and Eastern Mediterranean*, ed. S. Menchelli, S. Santoro, M. Pasquinucci, and G. Guiducci, 2 vols. BAR International Series 2185. Oxford: Archaeopress, 2010.

2014 A Sixth-century Context at Olympia (SW Building). Pp. 761–68 in *LRCW4: Late Roman Coarse Wares, Cooking Wares and Amphorae in the Mediterranean: Archaeology and Archaeometry. The Mediterranean: A Market without Frontiers*, ed. N. Poulou-Papadimitriou, E. Nodarou, and V. Kilikoglou, 2 vols. BAR International Series 2616. Oxford: Archaeopress.

Martin, A., Cuyler, M.J., and Banducci, L.

2020 Santa Maria in Aracoeli (Rome): Frank Brown's Excavation in 1963. *Archaeologiae: Research by Foreign Missions in Italy* 18.1–2: 11–80.

Martin, A., and De Sena, E.C.
2003 Ostia: Overview of the Pottery. *Rei Cretariæ Romanæ Favtorvm Acta* 38: 43–49.
2005 Agricultural and Craft Supplies in Late Roman Ostia: Pottery Evidence from the DAI/AAR Excavations. Pp. 385–93 in *LRCW1: Late Roman Coarse Wares, Cooking Wares, and Amphorae in the Mediterranean: Archaeology and Archaeometry*, ed. J.M. Gurt i Esparraguera, J. Buxeda i Garrigos, and M.A. Cau Ontiveros. BAR International Series 1340. Oxford: Archaeopress.

Martin-Kilcher, S.
1994 *Die römischen Amphoren aus Augst und Kaiseraugst.* Forschungen in Augst 7.1-3. Augst.

Martin-Kilcher, S., and Tchernia, A.
2021 Amphorae: Typology and Contents. Pp. 31–40 in *Roman Amphora Contents Reflecting on the Maritime Trade of Foodstuff in Antiquity. In Honour of Miguel Beltrán Lloris. Proceedings of the Roman Amphora Contents International Interactive Conference (RACIIC) (Cadiz, 5–7 October 2015)*, ed. D. Bernal Casasola, M. Bonifay, A. Pecci, and V. Leitch. Roman and Late Antique Mediterranean Pottery 17. Oxford: Archaeopress. https://doi.org/10.2307/j.ctv22zp41p.5.

Martindale, J.R.
2011 *The Prosopography of the Later Roman Empire III, A.D. 527–641.* Cambridge: Cambridge University Press.

Massa, S.
2020 Imported Wares in the Sudanese Eastern Desert: Finds from the CeRDO Survey 2004. Pp. 84–98 in *Travelling the Korosko Road: Archaeological Exploration in Sudan's Eastern Desert*, ed. W.V. Davies and D.A. Welsby. Sudan Archaeological Research Society Publication 24. Oxford: Archaeopress. https://doi.org/10.2307/j.ctv1bjc3dk.15.

Maurina, B., and Capelli, C.
2005 L'importazione di prodotti alimentari in anfore nell'arco alpino orientale fra tardoantico e altomedioevo: recenti dati da Loppio-S. Andrea (TN). *Archeologia Medievale* 32: 409–22.
2007 Anfore tardoantiche dall'insediamento fortificato di Loppio-S. Andrea (Trentino, Italia). Pp. 481–89 *LRCW2: Late Roman Coarse Wares, Cooking Wares and Amphorae in the Mediterranean: Archaeology and Archaeometry*, ed. M. Bonifay and J. C. Tréglia, 2 vols. BAR International Series 1662. Oxford: Archaeopress.

McCarthy, B.
2017 *Inis Cealtra: Appendix 2, Detailed Support Material.* Dublin: Solearth Architecture.

McCormick, M.
2001 *Origins of the European Economy: Communications and Commerce, A.D. 300–900.* Cambridge: Cambridge University Press.

McNicoll, A.W., Edwards, P.C., Hennessy, J.B., Potts, T.F., Smith, R.H., Walmsley, A., and Watson, P.
1992 *Pella in Jordan 2: The Second Interim Report of the Joint University of Sydney and College of Wooster Excavations at Pella 1982–1985.* Mediterranean Archaeology Supplement 2. Sydney: Meditarch.

Megaw, A.H.S., and Jones, R.E.
1983 Byzantine and Allied Pottery: A Contribution by Chemical Analysis to Problems of Origins and Distribution. *The Annual of the British School at Athens* 78: 235–63.

Menchelli, S.
2020 Marketing Roman Pottery along the Tyrrhenian Coast: The Case Studies of Vada Volaterrana, Pisae and Luna. *Rei Cretariæ Romanæ Favtorvm Acta* 46: 217–28. https://doi.org/10.2307/j.ctv1gt94kk.25.

Menozzi, O., Antonelli, S., Cinalli, A., Mancini, M.C., and Agostini, S.
2014 Lamluda: From the Excavation to the Archaeometric Analysis. *Libyan Studies* 45: 65–83. https://doi.org/10.1017/lis.2014.9.

Mills, P.J.E., and Beaudry, N.
2010 Pottery from Late Roman Ras el Bassit, Syria. Pp. 857–66 in *LRCW3: Late Roman Coarse Wares, Cooking Wares and Amphorae in the Mediterranean: Archaeology and Archaeometry. Comparison between Western*

and Eastern Mediterranean, ed. S. Menchelli, S. Santoro, M. Pasquinucci, and G. Guiducci, 2 vols. BAR International Series 2185. Oxford: Archaeopress.

Mitchell, S.

2015 *A History of the Later Roman Empire, AD 284–641: The Transformation of the Ancient World.* Blackwell History of the Ancient World. Oxford: Blackwell.

Modrijan, Z.

2011 4. The Pottery. Pp. 121–220 in *Poznoantična utrjena naselbina Tonovcov grad pri Kobaridu: Najdbe/Late Antique Fortified Settlement Tonovcov grad near Kobarid: Finds.* Opera Instituti archaeologici Sloveniae 24. Ljubljana: Institut za arheologijo – Založba ZRC.

2014 Imports from the Aegean Area to the Eastern Alpine Area and Northern Adriatic in Late Antiquity. *Ephemeris Napocensis* 24: 51–70.

Morris, C.E., and Peatfield, A.D.

1987 Pottery from the Cyprus Underwater Survey, 1983. *Report of the Department of Antiquities, Cyprus* 1987: 199–212.

Morselli, C., and Ricci, M.

2009 Nuove ricerche archeologiche a Elaiussa Sebaste. Pp. 99–112 in *Ideologia e cultura artistica tra Adriatico e Mediterraneo orientale (IV–X secolo): Il ruolo dell'autorità ecclesiastica alla luce di nuovi scavi e ricerche. Atti del Convegno Internazionale Bologna-Ravenna, 26–29 Novembre 2007*, ed. R. Farioli Campanati, C. Rizzardi, P. Porta, A. Augenti, and I. Baldini Lippolis. Studi e scavi 19. Bologna: Ante Quem.

Muçaj, S., Lako, K., Bushi, S., and Xhyheri, S.

2014 Monumenti i 40 Shenjtorëve, 2013. *Iliria* 38: 321–26. https://doi.org/10.3406/iliri.2014.2484.

Mukai, T.

2016 *La Céramique du Groupe épiscopal d'Aradi/Sidi Jdidi (Tunisie).* Roman and Late Antique Mediterranean Pottery 9. Oxford: Archaeopress.

Murcia Muñoz, A.J., Vizcaíno Sánchez, J., García Lorca, S., and Ramallo Asensio, S.F.

2005 Conjuntos cerámicos tardíos de las excavaciones en el teatro romano de Cartagena. Pp. 1–36 in *LRCW1: Late Roman Coarse Wares, Cooking Wares, and Amphorae in the Mediterranean: Archaeology and Archaeometry*, ed. J.M. Gurt i Esparraguera, J. Buxeda i Garrigos, and M.A. Cau Ontiveros. BAR International Series 1340. Oxford: Archaeopress 2005.

Nacef, J.

2007 Nouvelles données sur l'atelier de potiers de Henchir Ech Chekaf (Ksour Essef, Tunisie). Pp. 581–91 in *LRCW2: Late Roman Coarse Wares, Cooking Wares and Amphorae in the Mediterranean: Archaeology and Archaeometry*, ed. M. Bonifay and J.-C. Tréglia, 2 vols. BAR International Series 1662. Oxford: Archaeopress.

Nelson, M.C., Kelly, A., Ian Begg, D.J., and Brenningmeyer, T.

2015 The Early Byzantine Settlement at Leukos, Karpathos. *Annual of the British School at Athens* 110: 321–67. https://doi.org/10.1017/S0068245415000040.

Nagy, A.A., and Szakmány, G.

2019 Amphorae as Indicators of Trade and Diet in Cibalae (Pannonia). *ArcheoSciences* 43: 211–27. https://doi.org/10.4000/archeosciences.6793.

Naumenko, V.E.

2018 Укрепление сиваг-кермен в юго-западном крыму. Новая византийская крепость "страны дори" прокопия кесарийского (общие итоги археологического изучения памятника в 2015–2017). Античная древность и средние века. Вып 46: 54–72. https://doi.org/10.15826/adsv.2018.46.003.

2023 Застройка Ранневизантийского Времени в Центральной Части Мангупа-дороса. Новые Материалы Исследований/Development of the Early Byzantine Time in the Central Part of Mangupa-doros: New Research Materials. Pp. 223–33 in *Imperium et Barbaricum: Interaction of Civilizations.*

Papers Collected in Honour of Michel Kazanski's 70th Birthday, ed. A. Aibabin, and E. Khairedinova. Simferopol: Izdatel'stvo "Antika".

Negrelli, C.

2021 Le ceramiche tardoantiche e altomedievali. Pp. 201–76 in *Un emporio e la sua cattedrale, Gli scavi di piazza XX Settembre e Villaggio San Francesco a Comacchio*, ed. S. Gelichi, C. Negrelli, and E. Grandi. Florence: All'Insegna del Giglio.

Nervi, C.

2014 Local and Imported Pottery at Nora (Sardinia-Cagliari) from the 3rd to the 7th Centuries: Comparison between Urban and Rural Finds. Pp. 843–54 in *LRCW4: Late Roman Coarse Wares, Cooking Wares and Amphorae in the Mediterranean: Archaeology and Archaeometry. The Mediterranean: A Market without Frontiers*, ed. N. Poulou-Papadimitriou, E. Nodarou, and V. Kilikoglou. BAR International Series 2616, 2 vols. Oxford: Archaeopress.

O'Brien, W., and Hogan, N.

2021 *Garranes: An Early Medieval Royal Site in South-west Ireland.* Archaeopress Archaeology. Oxford: Archaeopress.

Oikonomou-Laniado, A.

2003 *Argos paleochretienne: Contribution à l'étude du Péloponnèse byzantin.* BAR International Series 1173. Oxford: Archaeopress.

Olcay Uçkan, B.Y., Oztaskin, G.K., Oztaskin, M., and Evcim, S.

2022 Olympos Kazisi 2019 ve 2020 Yılı Çalişmalari. *Yılı Kazı Çalışmaları* 4: 415–34.

Öniz, H.

2016 *Amphorae in the Eastern Mediterranean.* Archaeopress Archaeology. Oxford: Archaeopress.

Öncü, E., and Çölmekçi, S.

2018 Yenikapı Kazıları ve Bizans Dönemi Amphora Buluntuları. Pp. 15–28 in *XIth Congress AIECM3 on Medieval and Modern Period Mediterranean Ceramics Proceedings*, ed. T. Hazırlayan and F. Yenişehirlioğlu. Ankara: Koç Üniversitesi.

Opaiţ, A.

1991 Ceramica din Aşezarea şi cetatea de la Independenţa (Murighiol) secolele V Î.E.N.–VII E.N. *Peuce* 10: 133–216.

2004 *Local and Imported Ceramics in the Roman Province of Scythia.* BAR International Series 1274. Oxford: Archaeopress.

2009 Cilician LR Amphora 1? *Arheologia Moldovei* 32: 283–89.

2010 On the Origin of the Carthage LR Amphora 1. Pp. 1015–22 in *LRCW3: Late Roman Coarse Wares, Cooking Wares and Amphorae in the Mediterranean: Archaeology and Archaeometry. Comparison between Western and Eastern Mediterranean*, ed. S. Menchelli, S. Santoro, M. Pasquinucci, and G. Guiducci, 2 vols. BAR International Series 2185. Oxford: Archaeopress.

2017 On the Local Production and Imports of Wine in the Pontic and Lower Danube Regions (1st Century BC to 7th Century AD): An Overview. Pp. 579–612 in *LRCW5: Late Roman Coarse Wares, Cooking Wares and Amphorae in the Mediterranean: Archaeology and Archaeometry. La céramique commune, la céramique culinaire et les amphores de l'Antiquité tardive en Méditerranée*, ed. D. Dixneuf, 2 vols. Études Alexandrines 42/43. Alexandria: Centre d'Études Alexandrines.

2018 Local and Imported Wine at Pompeiopolis, Paphlagonia. *Rei Cretariæ Romanæ Favtorvm Acta* 45: 701–13.

2021 A Levantine Trade Diaspora at Pompeiopolis? *Ancient West and East* 20: 81–97. https://doi.org/10.2143/AWE.20.0.3289530.

2023 Some Thoughts on the Production, Distribution, and Consumption of Wine, Olive Oil, and Fish Products in the Pontic and Lower Danube Areas (1st–6th c. AD). Pp. 645–61 in *Aux sources des connaissances historiques: Épigraphie, textes littéraires et documents archéologiques. Volume dédié à la mémoire de Alexandru Avram*, ed. L. Buzoianu, V. Lungu, and D. Hălmagi. Pontica 56, Supplementum 10. Constanţa: Mega.

Opaiţ, A., Barnea, A., Barnea, I., Grigoraş, B., and Potra, I.
2020 Supplying Wine, Olive Oil and Fish Products to the Lower Danube Frontier (2nd–7th Century AD): The Case of Dinogetia. *Rei Cretariae Romanae Favtorvm Acta* 46: 381–94.
Opaiţ, A., Barnea, A., Grigoraş, B., Panaite, A., and Hălmagi, D.
2022 *Dinogetia II: Amforele romane*, ed. A. Panaite. Biblioteca Istro-Pontica Seria Arheologie 22. Cluj-Napoca: Mega.
Opaiţ, A., Davis, D., Brennan, M.L., and Kofahl, M.
2019 The Sinop F Shipwreck in the Black Sea: An International Cargo from Late Antiquity. Pp. 77–89 in *Proceeding of the International Symposium on Sinope and Black Sea Archaeology "Ancient Sinope and the Black Sea,"* ed. H. Kaba, G. Kan Şahin, B.M. Akarsu, and O. Bozoğlan. Sinop: Sinop Üniversitesi.
Opaiţ, A., and Ionescu, M.
2016 Contributions to the Economic Life of the City of Callatis in Light of New Ceramic Finds (2nd–6th Centuries AD). *Arheologia Moldovei* 39: 57–112. https://doi.org/10.11588/amold.2016.1.91740.
Opriş, I. C., and Ratiu, A.
2016 An Early Byzantine Amphorae Deposit from Capidava. *Journal of Ancient History and Archeology* 3.1: 24–42. https://doi.org/10.14795/j.v3i1.155.
2019 The Northern Supply Chain in *Quaestura Exercitus*. 6th to Early 7th Century Amphorae at Capidava – Archaeology of the *annona* for *Limes Scythicus*. *RAIA Bulletin: Romanian Archaeological Institute in Athens Bulletin* 1: 139–55.
Orssaud, D.
1992 Le passage de la céramique Byzantine à la céramique Islamique: Quelques hypothèses à partir du mobilier trouvé à Déhès. Pp. 219–28 in *La Syrie de Byzance à l'Islam 7e–8e siècles: Actes du colloque international Lyon–Maison de l'Orient méditerranéen, Paris – Institut du monde arabe (11–15 septembre 1990)*, ed. P. Canivet and J.-P. Rey-Coquais. Damascus: Institut français de Damas.
Pacetti, F.
1995 Appunti su alcuni tipi di anfore orientali della prima età bizantina: Centri di produzione, contenuti, cronologia e distribuzione. Pp 273–94 in *Agricoltura e commerci nell'Italia Antica*, ed. L. Quilici. Atlante tematico di topografia antica I supplemento. Rome: "L'Erma" di Bretschneider.
Panella, C.
1993 Merci e scambi nel Mediterraneo tardoantico. Pp. 613–97 in *Storia di Roma 3: L'età tardoantica. II. I luoghi e le culture*, ed. A. Carandini, L. Cracco Ruggini, and A. Giardina. Torino: Einaudi.
2013 Roma e gli altri: La cultura materiale al tempo del sacco di Alarico. Pp. 365–402 in *The Sack of Rome in 410 AD: The Event, Its Context and Its Impact. Proceedings of the Conference Held at the German Archaeological Institute at Rome, 04–06 November 2010*, ed. J. Lipps, C. Machado, and P. von Rummel. Palilia 28. Wiesbaden: Reichert.
Panella, C., Saguì, L., Casalini, M., and Coletti, F.
2010 Contesti tardoantichi di Roma: Una rilettura alla luce di nuovi dati. Pp. 57–78 in *LRCW3: Late Roman Coarse Wares, Cooking Wares and Amphorae in the Mediterranean: Archaeology and Archaeometry. Comparison between Western and Eastern Mediterranean*, ed. S. Menchelli, S. Santoro, M. Pasquinucci, and G. Guiducci, 2 vols. BAR International Series 2185. Oxford: Archaeopress.
Papadopoulos, J.K.
1989 Roman Amphorae from the Excavations at Torone. Αρχαιολογική εφημερίς 128: 67–103.
Papakosta, L.
2020 The Late Roman Anchorage of Cape Petounda, Cyprus. *"Under the Mediterranean": The Honor Frost Foundation Conference on Mediterranean Maritime Archaeology 20th–23rd October 2017 Short Report Series*. https://doi.org/10.33583/utm2020.09.
Paraschiv, I.D.
2006 *Amfore romane şi romano-bizantine în zona Dunării de Jos (sec. I–VII Chr.)*. Seria Istorie 64. Iaşi: Axis.

2014 Roman-Byzantine Pontic Amphorae Discovered at (L)Ibida, in the Province of Scythia. Pp. 425–32 in *LRCW4: Late Roman Coarse Wares, Cooking Wares and Amphorae in the Mediterranean: Archaeology and Archaeometry. The Mediterranean: A Market without Frontiers*, ed. N. Poulou-Papadimitriou, E. Nodarou, and V. Kilikoglou, 2 vols. BAR International Series 2616. Oxford: Archaeopress.

Papavassiliou, E., and Didioumi, S.

2017 Workshop Installations in the Dodecanese in Late Antiquity and the Early Byzantine Period. Pp. 43–60 in *Το Αρχαιολογικό Έργο στα Νησιά του Αιγαίου. Διεθνές Επιστημονικό Συνέδριο (Ρόδος, 27 Νοεμβρίου–1 Δεκεμβρίου 2013)*. Mytilene: Hellenic Ministry of Culture and Sports (Greek).

Papavassiliou, E., Sarantidis, K., and Papanikolaou, I.

2014 Ceramic Workshop of the Early Byzantine Period on the Island of Lipsi in the Dodecanese (Greece): A Preliminary Approach. Pp. 159–68 in *LRCW4: Late Roman Coarse Wares, Cooking Wares and Amphorae in the Mediterranean: Archaeology and Archaeometry. The Mediterranean: A Market without Frontiers*, ed. N. Poulou-Papadimitriou, E. Nodarou, and V. Kilikoglou, 2 vols. BAR International Series 2616. Oxford: Archaeopress.

Peacock, D.P.S., and Williams, D.F.

1986 *Amphorae and the Roman Economy: An Introductory Guide*. Longman Archaeology. London: Longman.

Pecci, A., Salvini, L., and Cantini, F.

2010 Residue Analysis of Some Late Roman Amphora Coming from the Excavations of the Historical Center of Florence. Pp. 363–67 in *LRCW3: Late Roman Coarse Wares, Cooking Wares and Amphorae in the Mediterranean: Archaeology and Archaeometry. Comparison between Western and Eastern Mediterranean*, ed. S. Menchelli, S. Santoro, M. Pasquinucci, and G. Guiducci, 2 vols. BAR International Series 2185. Oxford: Archaeopress.

Pedersen, R.K.

2000 Under the Erythrean Sea: An Ancient Shipwreck in Eritrea. *INA Quarterly* 27.2/3: 3–13.

2008 The Byzantine-Aksumite Period Shipwreck at Black Assarca Island, Eritrea. *Azania* 43: 77–94. https://doi.org/10.1080/00672700809480460.

Pellegrino, E.

2002 Le matériel céramique issu des fouilles menées en 1995 et 2000 sur l'acropole lycienne de Xanthos. *Anatolia Antiqua* 10: 245–60. https://doi.org/10.3406/anata.2002.985.

2003 Présentation des céramiques issues des fouilles menées en 1998–1999 sur l'acropole Lycienne de Xanthos. *Anatolia Antiqua* 11: 215–21. https://doi.org/10.3406/anata.2003.1004.

2011 Un lot de céramique de la collection Maurice Sechter Ier au XIIIe s. apr. J.-C. à Saint-Cassien (Mandelieu, Alpes-Maritimes). *Revue du Centre Archéologique du Var*: 113–38.

Penchev, V.

2021 An Interesting Early Byzantine Lead Seal. *Contributions to Bulgarian Archaeology* 11: 5–7. https://doi.org/10.53250/cba11.5-7.

Pensabene, P.

1981 Anfore tarde con iscrizioni cristiane dal Palatino. *Rivista di Studi Liguri* 47: 189–213.

Peña, J.T.

2021 The Reuse of Transport Amphora as Packaging Containers in the Roman World: An Overview. Pp. 77–91 in *Roman Amphora Contents Reflecting on the Maritime Trade of Foodstuff in Antiquity. In Honour of Miguel Beltrán Lloris. Proceedings of the Roman Amphora Contents International Interactive Conference (RACIIC) (Cadiz, 5–7 October 2015)*, ed. D. Bernal Casasola, M. Bonifay, A. Pecci, and V. Leitch. Roman and Late Antique Mediterranean Pottery 17. Oxford: Archaeopress. https://doi.org/10.2307/j.ctv22zp41p.9.

Perna, R.

2014 *Hadrianopolis* e la valle del Drino (Albania): Considerazioni sulle trasformazioni dell'insediamento e del territorio dall'età ellenistica a quella bizantina (campagne di scavo e surveys 2011–2015). *Annuario della Scuola Archeologica di Atene e delle Missioni Italiane in Oriente* 92 (Series 3.14): 195–260.

Perna, R., Çondi, D., Capponi, C., Lahi, B., Martinelli, C., Severini, S., Sforzini, D., Shkodra Rrugia, B., and Tubaldi, V.

2014 Ceramiche d'uso comune, anfore e materiali laterizi provenienti dall'Edificio Termale di Hadrianopolis (Sofratikë – Albania). Pp. 501–13 in *LRCW4: Late Roman Coarse Wares, Cooking Wares and Amphorae in the Mediterranean: Archaeology and Archaeometry. The Mediterranean: A Market without Frontiers*, ed. N. Poulou-Papadimitriou, E. Nodarou, and V. Kilikoglou, 2 vols. BAR International Series 2616. Oxford: Archaeopress.

Pettegrew, D.K.

2007 The Busy Countryside of Late Roman Corinth: Interpreting Ceramic Data Produced by Regional Archaeological Surveys. *Hesperia* 76: 743–84.

Philipson, D.W.

2000 *Archaeology at Aksum, Ethiopia, 1993-7.* 2 vols. Memoirs of the British Institute in Eastern Africa 17. Report 65, Research Committee of the Society of Antiquaries of London. London: The British Institute in Eastern Africa.

Pieri, D.

2005a *Le Commerce du Vin Oriental a l'Epoque Byzantine: Le témoignage des amphores en Gaule.* Bibliothèque archéologique et historique 174. Beirut: Institut français du Proche-Orient.

2005b Nouvelles productions d'amphores de Syrie du Nord aux époques protobyzantine et omeyyade. Pp. 583–96 in *Mélanges Jean-Pierre Sodini*, ed. F. Baratte. Travaux et mémoires 15. Paris: Collège de France, Centre de recherche d'histoire et civilisation de Byzance.

2007a Amphores de Méditerranée orientale durant l'Antiquité tardive (IVe–VIIe s.): Régions de production et commerce vers la Gaule. Pp. 149–52 in *Antiquité tardive, haut Moyen Âge et premiers temps chrétiens en Gaule méridionale, Seconde partie: Monde rural, échanges et consummation*, ed. M. Heijmans and J. Guyon. Gallia 64. Paris: CNRS.

2007b Les centres de production d'amphores en Mediterranée orientale durant l'antiquité tardive: Quelques remarques. Pp. 611–25 in *LRCW2: Late Roman Coarse Wares, Cooking Wares and Amphorae in the Mediterranean: Archaeology and Archaeometry*, ed. M. Bonifay and J.C. Tréglia, 2 vols. BAR International Series 1662. Oxford: Archaeopress.

2012 Regional and Interregional Exchanges in the Eastern Mediterranean during the Early Byzantine Period: The Evidence of Amphorae. Pp. 27–49 in *Trades and Markets in Byzantium*, ed. C. Morrison. Dumbarton Oaks Byzantine Symposia and Colloquia. Washington, DC: Dumbarton Oaks Research Library and Collection.

Pipere, M.F.

2018 Indagini subacquee presso la città di Elaiussa Sebaste (Turchia): Porto tra Oriente e Occidente. Pp. 371–79 in *Il patrimonio culturale sommerso: Ricerche e proposte per il futuro dell'archeologia subacquea in Italia*, ed. M. Capulli. Udine: Forum; Universitaria Udinese.

Piton, J.

2010 Mobilier, catalogue des céramiques. Pp. 169–87 in *Maisons de Clupea. Les maisons de l'école de pêche*, ed. J.-M. Lassère and H. Slim. Études d'Antiquités Africaines 1. Paris: CNRS Editions.

Plat Taylor, J., and Megaw, A.H.S.

1981 Excavations at Ayios Philon, the Ancient Carpasia, Part 2: The Early Christian Building. *Report of the Department of Antiquities Cyprus* 1981: 209–50.

Poblome, J., Corremans, M., Bes, P., Romanus, K., and Degryse, P.

2008 It Is Never Too Late...: The Late Roman Initiation of Amphora Production in the Territory of Sagalassos. Pp. 1001–12 in *Euergetes: Prof. Dr. Haluk Abbasoglu'na 65. Yas Armaganı/Festschrift für Prof. Dr. Haluk Abbasoglu zum 65. Geburtstag*, ed. İ. Delemen, S. Çokay-Kepçe, A. Özdibay, and Ö. Turak. Antalya: AKMED – Suna İnan Kıraç Akdeniz Medeniyetleri Araştırma Enstitüsü.

Polosa, A.
2003 Addendum ai rinvenimenti monetali delle campagne 1998–99: Ripostiglio di frazioni di bronzo. Pp. 557–69 in *Elaiussa Sebaste II: Un porto tra Oriente e Occidente*, ed. E. Equini Schneider. Bibliotheca Archaeologica 37. Rome: "L'Erma" di Bretschneider.

Popławski, S., Kraśniewska, U., Mi, F., and Oleksiak, J.
2021 Trash from a Temple: A Deposit Next to the Isis Temple at Berenike (Egypt). *Polish Archaeology in the Mediterranean* 30: 387–418. https://doi.org/10.31338/uw.2083-537X.pam30.2.18.

Popović, M.
1987 Svetinja. Contribution to the study of the early Byzantine Viminacium. (Serbian with English summary). *Starinar. Arheološki institut Beograd* 38: 1–37.

Portale, E.C.
2014 The Sunset of Gortyn: Amphorae in the 7th–8th Centuries AD. Pp. 477–89 in *LRCW4: Late Roman Coarse Wares, Cooking Wares and Amphorae in the Mediterranean: Archaeology and Archaeometry. The Mediterranean: A Market without Frontiers*, ed. N. Poulou-Papadimitriou, E. Nodarou, and V. Kilikoglou, 2 vols. BAR International Series 2616. Oxford: Archaeopress.

Portale, E.C., and Romeo, I.
2001 Contenitori da trasporto. Pp. 260–410 in *Gortina V. 3: Lo scavo del Pretorio (1989–1995). I materiali – tavole.* Monografie della Scuola Archeologica Italiana di Atene e delle Missioni Italiane in Oriente 12. Padova: Bottega D'Erasmo, Ausilio.

Poulou, N.
2017 Transport Amphoras and Trade in the Aegean from the 7th to the 9th Century AD: Containers for Wine or Olive Oil? *Byzantina* 35: 195–216.

Poulou-Papadimitriou, N.
2018 The Aegean during the "Transitional" Period of Byzantium: The Archaeological Evidence. Pp. 29–50 in *Naxos and the Byzantine Aegean: Insular Responses to Regional Change*, ed. J. Crow and D. Hill. Papers and Monographs from the Norwegian Institute at Athens 7. Athens: Norwegian Institute at Athens.

Poulou-Papadimitriou, N., and Didioumi, S.
2010 Nouvelles données sur la production de l'atelier céramique protobyzantin à Kardamaina (Cos - Grèce). Pp. 741–49 in *LRCW3: Late Roman Coarse Wares, Cooking Wares and Amphorae in the Mediterranean: Archaeology and Archaeometry. Comparison between Western and Eastern Mediterranean*, ed. S. Menchelli, S. Santoro, M. Pasquinucci, and G. Guiducci, 2 vols. BAR International Series 2185. Oxford: Archaeopress.
2015 Two Pottery Workshops of the Early Byzantine Period in the Island of Cos (Greece). Pp. 401–18 in *Tourner autour du pot: Les ateliers de potiers médiévaux de Ve au XIIe siècle dans l'espace européen. Actes du colloque international de Douai, 5–8 octobre 2010*, ed. F. Thuillier and É. Louis. Publications du CRAHAM. Série Antique et Médiévale. Caen: Presses universitaires de Caen.

Poulou-Papadimitriou, N., and Nodarou, E.
2007 La céramique protobyzantine de Pseira: La production locale et les importations, étude typologique et pétrographique. Pp. 755–66 in *LRCW2: Late Roman Coarse Wares, Cooking Wares and Amphorae in the Mediterranean: Archaeology and Archaeometry*, ed. M. Bonifay and J.C. Tréglia, 2 vols. BAR International Series 1662. Oxford: Archaeopress.
2014 Transport Vessels and Maritime Trade Routes in the Aegean from the 5th to the 9th c. AD. Preliminary Results of the EU Funded "Pythagoras II" Project: The Cretan Case Study. Pp. 873–83 in *LRCW4: Late Roman Coarse Wares, Cooking Wares and Amphorae in the Mediterranean: Archaeology and Archaeometry. The Mediterranean: A Market without Frontiers*, ed. N. Poulou-Papadimitriou, E. Nodarou, and V. Kilikoglou, 2 vols. BAR International Series 2616. Oxford: Archaeopress.

Poulter, A.
2019 *The Transition to Late Antiquity on the Lower Danube: Excavations and Survey at Dichin, a Late Roman to Early Byzantine Fort and a Roman Aqueduct.* Oxford: Oxbow.
Prausnitz, M. W.
1967 *Excavations at Shavei Zion: The Early Christian Church.* Monografie di Archeologia e d'Arte 2. Rome: Centro per le Antichità e la Storia dell'arte del Vicino Oriente.
Pulak, C.
1989 1988 Yılı Sualtı Araştırması. *Araştırma Sonuçları Toplantısı* 7: 73–79.
Pulak, C., and Rogers, E.
1994 The 1993–1993 Turkish Shipwreck Surveys. *INA Quarterly* 21.4: 17–21.
Purpura, G.
1977 Nuove anfore nell'Antiquarium di Terrasini. *Sicilia Archeologica* 10.35: 54–70.
1983 Il relitto bizantino di Cefalù. *Sicilia Archeologica* 16.51: 93–105.
2004a Il relitto bizantino di Cefalù: Ultimo atto? *Archaeologia Maritima Mediterranea* 1: 89–98.
2004b The Byzantine Shipwreck of Cefalù. Pp. 122–26 in *Barbarian Seas: Late Rome to Islam*, ed. S. Kingsley. Encyclopaedia of Underwater Archaeology 4. London: Periplus.
Quercia, A., Johnston, A., Bevan, A., Conolly, J., and Tsaravopoulos, A.
2011 Roman Pottery from an Intensive Survey of Antikythera, Greece. *Annual of the British School at Athens* 106: 47–98. https://doi.org/10.1017/S0068245411000037.
Quevedo, A., García-Sánchez, J., Khellaf, R., and Bensaidani, Y.
2023 The Territory of Ancient Tipasa, Algeria: Archaeological Survey, Material Culture, and Connectivity in Central Maghreb. *African Archaeology Review* 40: 673–709. https://doi.org/10.1007/s10437-023-09529-6.
Racheli, A.
1991 Osservazioni su alcune classi di materiali rinvenuti in territorio calabrese. *Mélanges de l'École française de Rome* 103: 709–29. https://doi.org/10.3406/mefr.1991.3196.
Rahtz, P.
1970 Excavations on Glastonbury Tor, Somerset, 1964–6. *Archaeological Journal* 127: 1–81. https://doi.org/10.1080/00665983.1970.11078389.
Rahtz, P., Hirst, S., and Wright, S.M.
2000 *Cannington Cemetery: Excavations 1962–3 of Prehistoric, Roman, Post-Roman, and Later Features at Cannington Park Quarry, Near Bridgwater, Somerset.* Britannia Monograph Series 17. London: Society for the Promotion of Roman Studies.
Raičković, A.
2012 Late Roman Pottery from Viminacium-Thermae: The Excavation of 2004. *Rei Cretariæ Romanæ Favtorvm Acta* 42: 147–54.
Rainbird, P., and Hughes, S.
2014 *The South West Coast Path "Unlocking Our Heritage" Project: High Peak Camp, Otterton, East Devon. NGR SY 10342 85956. Results of Archaeological Excavation.* Salisbury: AC Archaeology. https://doi.org/10.5284/1047648.
Ramstetter, K.
2018 Kaiserzeitliche und spätantike Gebäude ("Areal HA") auf dem Holzerberg in Teurnia/St. Peter in Holz. Pp. 405–15 in *Akten des 16. Österreichischen Archäologentages am Institut für Klassische Archäologie der Universität Wien vom 25. bis 27. Februar 2016*, ed. G. Schörner and K. Meinecke. Wiener Forschungen zur Archäologie 17. Vienna: Phoibos.
Ratzlaff, A., Galili, E., Waiman-Barak, P., and Yasur-Landau, A.
2017 The Plurality of Harbors at Caesarea: The Southern Anchorage in Late Antiquity. *Journal of Maritime Archaeology* 12: 125–46. https://doi.org/10.1007/s11457-017-9173-z.

Rauh, N.K.

2023 2023 Addendum to the Rough Cilicia Kiln Site Ceramics (Syedra, Delice, Biçkici, and Antiochia ad Cragum): An Update to the Kiln Sites. *Rough Cilicia Archaeological Survey Project, 1996–2011* Paper 17. https://doi.org/10.5703/1288284317638.

Rauh, N.K., Autret, C., and Lund, J.

2013 Amphora Design and Marketing in Antiquity. Pp. 145–81 in *Kauf, Konsum und Märkte Wirtschaftswelten im Fokus: Von der römischen Antike bis zur Gegenwart*, ed. M. Frass. Philippika Marburger altertumskundliche Abhandlungen 59. Wiesbaden: Harrassowitz.

Rautman, M.L.

1995 Two Late Roman Wells at Sardis. *Annual of the American Schools of Oriental Research* 53: 37–84.

Rautman, M.L., Neff, H., Gomez, B., Vaughan, S., and Glascock, M.D.

1999 Amphoras and Roof-tiles from Late Roman Cyprus: A Compositional Study of Calcareous Ceramics from Kalavasos-Kopetra. *Journal of Roman Archaeology* 12: 377–91. https://doi.org/10.1017/S1047759400018110.

Reddy, A.L.

2013 Looking from Arabia to India: Analysis of the Early Roman "India Trade" in the Indian Ocean during the Late Pre-Islamic Period (3rd Century BC–6th Century AD), 2 vols. Ph.D. dissertation, Deccan College Postgraduate and Research Institute.

Reed, S., Bidwell, P., and Allan, J.

2010 Excavation at Bantham, South Devon, and Post-Roman Trade in South-West England. *Medieval Archaeology* 55: 82–138. https://doi.org/10.1179/174581711X13103897378447.

Remolà Vallverdú, J.A.

2000 *Las ánforas tardo-antiguas en Tarraco (Hispania tarraconensis). Siglos IV–VII d.C.* Collectió Instrumenta 7. Barcelona: Publicacions Universitat de Barcelona.

Reynolds, P.

2004 13. The Roman Pottery from the Triconch Palace. Pp. 224–77 in *Byzantine Butrint: Excavations and Surveys 1994–99*, ed. W. Bowden, K. Lako, and R.D. Andrews. Butrint Archaeological Monographs 2. Oxford: Oxbow.

2005 Levantine Amphorae from Cilicia to Gaza: A Typology and Analysis of Regional Production Trends from the 1st to 7th Centuries. Pp. 563–611 in *LRCW1: Late Roman Coarse Wares, Cooking Wares, and Amphorae in the Mediterranean: Archaeology and Archaeometry*, ed. J.M. Gurt i Esparraguera, J. Buxeda i Garrigos, and M.A. Cau Ontiveros. BAR International Series 1340. Oxford: Archaeopress 2005.

2008 Linear Typologies and Ceramic Evolution. *FACTA* 2: 61–87.

2010a *Hispania and the Roman Mediterranean, AD 100–700: Ceramics and Trade.* London: Duckworth.

2010b Trade Network of the East, 3rd to 7th Centuries: The View from Beirut (Lebanon) and Butrint (Albania) (Fine Wares, Amphorae and Kitchen Wares). Pp. 89–114 in *LRCW3: Late Roman Coarse Wares, Cooking Wares and Amphorae in the Mediterranean: Archaeology and Archaeometry. Comparison between Western and Eastern Mediterranean*, ed. S. Menchelli, S. Santoro, M. Pasquinucci, and G. Guiducci, 2 vols. BAR International Series 2185. Oxford: Archaeopress.

2011 A 7th Century Pottery Deposit from Byzantine Carthago Spartaria (South-eastern Spain). Pp. 99–127 in *Late Roman Fine Wares 1. Solving Problems of Typology and Chronology. A Review of the Evidence, Debate, and New Contexts*, ed. M.A. Cau, P. Reynolds, and M. Bonifay. Roman and Late Antique Mediterranean Pottery 1. Oxford: Archaeopress. https://doi.org/10.2307/j.ctv177tjc9.12.

2013 Transport Amphorae of the First to Seventh Centuries: Early Roman to Byzantine Periods. Pp. 93–161 in *Excavations at Zeugma: Conducted by Oxford Archaeology*, vol. 2, ed. W. Aylward. Los Altos: Packard Humanities Institute.

2017 Butrint in the Late 6th to the 7th Centuries: Contexts, Sequences and Ceramics. Pp. 262–74 in *Encounters, Excavations and Argosies: Essays for Richard Hodges*, ed. J. Mitchell, J. Moreland, and B. Leal. Oxford: Archaeopress. https://doi.org/10.2307/j.ctv1pdrqgc.27.

2018 The Supply Networks of the Roman East and West: Interaction, Fragmentation, and the Origins of the Byzantine Economy. Pp. 353–95 in *Trade, Commerce, and the State in the Roman World*, ed. A. Wilson and A.K. Bowman. Oxford Studies on the Roman Economy. Oxford: Oxford University Press. https://doi.org/10.1093/oso/9780198790662.003.0012.

Reynolds, P., and Pavlidis, E.

2014 Nicopolis (*Epirus Vetus*): An Early 7th Century Pottery Assemblage from the "Bishop's House" (Greece). Pp. 451–67 in *LRCW4: Late Roman Coarse Wares, Cooking Wares and Amphorae in the Mediterranean: Archaeology and Archaeometry. The Mediterranean: A Market without Frontiers*, ed. N. Poulou-Papadimitriou, E. Nodarou, and V. Kilikoglou, 2 vols. BAR International Series 2616. Oxford: Archaeopress.

2017 An Early 5th Century AD Pottery Deposit from a Cloaca Cleaning Shaft of the Cardo Next to Basilica A, Nicopolis (Greece). Pp. 651–66 in *Σπείρα: Επιστημονική συνάντηση προς τιμήν της Αγγέλικας Ντούζουγλη και του Κωνσταντίνου Ζάχου; Πρακτικά, ed. Ε. Μέρμηγκα*. Athens: Έκδοση του Ταμείου Αρχαιολογικών Πόρων και Απαλλοτριώσεων.

Richarté, C.

2011 Proposition de périodisation des contextes tardo-antiques du théâtre d'Arles (Ve–VIe s.): Nouvelles données. Pp. 71–79 in *Contextes de consommation à Arles: Le point sur les connaissances céramiques; Contextes des villes portuaires et fluviales: Commerce, économie et société. Actualités des recherches céramiques, Actes du congrès de la SFECAG, Arles, 2011*, ed. L. Rivet and S. Saulnier. Marseilles: Société française d'étude de la céramique antique en Gaule, 2011.

Riley, J.A.

1979 Coarse Pottery. Pp. 91–467 in *Excavations at Sidi Khrebish Benghazi (Berenice) 2: Economic Life at Berenice – Sculpture and Terracottas – Coarse Pottery*, ed. J.A. Lloyd. Libya Antiqua Supplements 5.2. Tripoli: Department of Antiquities, People's Socialist Libyan Arab Jamahirya.

1981 The Pottery from Cisterns 1977.1, 1977.2 and 1977.3. Pp. 85–124 in *Excavations at Carthage 1977 Conducted by the University of Michigan 6*, ed. J.H. Humphrey. Ann Arbor: Kelsey Museum, University of Michigan.

1984 Abu Sha'ar Fort: The Pottery Report. Unpublished report dated 22 November 1984.

Rizzo, M.S., and Zambito, L.

2010 Ceramiche comuni ed anfore dal villaggio tardoantico di Cignana (Naro-agrigento, Sicilia, Italia). Pp. 293–300 in *LRCW3: Late Roman Coarse Wares, Cooking Wares and Amphorae in the Mediterranean: Archaeology and Archaeometry. Comparison between Western and Eastern Mediterranean*, ed. S. Menchelli, S. Santoro, M. Pasquinucci, and G. Guiducci, 2 vols. BAR International Series 2185. Oxford: Archaeopress.

Robinson, H.S.

1959 *Pottery of the Roman Period: Chronology.* Athenian Agora 5. Princeton: American School of Classical Studies at Athens.

Rodriguez Lopez, D.

2016 Etude du mobilier amphorique tardo-antique. Pp. 238–79 in *Fossae Marianae: Le système portuaire antique du golfe de Fos et le canal de Marius. Rapport 2016*, vol. 1. *Textes et figures*, ed. S. Fontaine. DRASSM—Département des recherches archéologiques subaquatiques et sous-marines.

Romanus, K., Baeten, J., Poblome, J., Accardo, S., Degryse, P., Jacobs, P., De Vos, D., and Waelkens, M.

2009 Wine and Olive Oil Permeation in Pitched and Non-pitched Ceramics: Relation with Results from Archaeological Amphorae from Sagalassos, Turkey. *Journal of Archaeological Science* 36: 900–909. https://doi.org/10.1016/j.jas.2008.11.024.

Romanowska, I., Lichtenberger, A., and Raja. R.

2021 Trends in Ceramic Assemblages from the Northwest Quarter of Gerasa/Jerash, Jordan. *Journal of Archaeological Science: Reports* 36: 102778. https://doi.org/10.1016/j.jasrep.2020.102778.

Rosenthal-Heginbottom, R.
1988 The Pottery. Pp. 78–97 in *Excavations at Rehovot-in-the-Negev*, vol. 1: *The Northern Church*, ed. Y. Tsafrir. Qedem 25. Jerusalem: Hebrew University.
Rosselló Mesquida, M., and Ribera I Lacomba, A.V.
2005 Las cerámicas del siglo VII d.C. en Valentia (Hispania) y su entorno. *Rei Cretariæ Romanæ Favtorvm Acta* 39: 155–64.
Rostovtzeff, M.
1957 *The Social and Economic History of the Roman Empire*, 2nd ed. Oxford: Clarendon.
Rousset, M.-O.
2012 La ceramique. Pp. 73–118 in *Al-Hadir: Étude archéologique d'un hameau de Qinnasrin (Syrie du Nord, VIIe–XIIe siècles)*, ed. M-O. Rousset. Travaux de la Maison de l'Orient et de la Méditerranée, Série recherches archéologiques 59. Lyon: Maison de l'Orient et de la Méditerranée.
Royal, J.G.
2006 Remote-sensing Survey of the South-eastern Bozburun Peninsula, Turkey. *International Journal of Nautical Archaeology* 35: 195–217. https://doi.org/10.1111/j.1095-9270.2006.00112.x.
Ruggiu, A.Z., and Cottica, D.
2007 Hierapolis di Frigia fra Tarda Antichità ed XI secolo: L'apporto dello studio degli spazi domestici nell'insula 104. *Rivista di Archeologia* 31: 139–89.
Rutgers, L.V.
2020 *The Jews in Late Ancient Rome: Evidence of Cultural Interaction in the Roman Diaspora.* Brill Scholar's List. Leiden: Brill.
Saguì, L.
2002 Roma, i centri privilegiati e la lunga durata della tarda antichità: Dati archeologici dal deposito di VII secolo nell'esedra della Crypta Balbi. *Archeologia Medievale* 29: 7–42.
Saguì, L., and Coletti, C.M.
2004 Contesti tardoantichi dall'area a S-E della *Crypta Balbi.* Pp. 242–77 in *Roma dall'antichità al medioevo: II, Contesti tardoantichi e altomedievali*, ed. L. Paroli and L. Vendittelli. Milan: Electa.
Saguì, L., Ricci, M., and Romei, D.
1997 Nuovi dati ceramologici per la storia economica di Roma tra VII e VIII secolo. Pp. 35–48 in *La céramique médiévale en Méditerranée: Actes du VIe Congrès de l'AIECM 2*, ed. G. Démians d'Archimbaud. Aix-en-Provence: Narration.
Saller, S.J.
1941 *The Memorial of Moses on Mount Nebo*, Part II: *The Plates.* Publications of the Studium biblicum franciscanum 1. Jerusalem: Studium Biblicum Franciscanum.
Salles, J.-F., and Sedov, A.V.
2010 *Qāni': Le port antique du Ḥaḍramawt entre la Méditerranée, l'Afrique et l'Inde. Fouilles russes, 1972, 1985–1989, 1991, 1993–1994.* Indicopleustoi: Archaeologies of the Indian Ocean. Turnhout: Brepols.
Sanders, G.D.R.
1999 A Late Roman Bath at Corinth: Excavations in the Panayia Field, 1995–1996. *Hesperia* 68.4: 441–80. https://www.jstor.org/stable/148411.
Sandhaus, D., and Balouka, M.
2015 The Pottery. Pp. 189–206 in *Bet She'an Vol. 3. Nysa-Scythopolis: The Southern And Severan Theaters. Part 1: The Stratigraphy and Finds*, ed. G. Mazor and W. Atrash. IAA Reports 58.1. Jerusalem: Israel Antiquities Authority.
Sänger, P., and Cesteros, H.G.
2019 Eine neue Spätantike Amphore mit Aufschriften aus Ephesos: Ein Beitrag zu der Problematik der Lr 1 Aufschriften. *Zeitschrift für Papyrologie und Epigraphik* 211: 137–42.

Sangineto, A.B.

2006 Anfore. Pp. 310–35 in *Blanda Julia sul Palecastro di Tortora: Scavi e ricerche (1990–2005)*, ed. G.F. La Torre and F. Mollo. Pelorias 13. Messina: Di.Sc.A.M.

Sanna, I., Soro, L., and Nervi, C.

2021 Amphorae with Residues from Southern Sardinia (Cagliari and Nora). Pp. 453–72 in *Roman Amphora Contents: Reflecting on the Maritime Trade of Foodstuffs in Antiquity. In Honour of Miguel Beltrán Lloris. Proceedings of the Roman Amphora Contents International Interactive Conference (RACIIC) (Cádiz, 5–7 october 2015)*, ed. D. Bernal Casasola, M. Bonifay, A. Pecci, and V. Leitch. Roman and Late Antique Mediterranean Pottery 17. Oxford: Archaeopress. https://doi.org/10.2307/j.ctv22zp41p.35.

Sarıkaya Levent, Y.

2022 What Happened in Soli-Pompeiopolis within the Last Two Centuries? *Trakya Üniversitesi Sosyal Bilimler Dergisi* 24: 273–304. https://doi.org/10.26468/trakyasobed.1038518.

Sazanov, A.

1999 Les amphores "LRA 1 Carthage" dans la région de la Mer Noire. Pp. 265–79 in *Production et commerce des amphores anciennes en Mer Noire*, ed. Y. Garlan. Aix-en-Provence: Publications de l'Université de Provence.

2017 Un ensemble de la fin du VIe siècle: Secteur nord de Chersonèse (Crimée). Pp. 651–69 in *LRCW5: Late Roman Coarse Wares, Cooking Wares and Amphorae in the Mediterranean: Archaeology and Archaeometry. La céramique commune, la céramique culinaire et les amphores de l'Antiquité tardive en Méditerranée*, ed. D. Dixneuf, 2 vols. Études alexandrines 42/43. Alexandrie: Centre d'Études Alexandrines.

2023 Керамические комплексы начала–третьей четверти V в. поселения "Ильич-1"/Pottery Contexts Dated to the Early–Third Quarter of the Vth Century AD Coming from Ilyich-1 Settlement. Древности Боспора/*Drevnosti Bospora* 28: 300–359. https://doi.org/10.25681/IARAS.2020.978-5-94375-339-8.142-165.

Schindler, D.

2017 Late Roman and Byzantine Galilee: A Provincial Case Study from the Perspective of the Imported and Common Pottery. Ph.D. dissertation, University of North Carolina.

Schneider, P.

2014 Diplomatie, commerce et savoir: Les Méditerranéens et l'océan Indien au temps de Justinien. *Sileno: Rivista di studi classici e cristiani* 40: 195–238.

Scorpan, C.

1975 Ceramica romano-bizantină de la Sacidava. *Pontica* 8: 263–313.

Sdrolia, S., Didioumi, S., and Koutsoyiannis, D.

2018 An Early Byzantine House in the Castle of Velika, Thessaly, Greece: A Possible Official Residence. Pp. 195–99 in *Abitare nel Mediterraneo tardoantico: Atti del 2. Convegno internazionale del Centro interuniversitario di studi sull'edilizia abitativa tardoantica nel Mediterraneo (CISEM) (Bologna 2–5 marzo 2016)*, ed. I. Baldini Lippolis and C. Sfameni. Insulae Diomedeae 35. Santo Spirito (BA): Edipuglia.

Seland, E.H.

2014 Early Christianity in East Africa and Red Sea/Indian Ocean Commerce/Les débuts du Christianisme en Afrique de l'est et le commerce de la mer Rouge et de l'Océan Indien. *African Archaeological Review* 13: 637–47. https://doi.org/10.1007/s10437-014-9172-5.

Şenol, A.K.

2009 *Taşucu Aslan Eyce Amfora Müzesi*. Silifke.

2015 Smyrna Kazılarında 2007–2011 yılları arasında bulunan Ticari Amphoralar. Pp. 243–56 in *Smyrna/İzmir Kazı ve Araştırmaları: I. Çalıştay bildirileri*, ed. A. Ersoy and G. Şakar. Antik Smyrna kazısı yayın çalışmaları 3. Istanbul: Ege Yayınları.

Şenol, A.K., and Alkaç, E.

2017 The Rediscovery of an LR 1 Workshop in Cilicia and the Presence of LRA 1 in Alexandria in the Light of New Evidence. Pp. 831–44 in *LRCW5: Late Roman Coarse Wares, Cooking Wares and Amphorae in the Mediterranean: Archaeology and Archaeometry. La céramique commune, la céramique culinaire et les amphores de l'Antiquité tardive en Méditerranée*, ed. D. Dixneuf, 2 vols. Études Alexandrines 42/43. Alexandria: Centre d'Études Alexandrines.

Shalev, E. A., Gambash, G., and Yasur-Landau, A.

2019 Disheveled Tenacity: The North Bay of Roman and Byzantine Dor. *Journal of Maritime Archaeology* 14: 205–37. https://doi.org/10.1007/s11457-019-09235-y.

Shkodra-Rugria, B.

2007 Një tip amfore i periudhës antike të vonë nga Durrësi/A Late Roman Amphora Type from Durrës. *Iliria* 33: 311–24. https://doi.org/10.3406/iliri.2007.1075.

2023 Roman and Late Roman Pottery. Pp. 213–31 in *Archaeological Investigations in a Northern Albanian Province: Results of the Projekti Arkeologjik i Shkodrës (PASH)*, vol. 2: *Artifacts and Artifact Analysis*, ed. M.L. Galaty, and L. Bejko. https://doi.org/10.3998/mpub.12208577.

Slane, K.W., and Sanders, G.D.R.

2005 Corinth: Late Roman Horizons. *Hesperia* 74: 243–97. https://doi.org/10.1353/hes.2005.0007.

Slim, H., Trousset, P., Paskoff, R., Oueslati, A., Bonifay, M., and Lenne, J.

2004 *Le littoral de la Tunisie: Étude géoarchéologique et historique.* Études d'antiquités africaines Paris: CNRS.

Smokotina, A.V.

2015 The Import of LR 1 Amphorae into Bosporus. Pp. 121–35 in *Per terram, per mare: Seaborne Trade and the Distribution of Roman Amphorae in the Mediterranean*, ed. S. Demesticha. Studies in Mediterranean Archaeology and Literature Pocket-book 180. Uppsala: Åströms.

2016 Late Roman Amphorae from Tyritake. *Rei Cretariæ Romanæ Favtorvm Acta* 44: 715–24.

2020 Амфоры позднеримского и ранневизантийского времени. Pp. 509–617 in *Тиритака Раскоп XXVI Том III: Археологические Комплексы Второй Половины III–VII Вв./Tyritake Excavation Trench XXVI*, vol. 3: *Archaeological Complexes Two Second* [second half of the] *III–VII Centuries. AD*, ed. V.N. Zinko, A.V. Zinko, and L. Yu. Ponomarev. Bosporos Studies Supplementum. Simferopol-Kerch.

Snyder, C.A.

1996 *Sub-Roman Britain (AD 400–600): A Gazetteer of Sites.* BAR British Series 247. Oxford: BAR.

Sodini, J.P., and Villeneuve, E.

1992 Le passage de la céramique Byzantine à la céramique Omeyyade en Syrie du nord, en Palestine at en Transjordanie. Pp. 195–218 in *La Syrie de Byzance a l'Islam. VIIe-VIIIe siècles. Actes du Colloque international*, ed. P. Canivet and J.-P. Rey-Coquais. Damascus: Institut Français de Damas.

Spahiu, H.

2011 Gjurmë të murit rrethues dhe të ndërtesave të Kohës së Vonë Antike në kështjellën e Beratit/Late Antique Wall and Buildings in the Castle of Berat. *Iliria* 35: 55–74. https://doi.org/10.3406/iliri.2011.1099.

Staffa, A.R., and Pellegrini, W.

1993 *Dall'Egitto copto all'Abruzzo bizantino. I Bizantini in Abruzzo (secc. VI-VII).* Crecchio: Soc. Coop. POLIS.

Starac, A.

2006 Promet amforama prema nalazima u Rovinjskome Podmorju/Transport of Amphorae according to Finds from the Waters of Rovinj. *Histria archaeologica* 37: 85–116.

Stănescu, R.O.

2018 Amphorae ex Aegysso: Fragments from Older Excavations. *Peuce* New Series 16: 205–226.

Steckner, C.

1989 Les amphores LR 1 et LR 2 en relation avec le pressoir du complexe ecclésiastique des thermes de Samos. Pp. 57–71 in *Recherches sur la céramique byzantine: Actes du colloque organisé par l'École française d'Athènes et l'Université de Strasbourg II, Athènes 8–10 avril 1987*, ed. V. Déroche, and J. Spieser. Bulletin de Correspondance Hellénique Supplément 18. Athens: École française d'Athènes.

Strouhal, E.

1984 *Wadi Qitna and Kalabsha-South: Late Roman–Early Byzantine Tumuli Cemeteries in Egyptian Nubia, 1: Ar-*

chaeology. Publications–Charles University of Prague, Czechoslovak Institute of Egyptology in Prague and Cairo. Prague: Charles University.

Swan, V.G.

2010 Dichin (Bulgaria): The Destruction Deposits and the Dating of Black Sea Amphorae in the Fifth and Sixth Centuries A.D. Pp. 107–18 in *Patabs I: Production and Trade of Amphorae in the Black Sea. Actes de la Table Ronde internationale de Batoumi et Trabzon, 27–29 avril 2006*. Varia Anatolica, 21. Istanbul: Institut Français d'Études Anatoliennes-Georges Dumézil.

Taşlıalan, M., and Drew-Bear, T.

2005 Fouilles de l'Agora de Smyrne: Rapport sur la campagne de 2004. *Anatolia Antiqua* 13: 371–434. https://doi.org/10.3406/anata.2005.1056.

Taxel, I.

2018 *Fragile Biography: The Life Cycle of Ceramics and Refuse Disposal Patterns in Late Antique and Early Medieval Palestine*. Babesch Supplement 35. Leuven: Peeters.

Tekocak, M., and Zoroğlu, K.L.

2013 Kelenderis'te Bulunan Bir Grup Roma Dönemi Ticari Amphorasi ve Düşündürdükleri. *Olba* 21: 109–40.

Theodoulou, T., Foley, B., Kourkoumelis, D., and Preka-Alexandri, K.

2015a Roman Amphora Cargoes in the Sea of Chios: The 2008 Mission. Pp. 41–54 in *Per terram, per mare: Seaborne Trade and the Distribution of Roman Amphorae in the Mediterranean*, ed. S. Demesticha. Studies in Mediterranean Archaeology and Literature Pocket-book 180. Uppsala: Åströms.

Theodoulou, T., Foley, B., Evagelistis, D., Koutsouflakis, G., Sakellariou, D., and Tourtas, A.

2015b Crete Project 2011: Underwater Archaeological Survey at the Area between Herakleion and Dia. A Preliminary Report. Pp. 615–25 in *Αρχαιολογικο Εργο κρητης: Πρακτικά της 3ης Συνάντησης Ρέθυμνο, 5–8 Δεκεμβρίου 2013*, ed. P. Karanasti, A. Tzigkounaki, and X. Tzigonaki. Rethymno: Crete University Publications.

Thomas, C.

1959 Imported Pottery in Dark-age Western Britain. *Medieval Archaeology* 3: 89–111. https://doi.org/10.1080/00766097.1959.11735586.

Thomas, R.

2018 Ptolemaic, Roman and Byzantine Amphorae and Stoppers. Pp. 2–19 in *Naukratis: Greeks in Egypt*, ed. A. Villing, M. Bergeron, G. Bourogiannis, A. Johnston, F. Leclère, A. Masson, and R. Thomas. British Museum, Online Research Catalogue. https://www.britishmuseum.org/research/online_research_catalogues/ng/naukratis_greeks_in_egypt/material_culture_of_naukratis/ptolemaic-byzantine_amphorae.aspx.

Tolbert, R.J.A.

2000 *Barrington Atlas of the Greek and Roman World*. Princeton: Princeton University Press.

Tomber, R.

2004 Amphorae from the Red Sea and Their Contribution to the Interpretation of Late Roman Trade beyond the Empire. Pp. 393–402 in *Transport Amphorae and Trade in the Eastern Mediterranean: Acts of the International Colloquium at the Danish Institute at Athens, September 26–29, 2002*, ed. J. Eiring and J. Lund. Monographs of the Danish Institute at Athens 5. Aarhus: Aarhus University Press.

2008 *Indo-Roman Trade: From Pots to Pepper*. Duckworth Debates in Archaeology. London: Duckworth.

2010 Beyond Western India: The Evidence from Imported Amphorae. Pp. 42–57 in *Migration, Trade and Peoples*, Part 1: *Indian Ocean Commerce and the Archaeology of Western India*, ed. R. Tomber, L. Blue, and S. Abraham. British Association for South Asian Studies. London: British Academy.

Topoleanu, F.G.

2000 *Ceramica romana si romano-bizantina de la Halmyris (sec. I–VII d.Ch.)/Roman and Roman-Byzantine Pottery from Halmyris (1st–7th centuries AD)*. Tulcea: Ministerului Culturii, Serviciul Arheologie (Romanian).

Tosti, T.

2014 Le anfore dagli scavi di Paola (CS). Graduation Thesis. Corso di Laurea Magistrale in Archeologia, Dipartimento di Studi Umanistici, Università della Calabria, 2013–2014.

Totten, D.M., De Mitri, C., and Loprieno, S.

2023 The Late Antique Town of Salapia: Midden Data as an Indicator of Exchange and Daily Life. Pp. 103–13 in *LRCW6: Late Roman Coarse Wares, Cooking Wares and Amphorae in the Mediterranean: Archaeology and Archaeometry. Land and Sea: Pottery Routes*, ed. V. Caminneci, E. Giannitrapani, M.C. Parello, and M.S. Rizzo, 2 vols. Roman and Late Antique Mediterranean Pottery 19. Oxford: Archaeopress.

Trabelsi, S.

2019 Le port antique de Missua (Sidi Daoud), découvertes sous-marines récentes. *Méditerranée* 2019: 1–25. https://doi.org/10.4000/mediterranee.10799.

Tréglia, J.-C., and Berthier, S.

2010 Amphores, céramiques communes et céramiques culinaires byzantines de la citadelle de Damas (Syrie). Pp. 867–76 in *LRCW3: Late Roman Coarse Wares, Cooking Wares and Amphorae in the Mediterranean: Archaeology and Archaeometry. Comparison between Western and Eastern Mediterranean*, ed. S. Menchelli, S. Santoro, M. Pasquinucci, and G. Guiducci, 2 vols. BAR International Series 2185. Oxford: Archaeopress.

Tubb, J.N.

1986 The Pottery from a Byzantine Well near Tell Fara. *Palestine Exploration Quarterly* 118: 51–65. https://doi.org/10.1179/peq.1986.118.1.51.

Twardecki, A., and Buiskikh, A.

2021 The Cherniakhov Culture in Olbia Pontica in the Light of the Polish-Ukrainian Excavations 2016–2018. *Sprawozdania Archeologiczne* 73: 251–73. https://doi.org/10.23858/SA/73.2021.2.2166.

Tzavella, E., Trainor, C., and Maher, M.

2014 Late Roman Pottery from the Sikyon Survey Project: Local Production, Imports, and Urban Evolution (4th–7th c. AD) (Greece). Pp. 91–102 in *LRCW4: Late Roman Coarse Wares, Cooking Wares and Amphorae in the Mediterranean: Archaeology and Archaeometry. The Mediterranean: A Market without Frontiers*, ed. N. Poulou-Papadimitriou, E. Nodarou, and V. Kilikoglou, 2 vols. BAR International Series 2616. Oxford: Archaeopress.

Vaccaro, E.

2014 Patterning Late Roman Ceramic Exchange in Southern Tuscany (Italy): The Coastland and Inland Evidence, i.e., Centrality vs. Marginality. Pp. 11–26 in *LRCW4: Late Roman Coarse Wares, Cooking Wares and Amphorae in the Mediterranean: Archaeology and Archaeometry. The Mediterranean: A Market without Frontiers*, ed. N. Poulou-Papadimitriou, E. Nodarou, and V. Kilikoglou, 2 vols. BAR International Series 2616. Oxford: Archaeopress.

2017 Philosophiana in Central Sicily in the Late Roman and Byzantine Periods: Settlement and Economy. Pp. 300–313 in *Encounters, Excavations and Argosies: Essays for Richard Hodges*, ed. J. Moreland, J. Mitchell, and B. Leal. Archaeopress Archaeology. Oxford: Archaeopress.

Van den Berg, J.

2023 The Amphorae. Pp. 587–614 in *Excavations of a Late Iron Age Enclosure, a Roman Villa Complex, a Late Roman-Early Medieval Settlement and Burials Part III-A: Specialist Analyses*, ed. H.A. Hiddink. Nederlandse Oudheden 20. Amersfoort: Cultural Heritage Agency of the Netherlands.

Van den Brink, E.C.M., Rutgaizer, O., Gorin-Rosen, Y., Horwitz, L.K., Liphschitz, N., Mienis, H.K.

2013 Two Roman-Byzantine Subsurface Features at Horbat Qastra (Castra), at the Foot of Mount Carmel. *'Atiqot* 75: 71–127.

Varinlioğlu, G.

2013 Rural Habitat in the Hinterland of Seleucia ad Calycadnum during Late Antiquity. Pp. 199–209 in *Rough Cilicia: New Historical and Archaeological Approaches*, ed. M.C. Hoff and R.F. Townsend. Oxford: Oxbow. https://doi.org/10.2307/j.ctvh1dhr3.21.

Varinlioğlu, G., Kaye, N., Pejša, S., and Rauh, N.K.

2023 *Ovacık (Aphrodisias) Archaeological Survey: Processed Ceramics, 2017 through 2019.* Purdue University Research Repository. https://doi.org/10.4231/0EAN-DE59.

Varinlioğlu, G., Rauh, N.K., and Pejša, S.

2022 *Dana Island Archaeological Survey: Processed Ceramics, 2016 through 2019.* Purdue University Research Repository. https://doi.org/10.4231/WGXJ-TE67.

Varinlioğlu, G., Rauh, N.K., Pejša, S., and Wohmann, R.

2020 *Boğsak Archaeological Survey: Processed Ceramics, 2016 and 2017.* Purdue University Research Repository. https://doi.org/10.4231/WF3E-2W39.

Vasiliou, S., and Tsigarida, E.B.

2014 Late Roman Pottery from Recent Excavations at Cassandra in Chalcidice. Pp. 723–35 in *LRCW4: Late Roman Coarse Wares, Cooking Wares and Amphorae in the Mediterranean: Archaeology and Archaeometry. The Mediterranean: A Market without Frontiers*, ed. N. Poulou-Papadimitriou, E. Nodarou, and V. Kilikoglou, 2 vols. BAR International Series 2616. Oxford: Archaeopress.

Vatta, G., and Bertoldi, T.

2004 Celio. *Basilica Hilariana*: scavi 1997. Pp. 458–79 in *Roma dall'antichità al medioevo, II: Contesti tardoantichi e altomedievali*, ed. L. Paroli and L. Vendittelli. Milan: Electa.

Vaz Pinto, I., Magalhães, A.P., and Brum, P.

2012 Un Depotoir du Ve Siecle dans l'Officine de Salaisons 1 de Troia (Portugal). *Rei Cretariæ Romanæ Fautorum Acta* 42: 397–407 (French).

Vidrih Perko, V., and Župančič, M.

2005 Amphorae in Western Slovenia and in Northern Istra. Pp. 521–36 in *LRCW1: Late Roman Coarse Wares, Cooking Wares, and Amphorae in the Mediterranean: Archaeology and Archaeometry*, ed. J.M. Gurt i Esparraguera, J. Buxeda i Garrigos, and M.A. Cau Ontiveros. BAR International Series 1340. Oxford: Archaeopress 2005.

de Vincenz, A.

2020 Byzantine- and Ottoman-Period Pottery Assemblages from Rabbi Yehuda Me-Raguza Street, Yafo (Jaffa). *'Atiqot* 100: 75–120.

2024 The Ceramic Assemblages. Pp. 263-441 in *Sepphoris 3: the Temple and the Eastern Church in the Lower City*, ed. by Z. Weiss and S. Miller. Qedem Reports 15. Jerusalem: Hebrew University of Jerusalem.

Vionis, A.

2017 Understanding Settlements in Byzantine Greece: New Data and Approaches for Boeotia, Sixth to Thirteenth Century. *Dumbarton Oaks Papers* 71: 127–73.

2023 A Boom-bust Cycle in Cyprus at the End of Antiquity: Landscape Perspectives for Settlement Transformation. Pp. 161–74 in *Cyprus in the Long Late Antiquity*, ed. P. Panayides. https://doi.org/10.2307/jj.1791895.14.

Vokaer, A.

2013 Continuity and Changes in Ceramic Production and Exchange in Syria during the Byzantine and Early Islamic Periods (5th–8th c. A.D.). Pp 483–510 in *Proceedings of the International Symposium Byzantium and the Arab World: Encounter of Civilizations (Thessaloniki, 16–18 December 2011)*, ed. A. Kralidis and A. Gkoutzioukostas. Thessaloniki.

2017 Late Roman Amphorae from Apamea, Syria. Pp. 779–805 in *LRCW5: Late Roman Coarse Wares, Cooking Wares and Amphorae in the Mediterranean: Archaeology and Archaeometry. La céramique commune, la céramique culinaire et les amphores de l'Antiquité tardive en Méditerranée*, ed. D. Dixneuf, 2 vols. Études Alexandrines 42/43. Alexandria: Centre d'Études Alexandrines.

Volpe, G.

1989 La circolazione delle anfore romane nella Daunia: Dati preliminari. Pp. 629–32 in *Amphores romaines et histoire* économique*: Dix ans de recherche. Actes du colloque de Sienne (22–24 mai 1986).* Publications de l'École française de Rome 114. Rome: École française de Rome.

Vroom, J.

2007 Limyra in Lycia: Byzantine/Umayyad Pottery Finds from Excavations in the Eastern Part of the City. Pp. 261–92 in *Céramiques antiques en Lycie (VIIe s. a.C. – VIIe s. p.C.): Les produits et les marches. Actes de la table ronde de Poitiers, 21–22 mars 2003*, ed. S. Lemaître. Bordeaux: de Boccard.

Waksman, S.Y., Morozova, Y., Zelenko, S., and Çolak, M.

2014 Archaeological and Archaeometric Investigations of the Amphorae Cargo of a Late Roman Shipwreck Sunk near the Cape of Plaka (Crimea, Ukraine). Pp. 919–929 in *LRCW4: Late Roman Coarse Wares, Cooking Wares and Amphorae in the Mediterranean: Archaeology and Archaeometry. The Mediterranean: A Market without Frontiers*, ed. N. Poulou-Papadimitriou, E. Nodarou, and V. Kilikoglou, 2 vols. BAR International Series 2616. Oxford: Archaeopress.

Waliszewski, T.

2014 *Elaion: Olive Oil Production in Roman and Byzantine Syria-Palestine.* Polish Centre of Mediterranean Archaeology 6. Warsaw: Warsaw University Press.

Ward, C.A.

2015 Plant Remains from the Old Wine Jars on the Byzantine Ship at Yassıada. Pp. 55–62 in *Maritime Studies in the Wake of the Byzantine Shipwreck at Yassıada, Turkey*, ed. D.N. Carlson, J. Leidwanger, and S.M. Kampbell. College Station: Texas A&M University Press.

Ward, C., and Ballard, R.D.

2004 Deep-water Archaeological Survey in the Black Sea: 2000 Season. *International Journal of Nautical Archaeology* 33.1: 2–13. https://doi.org/10.1111/j.1095-9270.2004.00002.x.

Weadick, S.

n.d. Late Roman Amphora Sherds from Co. Waterford. *National Museum of Ireland.* https://www.museum.ie/en-IE/Collections-Research/Collection/Documentation-Discoveries/Artefact/Late-Roman-Amphora-Sherds-from-Co-Waterford/14402eb2-27e7-4b42-b7ca-b0a6020353b5.

Weiss, Z.

2010 From Roman Temple to Byzantine Church: A Preliminary Report on Sepphoris in Transition. *Journal of Roman Archaeology* 23: 196–218. https://doi.org/10.1017/S1047759400002361.

Whitbread, I.

1995 *Greek Transport Amphorae: A Petrological and Archaeological Study.* Fitch Laboratory Occasional Paper 4. Exeter: British School at Athens.

Whitehouse, D., Costantini, L., Guidobaldi, F., Passi, S., Pensabene, P., Pratt, S., Reece, R., and Reese, D.

1985 The Schola Praeconum II. *Papers of the British School at Rome* 53: 163–210. https://doi.org/10.1017/S0068246200011533.

Wicenciak, U.

2019 Aspects of Economic Activity in Phoenicia during Roman and Byzantine Times: The Case of Olive Oil and Amphora Production in Chhim, in the Chora of Sidon. *Levant* 51: 314–36. https://doi.org/10.1080/00758914.2020.1854973.

2021a *From Sacred to Everyday: Common Wares and Amphorae from Chhim in the Sidon Hinterland.* Polish Publications in Mediterranean Archaeology 4. Leuven: Peeters.

2021b *Porphyreon: Hellenistic and Roman Pottery Production in the Sidon Hinterland.* Polish Centre of Mediterranean Archaeology 7. Warsaw: Polish Centre of Mediterranean Archaeology, University of Warsaw.

Wieczorek, M.

2023 The Importance of the City of Petra Pia Justiniana in the Caucasian Policy of Justinian I. Pp. 84–91 in *Heritage: Proceedings of the 10th International Symposium on Byzantine and Medieval Studies "Days of Justinian I," Skopje, 10–13 November, 2022*, ed. M.B. Panov. Skopje: Institut za nacionalna istorija-Skopje.

Wijnendaele, J.W.P., ed.

2023 *Late Roman Italy: Imperium to Regnum.* Edinburgh: Edinburgh University Press.

Williams, C.

1989 *Anemurium: The Roman and Early Byzantine Pottery.* Subsidia Mediaevalia 16. Toronto: Pontificial Institute of Mediaeval Studies.

Williams, D.F.

1980 The Petrology of Certain Byzantine Amphorae: Some Suggestions as to Origins. *Ancient Monuments Laboratory Report* 3115: 1–12.

2000 Petrology of Imported Amphorae. Pp. 494–96 in *Archaeology at Aksum, Ethiopia, 1993–7*, ed. D.W. Philipson, 2 vols. Memoirs of the British Institute in Eastern Africa 17. Report 65, Research Committee of the Society of Antiquaries of London. London: British Institute in Eastern Africa.

2005a Late Roman Amphora 1: A Study of Diversification. Pp 157–68 in *Trade Relations in the Eastern Mediterranean from the Late Hellenistic Period to Late Antiquity, the Ceramic Evidence: Acts from a Ph.D.-seminar for Young Scholars, Sandbjerg Manorhouse, 12–15 February 1998*, ed. M.B. Briese and L.E. Vaag. Halicarnassian Studies 3. Odense: University Press of Southern Denmark.

2005b An Integrated Approach to Ceramic Fabric Recognition: A Study Case on Late Roman Amphora 1 from the Eastern Mediterranean. Pp. 613–24 in *LRCW1: Late Roman Coarse Wares, Cooking Wares, and Amphorae in the Mediterranean: Archaeology and Archaeometry*, ed. J.M. Gurt i Esparraguera, J. Buxeda i Garrigos, and M.A. Cau Ontiveros. BAR International Series 1340. Oxford: Archaeopress 2005.

Wilson, A.

2012 Saharan Trade in the Roman Period: Short-, Medium- and Long-distance Trade Networks. *Azania* 47: 409–49. https://doi.org/10.1080/0067270X.2012.727614.

Winther-Jacobsen, K.

2005 Transport Amphorae. Pp. 303–38 in *Panayia Ematousa I. A Rural Site in South-eastern Cyprus*, ed. L. Wright Sørenson and K. Winther-Jacobsen. Monographs of the Danish Institute at Athens 6. Athens: Danish Institute at Athens.

2022 Ceramic Assemblages and Material Connections in Late Roman North-western Cyprus and Beyond. *Annual of the British School at Athens* 117: 353–91. https://doi.org/10.1017/S0068245422000065.

Wohmann, R.

2016 Tableware and Cargo Amphorae of the Late Antique to Late Byzantine Periods from Küçükyali (İstanbul): A Ceramic Assemblage from the Asian Hinterland of Constantinople (4th–14th centuries CE). M.A. thesis, Koç University.

Wohmann, R., Rauh, N.K., and Varinlioğlu, G.

2023 Amphorae and Coarse Wares from Boğsak Island in South Turkey, 4th–9th Centuries AD. Pp. 928–35 in *LRCW6: Late Roman Coarse Wares, Cooking Wares and Amphorae in the Mediterranean: Archaeology and Archaeometry. Land and Sea: Pottery Routes*, ed. V: Caminneci, E. Giannitrapani, M.C. Parello, and M.S. Rizzo, 2 vols. Roman and Late Antique Mediterranean Pottery 19. Oxford: Archaeopress.

Xhyheri, S., Muçaj, S., Halilaj, E., Sheremetaj, L.

2012 Kërkime arkeologjike në zonën e Vlorës – 2012. *Iliria* 37: 437–58. https://doi.org/10.3406/iliri.2013.2458.

Yaman, A.

2018 Arykanda Geç Antik Dönem Mahallesi Seramikler. Ph.D. dissertation, T.C. Muğla Sitki Koçman Üniversitesi Sosyal Bilimler Enstitüsü Arkeoloji Anabilim Dali.

Yashna, O.

2019 Trade Contacts of Mangup-Kale Population in the 5th Century on the Materials of Amphorae and Red-figure Pottery. *Eminak: Scientific Quarterly Journal* 3 (27): 47–59. https://doi.org/10.33782/eminak2019.3(27).310.

Zachariadis, S.

2014 Pottery from the Workshop Building in the Early Byzantine City of Philippi, Greece. Pp. 705–13 in

LRCW4: Late Roman Coarse Wares, Cooking Wares and Amphorae in the Mediterranean: Archaeology and Archaeometry. The Mediterranean: A Market without Frontiers, ed. N. Poulou-Papadimitriou, E. Nodarou, and V. Kilikoglou, 2 vols. BAR International Series 2616. Oxford: Archaeopress.

Zacharopoulou, E.

2016 The Emergence of the State of Nobadia and the Byzantine Policy. *Proceedings Ekklesiastikos Pharos* 2014: 231–49. https://journals.co.za/doi/epdf/10.10520/EJC-759cbe3f5.

Zemer, A.

1977 *Storage Jars in Ancient Sea Trade*. Haifa: National Maritime Museum Foundation.

Zerai, A., Guerrini, C., Łucejko, J.J., Ribechini, E., Piccirillo, A., Massa, S., Mandelli, C., Medin, T., Re, A., Lo Giudice, A., Davit, P., and Gulmini, M.

2022 The Organic Residues of Lining in Transport Vessels from the Red Sea Coast of Eritrea: A Further Element to Understand Past Commercial Relations. *Heritage Science* 10: 162. https://doi.org/10.1186/s40494-022-00801-7.

Zoroğlu, K.L.

2020 A New Context of Late Roman Pottery from Kelenderis: A Preliminary Discussion. Pp. 27–37 in *Men, Goods and Ideas Travelling over the Sea: Cilicia at the Crossroad of Eastern Mediterranean Trade Network. Proceedings of the 19th International Congress of Classical Archaeology, Cologne/Bonn 2018*, ed. E. Equini Schneider. Archaeology and Economy in the Ancient World 35. Heidelberg: Propylaeum. https://doi.org/10.11588/propylaeum.554.

Zviely, D., Galili, E., Ronen, A., Salamon, A., and Ben-Avraham, Z.

2009 Reevaluating the Tectonic Uplift of Western Mount Carmel, Israel, since the Middle Pleistocene. *Quaternary Research* 71: 239–45. https://doi.org/10.1016/j.yqres.2008.11.008.

Indexes

List of Contributors and Acknowledgments

LCP Contributors

Caroline Autret
Safiye Aydin
Phillip Bes
Dennis Braekmans
Clementina Caputo
William Caraher
Michelle Creisher
Patrick Degryse
Stella Demesticha
Maria Dikiomitou Eliadou
Matthew Dillon
Peter Gendelman
Grady Gillett
Sasha Greenhall
John Hayes
Sebastian Heath
Veronica Iacomi
Mark Jackson
Anthi Kaldelis
Dominique Kassab Tezgör
Asena Kızılarslanoğlu
Bernard Knapp
Grzegorz Majcherek
R. Scott Moore
Eilat Mazar
Andrei Opaiţ
Stanislav Pejsa
Dominque Pieri
Alexandra Ratzlaff
Nicholas K. Rauh
Paul Reynolds
Renate Rosenthal-Heginbottom
Marie Odile Rousset
Debora Sandhaus
Andrei Sazanov
Itamar Taxel
Mehmet Tekocak
Agnes Vokaer
Paula Waiman-Barak
Yona Waksman
Urszula Wicenciak
Kristina Winther-Jacobsen
Assaf Yasur-Landau

Acknowledgments

Matthew Adams
Andrea Berlin
Bill Caraher
Alexander Dorr
Maria Duggan
Asena Kızılarslanoğlu
Shulamit Miller
Andrei Opaiţ
Laura Rembart
Anna de Vincenz
Alice Waldern
Zeza Zomeni

List of LRA1 Consumption Sites

Sites discussed in the text and/or reported in our maps are listed here in alphabetical order; letters and numbers as in our macroregions and related tables.

Site	Code
Abu Mina	I01
Abu Sha'ar	I02
Adoulis	N01
Aegyssus	D01
Agios Ioannis	F01
Agnuli	H01
Aigues-Vives	L01
Aila/Aqaba	C01
Aix-en-Provence/Aquae Sextae	L02
Ajdabiyah	I03
Akragas/Agrigento	H02
Aksum	N02
Alassa	B01
Albenga	H03
Alexandria	I04
Aliki (Thasos)	G01
Alt Glut	M01
Amathus	B02
Anchialos	D03
Andriake	F02
Androna	A01
Anemurium	A02
Antibes/Antipolis	L03
Antikythera	G02
Antinoupolis	I05
Antioch	A04
Antiocheia ad Cragum	A03
Apamea	A05
Aphendrika	B03
Aphrodisias	F03
Aphrodisias/Ovacık	A06
Apolakkia	F04
Apollonia Pontica	D02
Apsaros/Gonio	E01
Aquae/Prahovo	G03
Aquileia	H04
Arap Island (? shipwreck)	F05
Arelatum/Arles	L04
Argos	G04
Arikamedu	O01
Armant/Hermonthis	I06
Arsuz	A07
Arykanda	F06
Asar Tepe	A08
Ashdod	C02
Ashkelon	C03
Askra	G05
Assos	F07
Athens	G06
Aubigné-Racan	L05
Augst/Augusta Raurica	L06
Avdimou Bay (shipwreck)	B06
Avignon	L07
Ayia Marina-Mavrovouni	B04
Ayios Philon	B05
Bad Kreuznach	L08
Ballana	N03
Ballygarran	M02
Bantham	M03
Baouît/Abba Apollotos	I07
Barcino/Barcelona	K01
Baux-de-Provence	L09
Beaucaire	L10
Beirut	C04
Beisan/Scythopolis	C05
Belgrad	G07
Benalùa	K02
Berat	G08
Berenice/Benghazi	I08
Berenike/Bender el-Kebir	I09
Bethany	C06
Bharuch (?)	O02
Bir Flaguess	J01
Bivona	H05
Bjolgrad	D04
Blanchfieldsland	M04

Site	Code
Dime/Soknopaiou Nesos	I13
Dinas Powys	M13
Dinogetia	D12
Diocaesarea	A15
Dion	G18
Djerba	J04
Dodekaskala	B12
Dor	C12
Dranda	E05
Dyrrachium, Epidamnos	G19
Egnatia	H22
Ein Boqeq	C14
El Aouabed, Koudiat Jaber	J05
Elaiussa Sebaste	A16
Elephanta	O03
Elephantine	I14
Elne	L18
Elusa	C13
Emporiae/Emporion	K13
Emporio	F11
En Nadour	J06
Ephesus	F12
Epomanduodurum	L19
Esna/Latopolis	I15
Faras/Pachora	N04
Favatrix (shipwreck)	K14
Finale Ligure (S. Antonino di Perti)	H23
Firka	N05
Florentia	H24
Fossae Marianae	L20
Frejús	L21
Gajtan	G20
Gap	L22
Garranes (Lisnacaheragh)	M14
Gasr el-Atallat	I16
Genoa	H25
Giancola	H26
Giglio Island	H27
Giurdignano	H28
Giza	I17
Glastonbury Tor	M15
Gocuk Asari	A17
Gortyn	G21
Gourine est	J07
Gradiste	D13
Grumentum	H29
Gumenicë	G22
Gwithian	M16
Hadir	A18
Hadrianopolis	G23
Hala Milieri	H30
Halabiye/Zenobia	A19
Halasarna	F13
Halmyris/Murighiol	D14
Haskovo	D15
Hathab	O04
Hawarte	A20
Henchir Chougaf	J08
Henchir Ech Cheggaf, Sidi Mansour	J13
Henchir El Flouss	J09
Henchir El Hefair	J10
Henchir El Kebir	J11
Henchir Ferchatt	J12
Henchir Leich	J14
Hermonassa	E06
Hermopolis/El-Ashmunein	I18
Hierapolis/Pamukkale	F14
High Peak, Sidmouth	M17
Hippos-Sussita	C15
Hispalis/Seville	K15
Histria	D16
Horbat ʻAqav	C16
Horbat Castra	C17
Horrea Caelia	J15
Huqoq	C18
Iasos	F15
Iatrus	D17
Ibiza	K16
Içmeler, Ismeler	F16
Il'ich	E07
Iluro	K17
Imola	H31
Inis Cealtra	M18
Invilino-Ibligo	H32
Iotape	A21
Iraq al-Amir	C19

Maroni-Petrera	B20	Oppidum de Constantine	L36
Marsa Nakari/Nechesia(?)	I25	Orbetello	H44
Massalia/Marseille	L29	Orgame/Argamum	D27
Mastichari	F33	Orikos	G39
Menerbes	L30	Ossonoba/Faro	K21
Metapontum	H39	Ostia	H45
Mezad Yerouham	C26	Ostrakine	C30
Milan	H40	Otranto	H46
Miletos	F34	Oued Maltine	J24
Misenum	H41	Ovech Fortress (Provadia)	D28
Missua/Sidi Daoud	J21	Oxyrhynchos/Bahnasa	I27
Montille d'Ulmet	L31	Palike	H47
Mothecombe	M20	Palmyra	A32
Mount Nebo	C27	Panayia Ematousa	B22
Myndos	F35	Pano Limna	B23
Myrmekion	E11	Pantikapaion, Bosporos/Kerch	E14
Nabeul/Neapolis	J22	Paola	H48
Nahal Beqa'	C28	Parion	F37
Nantes	L32	Paris	L37
Naoura	J23	Patara	F38
Narbo	L33	Pefkochori	G40
Naukratis	I28	Pella	C31
Naula	A29	Perge	F39
Nea Paphos	B21	Petra/Tsikhisdziri	E15
Neapolis/Nablus	C29	Phanagoria	E16
Neapolis/Naples	H42	Phaselis	F40
Nephelion	A30	Philippi	G41
Nikopolis	G36	Philosophiana	H49
Nîmes	L34	Phoinike	G42
Nokalakevi/Archaiopolis	E12	Phoukasa	B24
Nora	H43	Piatra Frecăţei/Beroe	D29
Novae	D24	Pievina	H50
Odessos	D25	Piran	H51
Olba	A31	Pisa	H52
Olbia/Hyères	L35	Piscino di Piscopio	H53
Olbia Pontica, Borysthenes	E13	Pitiunt/Bichvinta	E17
Old Cairo	I26	Plaka (shipwreck)	E18
Old Dongola	N07	Pollena Trocchia	H54
Olisipo	K20	Pompeiopolis	E19
Oltina	D26	Porphyreon	C32
Olympia	G37	Port-Vendres	L38
Olympos	F36	Portmarnock	M21
Onchesmos/Saranda	G38	Porto Torres	H55

Portus	H56
Portus Pisanus	H57
Predloka	H58
Pseira	G43
Puig Rodon villa (Corça)	K22
Punta del Serrone (shipwreck)	H59
Pyla-Koutsopetria	B25
Qal'at Sem'an	A33
Qana	N08
Qasrawet	C33
Qusair al-Saila	A34
Qustul	N09
Ras el Ain	J25
Ras el Bassit	A35
Ras el Koran	J26
Ras Ibn Hani	A36
Rass Enghela	J27
Rass Jezira	J28
Ravenna	H60
Razgrad	D30
Reask	M22
Rehovot	C34
Resafa/Sergiopolis	A37
Rhegion	H61
Rhodiapolis	F41
Rifnik	G44
Rimini	H62
Rome/Roma	H63
Romuliana/Gamzigrad	G45
Roselle/Rusellae	H64
Ruginium	G46
S. Giacomo degli Schiavoni	H66
Sabratha	J29
Sacidava	D31
Sadovec	D32
Sagalassos	F42
Saint Jeremiah's Monastery, Saqqara	I29
Saint-Blaise	L39
Saint-Cassien/ad horrea (Cannes)	L40
Saint-Julien-les-Martigues	L41
Saint-Martin-de-Crau	L43
Saint-Raphaël	L44
Saint-Tropez/Athenopolis	L45
Saintes-Maries de la Mer	L42
Salamis	B26
Salapia	H65
Salona	G47
Samos	F43
San Giusto	H67
Sardis	F44
Sayala	N10
Schedia	I30
Scodra	G48
Scolacium	H68
Segesta	H69
Seleucia Pieria	A38
Selinus	A39
Septem/Ceuta	K23
Sergilla	A40
Shelomi	C35
Shavei Zion	C36
Shuni	C37
Sibari	H70
Side	F45
Sidi Aamer	J30
Sidi Ali Moujehed Sud	J31
Sidi Jdidi/Aradi	J32
Sikyon	G49
Sillina	M23
Sinop	E20
Sinop B (shipwreck)	E21
Sion-sous-le-Scex	L46
Sirmium	G50
Sivag-Kerman	E22
Skouriotissa-Vouppes	B27
Skyros	F46
Sliven	D33
Smyrne	F47
Solenzara	L47
Soli-Pomepiopolis	A41
Somnath	O07
Stara Zagora	D34
Sucidava/Corabia	D35
Sudanese Mine R37	N11
Sudanese Mine R45	N12
Sudanese Mine R57	N13